Looking Back

150 Years of Memories and a Pictorial History of Midland County

Presented by the Midland Daily News

Acknowledgments

Putting together a book depicting the history of Midland County in conjunction with the 150th anniversary of the *Midland Daily News* (which over the years also has been known as the *Midland Sentinel, Midland Independent, Midland Republican* and the *Midland Sun*) is a big undertaking, one that could not be accomplished without the help of a number of people.

Topping that list are the folks at the Midland County Historical Society, who provided photos that are featured prominently throughout this book. Without their support, particularly in providing pictures from the early days of Midland County, our history book would not have been possible. We are greatly indebted to the people at the Historical Society for their assistance and support.

Next on the list is our very own Doug Winger, the *Daily News* librarian, who pulled photographs from our archives so that readers could get a better sense of the newspaper's history. As you look through this book, you will see pictures of some of the key people who were responsible for making this a daily newspaper.

Daily News photographers over the past several years also deserve our thanks, as they took many of the color pictures that you see toward the end of the book that help depict our county's more recent history.

Finally, a history book such as the one you hold in your hands would not be possible without contributions from a number of local residents who shared their family photographs with the *Daily News*. We thank each and every person who contributed a picture to help make this book a success.

We hope you enjoy this look back at the history of Midland County and the people who made it such a great place to live. And we thank you for 150 years of supporting your *Midland Daily News*.

John "Jack" Telfer
Editor, *Midland Daily News*

 • ISBN: 978-1-59725-166-2

Published by Pediment Publishing, a division of The Pediment Group, Inc. Vancouver, Washington. Printed in Canada.

Contents

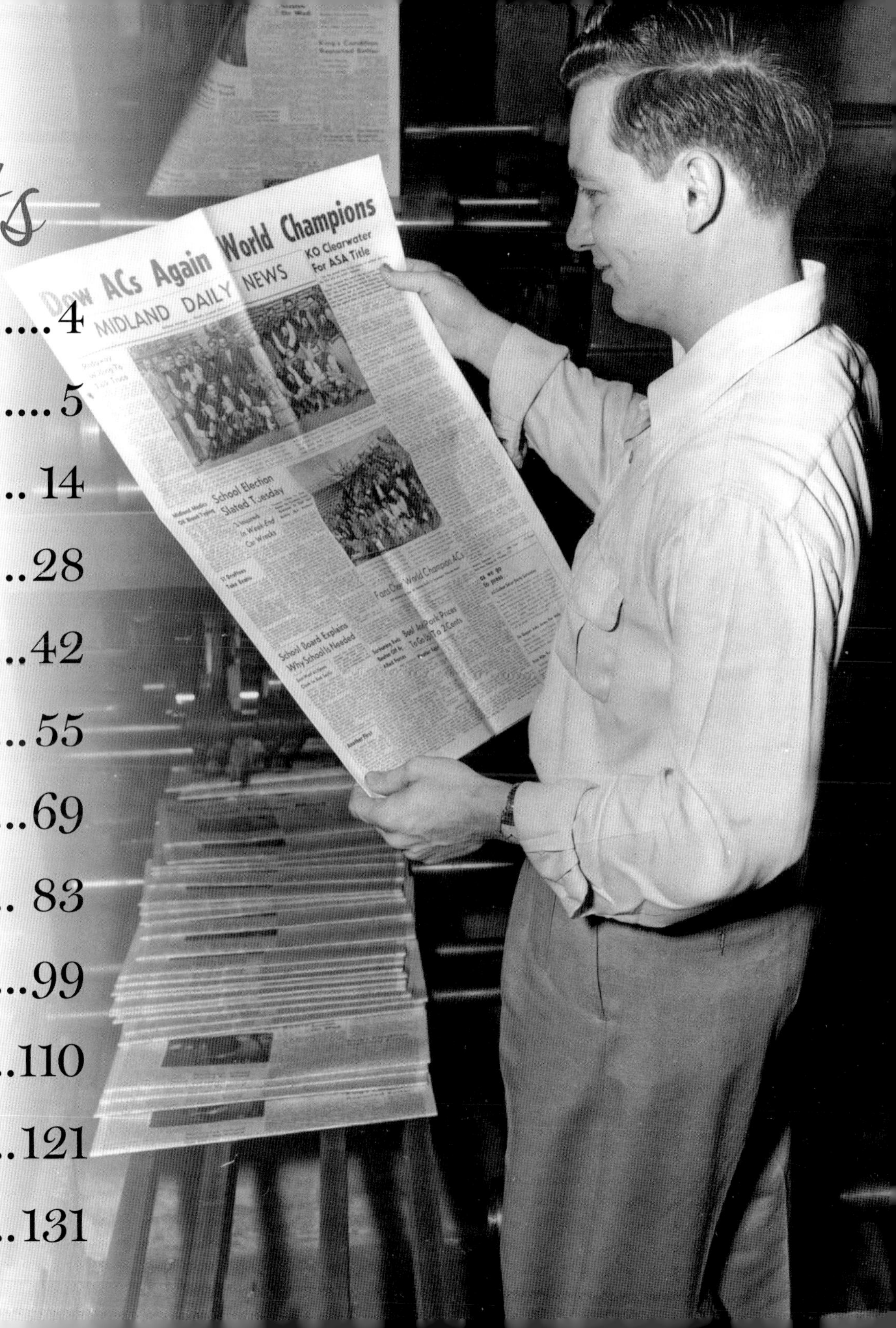

Dow ACs Again World Champions
MIDLAND DAILY NEWS
KO Clearwater For ASA Title
School Election Slated Tuesday
School Board Explains Why School Is Needed

Foreword

Everyone loves history, and the *Midland Daily News* loves to be a primary chronicler of that history. As we celebrate our 150th anniversary of newspaper publishing this year, we could not think of a better way to acknowledge this historic event than by producing a book depicting life through the years in Midland County.

But this book is different than one we produced several years ago. This book takes a look at Midland County in a series of chapters, starting with the early years of the county, the 1800s, and then progressing through the decades right up to the present. Along the way, we pulled out some old photos of life here at the *Daily News*. We thought it was only fitting, this being our 150th anniversary and all.

As you go through our pictorial history of Midland County, you might see someone from your own past, as our book contains a number of class photographs from area schools and other types of group shots. No doubt you also will learn something about the people and places of our community, from the past right up through this year.

And that, my friends, is what makes history so enjoyable.

Jenny Anderson
Publisher, *Midland Daily News*

The 1800s

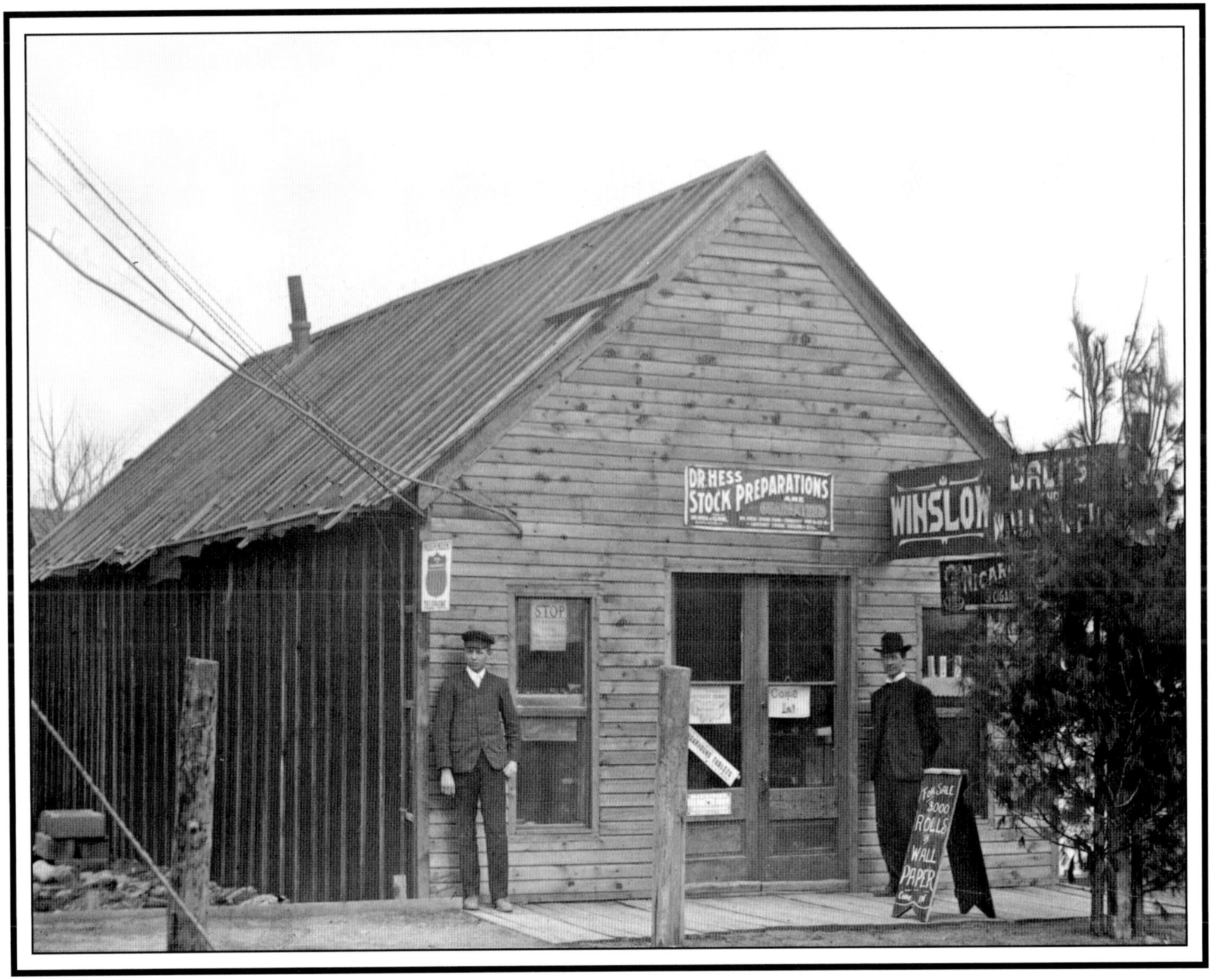

C. J. Winslow Drug Store, circa 1890. *Courtesy of Midland County Historical Society*

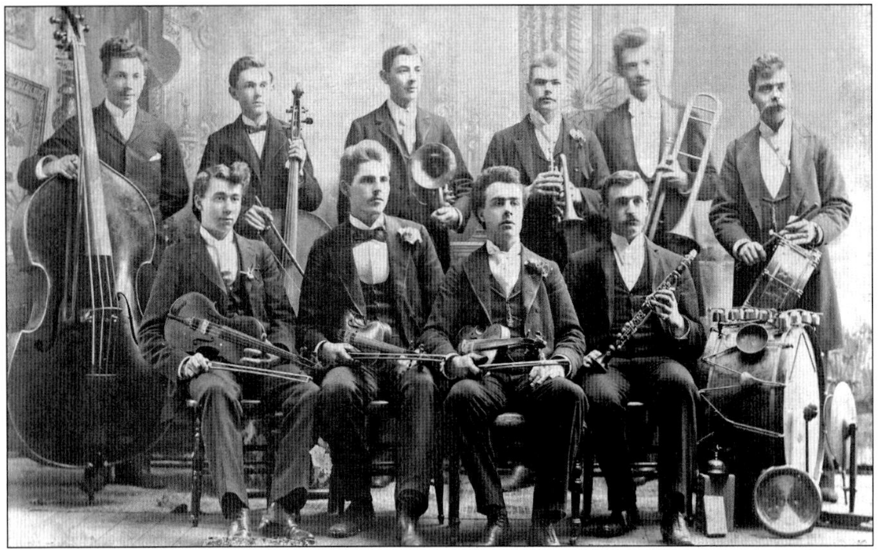

Midland Orchestra, circa 1885. Front row, left to right: Dewey D. Rockwell, Frank Johnson, leader G. Frank Teal and John Q. Matzinger. Second row: Cash C. Anderson, Ewart L. Gardiner, John H. Anderson, Elmer Johnson, Arthur Rumrill and Curt Lingle. *Courtesy of Midland County Historical Society*

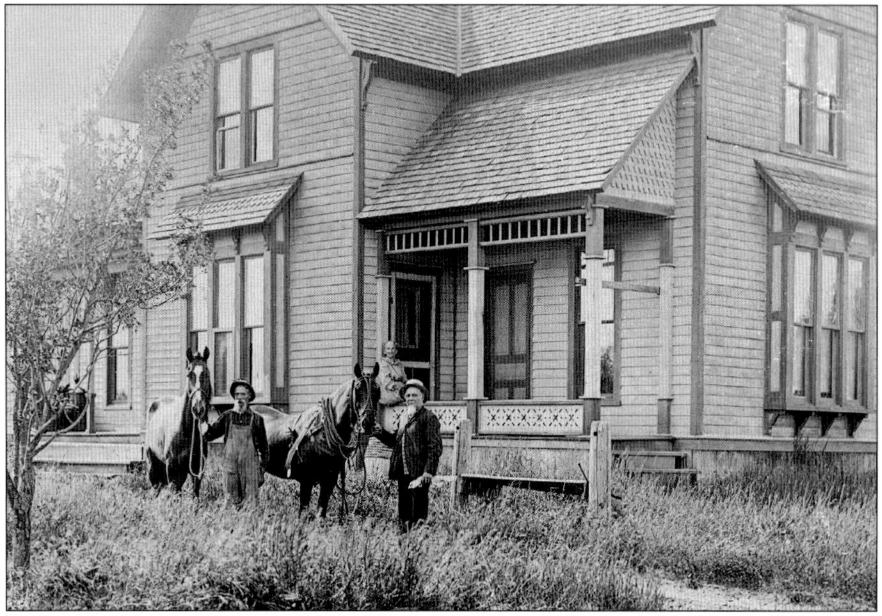

Fred Barth home on the county line, circa 1885.
Courtesy of Midland County Historical Society

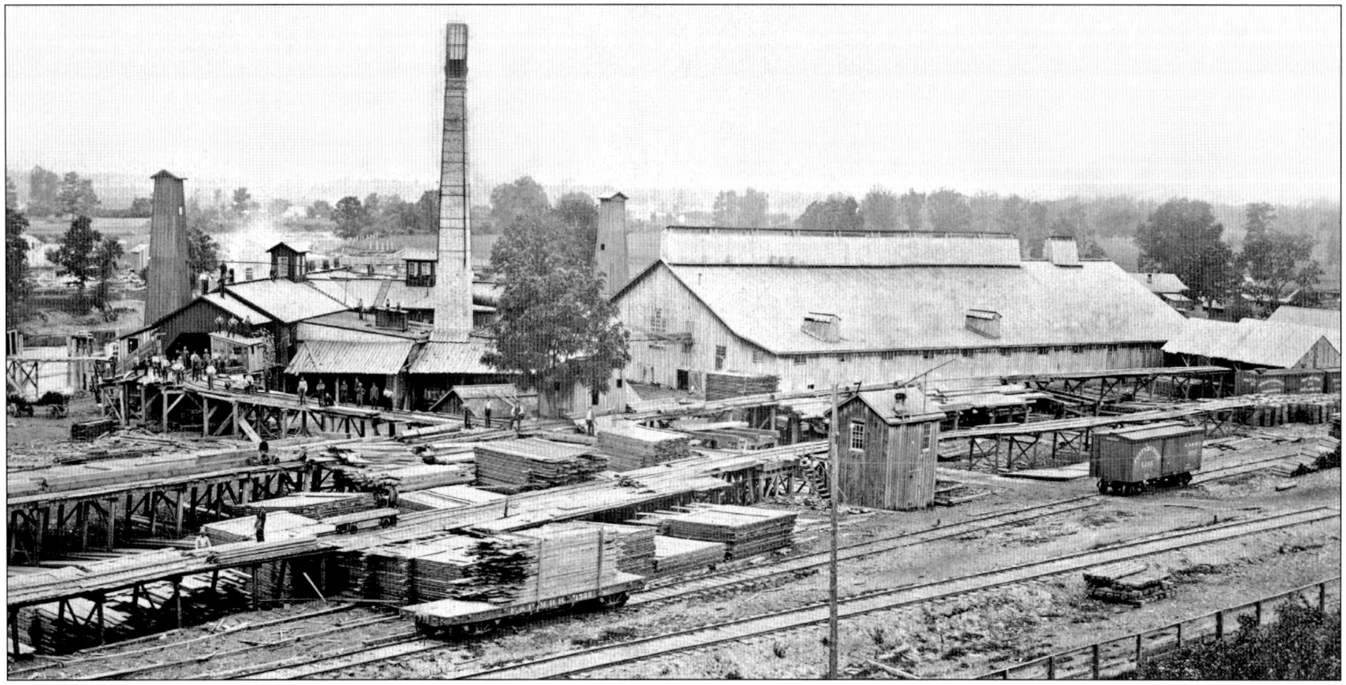

Larkin Mill at the foot of Ashman Street in Midland, circa 1885.
Courtesy of Midland County Historical Society

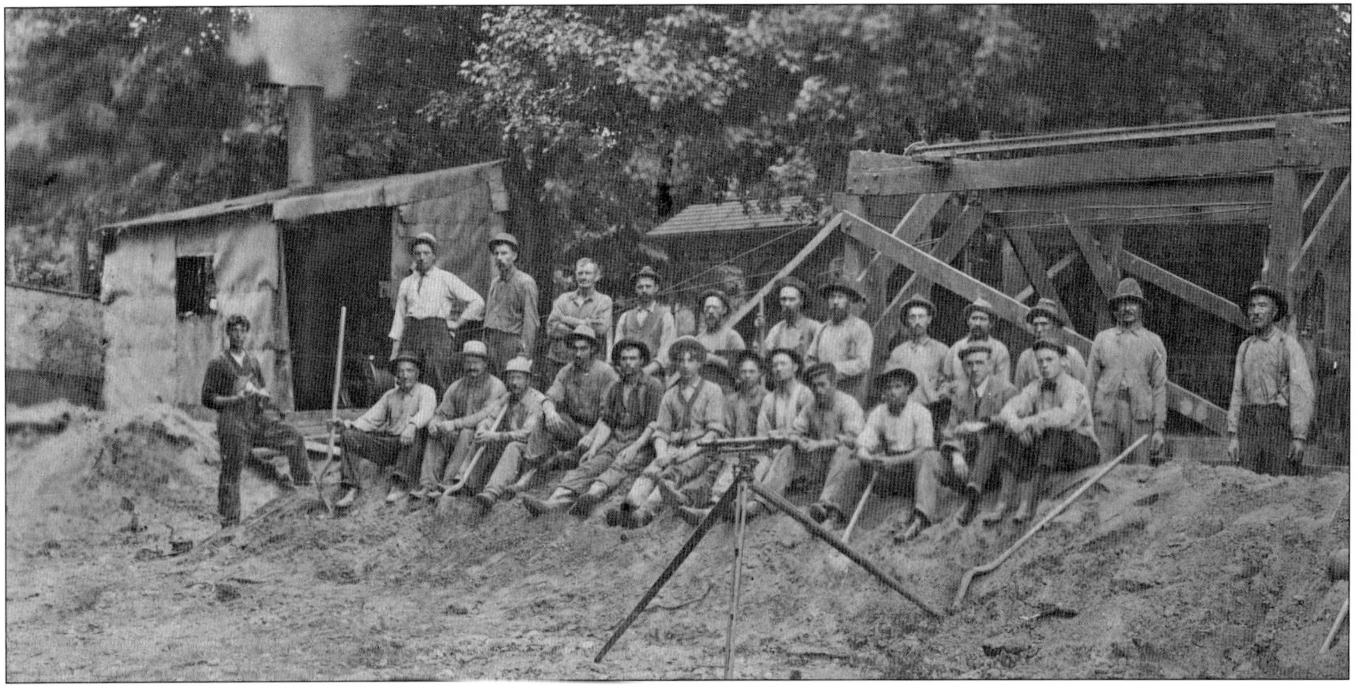

Workers for Larkin and Patrick Sawmill at the foot of Ashman Street, circa 1885. James Brose is in the back row third from the left with his arms folded. John Larkin founded the mill in 1855, and in 1877 William Patrick became partner. Covering ten acres, the mill was the largest industry by 1884 with a total of 90 employees. The mill was destroyed May 11, 1892, by an explosion that injured eight and killed Charles Allen, Richard Steers and Eugene Von Valkenburg. *Courtesy of Ruth E. Hozak*

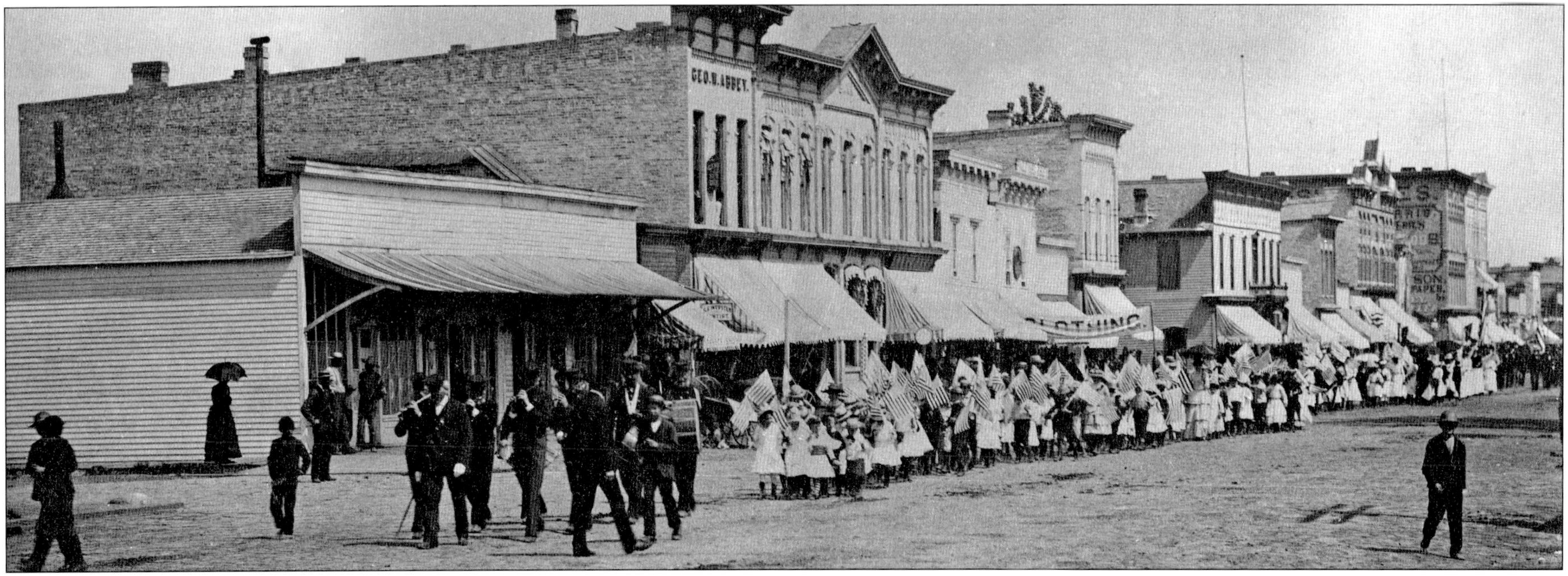

Memorial Day parade on Main Street in Midland, 1886. *Courtesy of Midland Daily News*

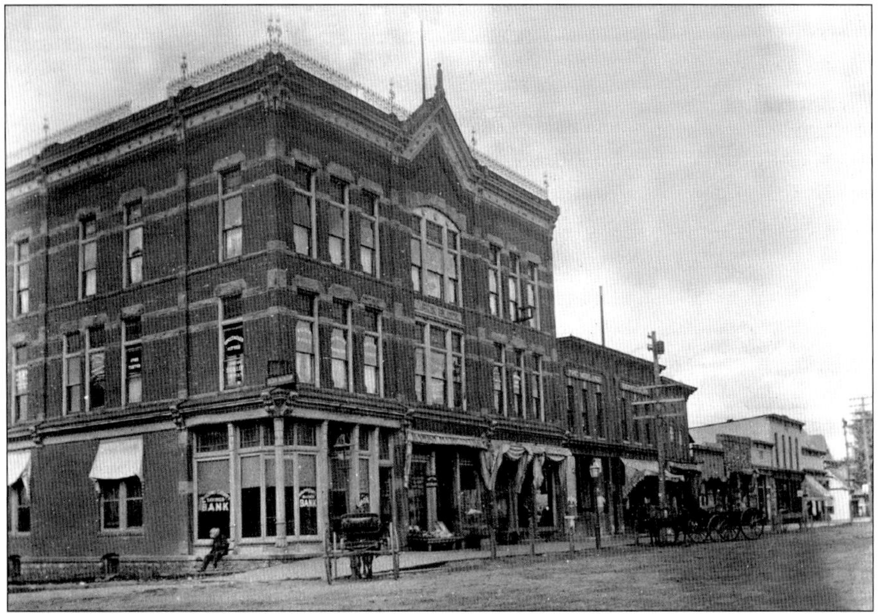

The Larkin Block, constructed by John Larkin in 1886, at the corner of Main and McDonald streets. *Courtesy of Midland County Historical Society*

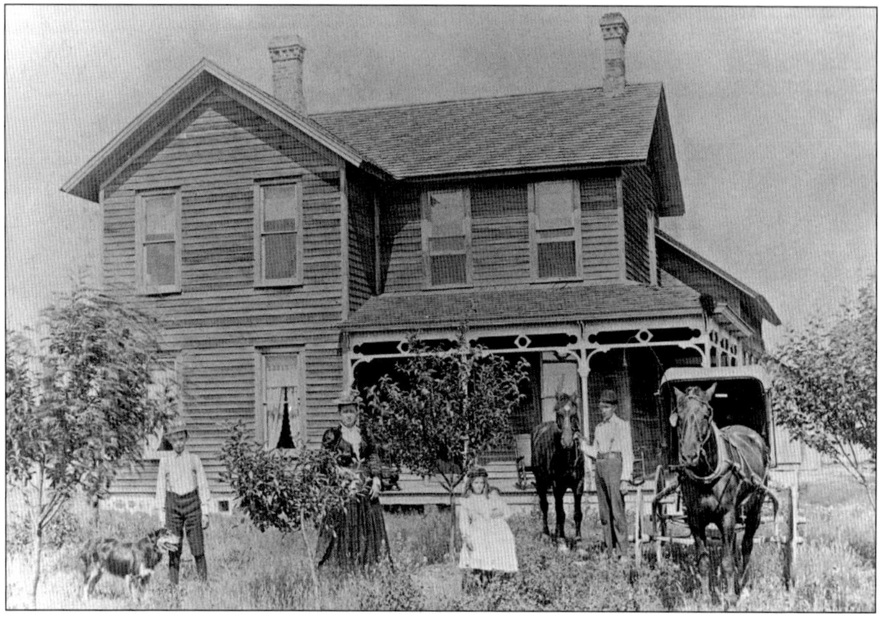

Higgins House, a hotel at Averill, circa 1890.
Courtesy of Midland County Historical Society

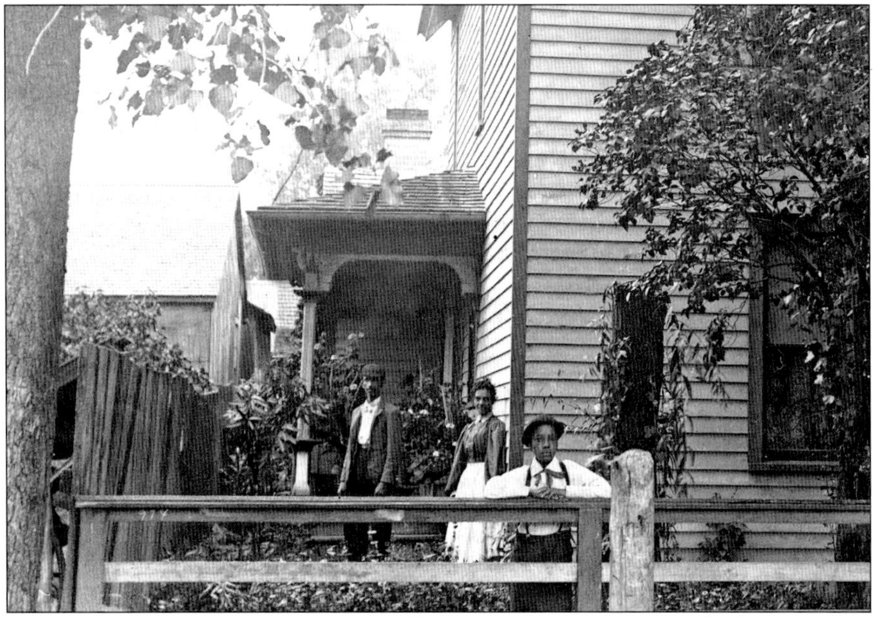

Residence of John Johnson, Midland, 1892.
Courtesy of Midland County Historical Society

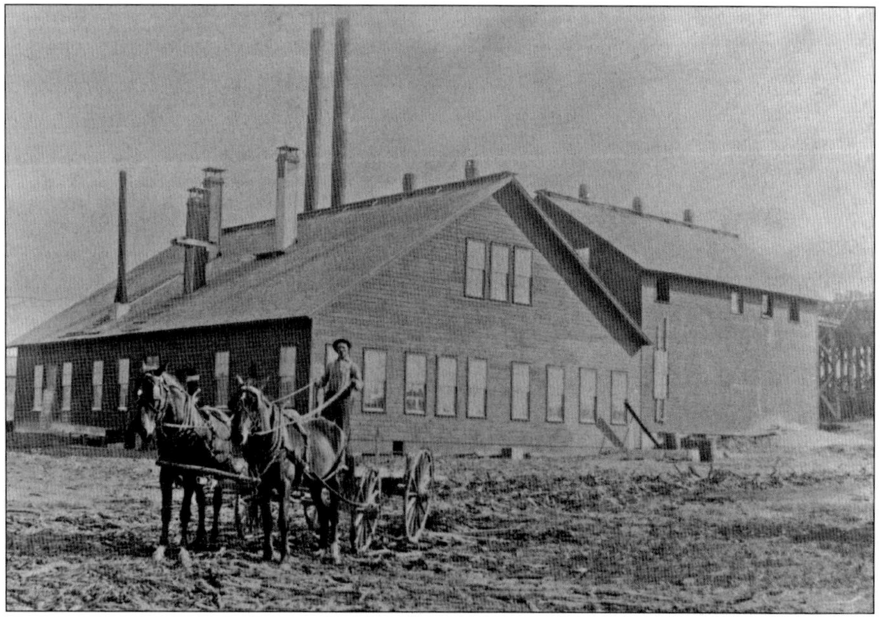

The Mildand Chemical Company, circa 1894.
Courtesy of Midland County Historical Society

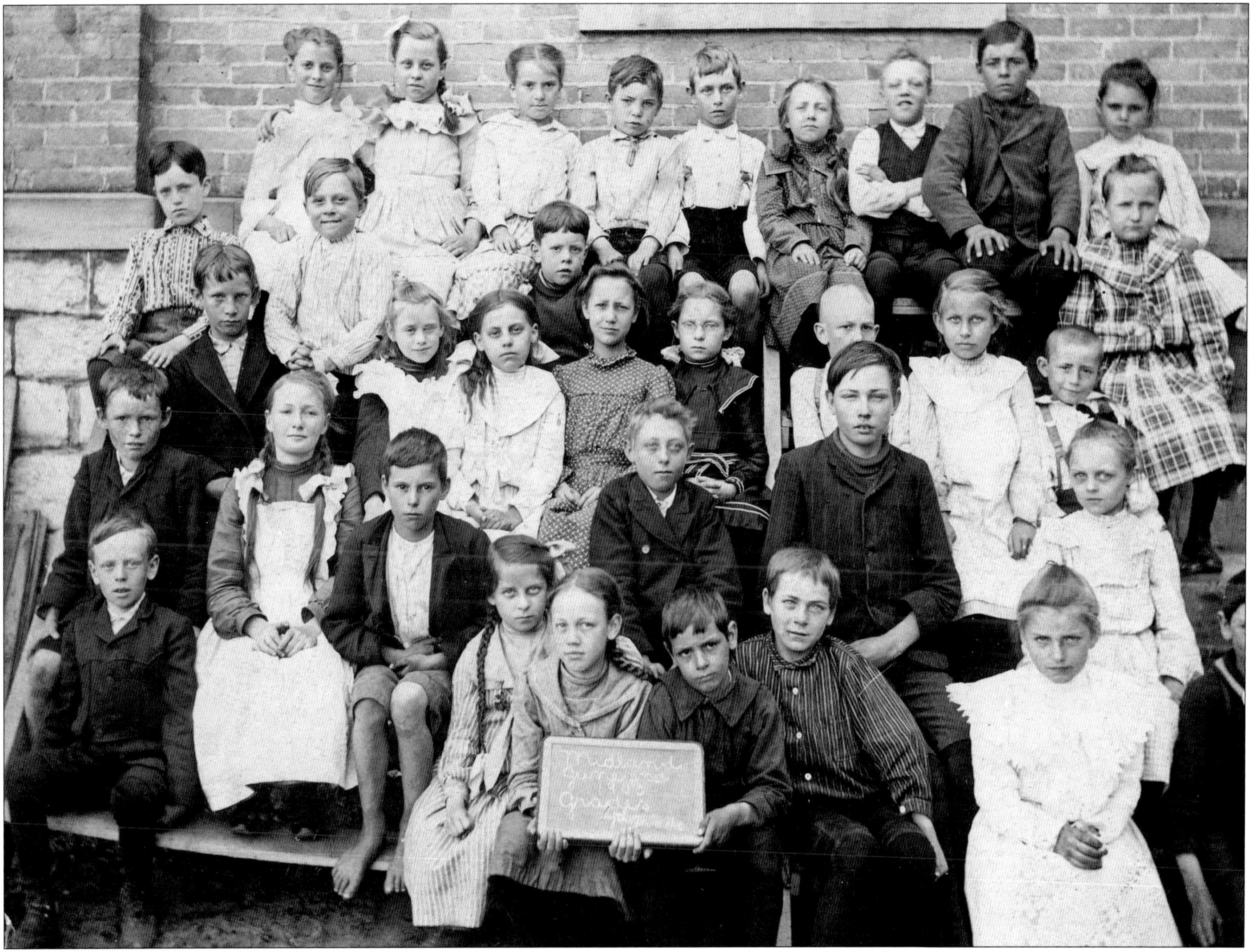

Third Ward School, 1890. *Courtesy of Midland County Historical Society*

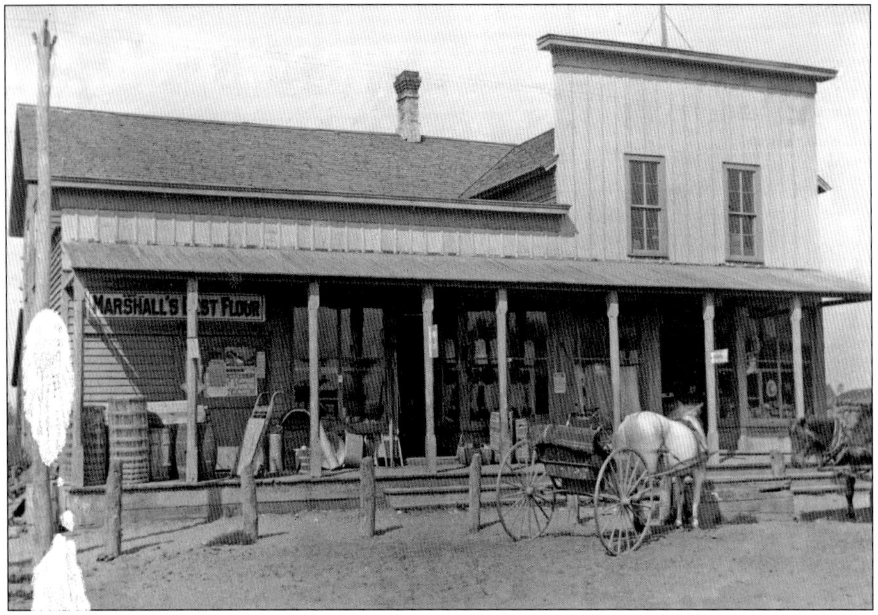

Charles Harper General Store in Edenville before 1900.
Courtesy of Midland County Historical Society

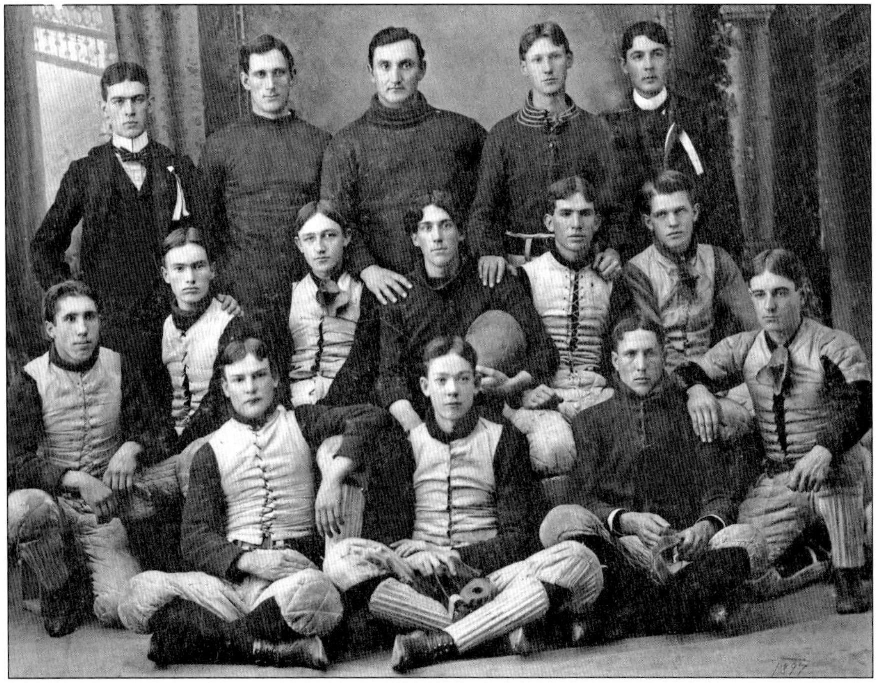

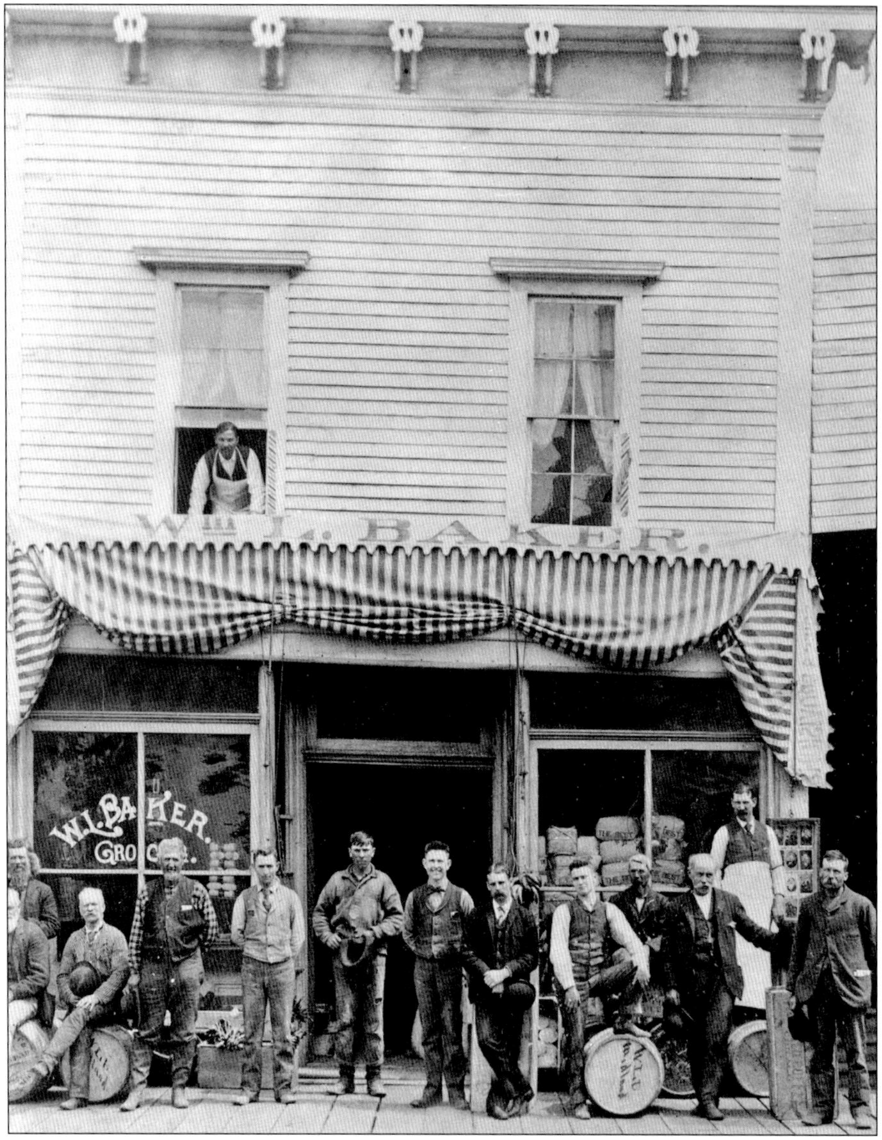

W. L. Baker Grocery, 1890. *Courtesy of Midland County Historical Society*

Midland High School football team, 1897. Front row, left to right: John Shaw, John Lane and Charles Dwyer. Second row: William Wismer, Clarence Dent, Luther Dickey, James Foreman, William Haley, Clem Shoup and Silas Hart. Third row: Claude Crissey, Bill Hanna, Ray Hart, James Bradley and John H. Anderson. Those not included are C.G. Olmsted, C.C. Anderson, Neil C. McKay and Earnest Mills. *Courtesy of Midland County Historical Society*

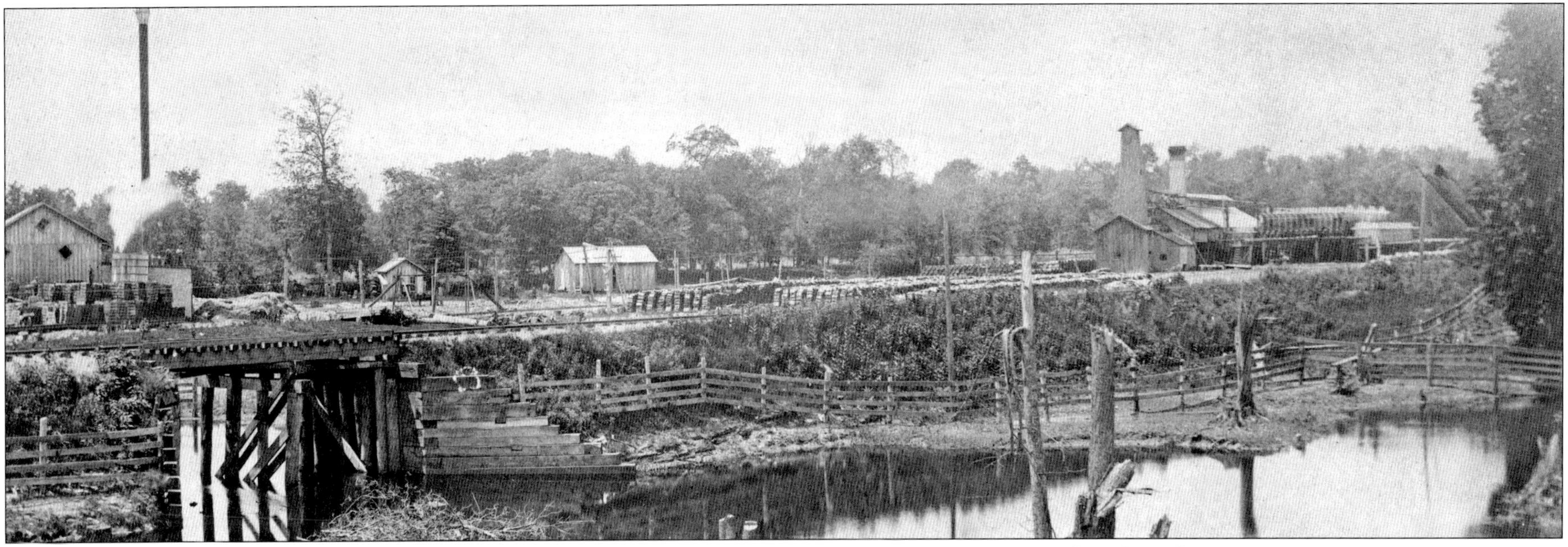

Looking toward the Larkin and Patrick Mill in the 1890s. The Snake Creek bridge and Pere Marquette Railroad can be seen.
Courtesy of Midland County Historical Society

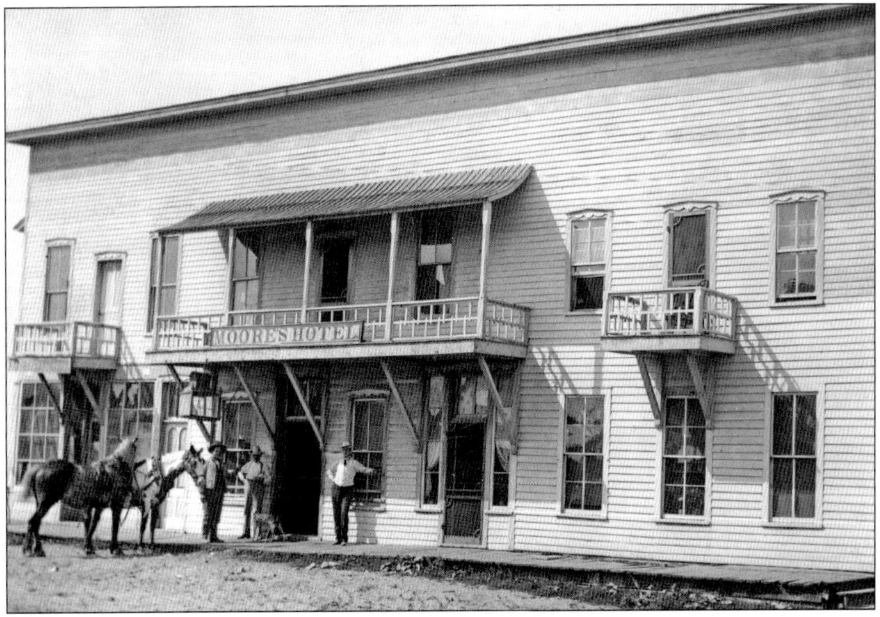

Moore's Hotel in Edenville, circa 1895. Thomas Moore is standing in the white jacket. The hotel was built in 1867. *Courtesy of Midland County Historical Society*

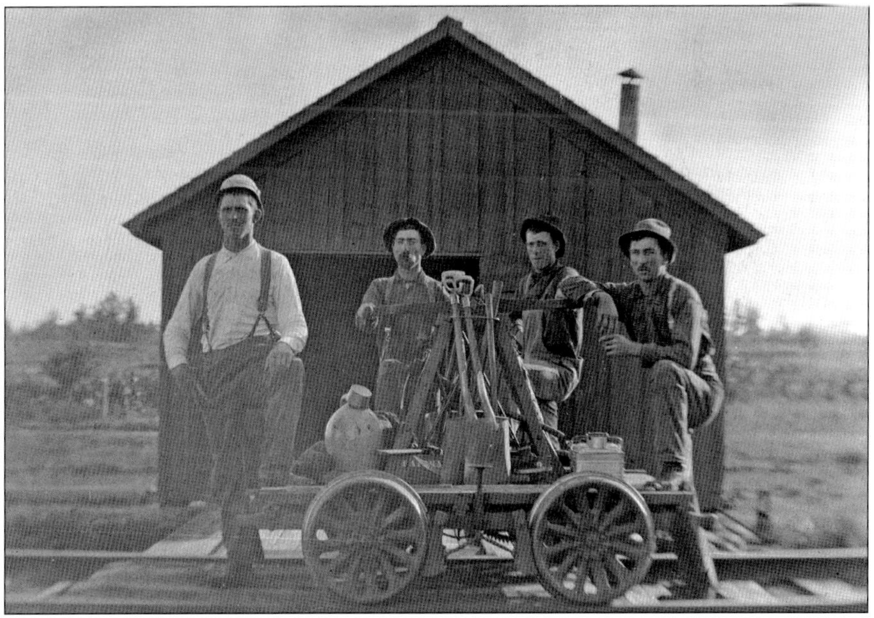

Section crew on the Pere Marquette Railroad at Averill, 1899.
Courtesy of Midland County Historical Society

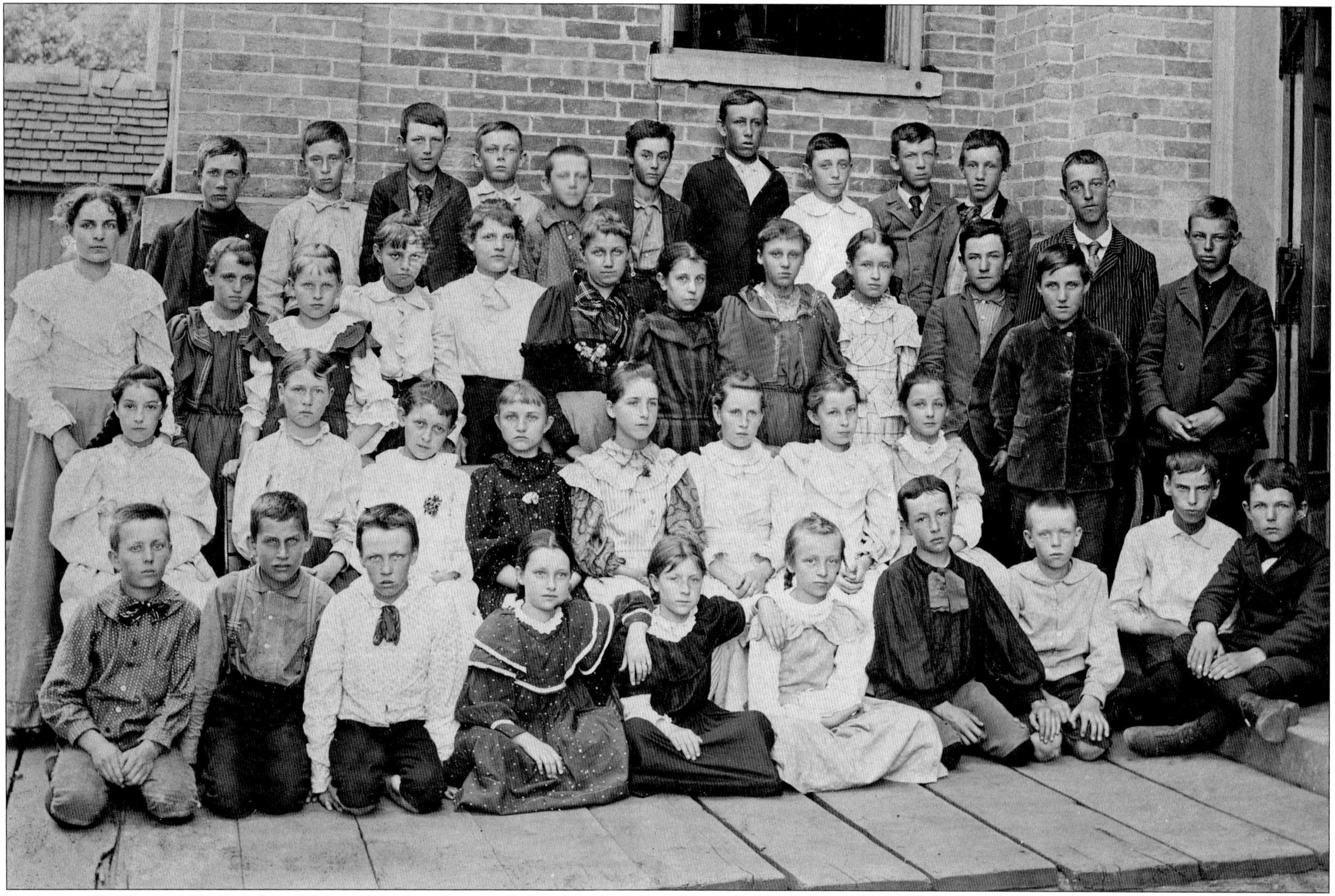

Sixth-grade class, 1895. Teacher Mildred Waldron is standing on the left. Front row, left to right: Frank Thompson, John Ryan, Jim Budd, Fay Thompson, Addie Duberville, Grace Corselius, Gene O'Neil, Ralph Rice, Will Ross and Art Sias. Second row: Maggie Harper, Grace Lewis, Jessie Reed, Cora Hale, Jessie Dean, Edith McCallum, Maude Chesney and Ethel Rice. Third row: Eliza Wilford, Bertha Wilson, Mimi VanOcker, Bell Shaw, (unknown) Boughner, Gertie Hill, Lucy Wilford, Ella McGregor, Neil McKay, Guy Evans and Earl McCartney. Fourth row: Barkley Shepard, Pat Witham, Charley Elston, Harry Sias, Jim Corselius, Andrew W. McDonald, "Phetty" Stewart, George Covert, Will Forman, Fred Lillibridge and Edwin Beardsley.

Courtesy of Midland County Historical Society

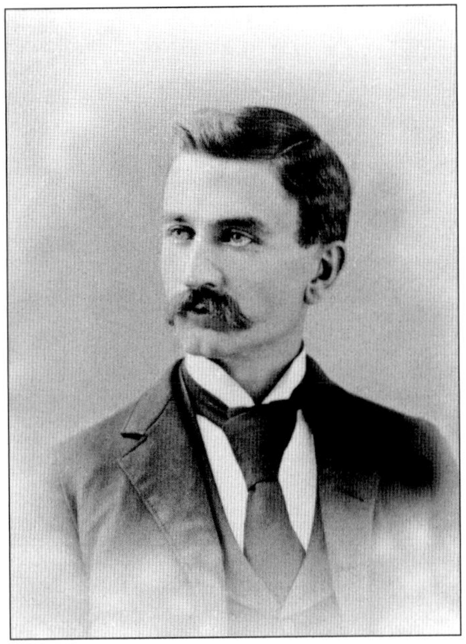

Herbert H. Dow, 1897.
Courtesy of Post Street Archives

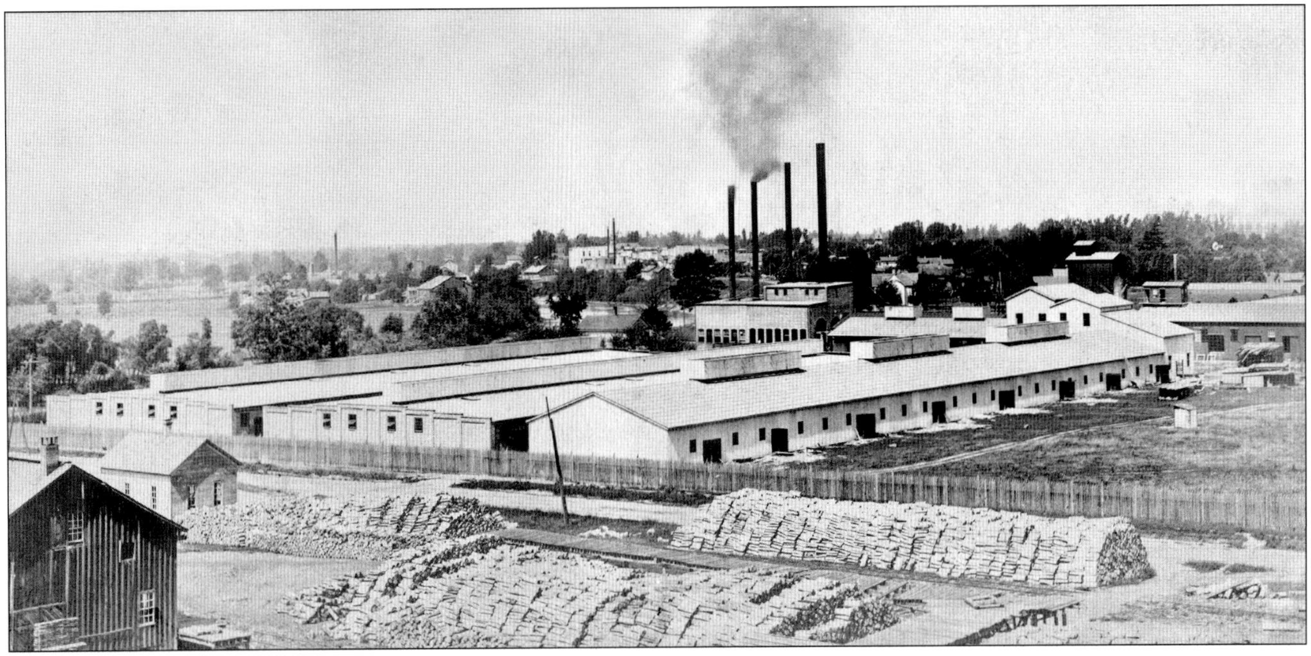

Dow Chemical, circa 1898. *Courtesy of Midland County Historical Society*

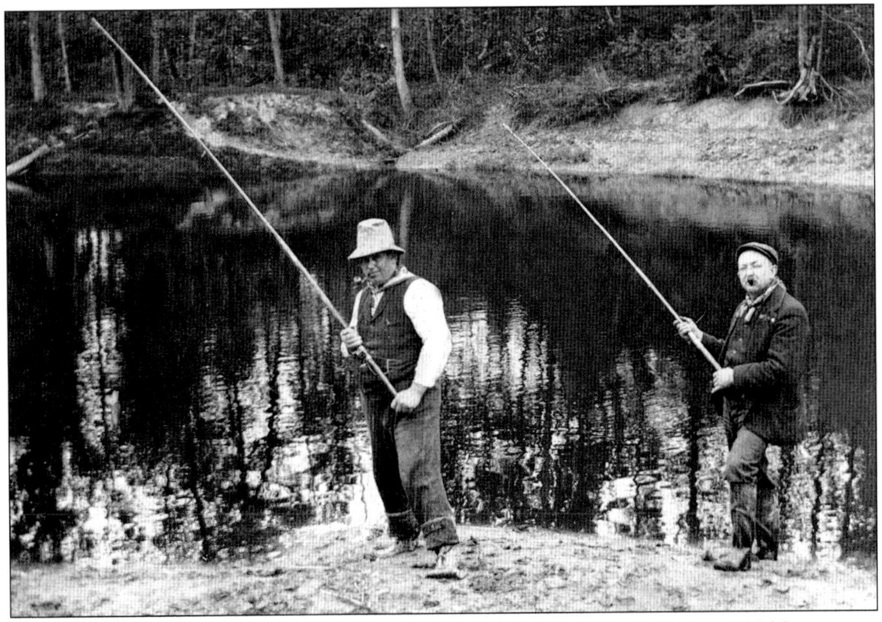

Sam Petrie and Bill Ellsworth fishing on the Salt River, May 22, 1898.
Courtesy of Midland County Historical Society

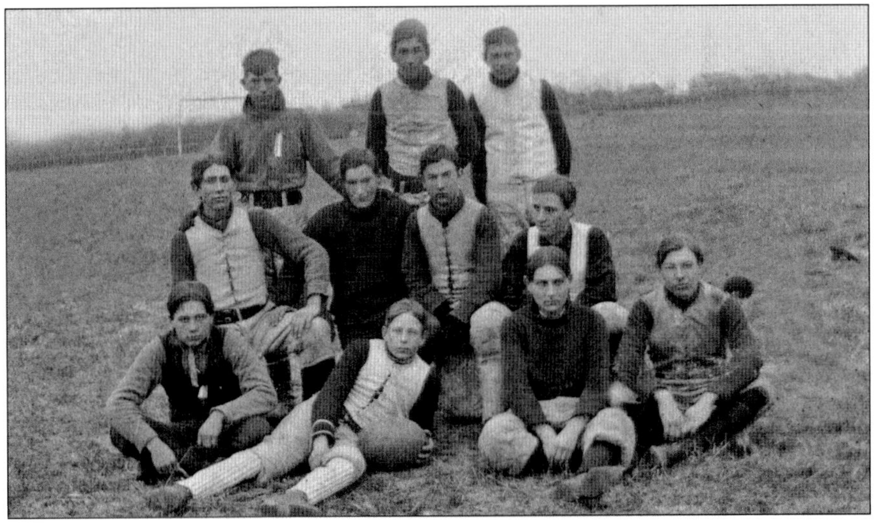

Midland football team, 1898. Front row, left to right: George Boughner, Thomas Walkling, Roy Fleming and Earl McCartney. Second row: Berkley Shepherd, Fred Shaw, Neil C. McKay and Guy Evans. Third row: Guy Harcourt, Thomas Williams and John Ryan.
Courtesy of Midland County Historical Society

The Early 1900s

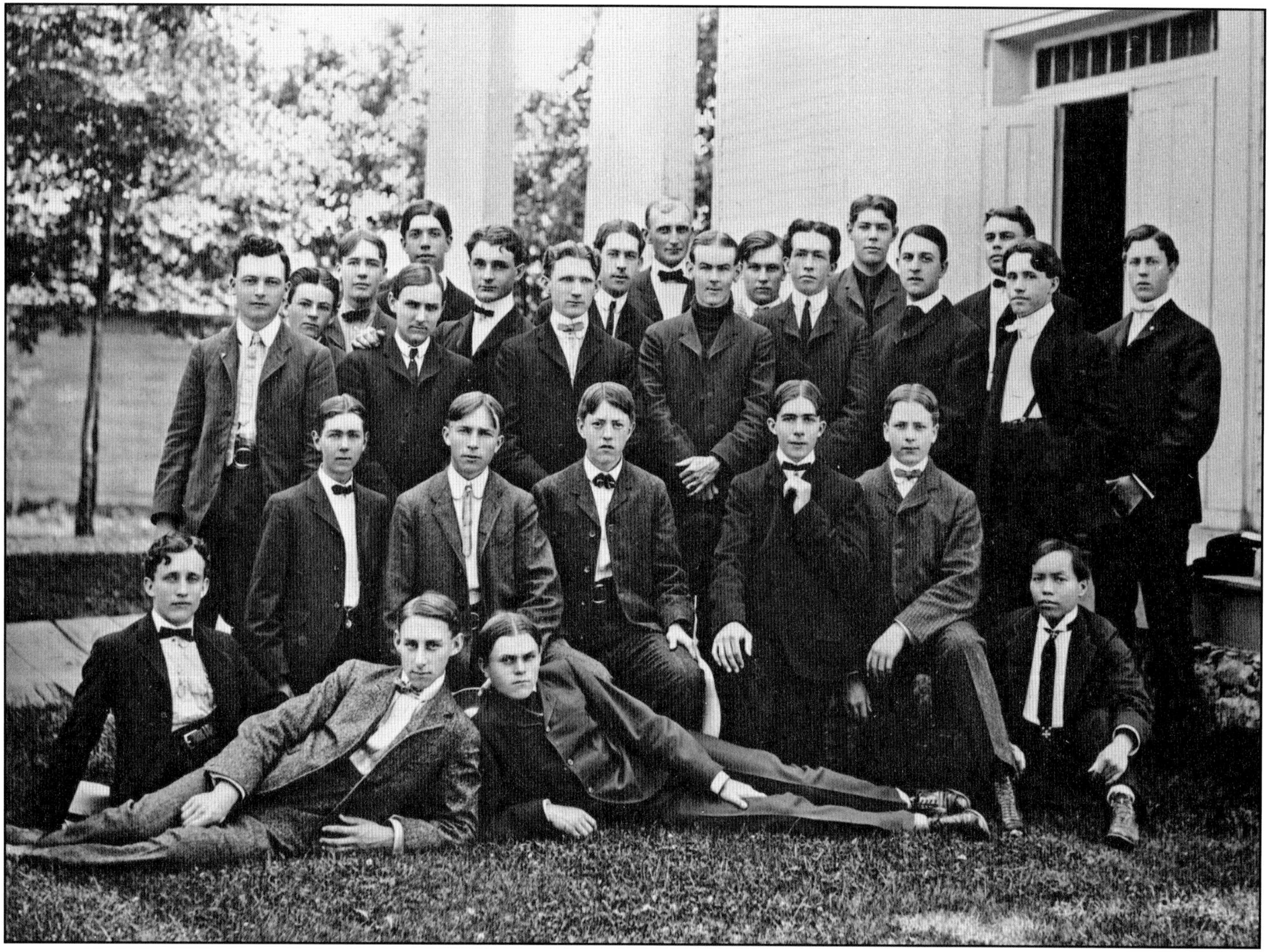

Midland Men About Town on a Sunday afternoon in front of the Midland County Courthouse, 1900. Front row, left to right: Lewis Easley and Miles Maine. Second row: Herbert Price, Harry Hinds, Jay Smith, Lynn Northway, William E. Hinds, Mark Thompson and Duck Lay. Third row: John H. Mustard, Roy Hinds, Wilbur McGregor, Roy Flemming, Clarence Anderson, Erwin Leiphart, Gus Winkler, James Davidson, Andrew S. Arbury, W. S. Hinds, Floyd Lehmer, Michael O'Neil, Dexter Anderson, Ray Ball, Fred V. Sayles, Bert Wismer and Frank Thompson. *Courtesy of Midland County Historical Society*

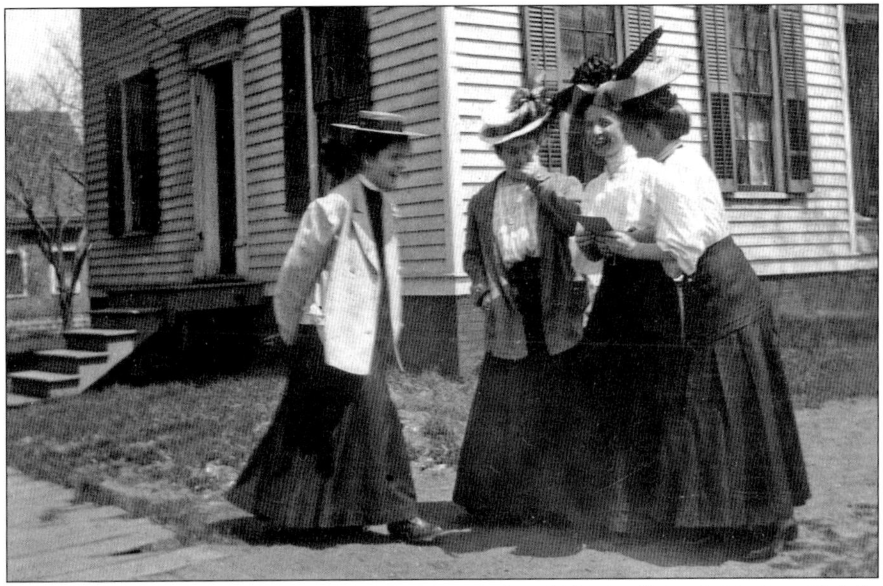

In front of the Dixon home at 201 Ellsworth St., 1900. Left to right: Ann Nehil, Mary Davidson, Florence Broderick and Ethel Dixon.

Courtesy of Midland County Historical Society

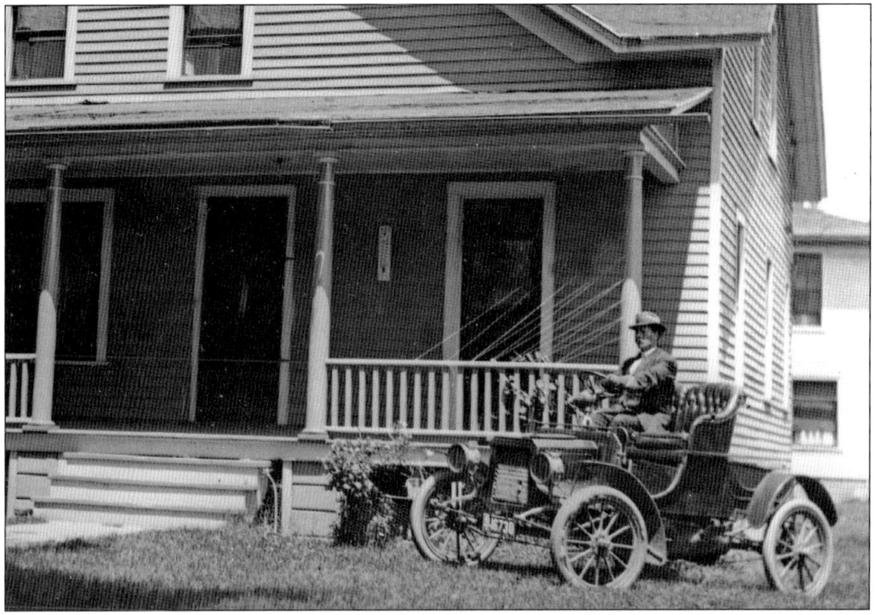

Dr. E. J. Dougher in his car in front of his home on Jerome Street, 1900.

Courtesy of Midland County Historical Society

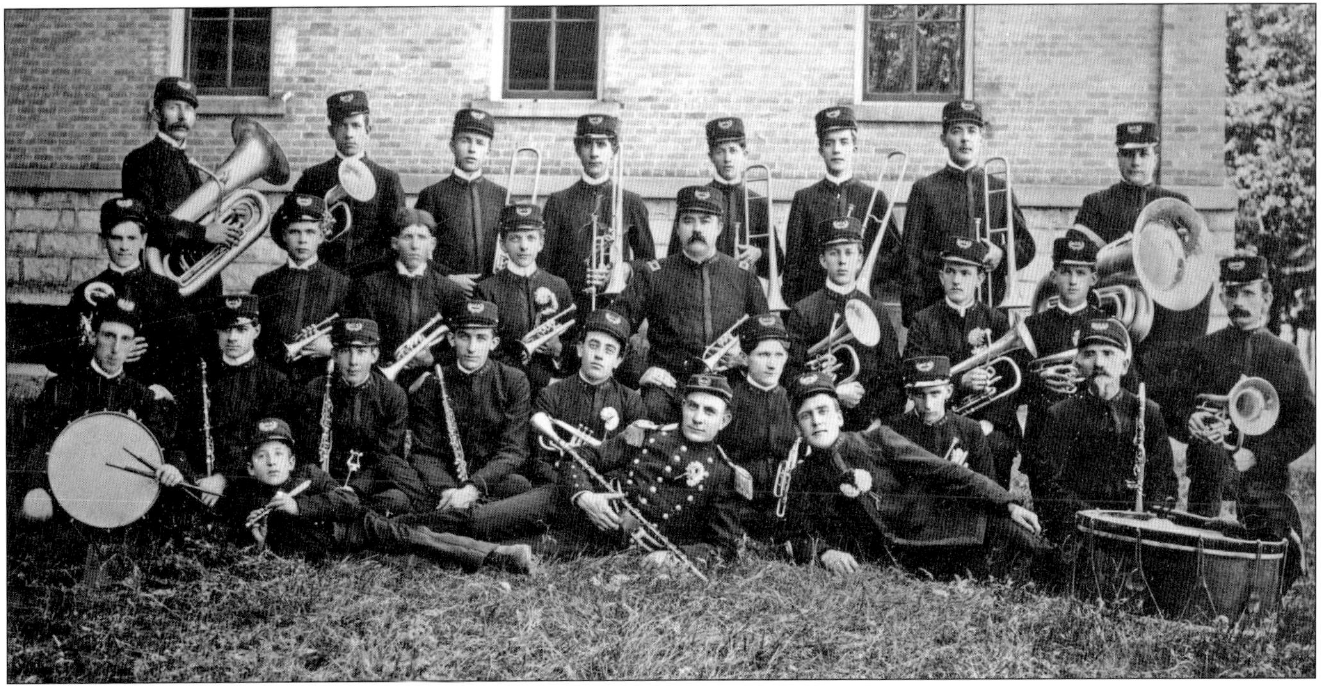

Midland's Big "Red" Band, 1900. Front row, left to right: (unknown) Miller, drum major Harry Burnett and Earl Aldrich. Second row: Frank Short, G. Reid Richardson, (unknown) Miller, George Burd, Einer Oderkirck, Gus Winkler, Harold Burd, (unknown) Burd Sr. and Ben Hammond. Third row: Patrick Fitzgibbon Jr., Ray Stevens, Otto Pomranky, Lorenzo Roeller, Henry Heisman, Frank Thompson, Frank McMullen and Herman Winkler. Fourth row: Charles Verick, Harry Aldrich, Jay Smith, Berkley Shepherd, Harry Comerford, Robert Heisman, John H. Anderson and Cash C. Anderson.

Courtesy of Midland County Historical Society

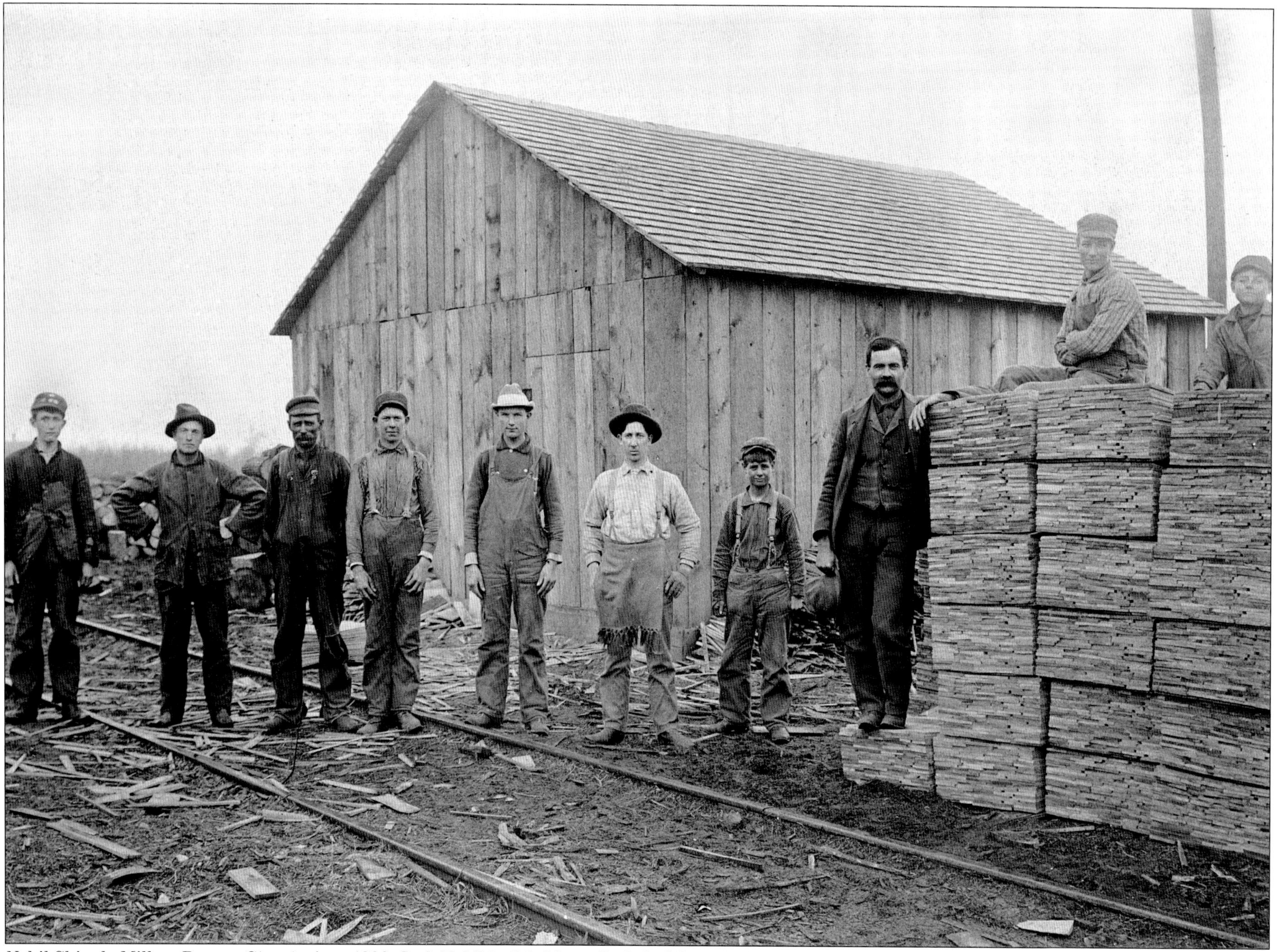

Nehil Shingle Mill on Benson Street, circa 1900. Jack Nehil is third from the left. Others include Roy Hicks and Fred Letts.

Courtesy of Midland County Historical Society

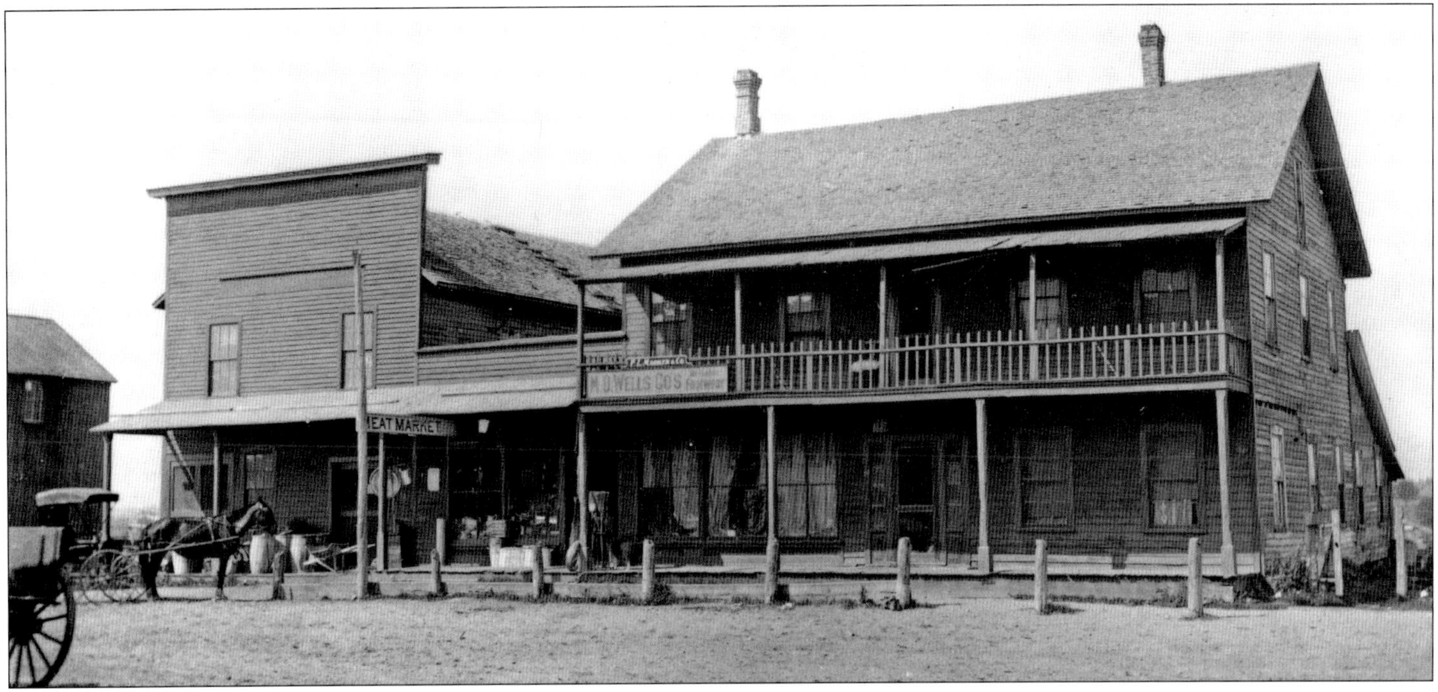

Axford House hotel in Edenville, circa 1900. The hotel was owned by Charlie Axford and run by Tom Gransden and Luther G. Carter. Charlie Axford was also Justice of the Peace. *Courtesy of Midland County Historical Society*

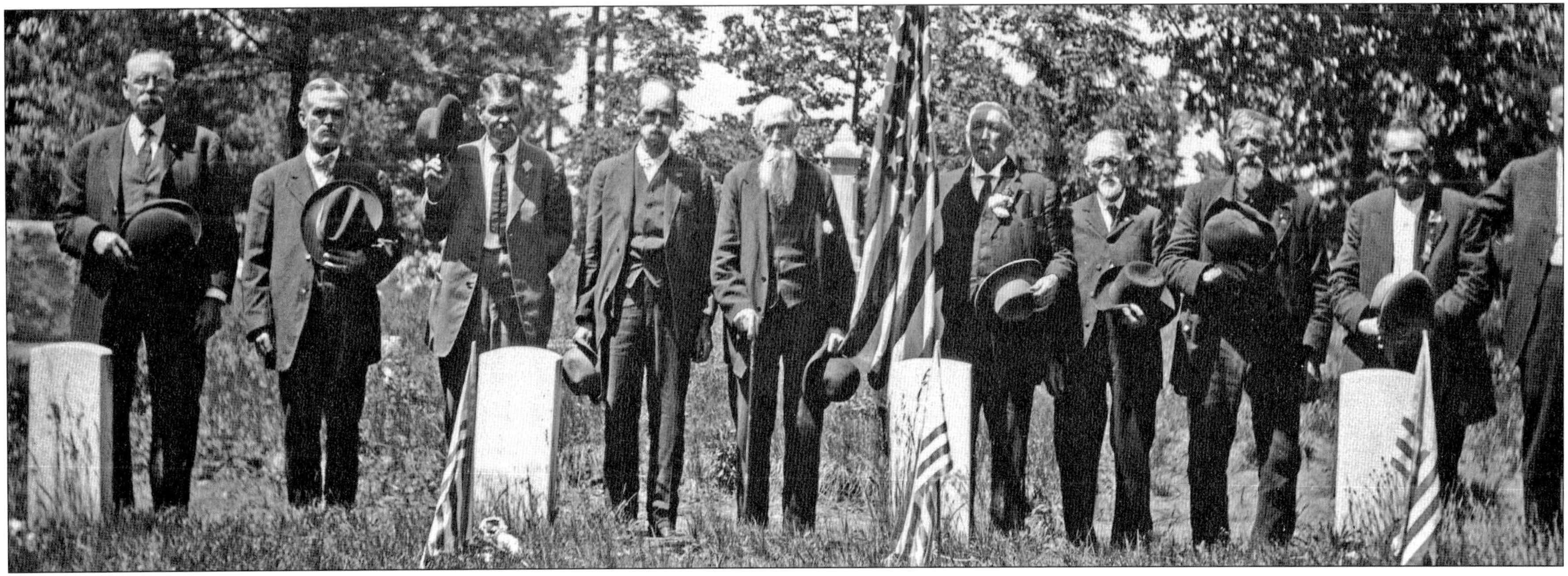

Midland County Civil War veterans, circa 1900. *Courtesy of Midland County Historical Society*

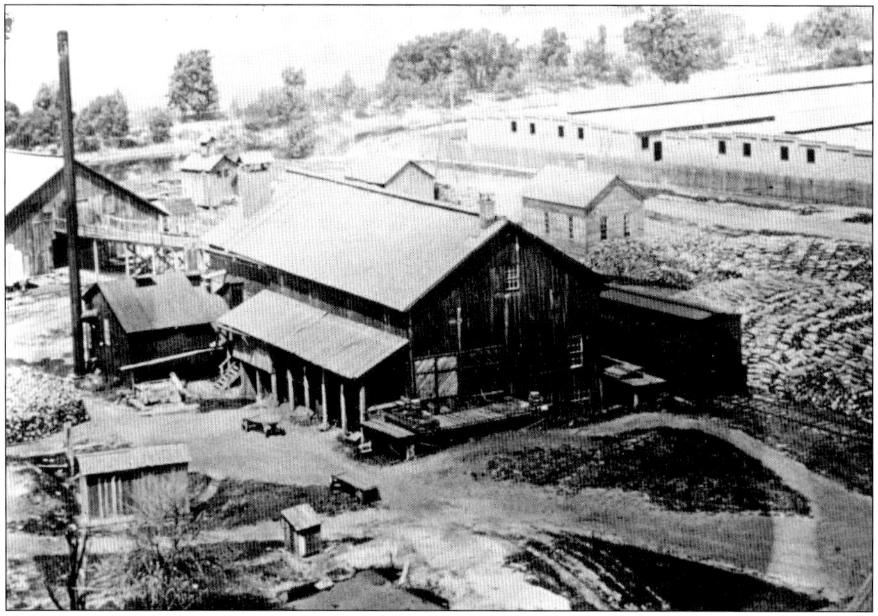

Elm Works Mill in Midland, 1900. It was at the corner of Main Street and Bay Road. *Courtesy of Midland County Historical Society*

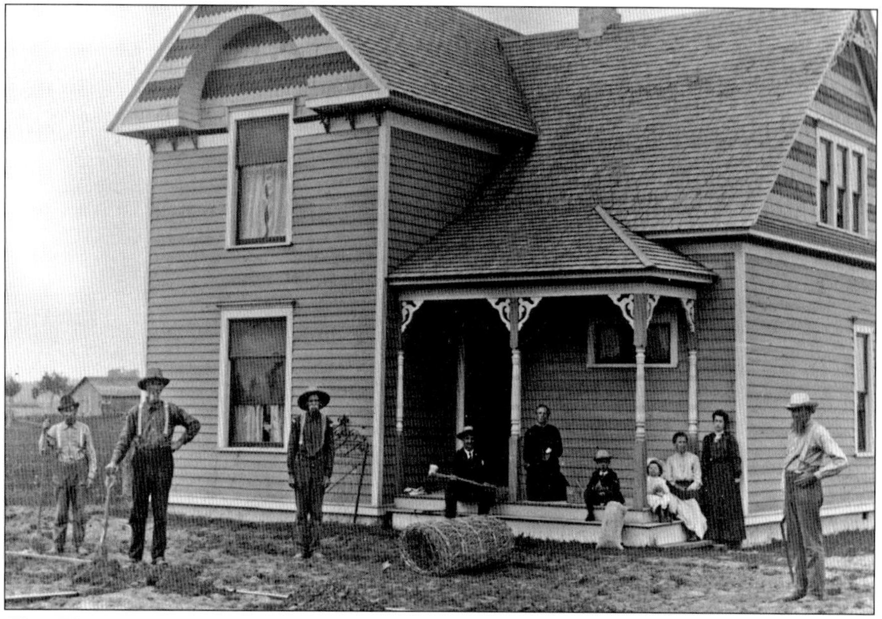

The Shearer family home in Hope, circa 1900.
Courtesy of Midland County Historical Society

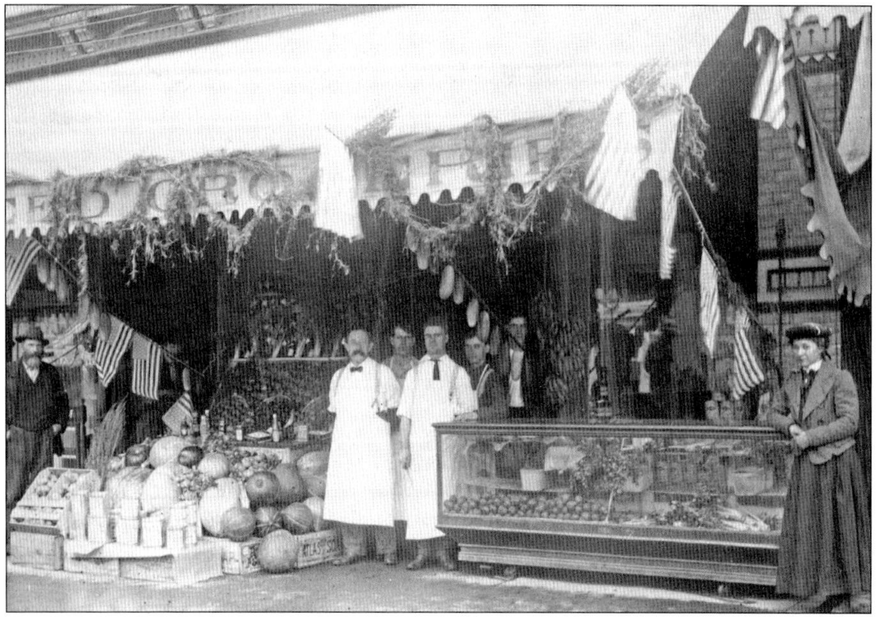

Reardon Bros. Dry Goods and Grociers on Main Street in Midland, 1900.
Courtesy of Midland County Historical Society

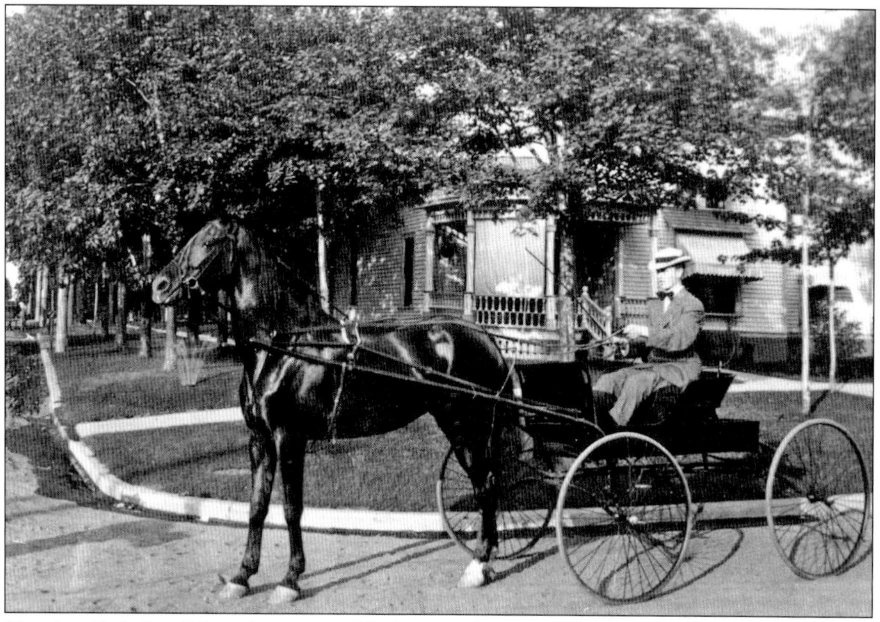

Dexter Reinhart in a buggy at Main and George streets, circa 1900.
Courtesy of Midland County Historical Society

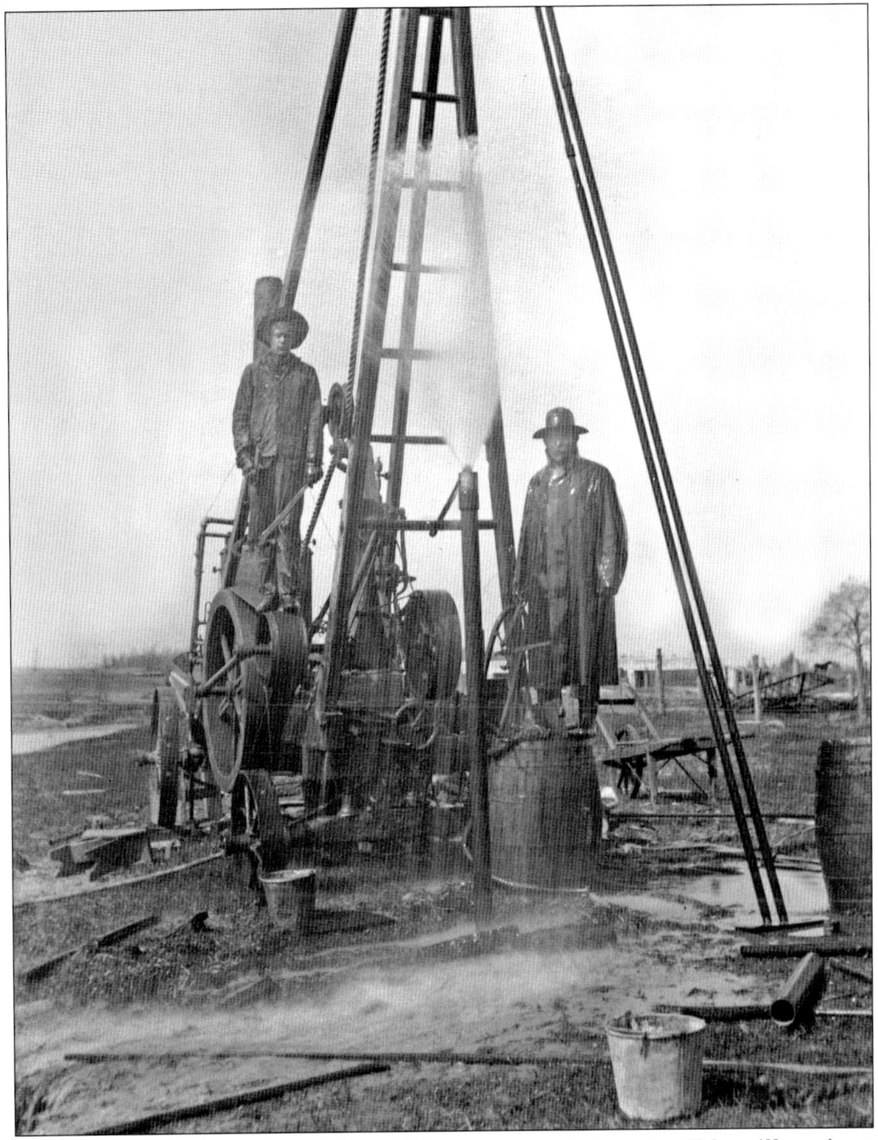

Oil well on the banks of the Tittabawassee River in Edenville, circa 1900. *Courtesy of Midland County Historical Society*

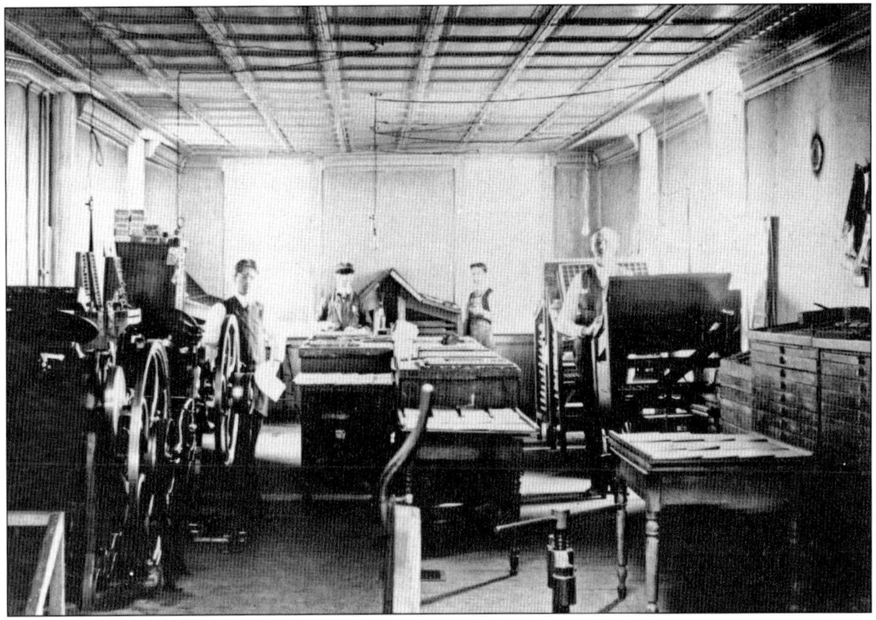

Interior of the *Midland Republican* newspaper office, 1902.
Courtesy of Midland County Historical Society

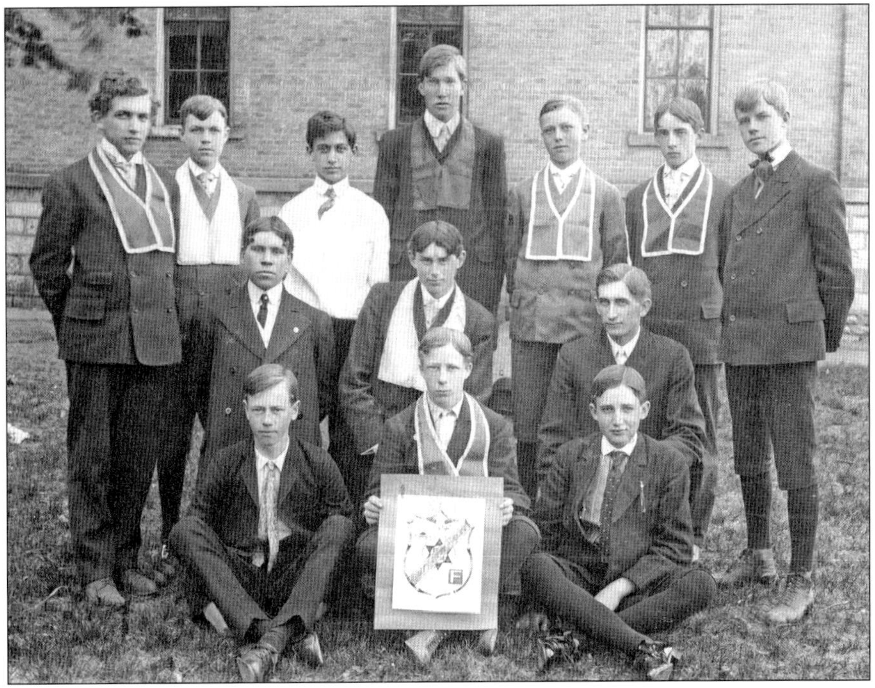

Coming Men of America, circa 1900. Front row, left to right: Eliot Rice, William E. Thompson and Rollin Gordon. Second row: A. D. Peterson, Ernest Ryan and Carl Kinerk. Third row: Paul Olmstead, Russell McCann, Seal Lewinstein, R. B. King, Dexter Reinhart, Cash H. Rice and W. D. G. McCann. *Courtesy of Midland County Historical Society*

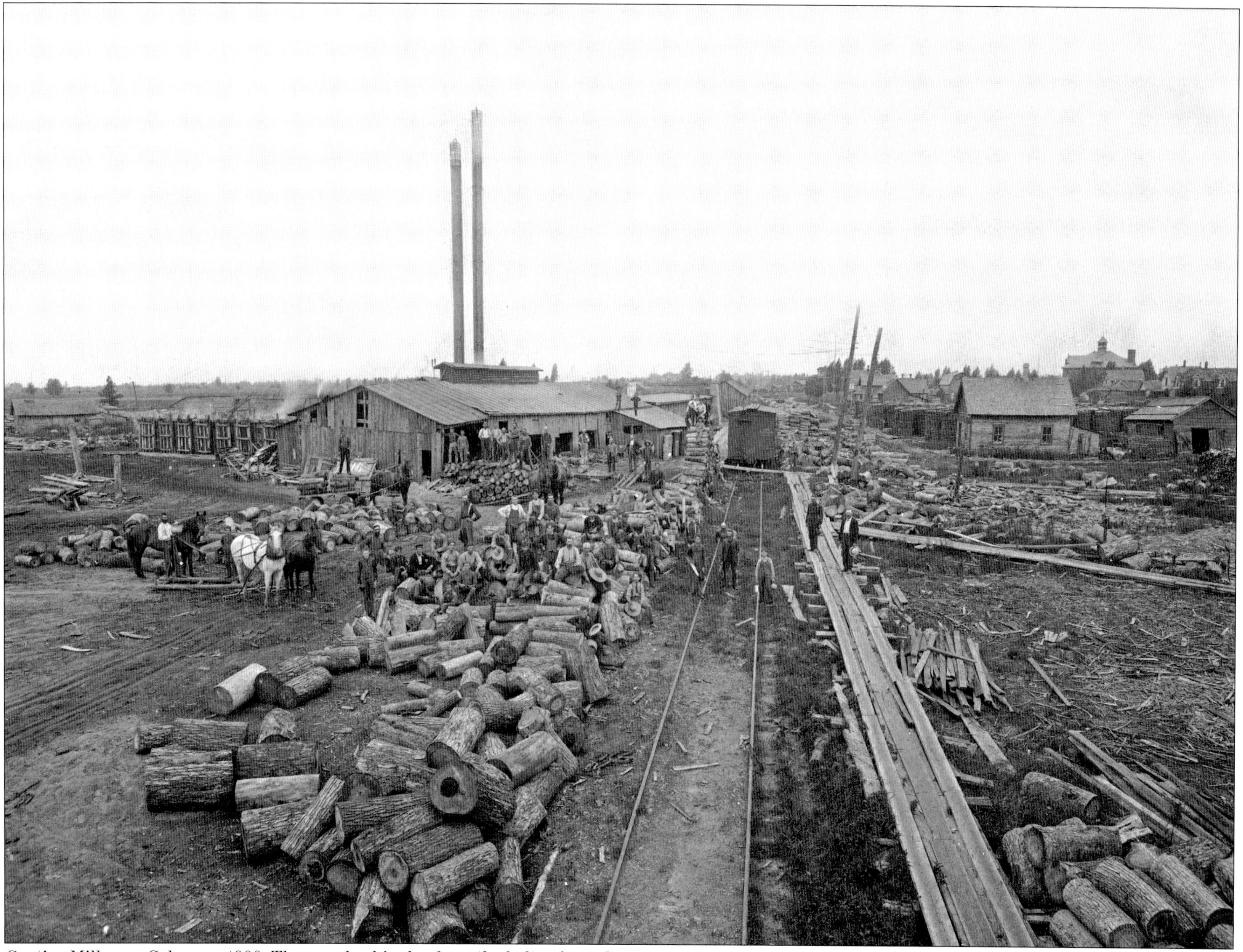

Curtice Mill near Coleman, 1900. They made shingles from the bolts of wood. *Courtesy of Midland County Historical Society*

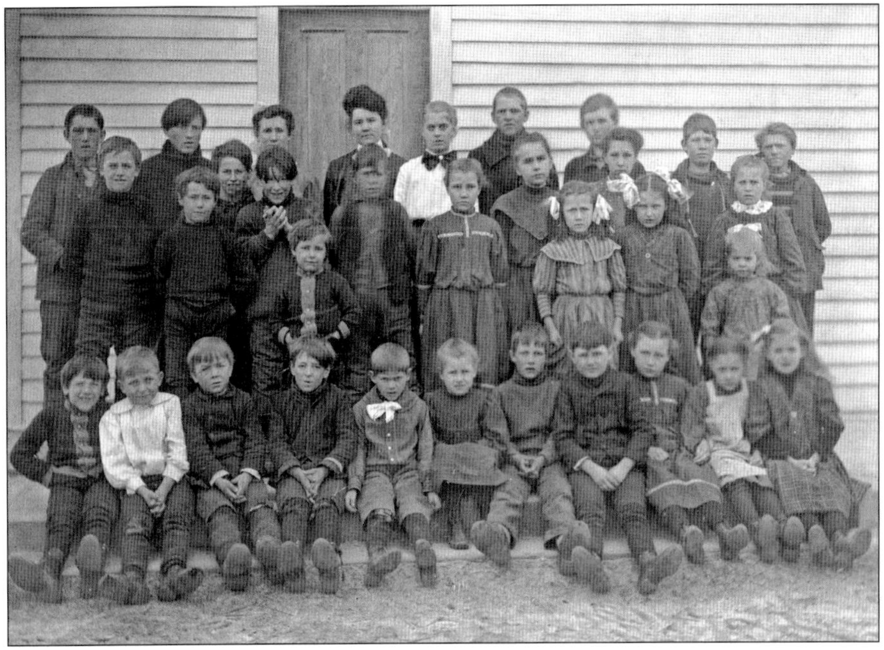

Mills Township school, 1902. *Courtesy of Midland County Historical Society*

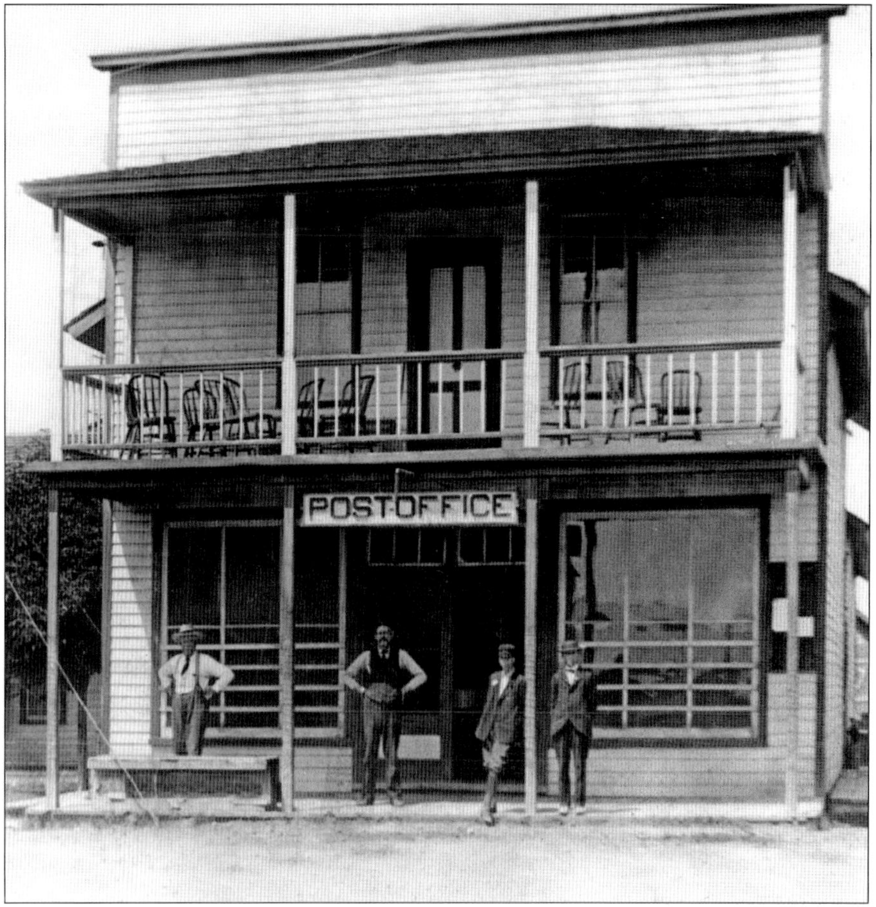

Post Office at Sanford, circa 1900. *Courtesy of Midland County Historical Society*

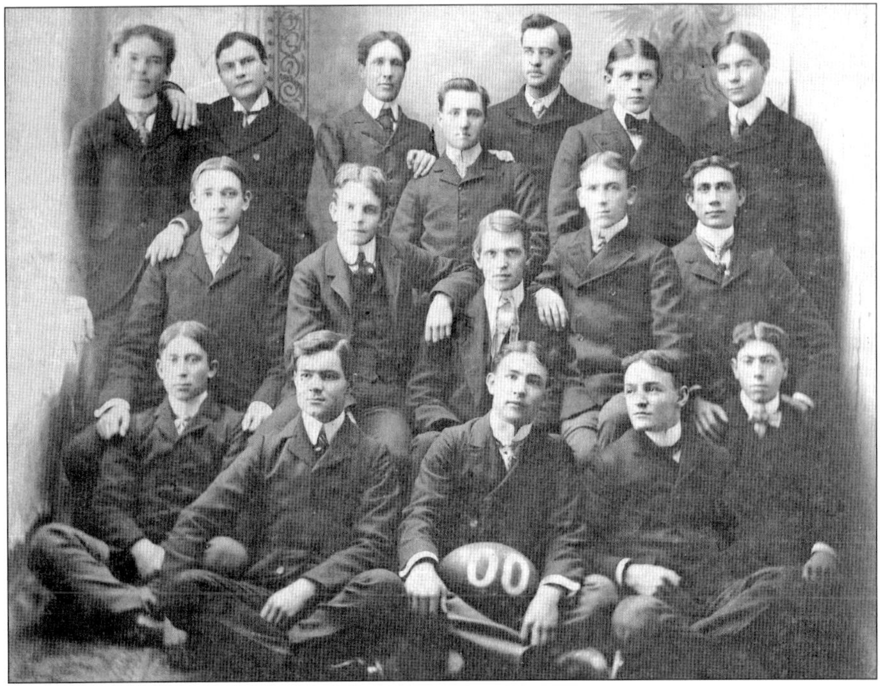

Midland High School football team, 1900. Front, left to right: George Whitman, G. Richardson, Neil McKay, Earl W. Bennett and Harry Ferries. Second row: George Johnson, Robert Davidson, Clem Shoup, William Forman and Barkley Shepherd. Third row: Gilbert A. Currie, John Shaw, Charles Dwyer, Guy Evans, G. L. Jenner, Harry Sias and George Walton. *Courtesy of Midland County Historical Society*

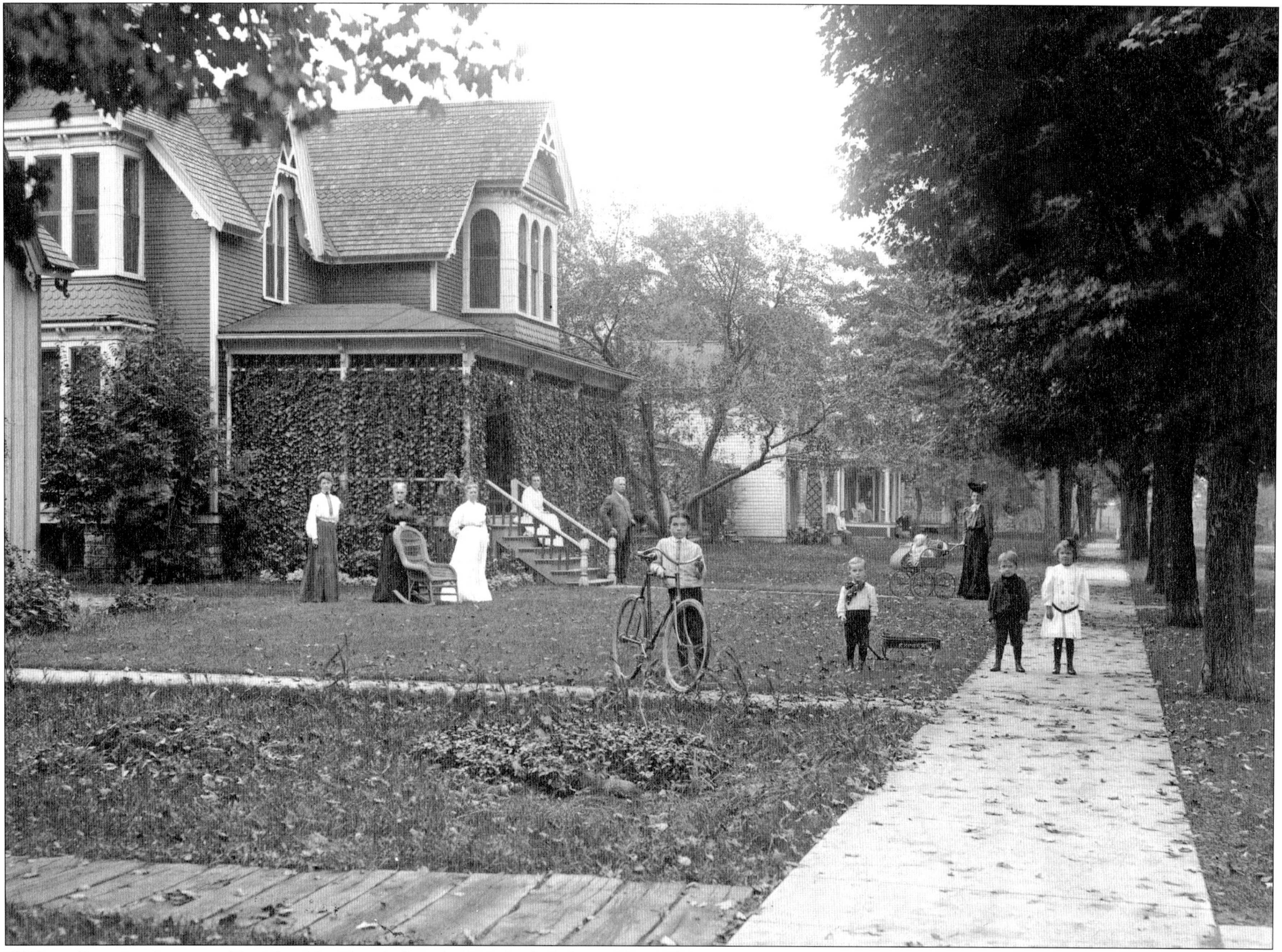

William Reardon home on East Larkin Street, Oct. 1, 1903. Included are Mrs. William Reardon, Mrs. Hiryek, Mrs. Baple, William Reardon Sr., William Reardon III, Mrs. Thomas Griswold, Mr. and Mrs. B. B. Ball and Mrs. J. W. Grissey. *Courtesy of Midland County Historical Society*

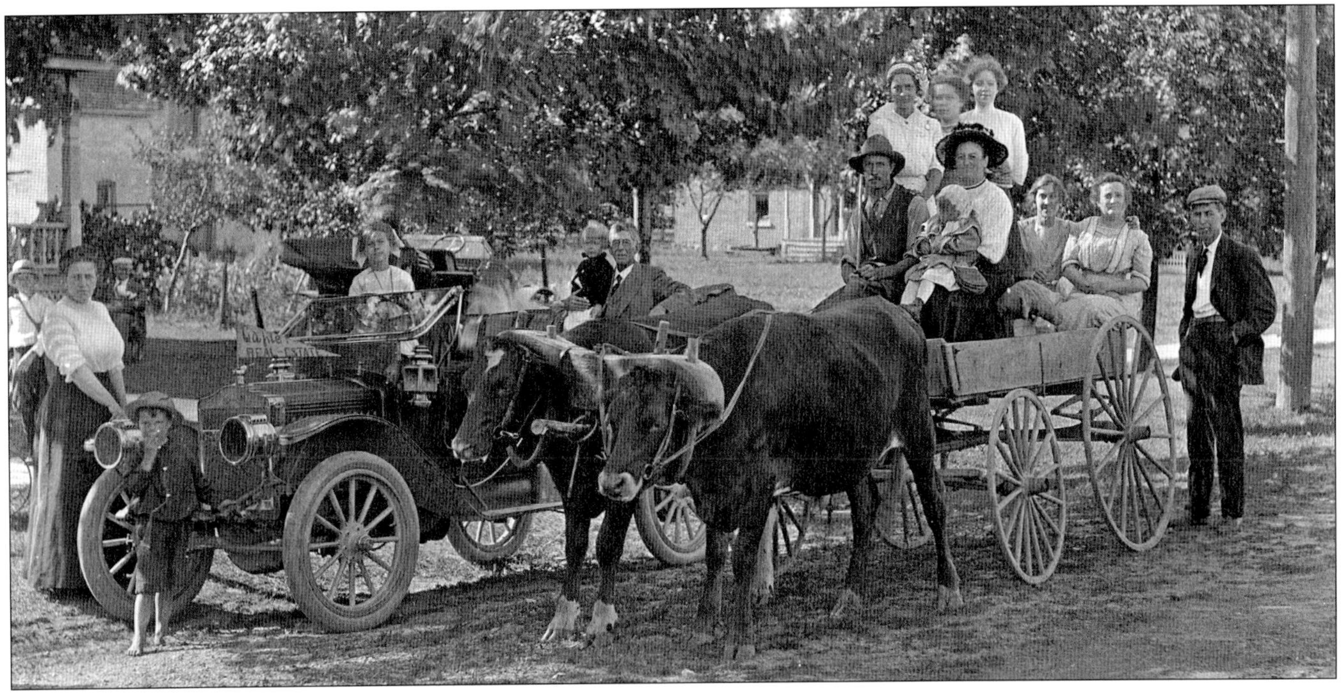

William Capel, standing on the far right, with his family in the car, circa 1905.
Courtesy of Midland County Historical Society

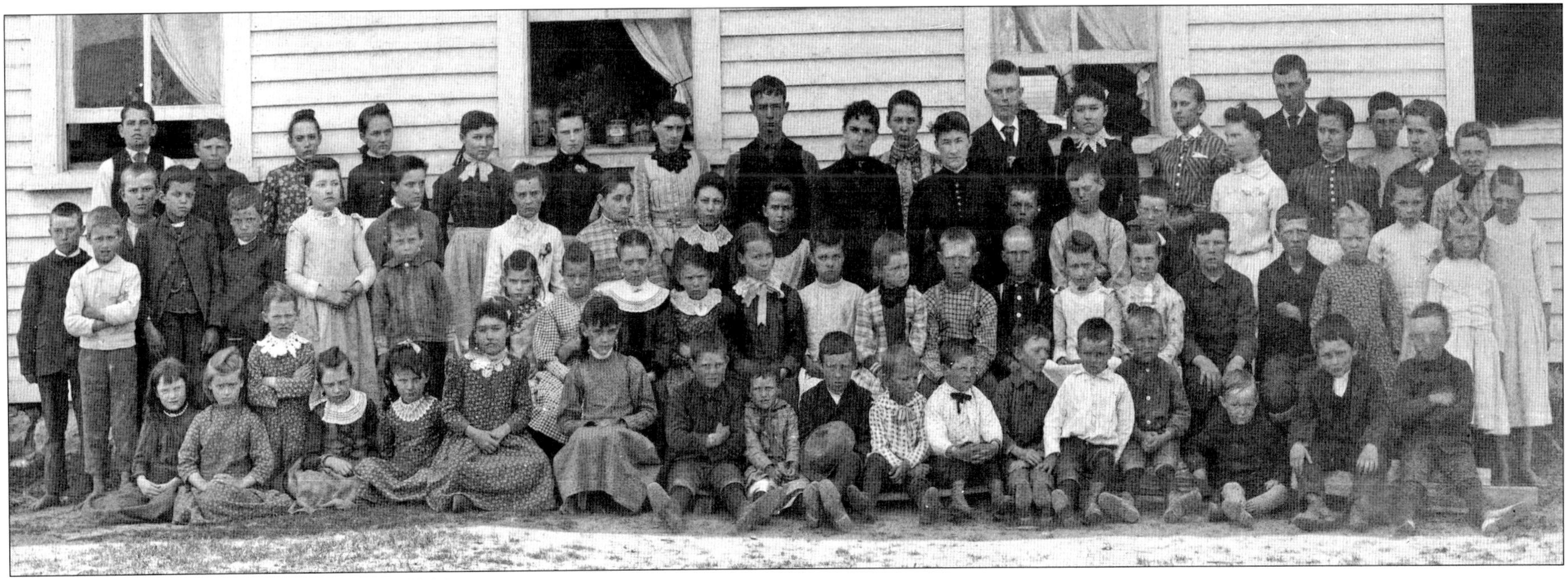

LaPorte Primary Sunday School class, 1904. *Courtesy of Midland County Historical Society*

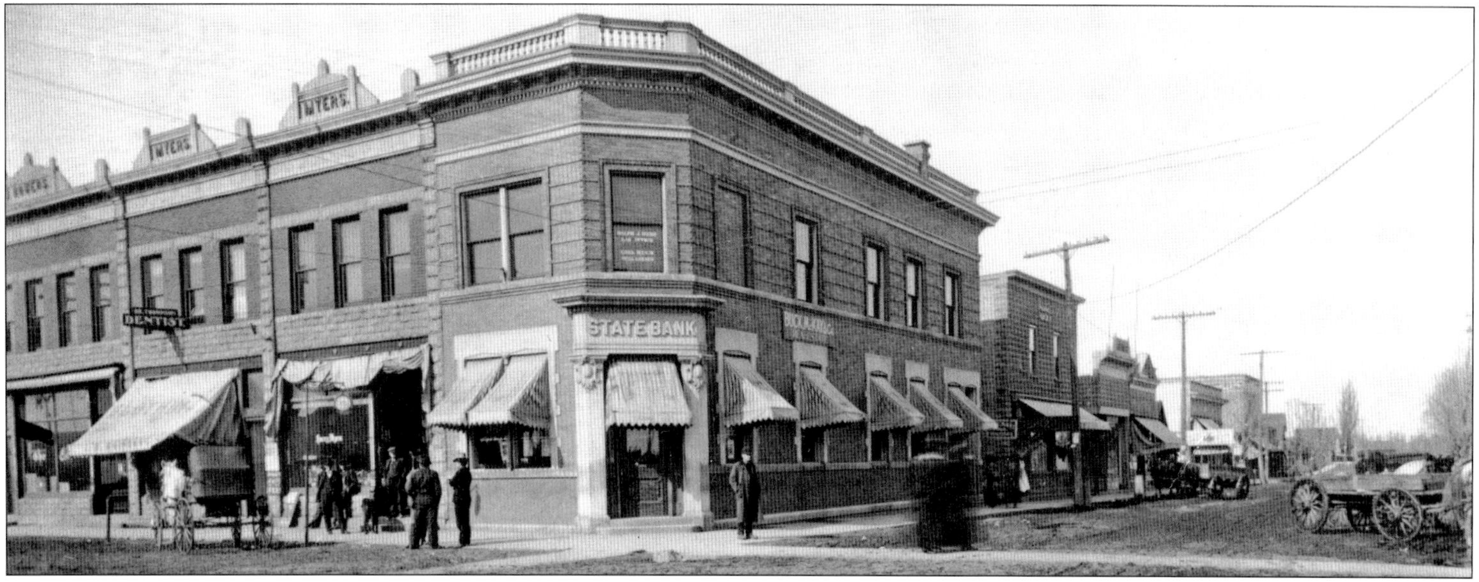

Looking down the main street of Coleman, 1905. *Courtesy of Midland County Historical Society*

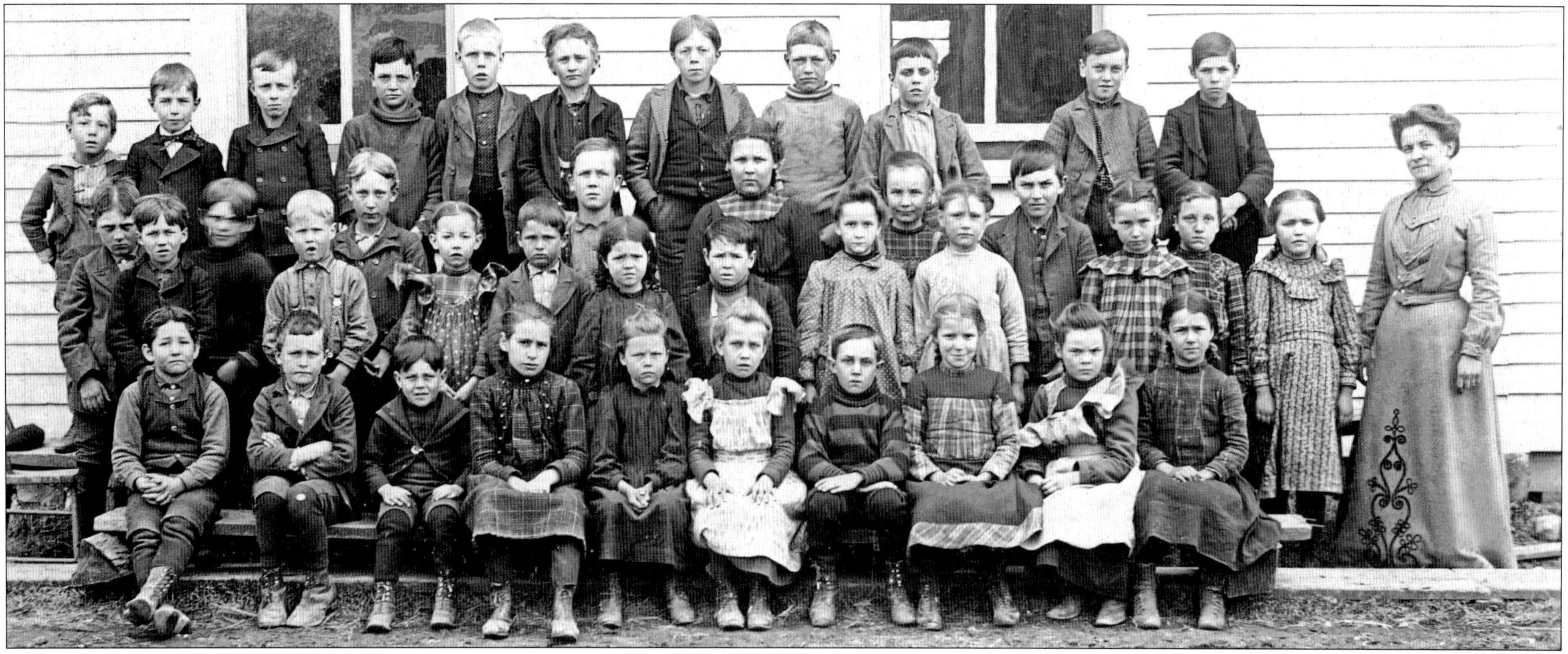

LaPorte School, circa 1905. *Courtesy of Midland County Historical Society*

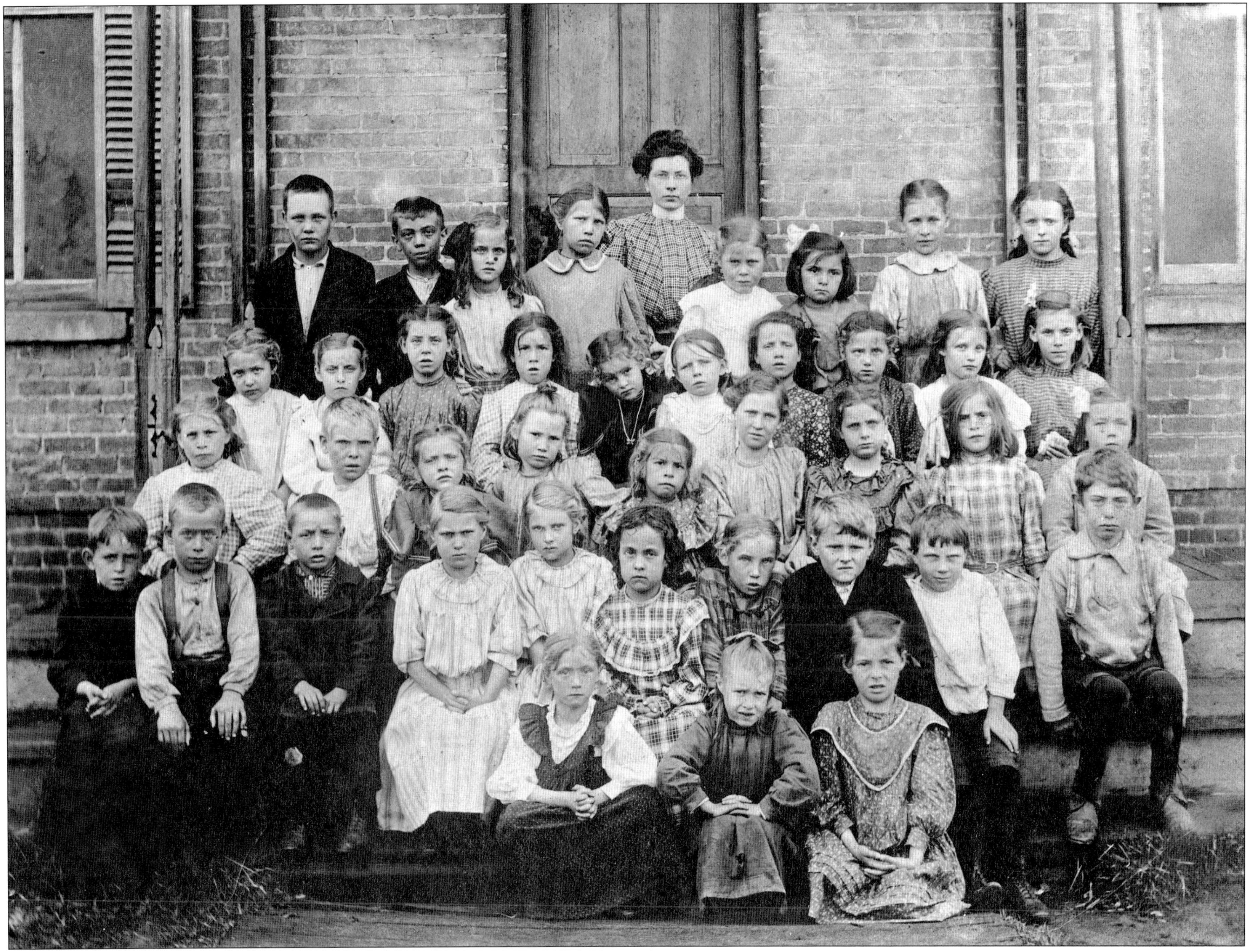

Bailey School in Ingersoll Township, 1907. *Courtesy of Midland County Historical Society*

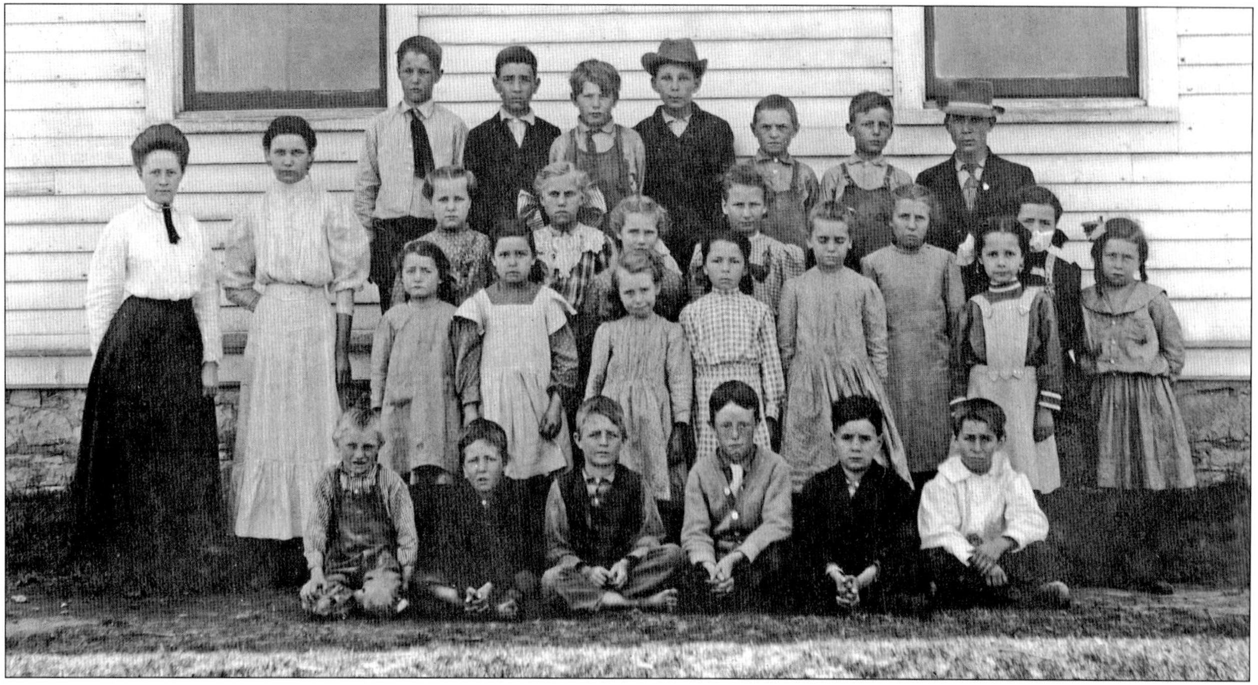

Sugnet School students and teacher, 1909.
Courtesy of Midland County Historical Society

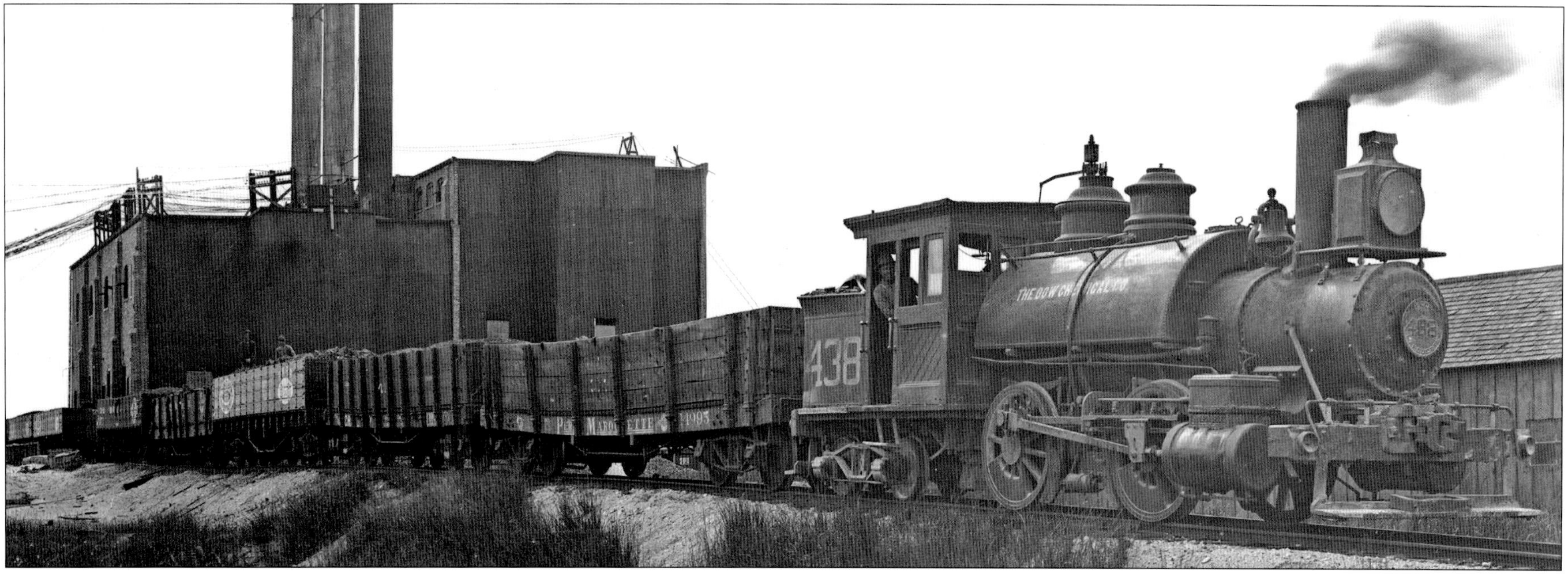

The first locomotive at Dow hauling coal to Dow's "E" powerhouse, 1905. *Courtesy of Midland County Historical Society*

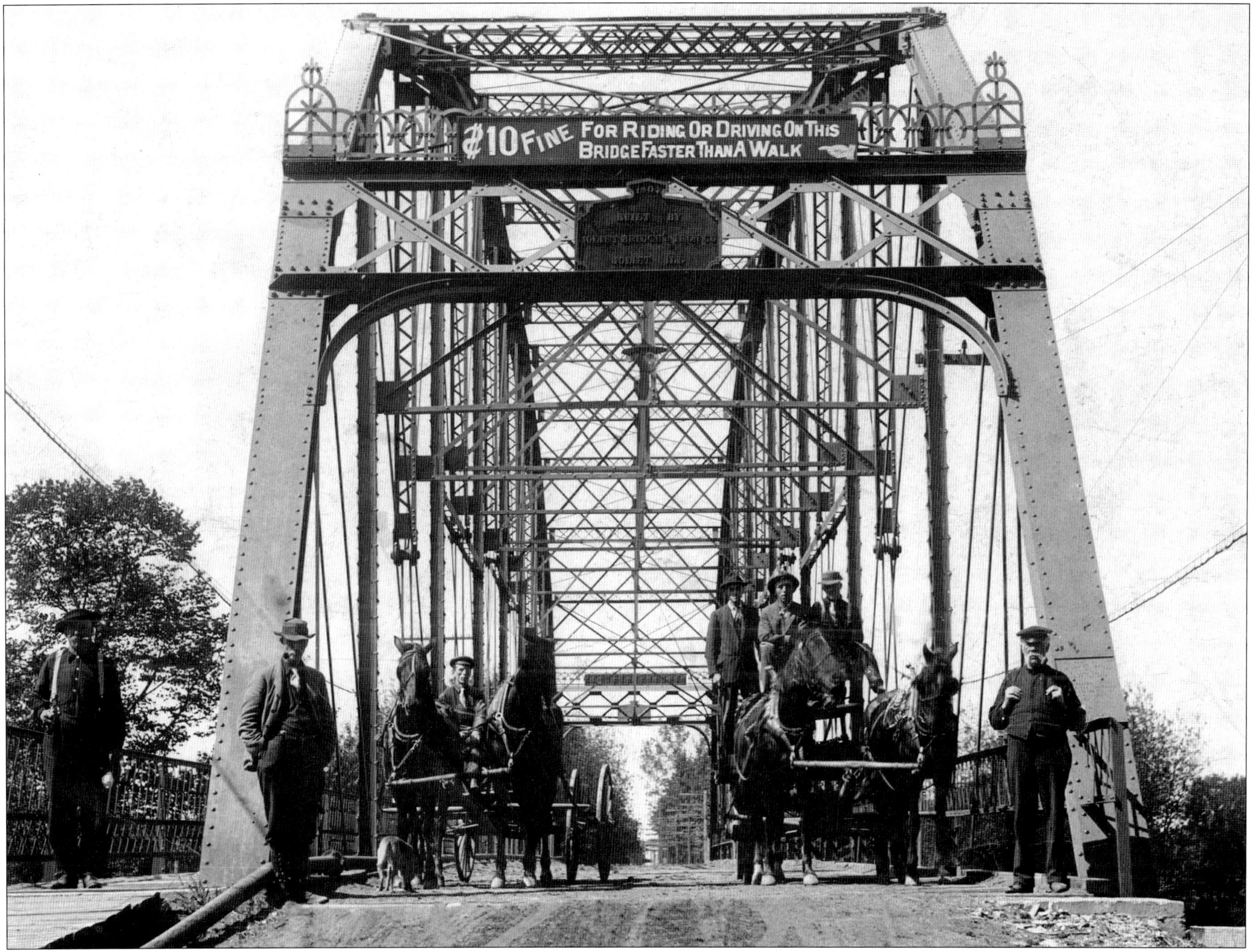

Benson Street Bridge built in 1908. This bridge replaced the Covered Bridge, built in 1871, which was destroyed by the flood of 1907. *Courtesy of Naomi Haebler*

1910-1919

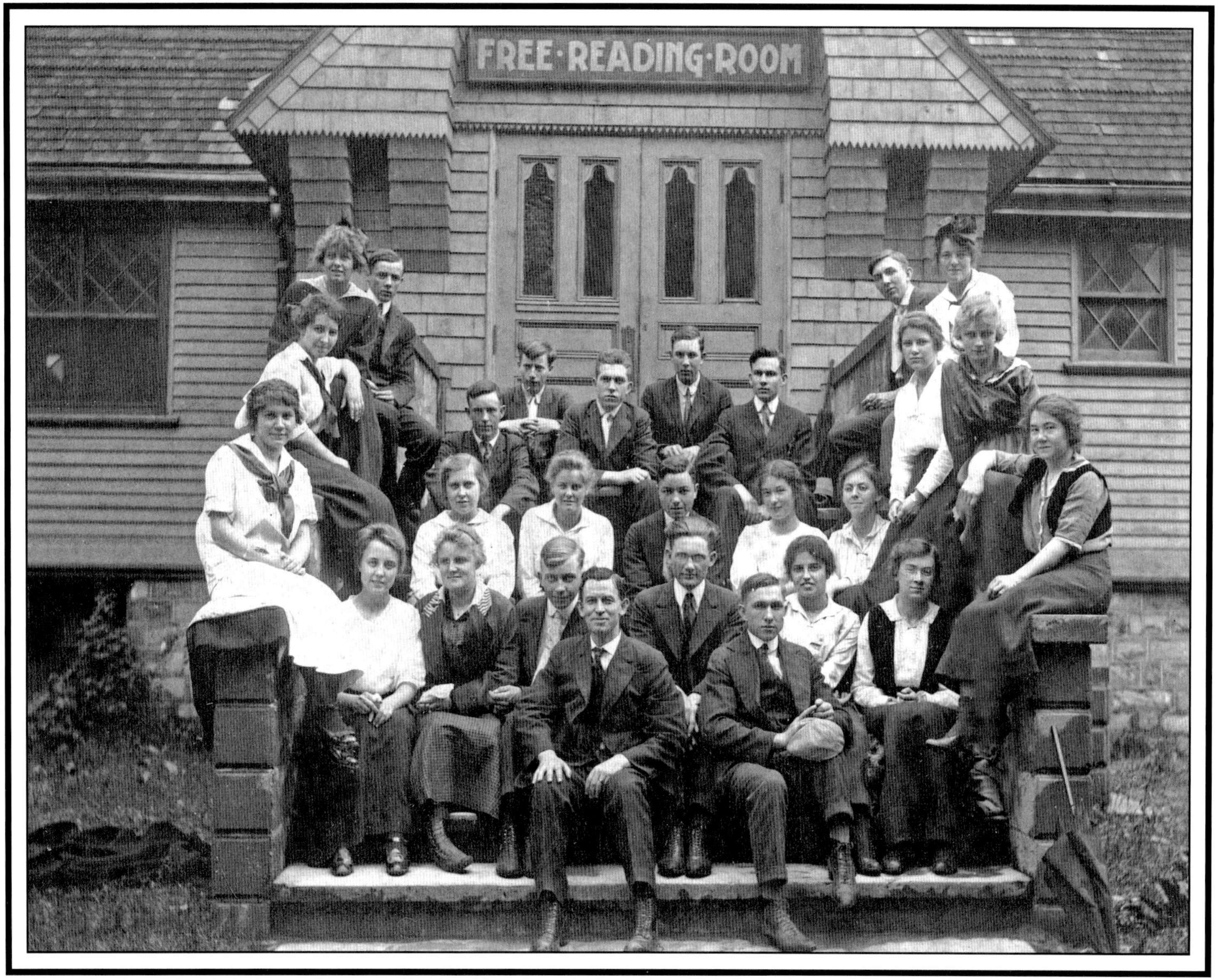

Midland High School class of 1916 in front of Midland's first library, The Free Reading Room, on the corner of Ashman and Ellsworth streets, 1916. *Courtesy of Midland County Historical Society*

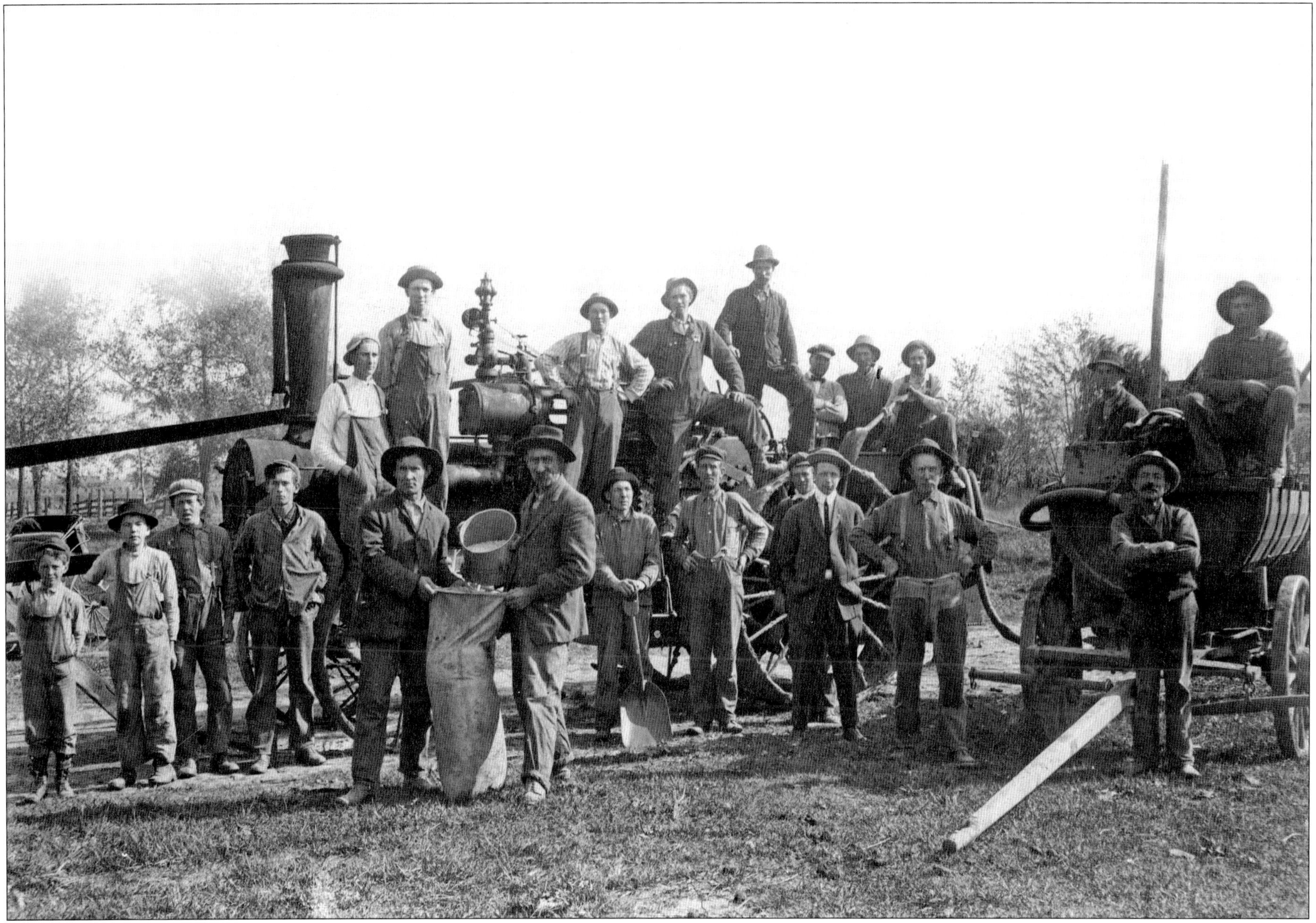

Threshing crew at the Louis Weaver farm on East Ashman the year the armyworms went through Midland, circa 1910. Those included: William Dehn, Roy Blake, Clyde Roberson, Julius Samper, Frank Martin, Scott Wilson, Harry Cox, Fred Opperman, Orian Robenson, Albert Brandt, Frank Robenson, Charles Dehn, Harman Upperman, Charles Schultz, Billie Thompson, Billie Findes, Louis Upperman, Louis Weaver and Roy Collins. *Courtesy of Richard Blake*

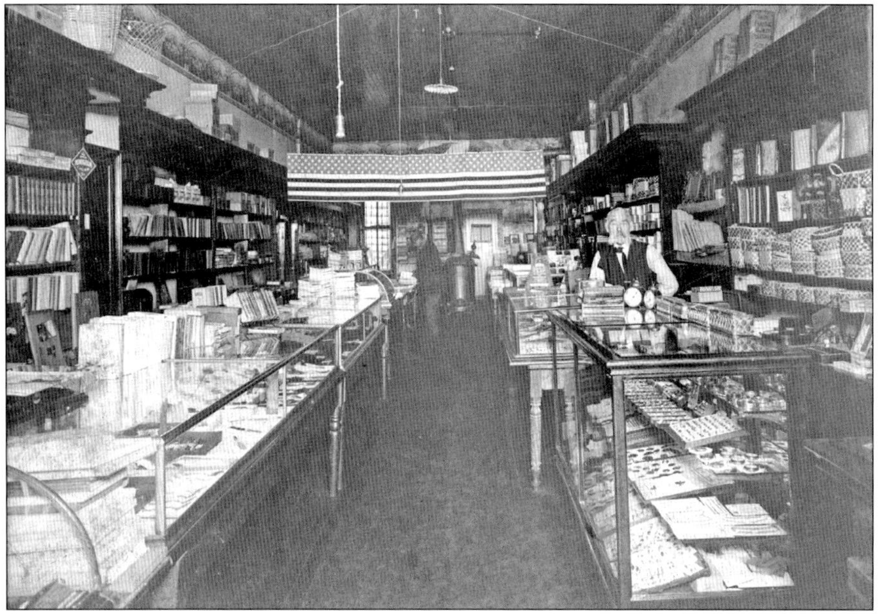

George Thompson behind the counter at Thompson Mercantile on Main Street, circa 1910. *Courtesy of Midland County Historical Society*

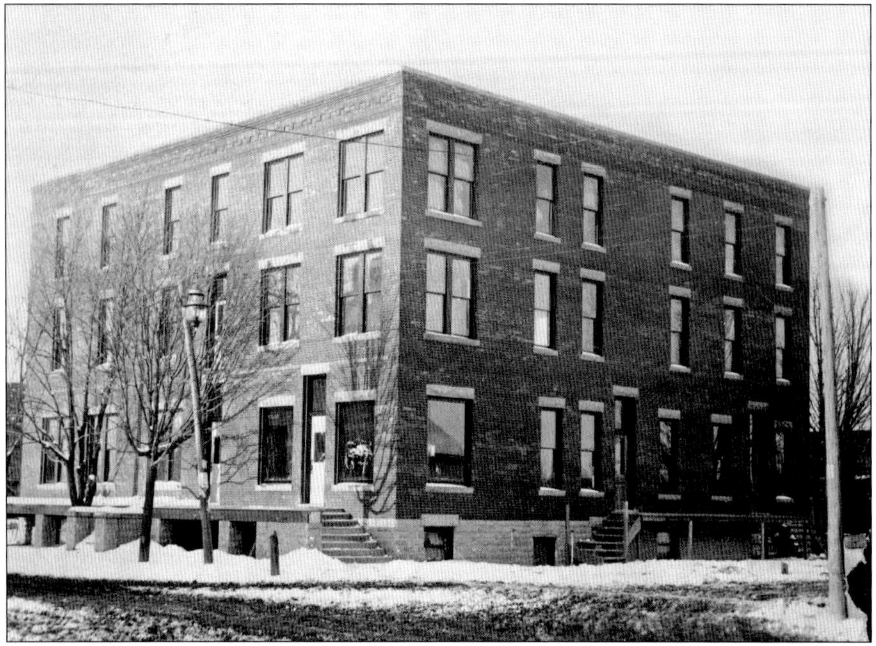

Hecox Hotel in Coleman, circa 1910. *Courtesy of Midland County Historical Society*

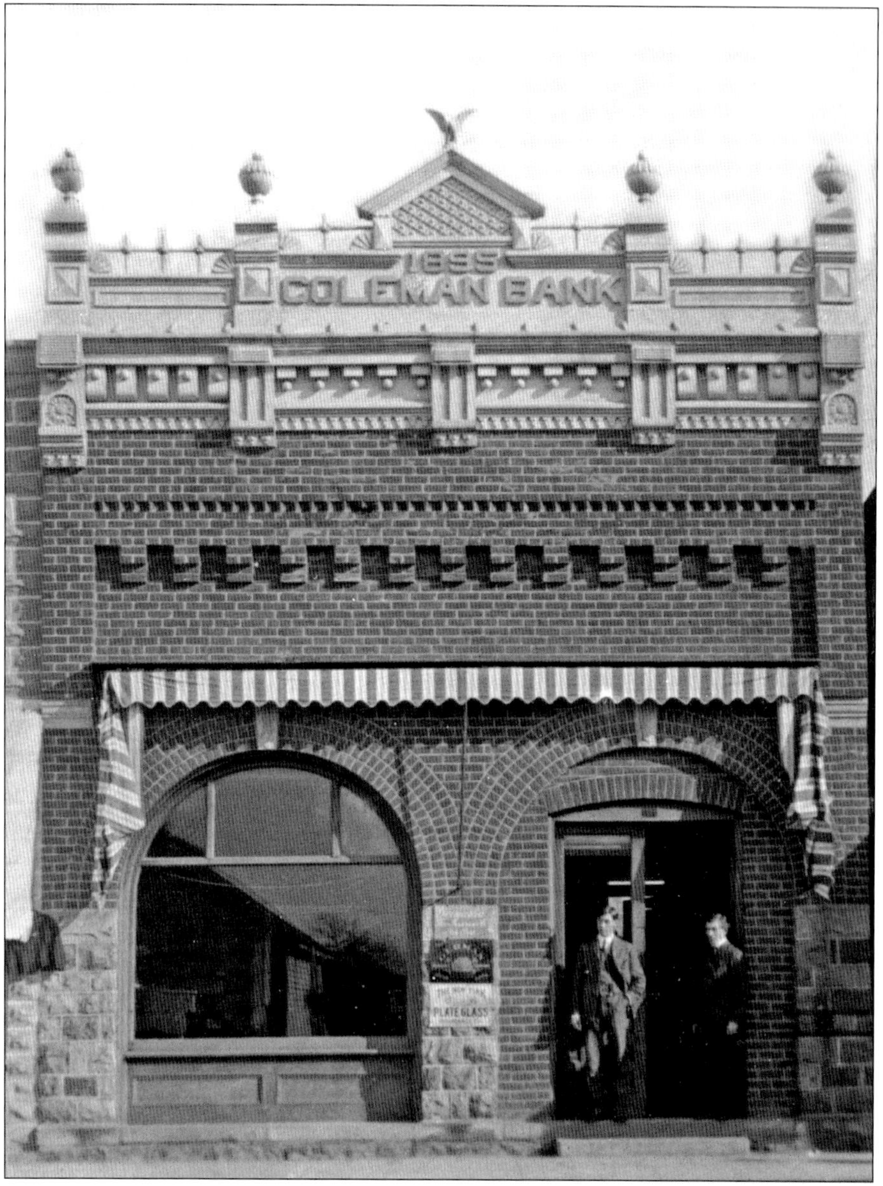

Coleman Bank, circa 1910. The bank was built by Charles Niggeman and B. R. Noble. *Courtesy of Midland County Historical Society*

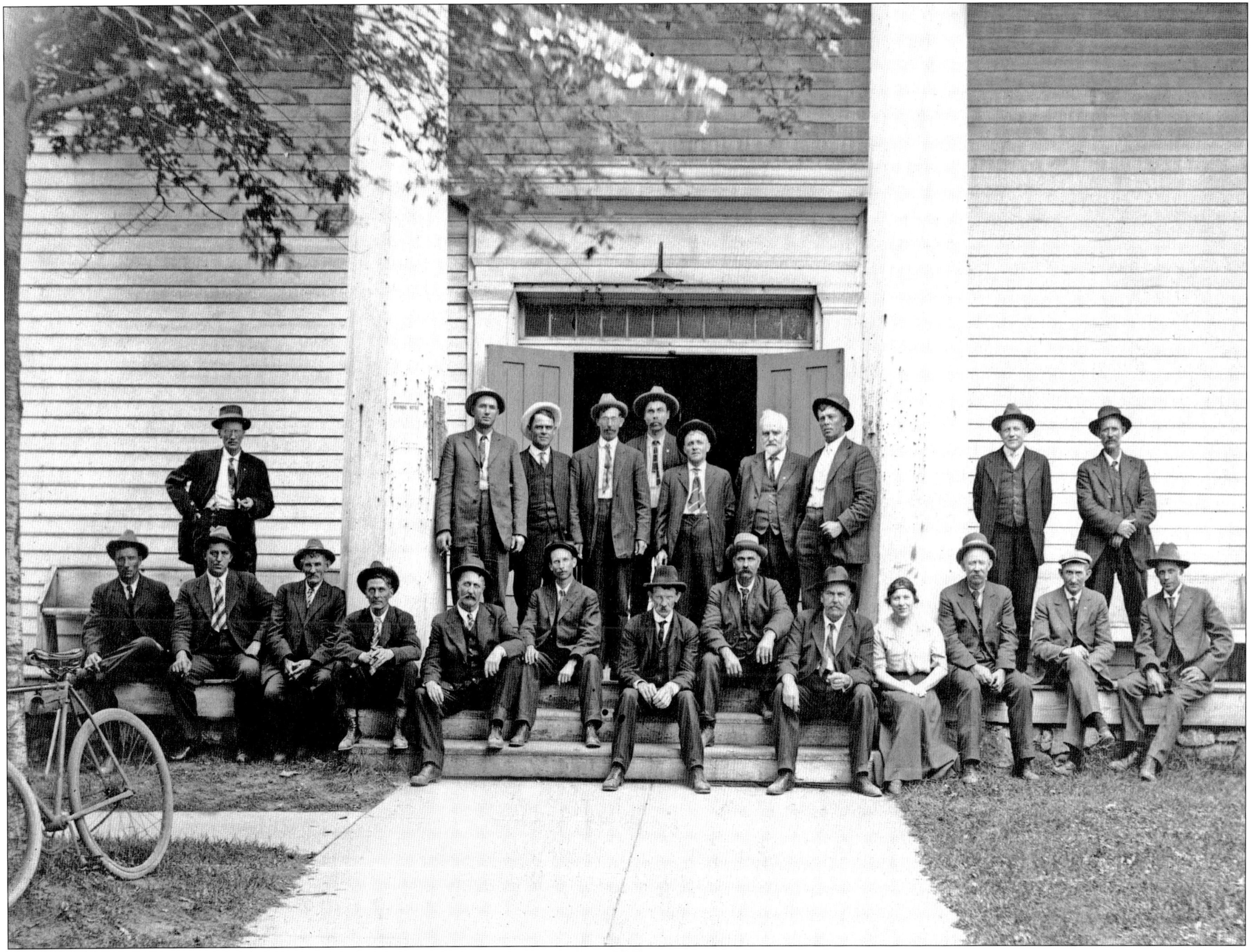

Midland County Board of Supervisors in front of the first courthouse, circa 1910. *Courtesy of Midland County Historical Society*

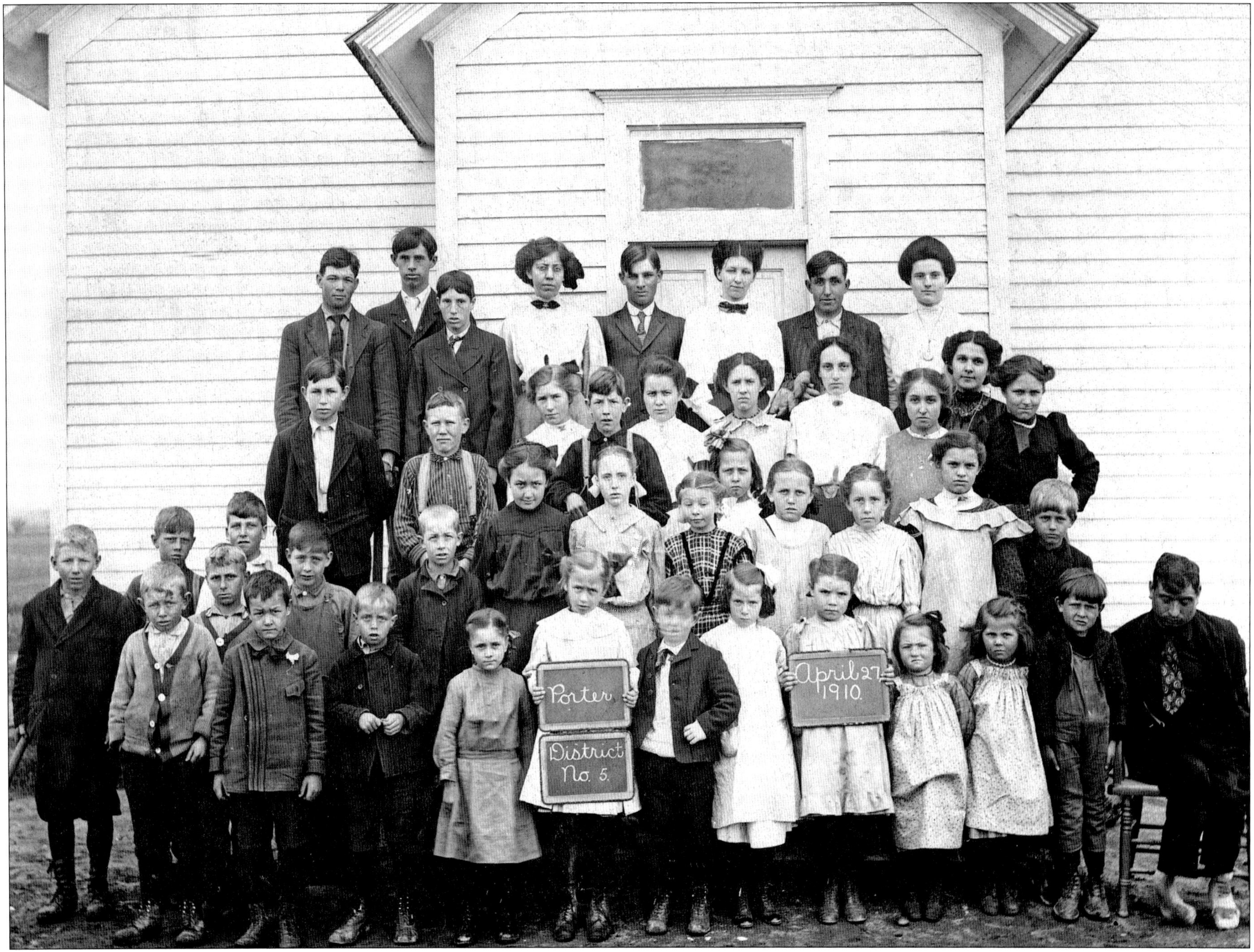

District #5 school, Porter Township, April 27, 1910. Bessie Gray was their teacher. *Courtesy of Midland County Historical Society*

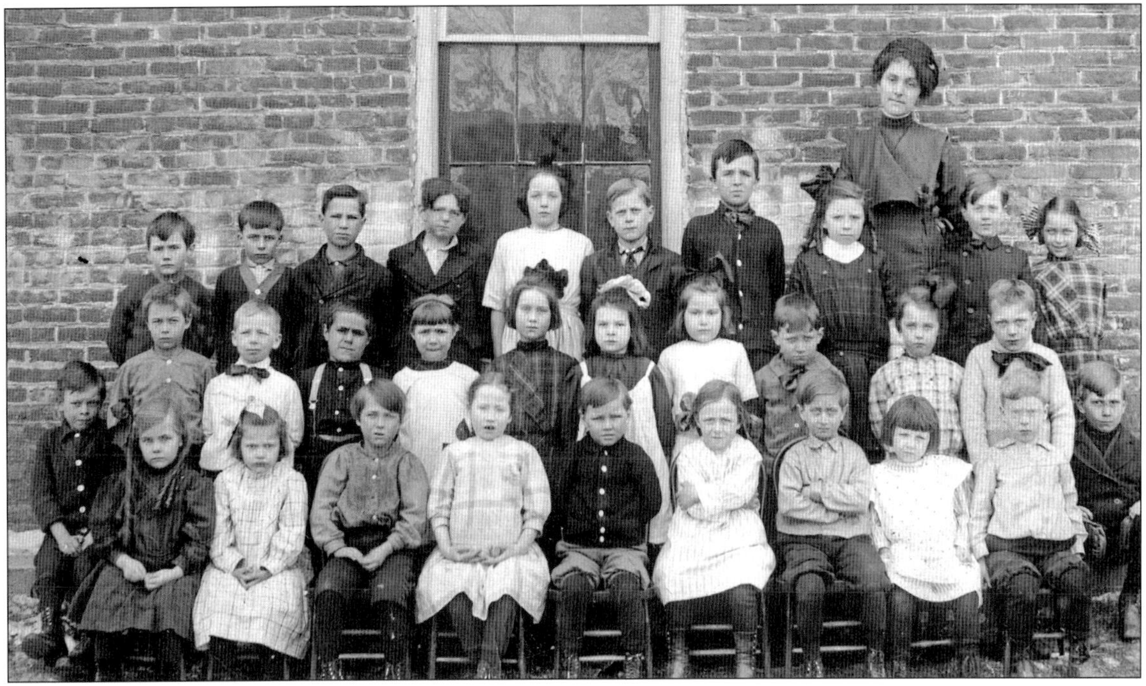

Fourth Ward School in Midland, March 14, 1912. The teacher is Miss Lydia Wade. Front row, left to right: unidentified, Ruth Robinson, Florence Brown, Lee Brink, Carrie Goodwin, Fred Slaw, Myrtle Ostrander, Harold Taylor, Zeta Sherwood and Leslie Howard. Second row: unidentified, Harry Lowsley, Richard Kenyon, Ruth Schwartz, Catherine Callahan, Bonnie Dorr, Harriet Shaw, Clarence Ostrowder, Dorothy Brooks, Arthur Brown and unidentified. Third row: Thomas Shaw, unidentified, Glenn Kenyon, unidentified, Olive Goodwin, Ray Hickling, Doran West, Hazel Sherwood, Bobbie Dour and Margaret Callahan. *Courtesy of Midland County Historical Society*

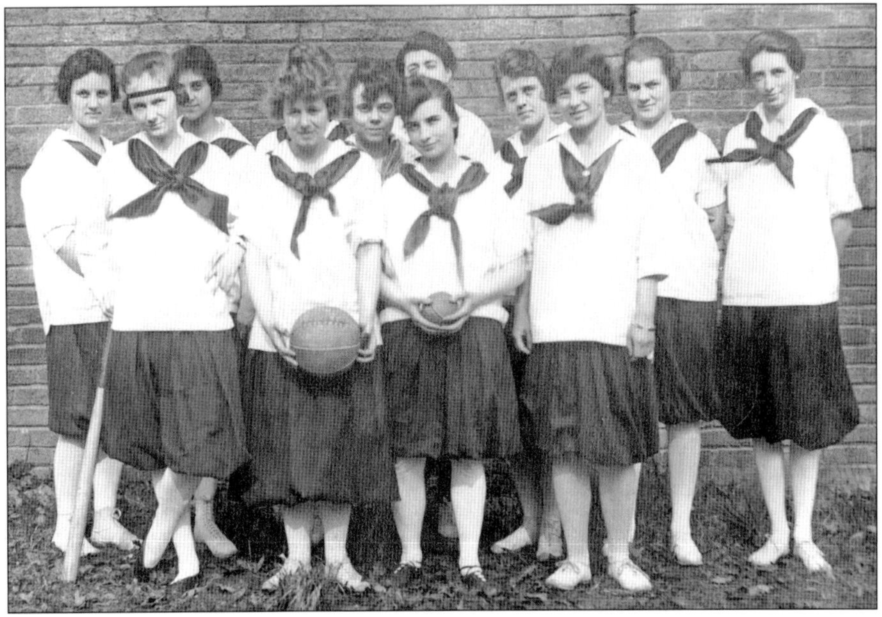

Midland High School girls' physical education class, circa 1915.

Courtesy of Midland County Historical Society

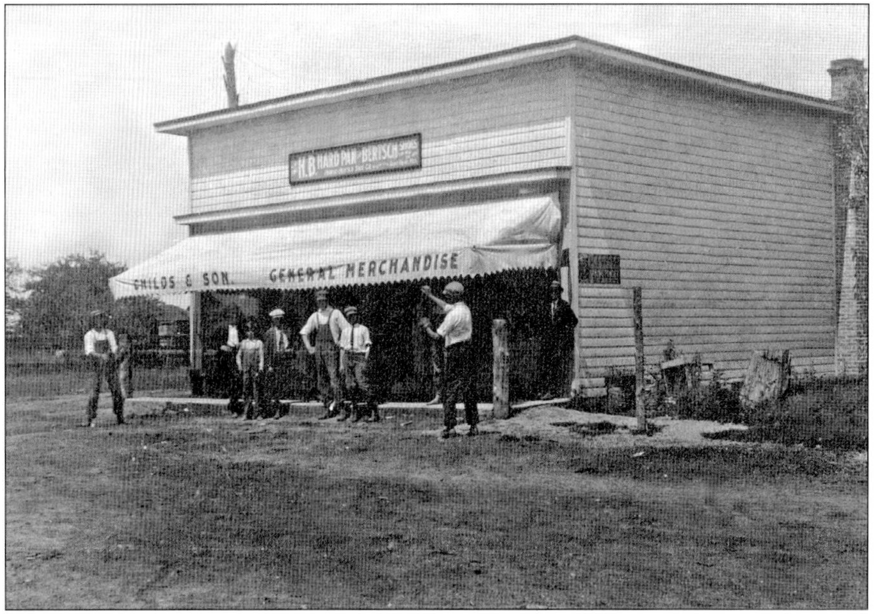

Childs & Son General Merchandise in North Bradley, 1915.

Courtesy of Judy Winter

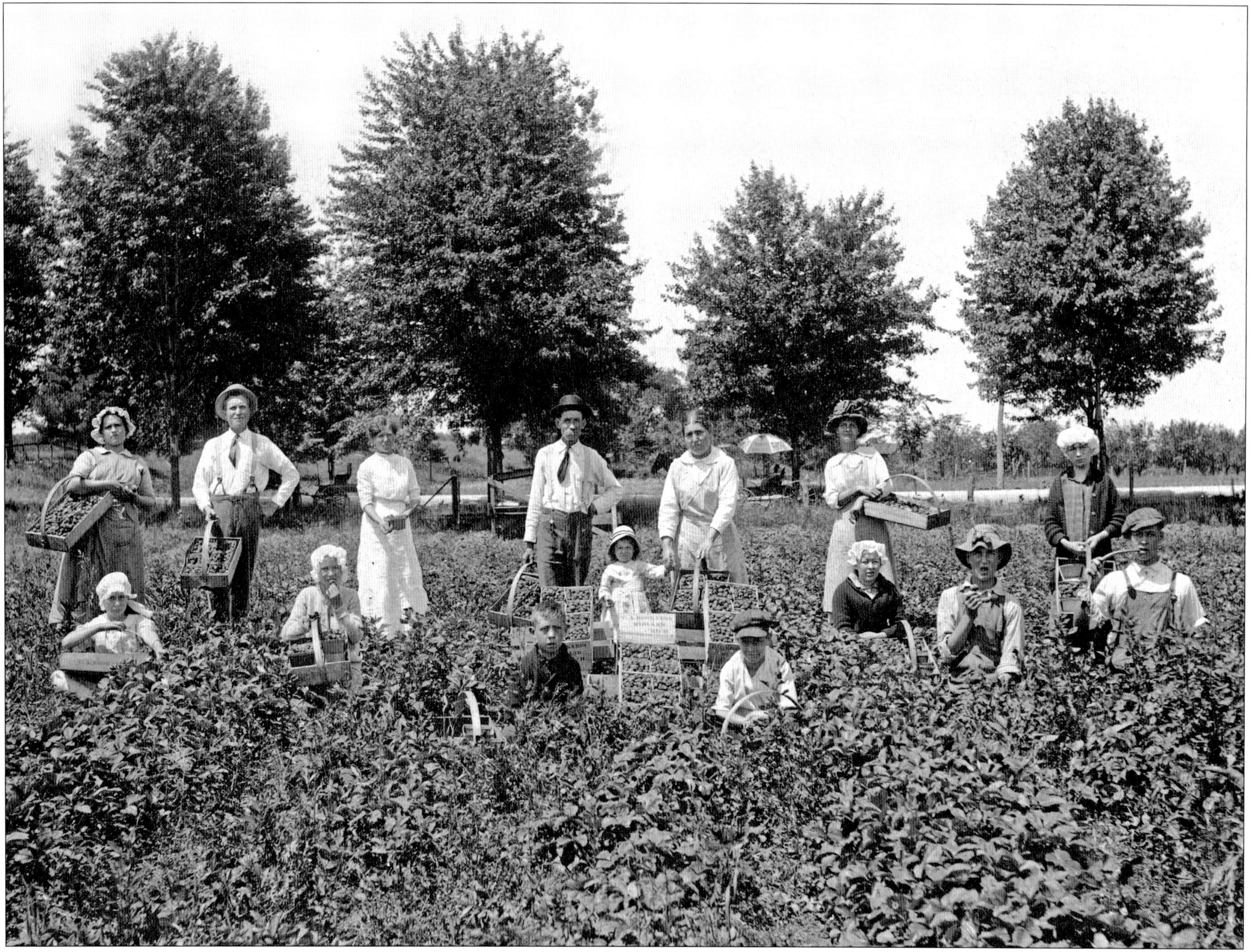

Harvesting on the C. A. Bookness farm, circa 1910. Eastman Road and Dow orchards are in the background. *Courtesy of Midland County Historical Society*

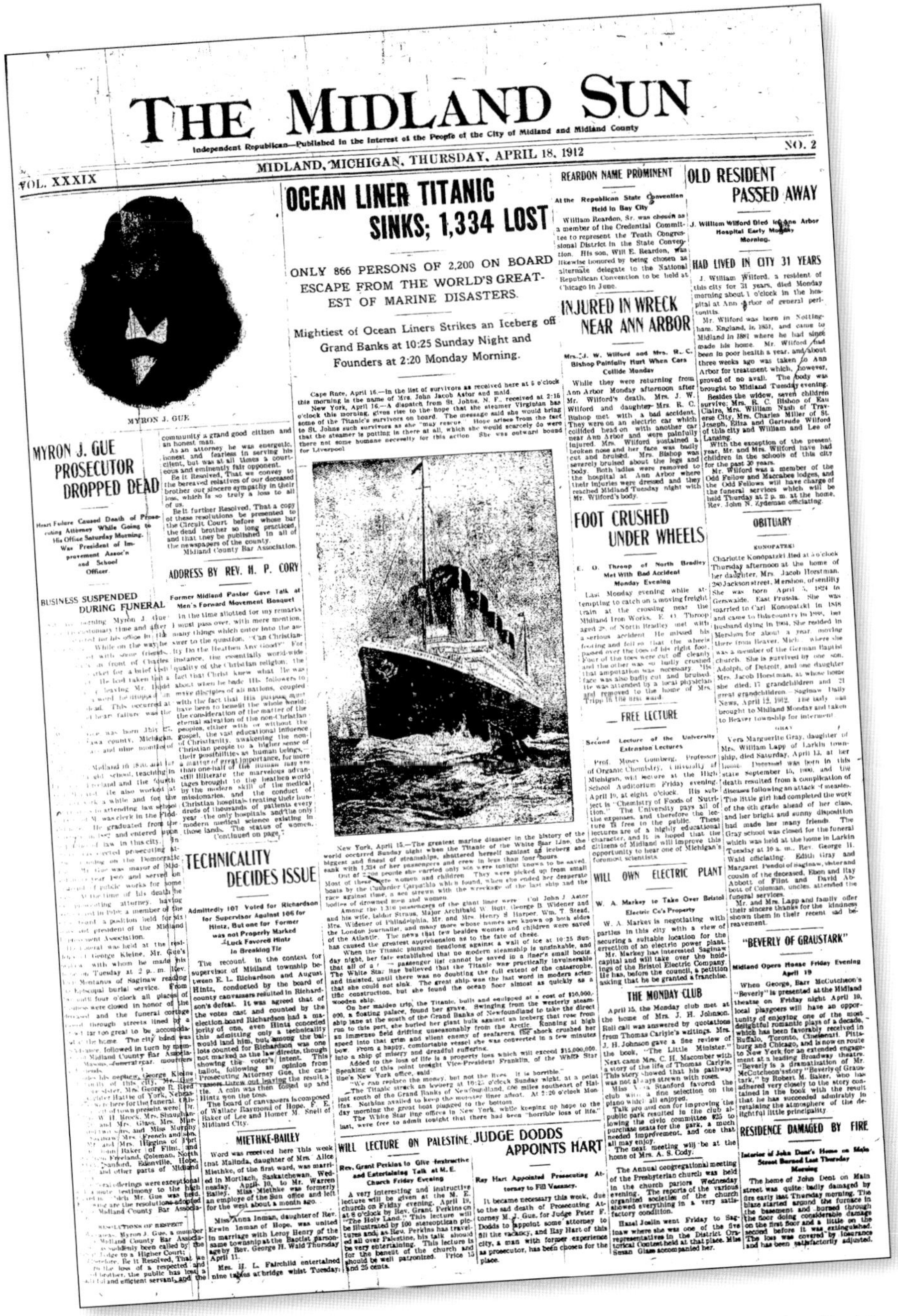

THE MIDLAND SUN

Independent Republican—Published in the Interest of the People of the City of Midland and Midland County

VOL. XXXIX MIDLAND, MICHIGAN, THURSDAY, APRIL 18, 1912 NO. 2

OCEAN LINER TITANIC SINKS; 1,334 LOST

ONLY 866 PERSONS OF 2,200 ON BOARD ESCAPE FROM THE WORLD'S GREATEST OF MARINE DISASTERS.

Mightiest of Ocean Liners Strikes an Iceberg off Grand Banks at 10:25 Sunday Night and Founders at 2:20 Monday Morning.

MYRON J. GUE

MYRON J. GUE PROSECUTOR DROPPED DEAD

ADDRESS BY REV. H. P. CORY

BUSINESS SUSPENDED DURING FUNERAL

TECHNICALITY DECIDES ISSUE

MIETHKE-BAILEY

REARDON NAME PROMINENT

INJURED IN WRECK NEAR ANN ARBOR

FOOT CRUSHED UNDER WHEELS

FREE LECTURE

WILL OWN ELECTRIC PLANT

THE MONDAY CLUB

WILL LECTURE ON PALESTINE

JUDGE DODDS APPOINTS HART

OLD RESIDENT PASSED AWAY

HAD LIVED IN CITY 31 YEARS

OBITUARY

"BEVERLY OF GRAUSTARK"

RESIDENCE DAMAGED BY FIRE

The Midland Sun reporting on the sinking of the *Titanic*, April 18, 1912. *Courtesy of Midland Daily News*

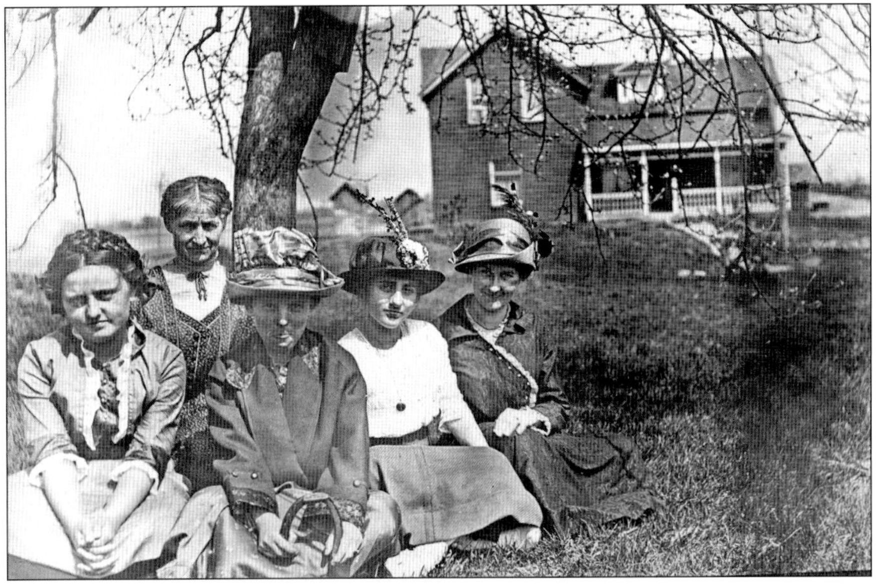

At the Franklin farm on Poseyville Road, circa 1914. Included are Helen Pritchard and Mina Franklin. A. J. Franklin built the house making the blocks by hand using a machine. *Courtesy of James J. Dion*

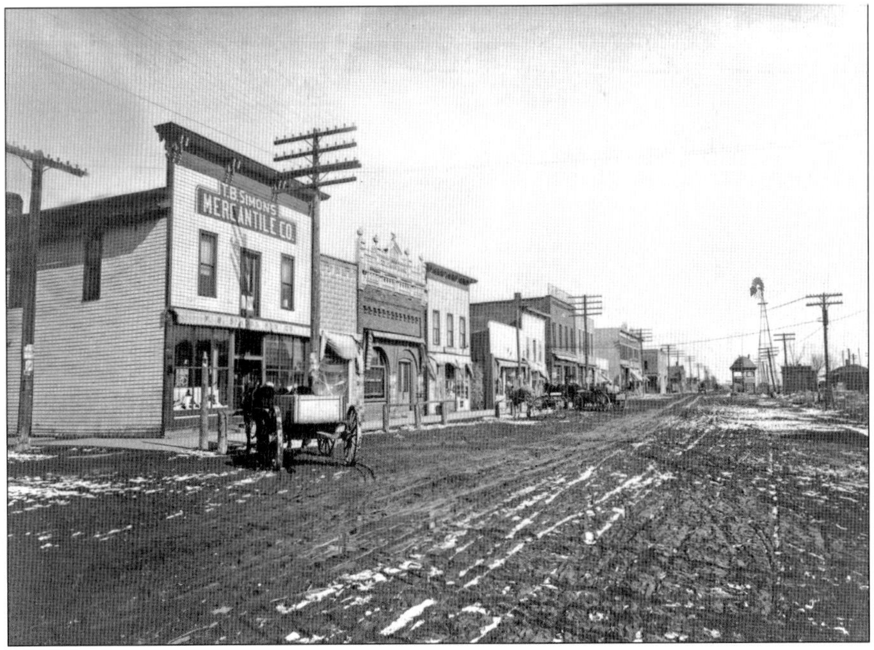

Main Street in Coleman, circa 1915. *Courtesy of Midland County Historical Society*

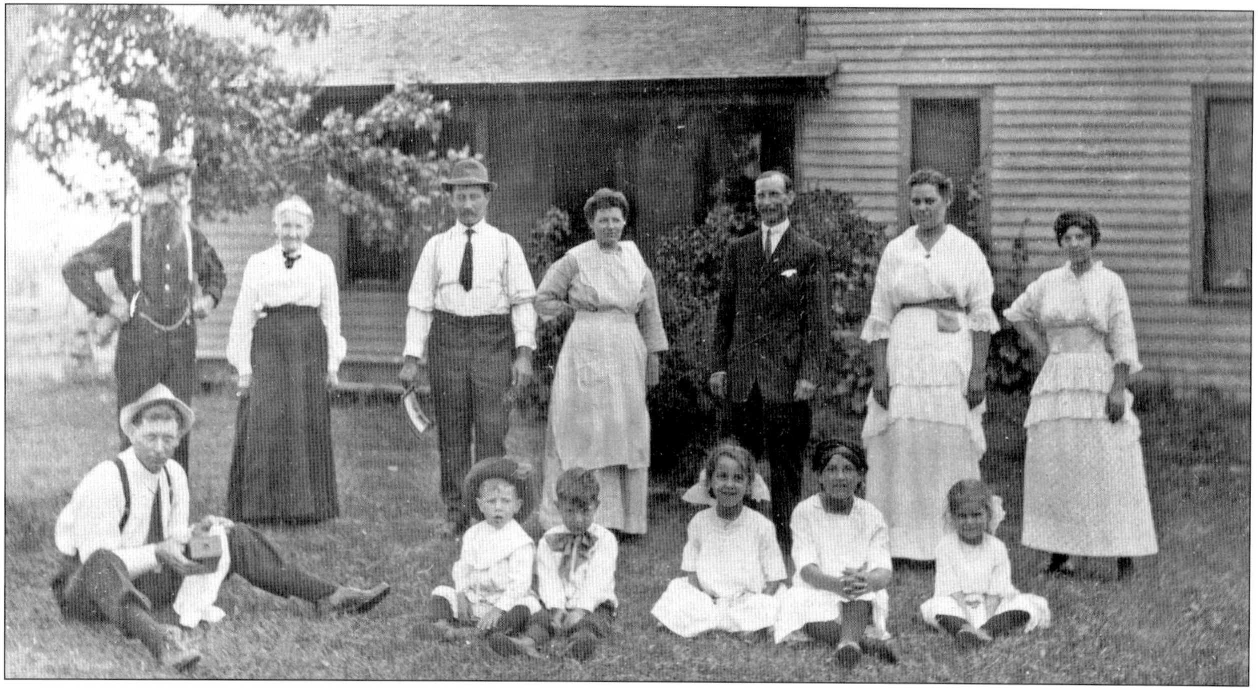

At the Frank Schlader farm at 4151 Kent Rd., circa 1912. Front row, left to right: George Schlader, Clarence Schlader, Willie Schlader, Evelyn Schlader, Ida Reid and Grace Schlader. Back row: William Schlader, Katherine Schlader, Frank Schlader, Minnie Schlader, Andy Schlader, Charlotte Schlader and Jessie Reid. *Courtesy of Janet Rice*

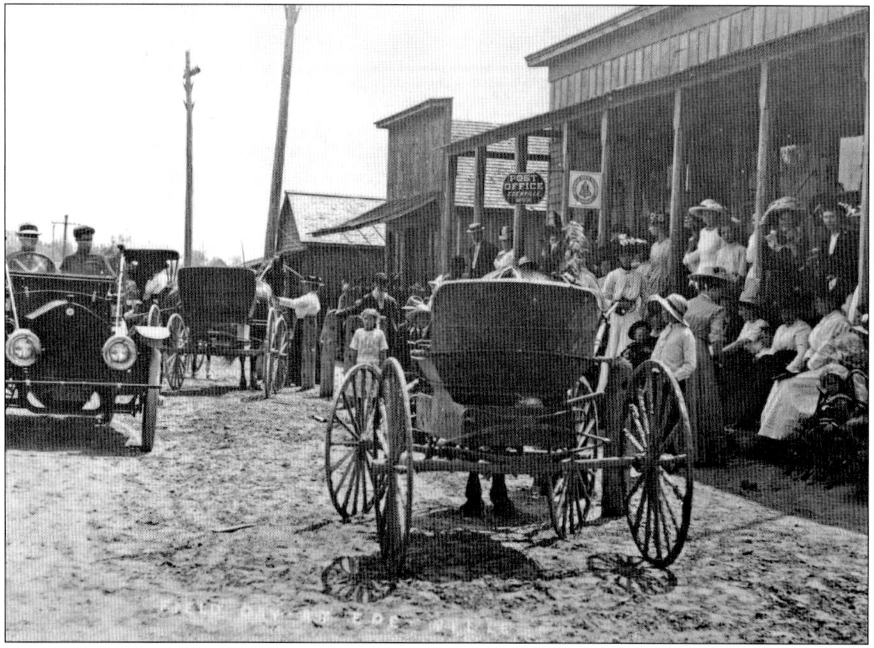

Street scene in Edenville, circa 1915. *Courtesy of Midland County Historical Society*

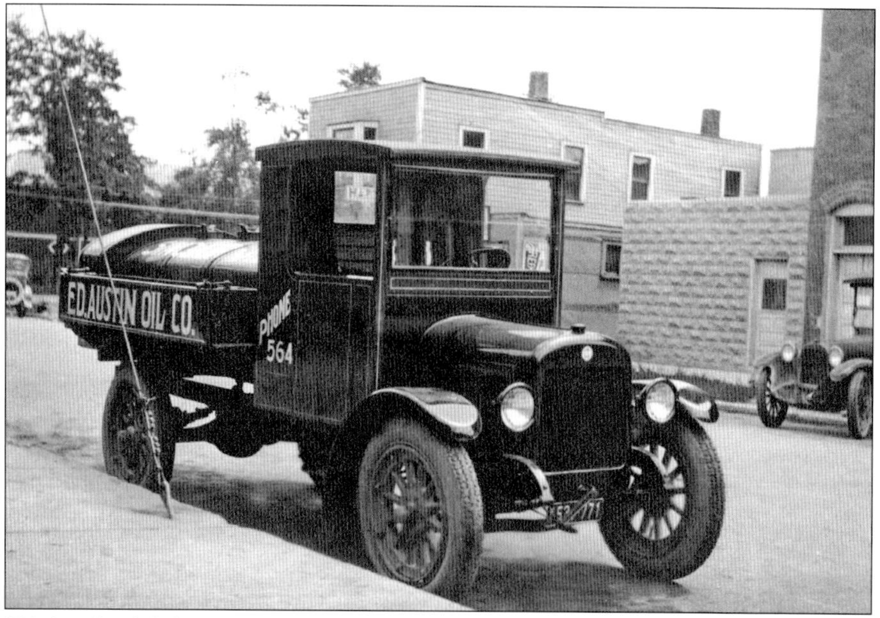

Ed Austin Oil Co. truck along the side of Austin Drug Store on Rodd Street, circa 1915. *Courtesy of Midland County Historical Society*

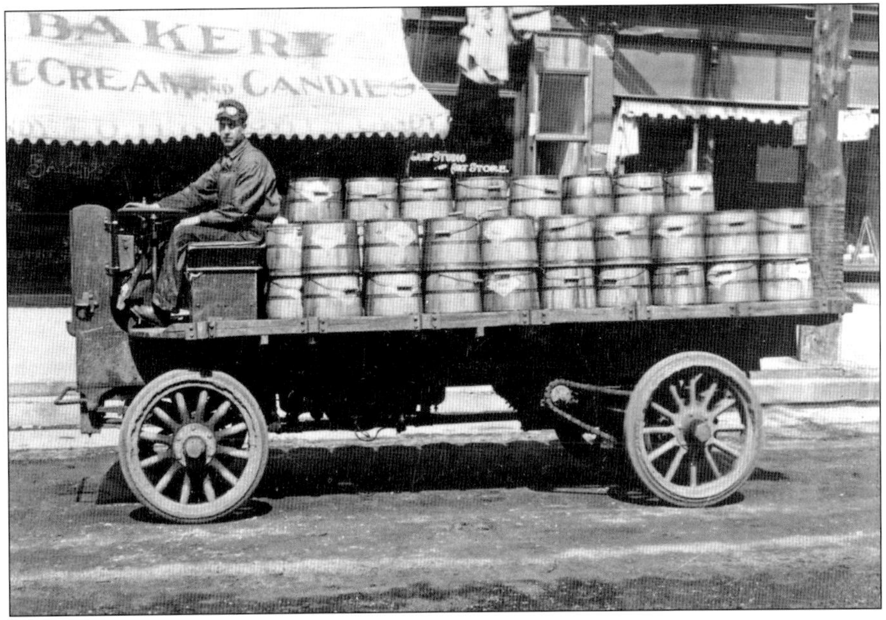

Dow's first motorized truck, circa 1915.

Courtesy of Midland County Historical Society

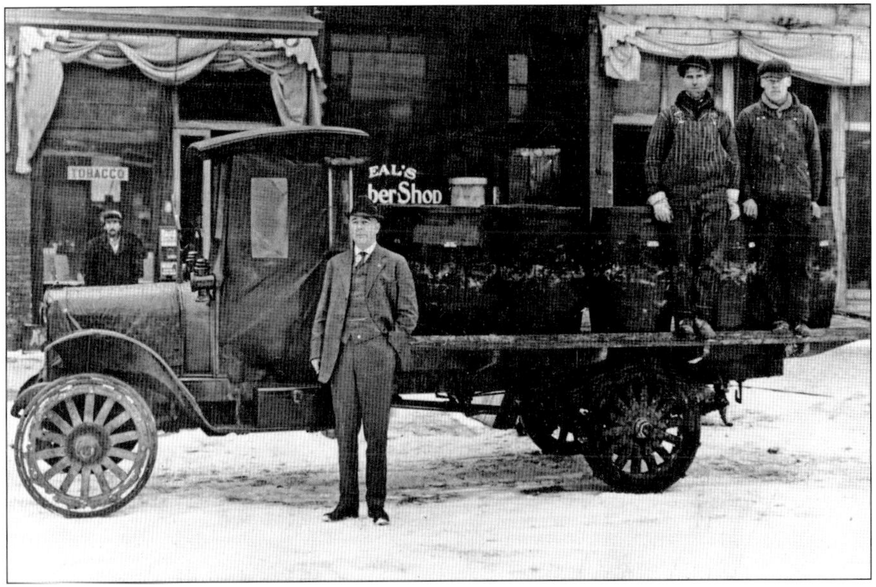

First shipment of synthetic indigo to leave the Dow plant, 1917. Germany had cut off the supply of indigo, which was essential to the textile and printing industries. *Courtesy of Midland County Historical Society*

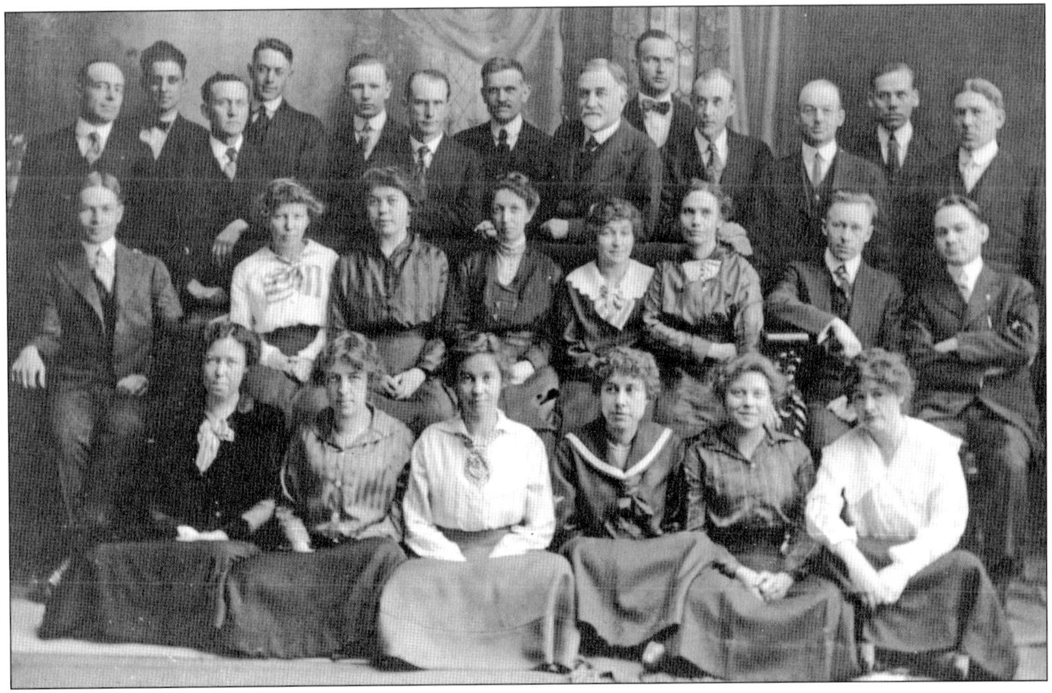

The Dow Chemical Company's office force, 1916. Front row, left to right: Mrs. Mae DeFoe, Gertrude Callahan, Carrie Smith, Winifred Thayer, Mary Burow and Kathryn Goodwin. Second row: Clyde Bordner, Vera Hadsall, Flora Currie, Roena Graves, Ethel McKarp, Clara Turner, F. J. Nelson and Carl E. Barnes. Third row: William Nash, William Bay, J. P. Holmes, Perley Wayne, A. C. Beckert, Joseph E. LeFevre, Thomas Griswold, Herbert H. Dow, C. R. Hunsicker, Arthur N. Patriache, Fred N. Lowry, Norman Best and E. M. Littlefield.

Courtesy of Midland County Historical Society

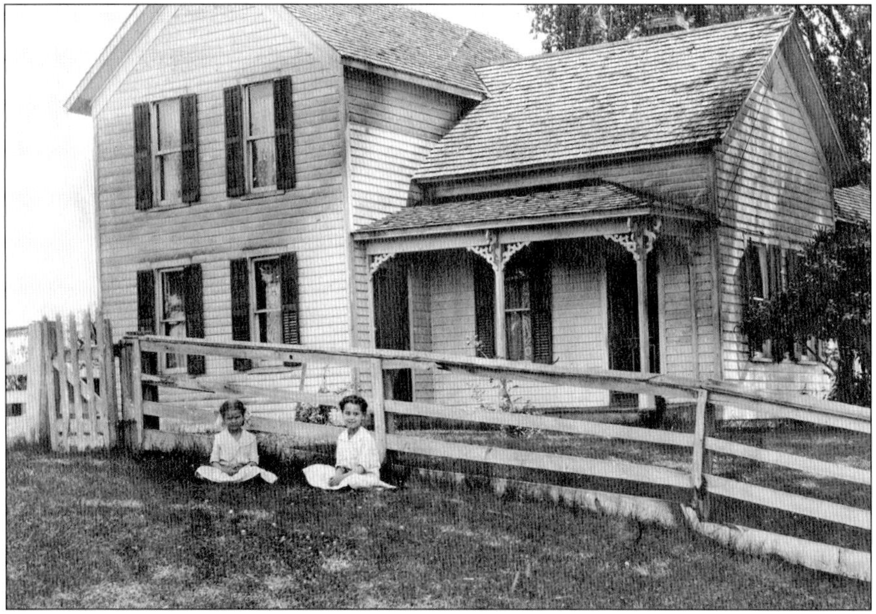

Grace and Evelyn Schlader at the home of their grandparents, William and Katherine Schlader, 3635 Smith Crossing Rd., circa 1918. *Courtesy of Janet Rice*

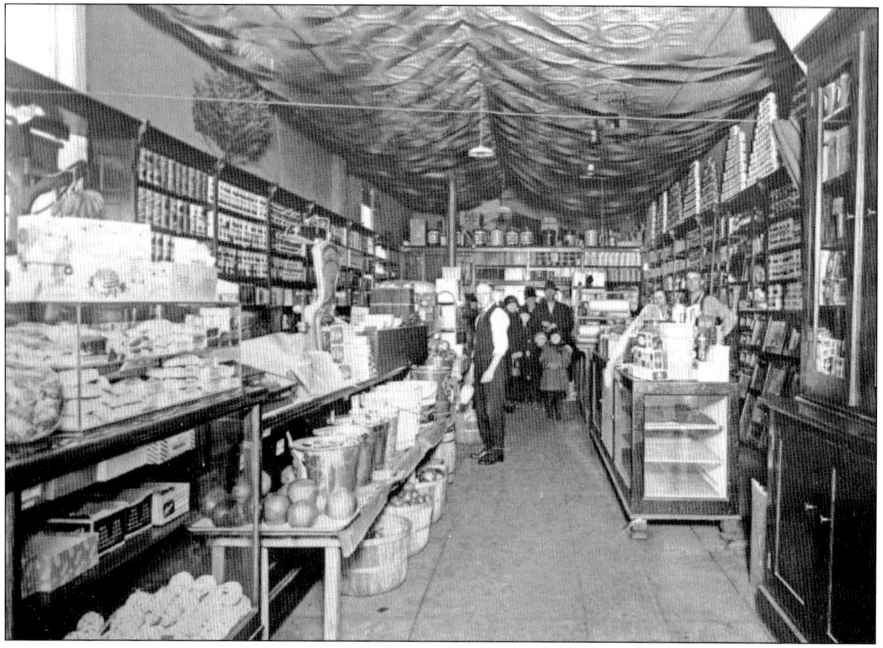

J. E. Barret's store, 1918. *Courtesy of Midland County Historical Society*

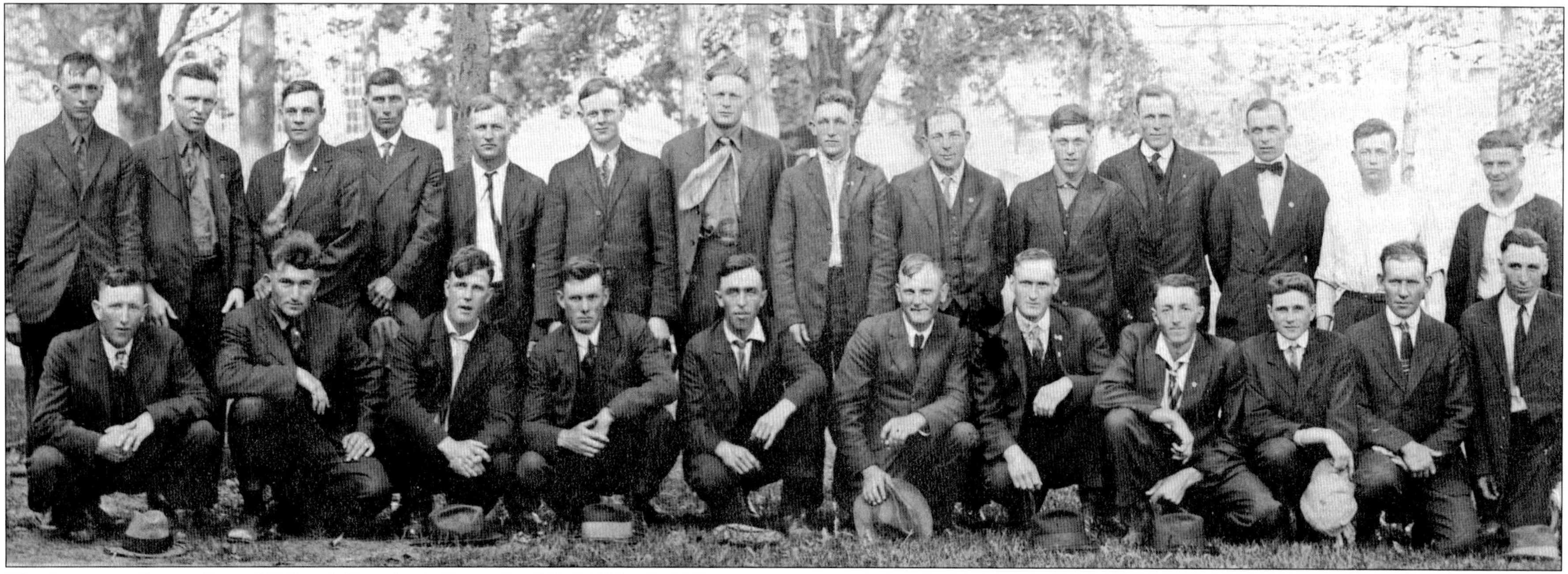

First group of men from Midland County to leave for World War I, 1917. *Courtesy of Midland County Historical Society*

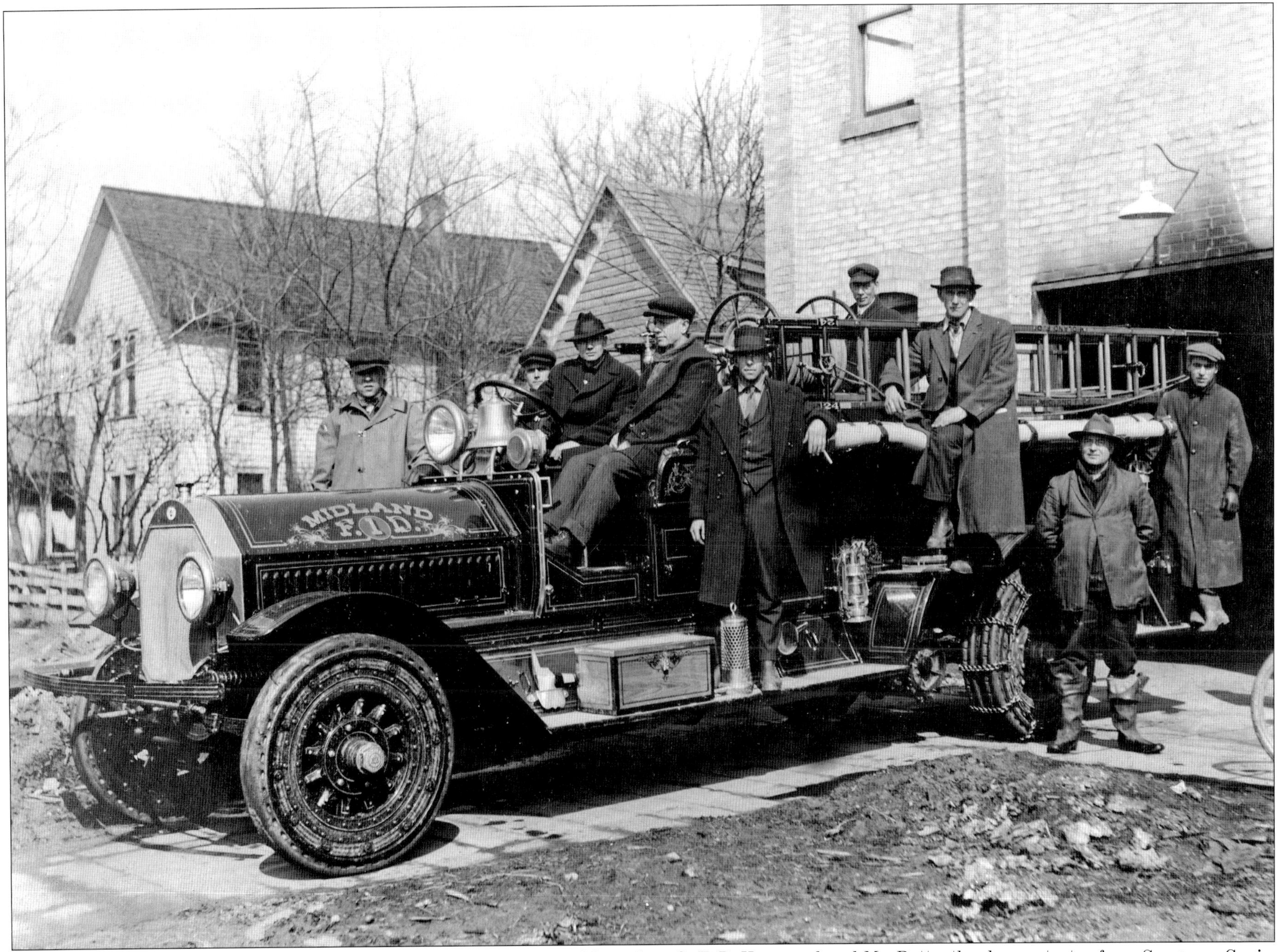

Midland's first fire truck arrived March 1, 1917. Included are Mayor Macomber, C. F. D. Hamsneel and Mr. Butts, the demonstrator from Seagrave Co. in Columbus, Ohio. The first alarm it answered was at The Dow Chemical Company. *Courtesy of Midland County Historical Society*

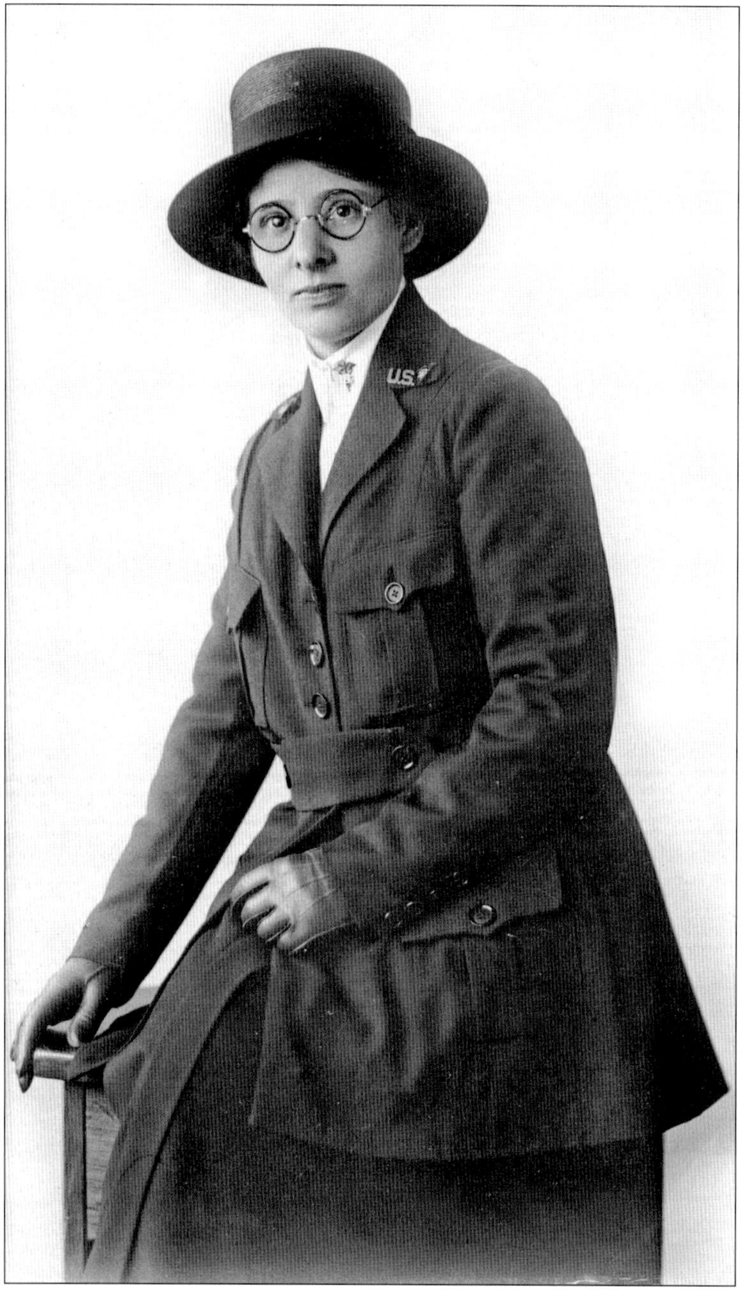

Clara Franklin in 1917. She served as an Army nurse in France during World War I. After returning to Midland, she worked as a private duty nurse. *Courtesy of James J. Dion*

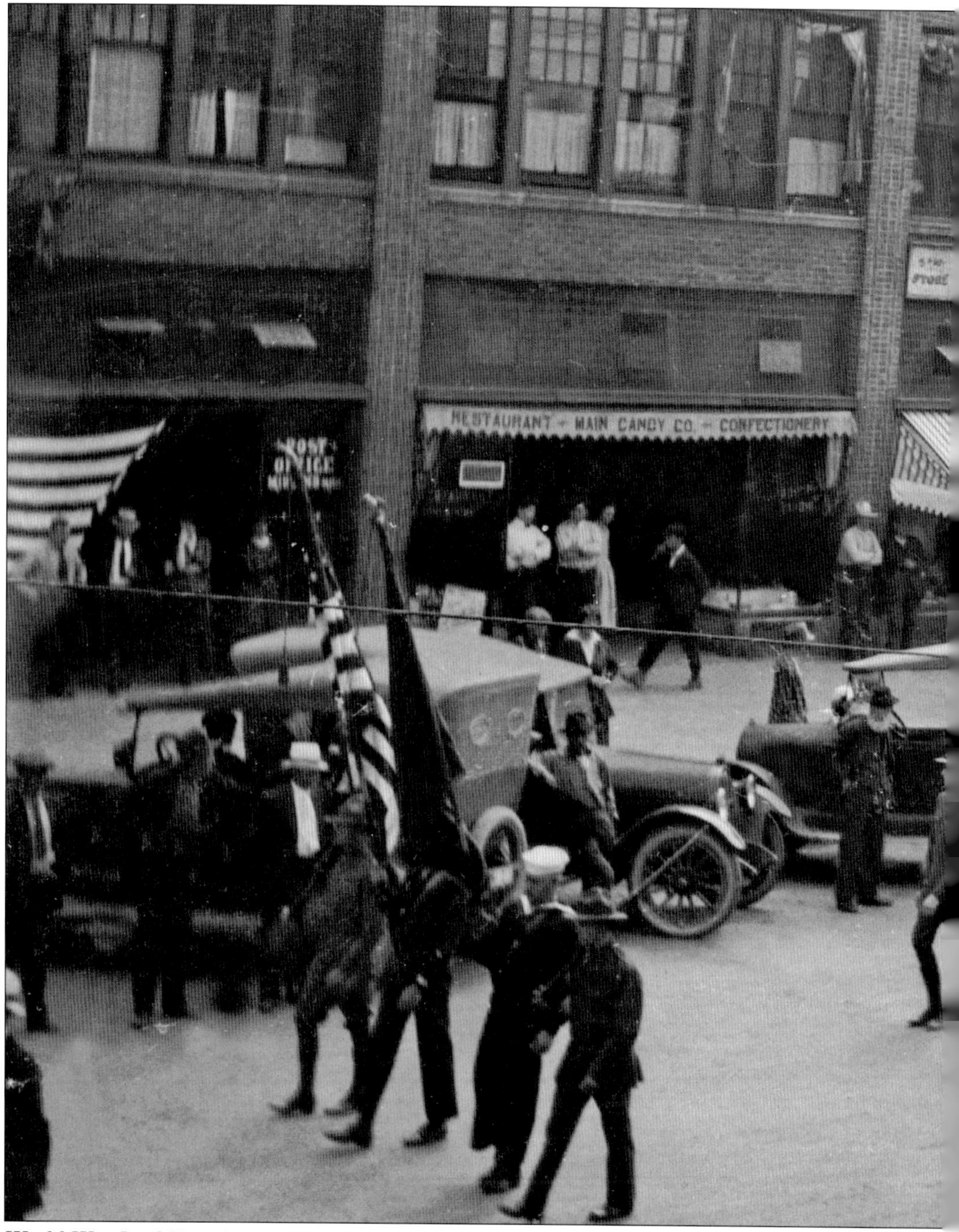

World War I soldiers in a parade in Midland, 1918. *Courtesy of Midland County Historical Society*

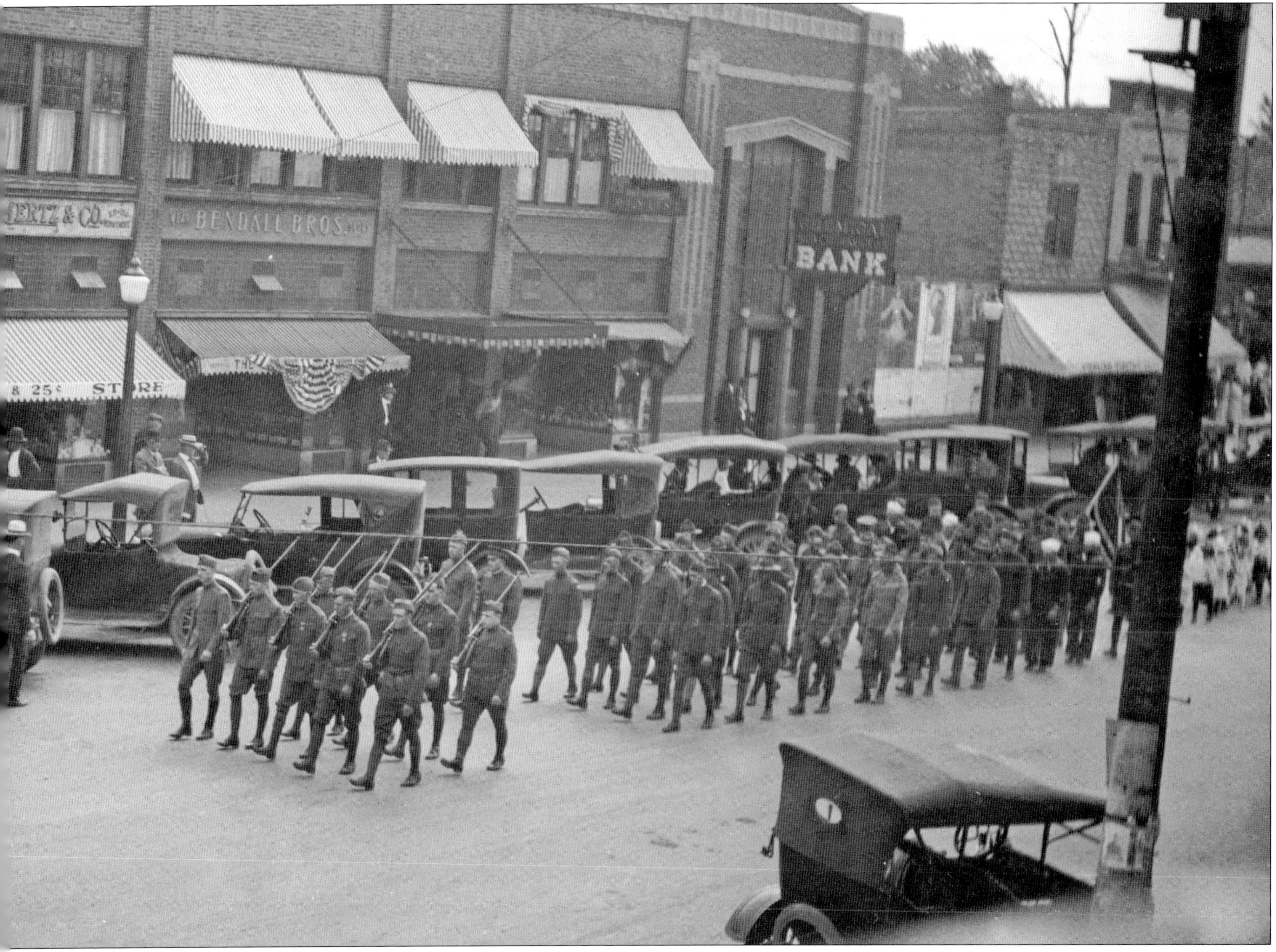
BENDALL BROS
BANK
& 25¢ STORE

The 1920s

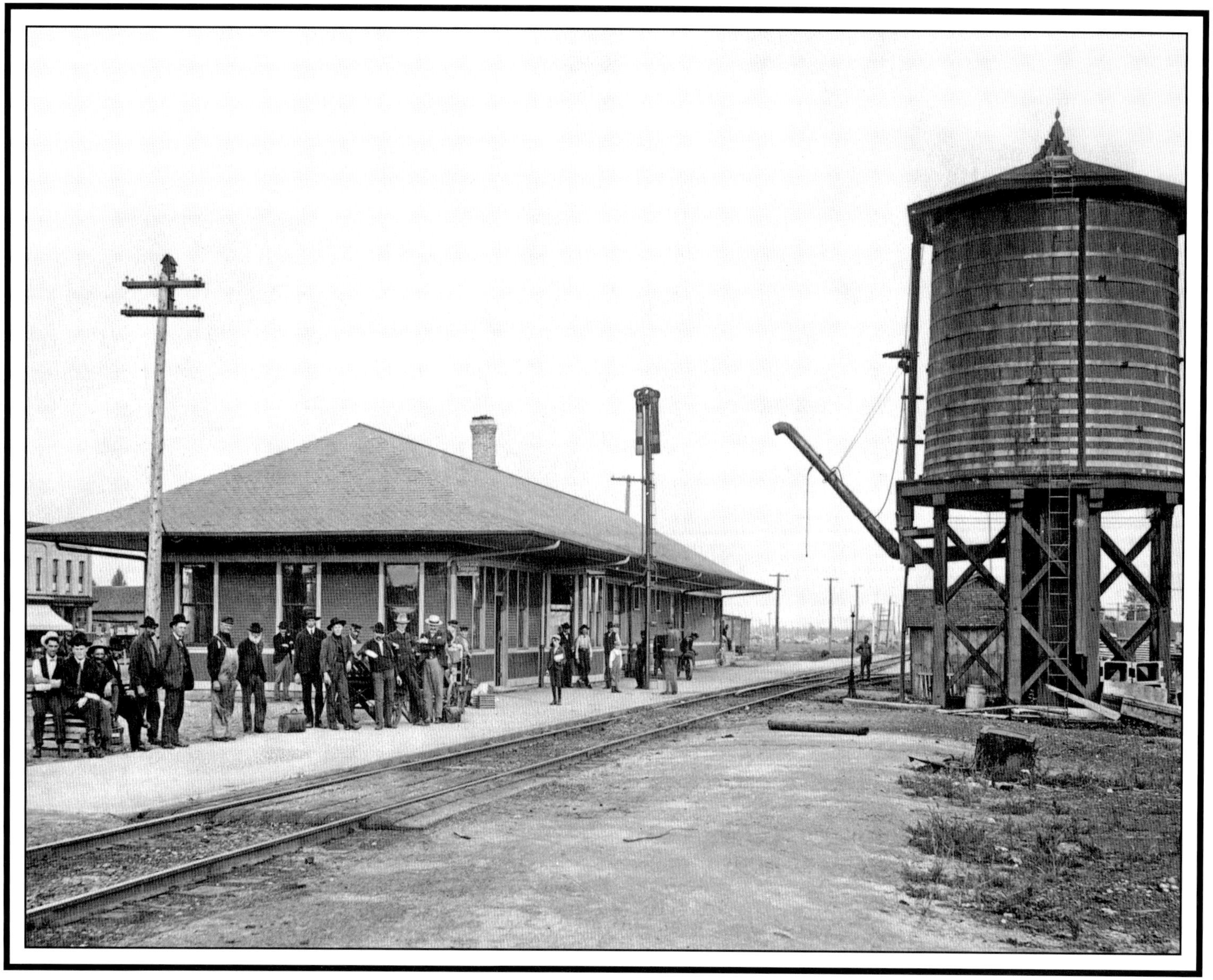

Depot at Coleman, circa 1920. *Courtesy of Midland County Historical Society*

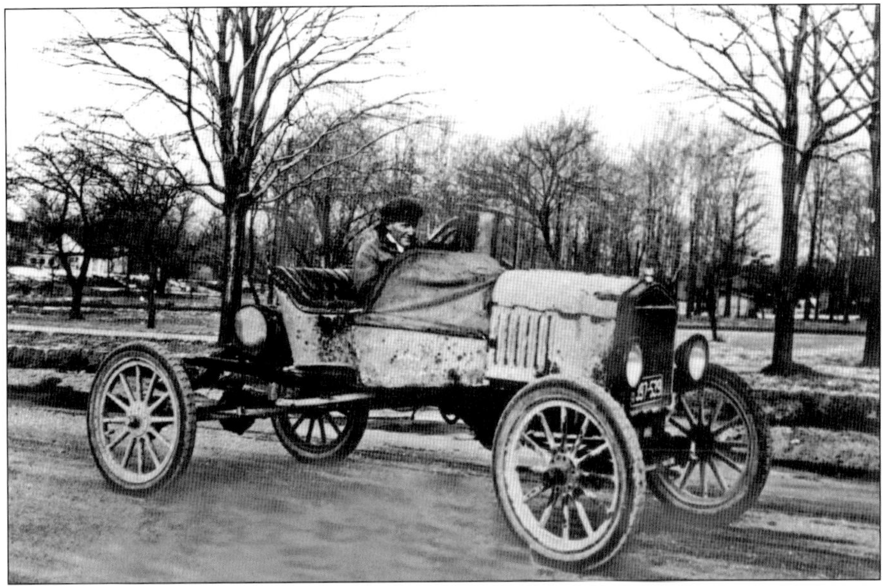

John E. Hoy in a Dow Chemical Company test car, circa 1922. It was an ordinary Ford car except it had Dow metal pistons and rings. The car could reach speeds of 60 miles per hour. *Courtesy of Mike and Tina Hoy*

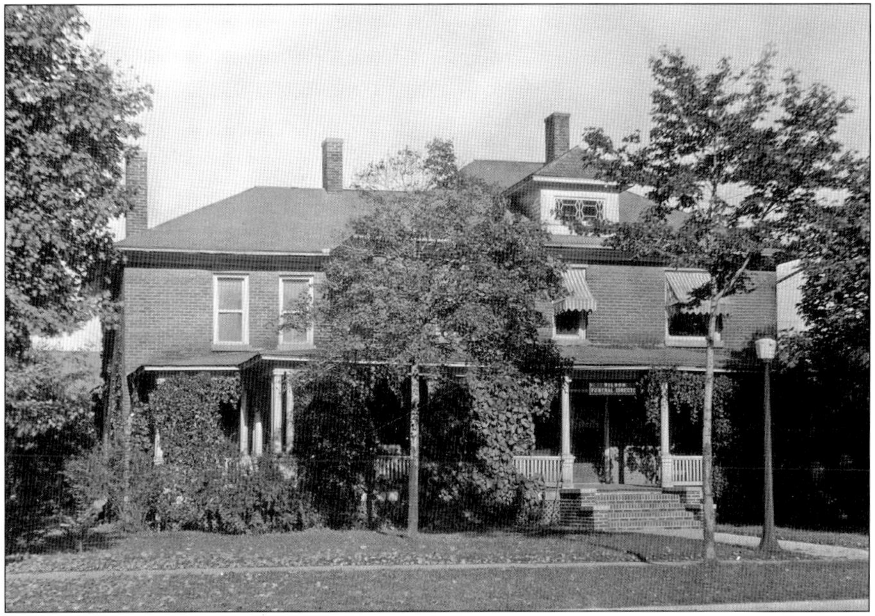

Wilson Funeral Home at Main and Fitzhugh streets, circa 1920.
Courtesy of Midland County Historical Society

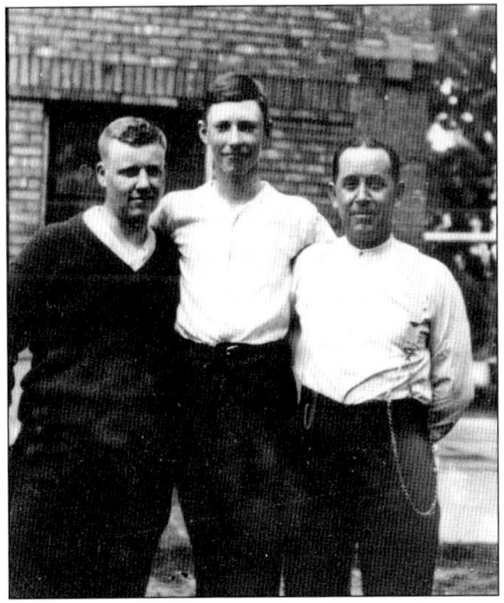

Custodial staff of Midland High School on Grove Street, circa 1921. Standing left to right: Joe Bradley, Art Collins and Jess Roe.
Courtesy of Joseph C. Bradley

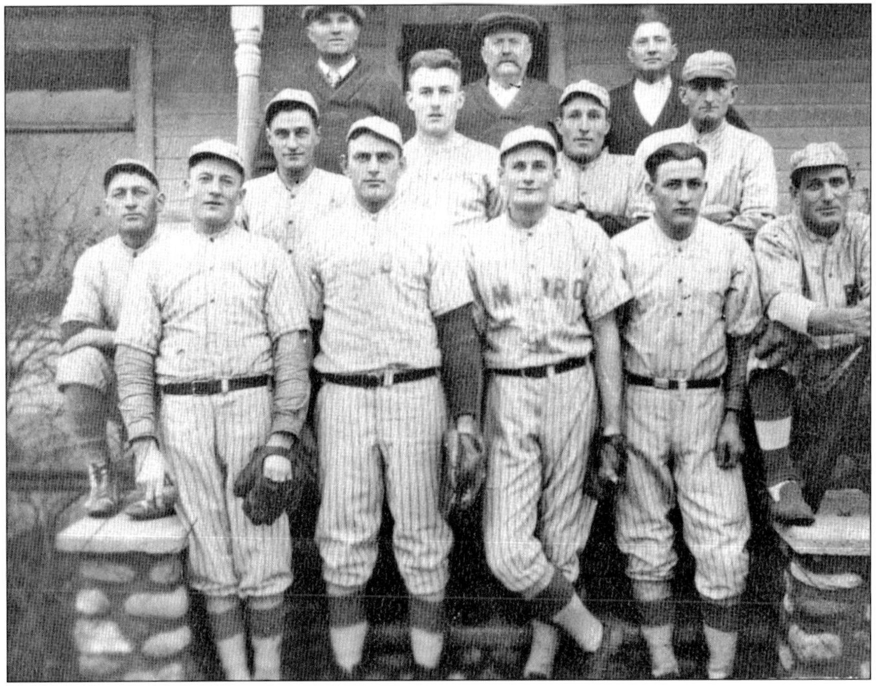

Frederick Methner with his twelve sons on the Methner farm, circa 1920. Front row, left to right: August, Joseph, Edward, Floyd "Pat", Elmer and William. Second row: Jason, Henry, Fritz and Otto. Third row: John, Frederick, and Frank. They were five county All-Stars four years in a row in the early 1920s.
Courtesy of Don and Sandy Methner Moore

Eighth- and tenth-grade graduation of LaPorte School in Ingersoll Township, 1923. Front row, left to right: Ruth Stearns, Dorothy Delong, teacher Margaret Overton, Clea Garrett and Katheryn Joynt. Back row: Ione Gould, Clifford McNett, Lillian Johnson, David Anger, Grace Schlader and George Brandt. *Courtesy of Janet Rice*

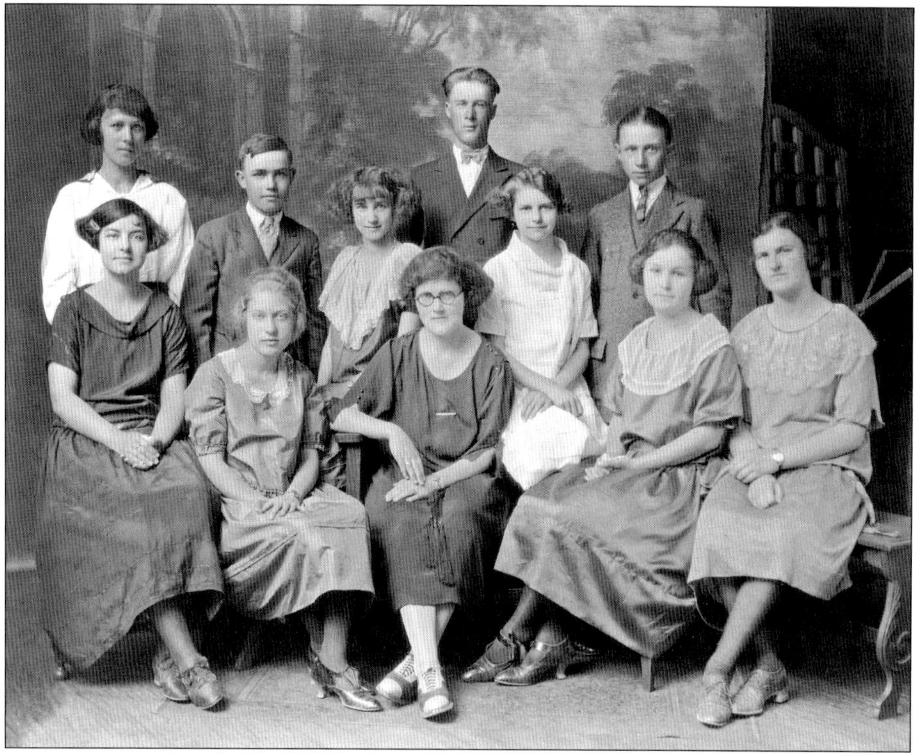

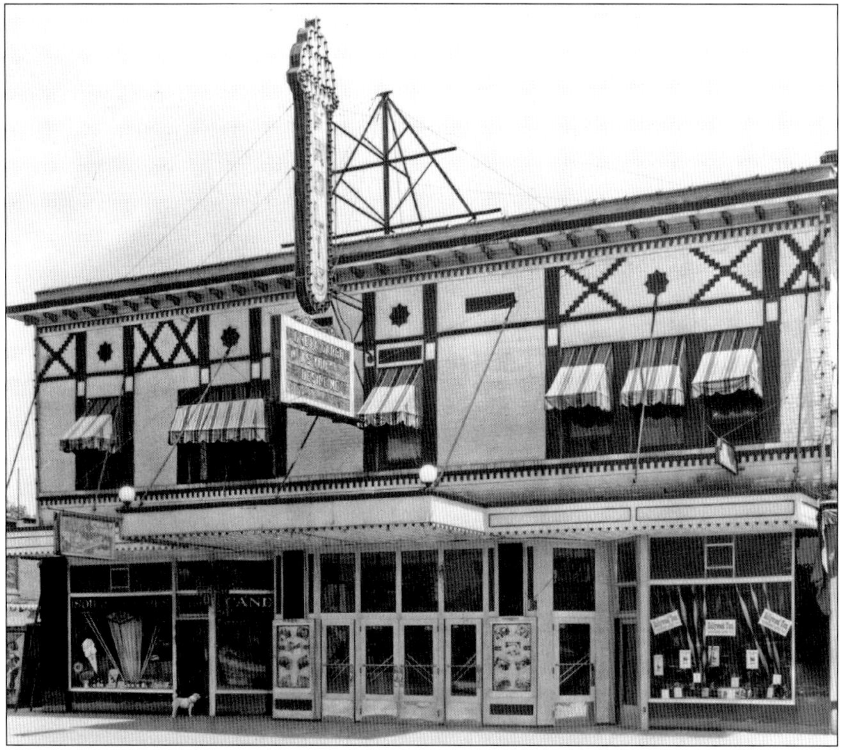

First Frolic Theater on the corner of Gordon and Main streets, circa 1925. Owner, Bill Cassidy, opened the theater Oct. 19, 1921.
Courtesy of Thomas J. Cox

Curtice School in Edenville Township, 1925. In the front row are Waldo Staley, Harold Procknow, Roy Procknow, Clarence Burch, Forest Staley, Emory Sprague, Sam Kushmaul, Gladys Finney, Lawrence Forsythe, Wava Hund, Pete Bergman, Ona Staley, Carrie Hund, Jennie Guest, Clara Hebner and Beryl Bergman. Second row: Franklin Hebner, Olive Finney, Martha Hebner, Muriel Reymore, Lila Guest, Elwood Hund, Jake Staley, Laurence Hund, Harold Zimmerman, Albert Kushmand and Iva Staley. Third row: Anna Hebner, Edith Zimmerman, Sophia Hebner, Florence Sprague, Mary Kushmaul, Violet Zacariah and Maybelle Guest.
Courtesy of Olive Deitsch

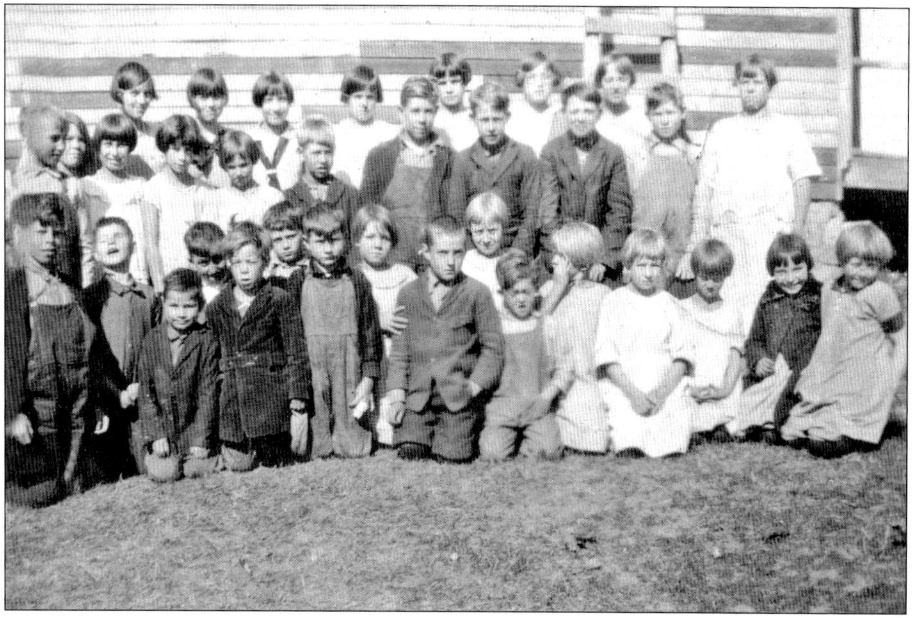

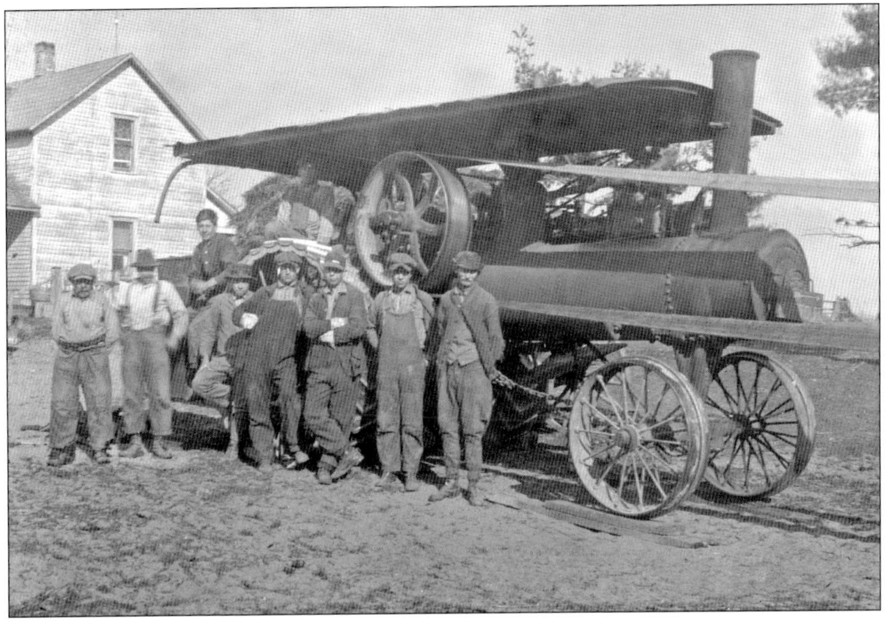

Threshing crew at the Echmain farm in Midland County, 1924.

Courtesy of Midland County Historical Society

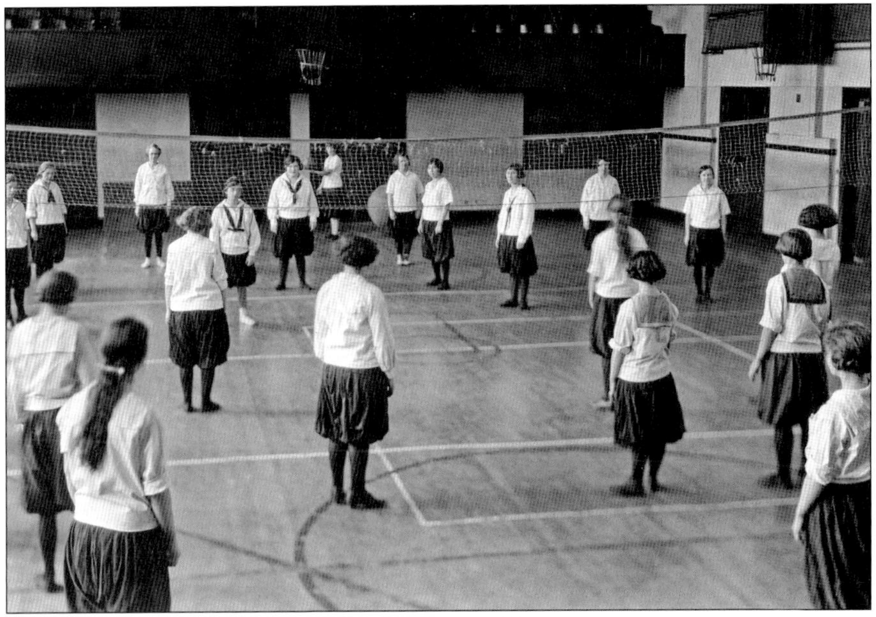

Volleyball at the Community Center, circa 1925.

Courtesy of Midland County Historical Society

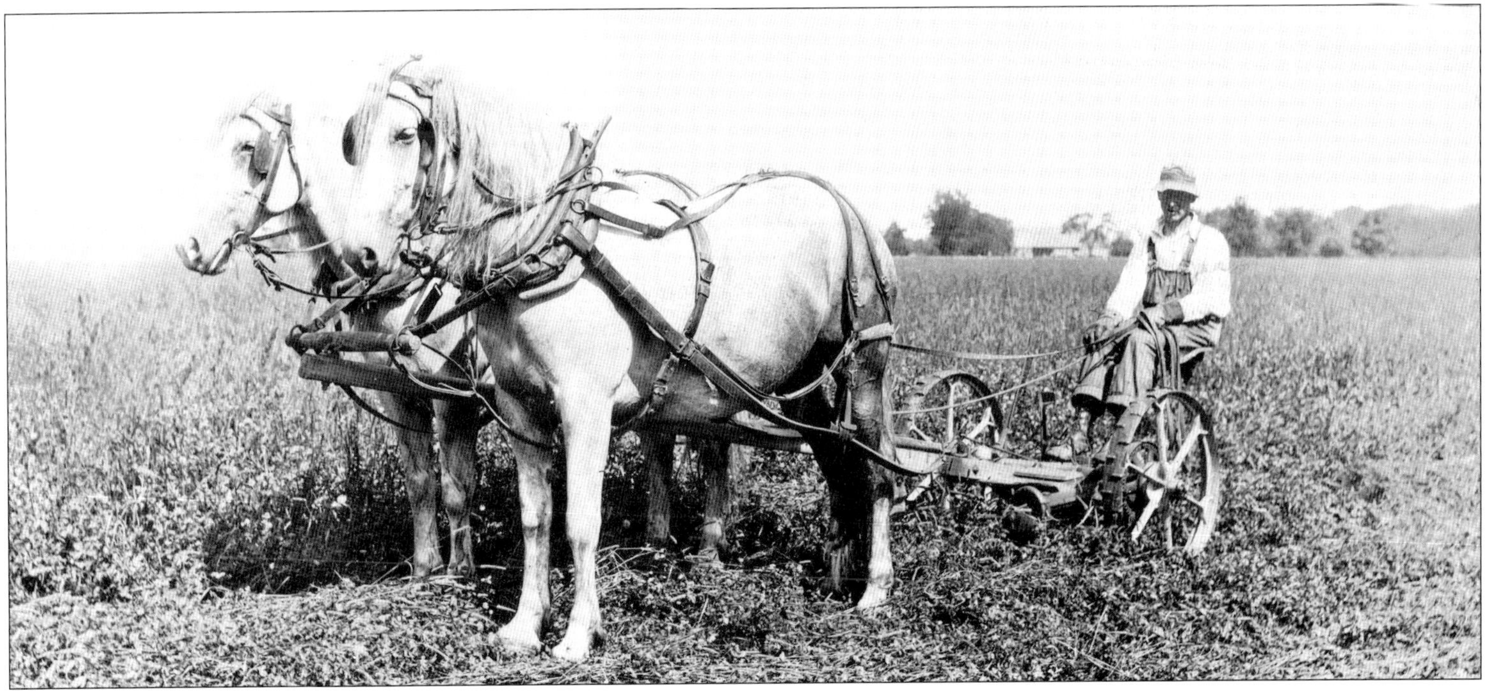

George Schlader farming with his team horses, Dick and Beauty, at 3830 Smith Crossing Rd. in Ingersoll Township, circa 1923.

Courtesy of Janet Rice

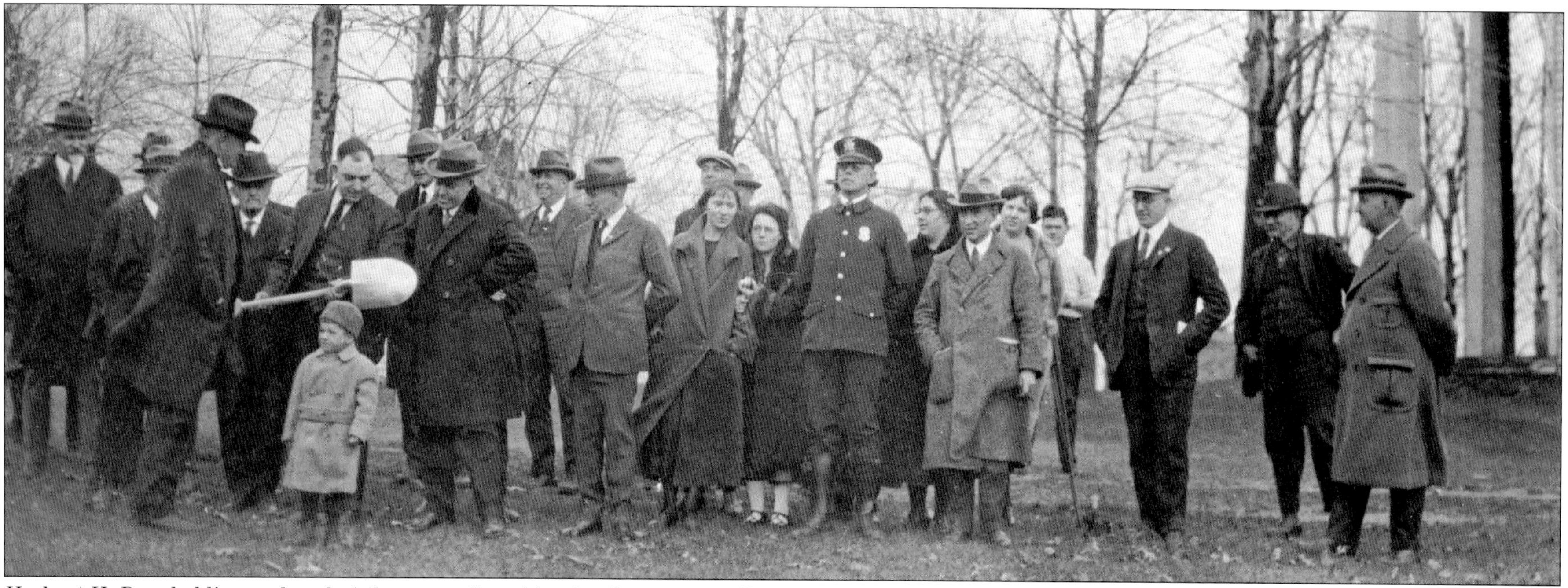

Herbert H. Dow holding a shovel at the groundbreaking for the new courthouse, Nov. 6, 1924. Those included are Aaron R. Bliss, Gilbert A. Currie, Officer Fred Sayles, C. H. Macomber, T. E. Main, A. S. Arbury and B. Carter. *Courtesy of Midland County Historical Society*

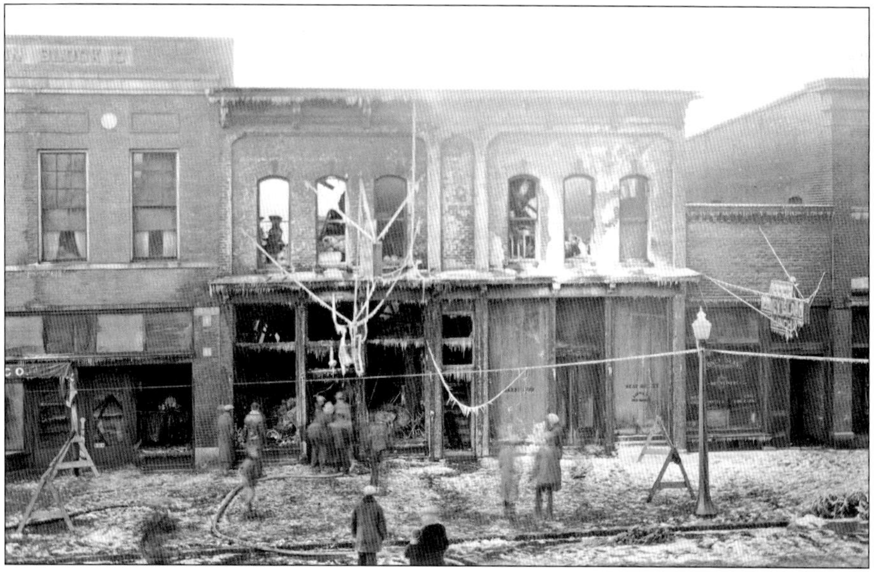

Fire destroyed the Rockwell Building on Main Street east of McDonald Street in the 1920s. *Courtesy of Midland County Historical Society*

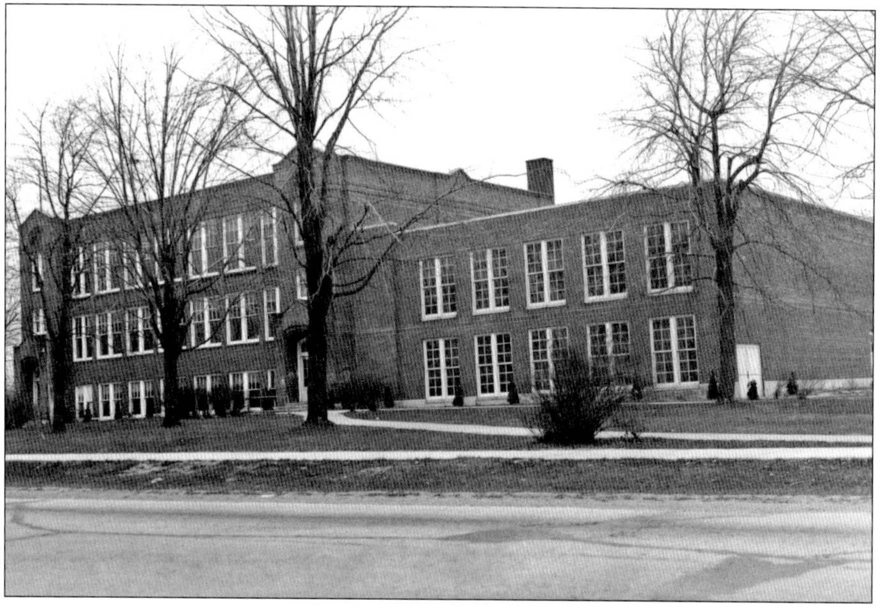

Coleman High School, circa 1924. *Courtesy of Don and Sandy Methner Moore*

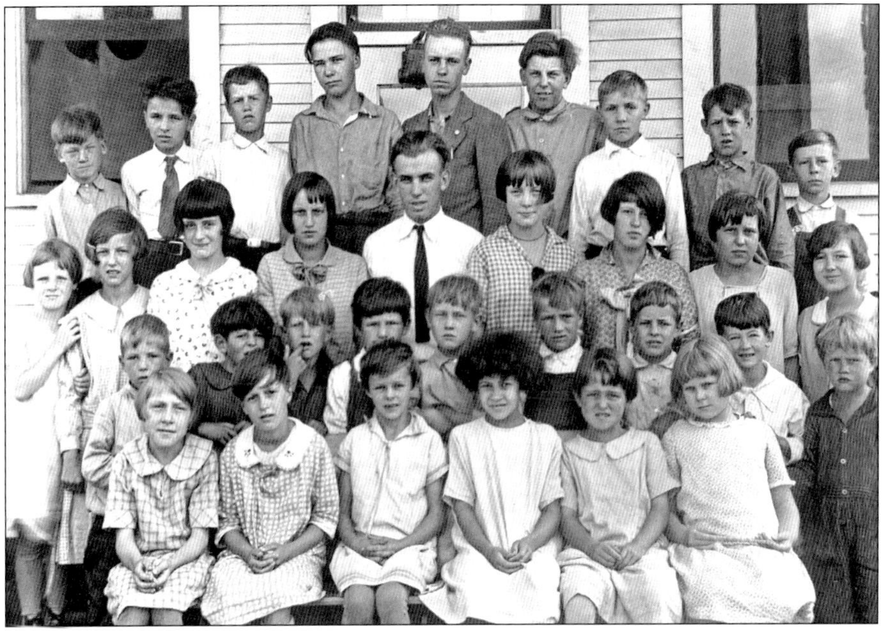

Averill School in Lincoln Township, 1925. First row, left to right: Rose Lamphierd, Flora Draves, Gene Briggs, Weona Proctor, Celina Draves and Alice Adams. Second row: Bill Briggs, Malcom Stephson, Floyd Draves, Fletcher Draves, unidentified, Clyde Draves, Bob Briggs, Jack Burro, unidentified and Loren Draves. Third row: Ruth Hockmeyer, Edna Jean Briggs, Verna Stephson, Vida Draves, teacher Bud Blackeley, Freda Lamphierd, Helen Stephson, Julia Draves and Shirlee Valentine. Fourth row: unidentified, Clarence Varner, Ed Draves, Bob Finney, Elmer Valentine, Jot Draves, Glen (unknown), Earl Draves and Bob Valentine. *Courtesy of Connie Moe*

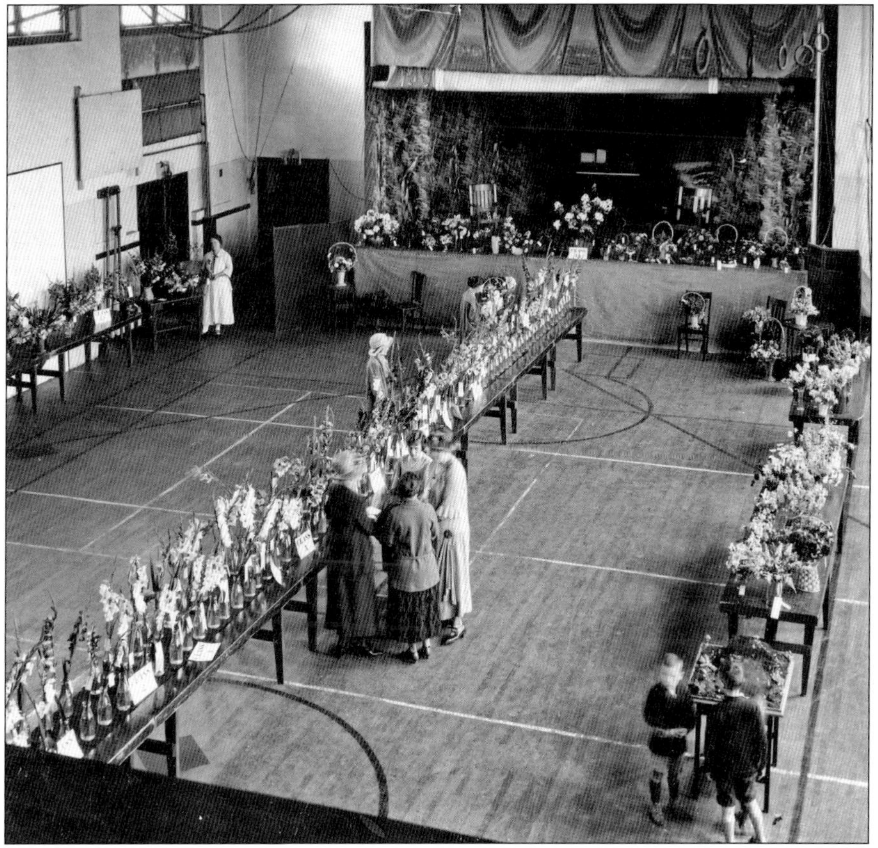

Flower show at the Midland Community Center, circa 1925. The building was built in 1917. *Courtesy of Midland County Historical Society*

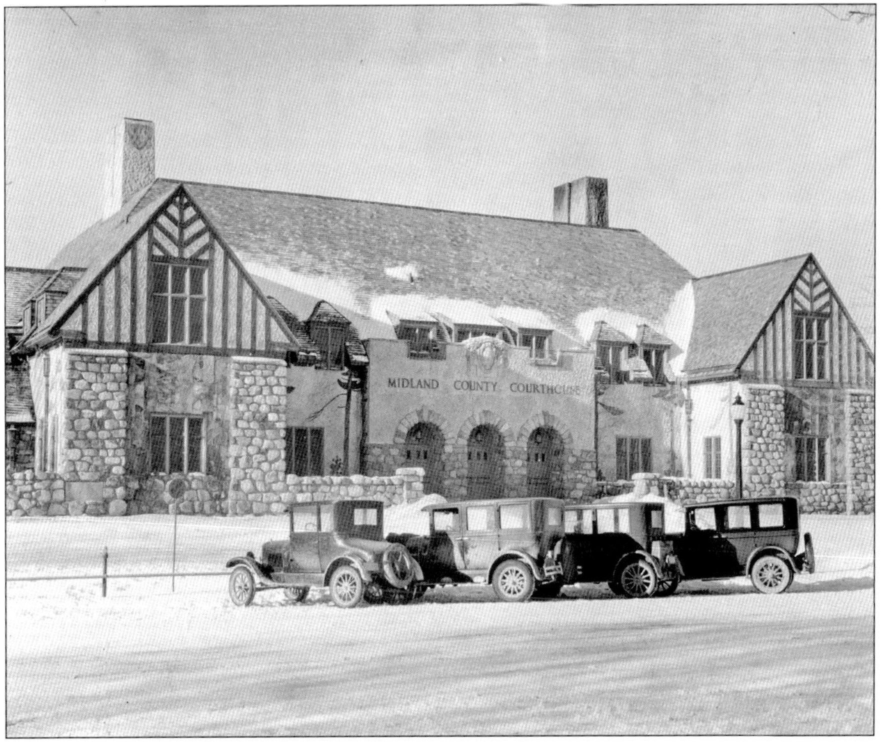

Midland County Courthouse shortly after it was built, February 1926. Bloodgood Tuttle was the architect to design the $225,000 building. Since 1858 there has been continual county government activity on the same block. *Courtesy of Midland County Historical Society*

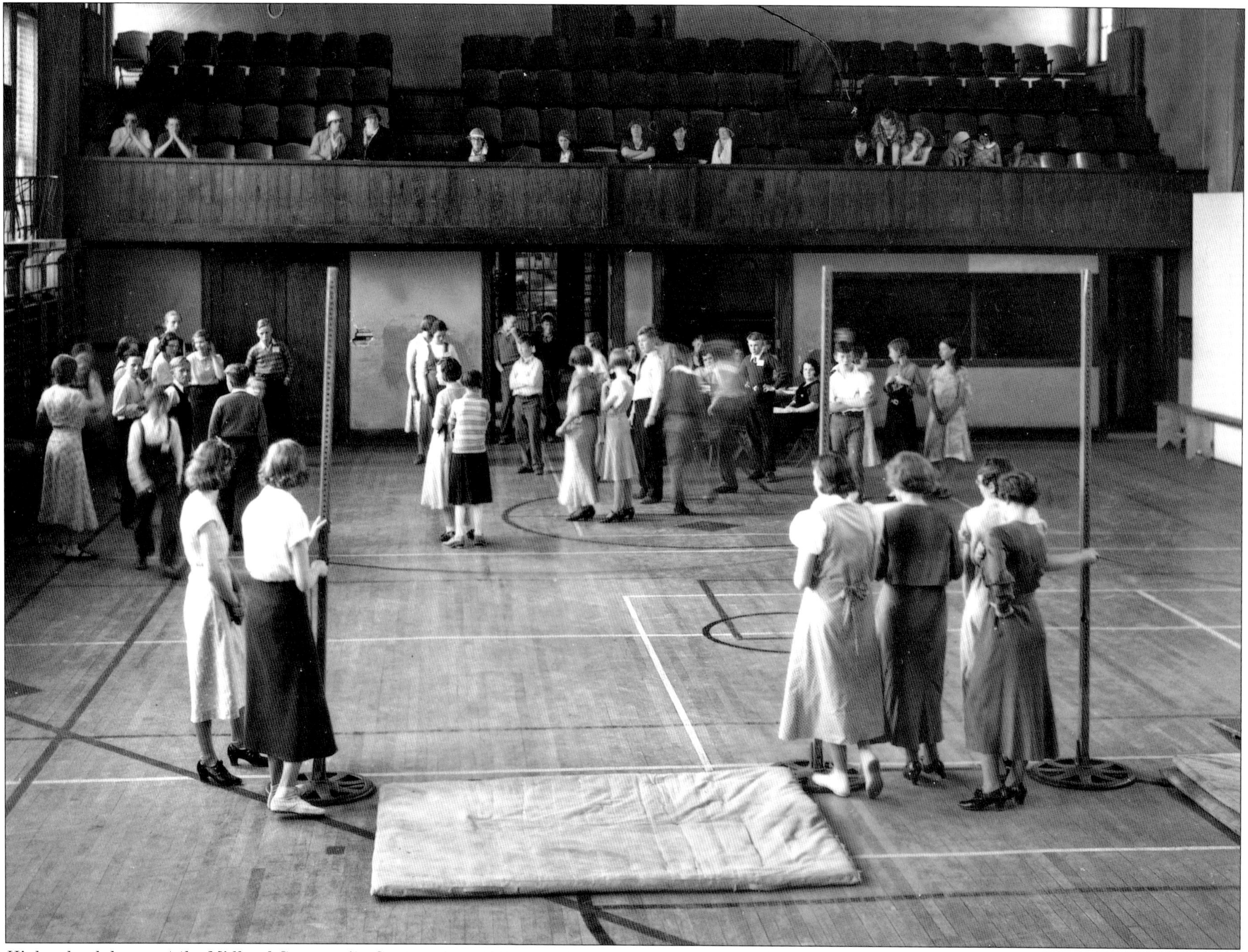

High school dance at the Midland Community Center, circa 1925. The Center was on Townsend Street. *Courtesy of Midland County Historical Society*

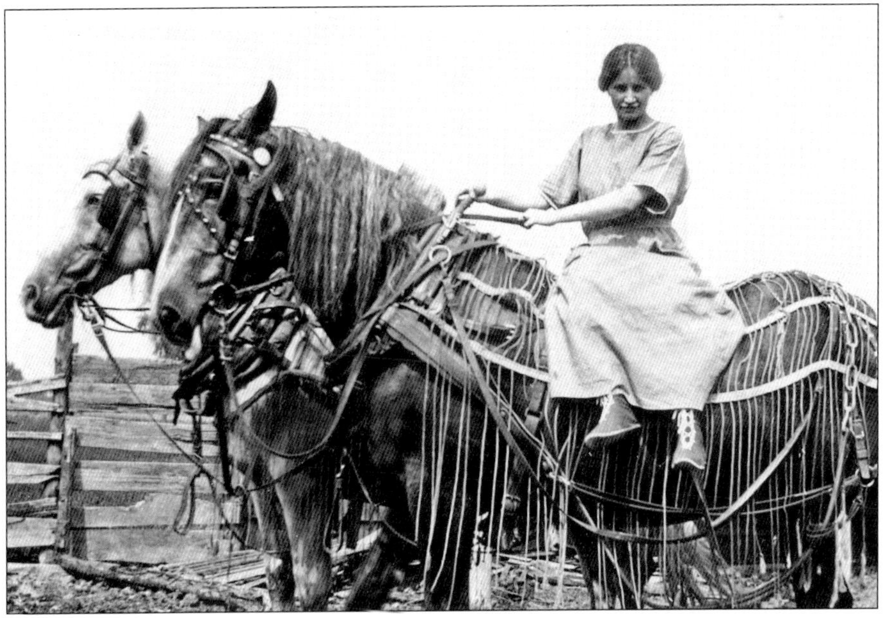

Stella Killian riding the work horse on Smith Crossing Road in Ingersoll Township, circa 1925. *Courtesy of Janet Rice*

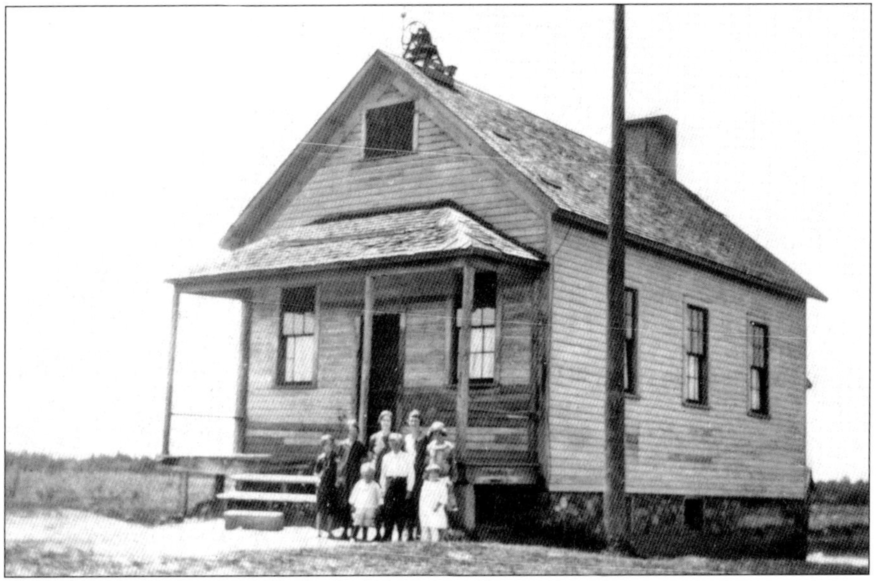

Curtice School in Edenville Township, 1925. Those included are Olive Finney, Leo Finney, Gladys Finney, Esther Miller, Millie Hill and Mildred Hill. *Courtesy of Olive Deitsch*

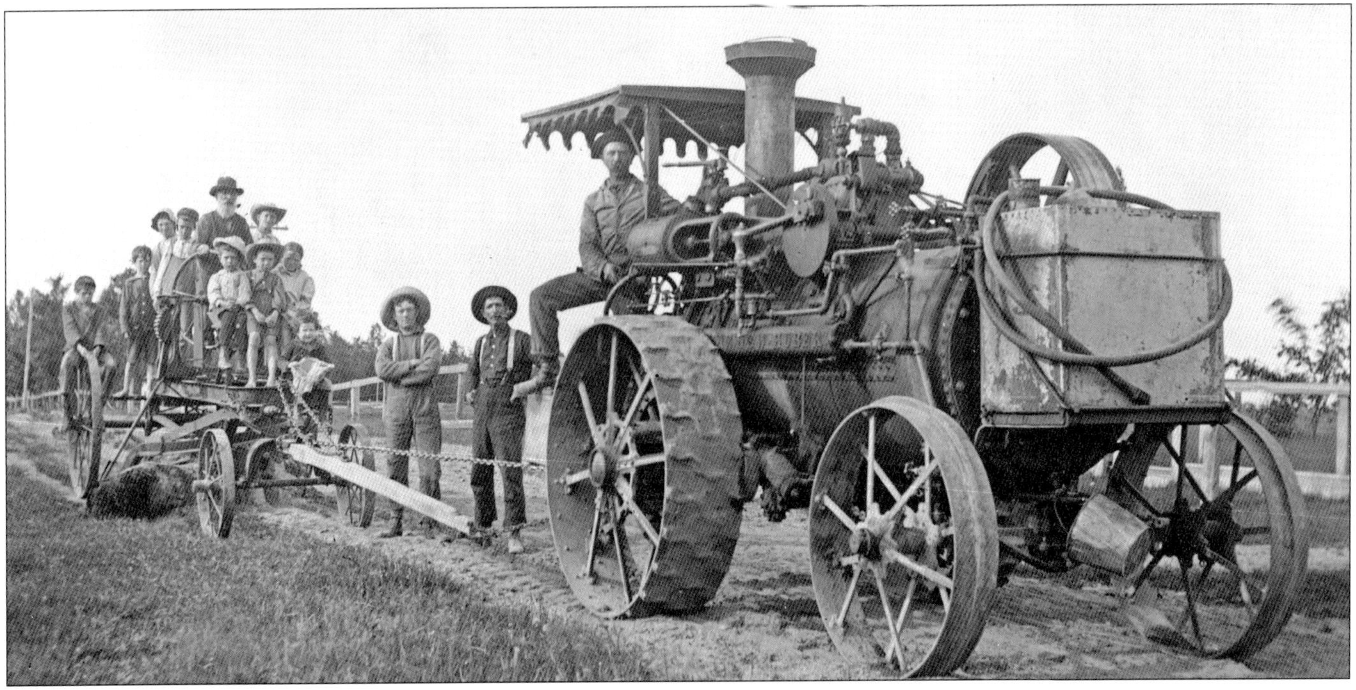

George W. Kent in the cab of his steam engine, circa 1925.
Courtesy of Midland County Historical Society

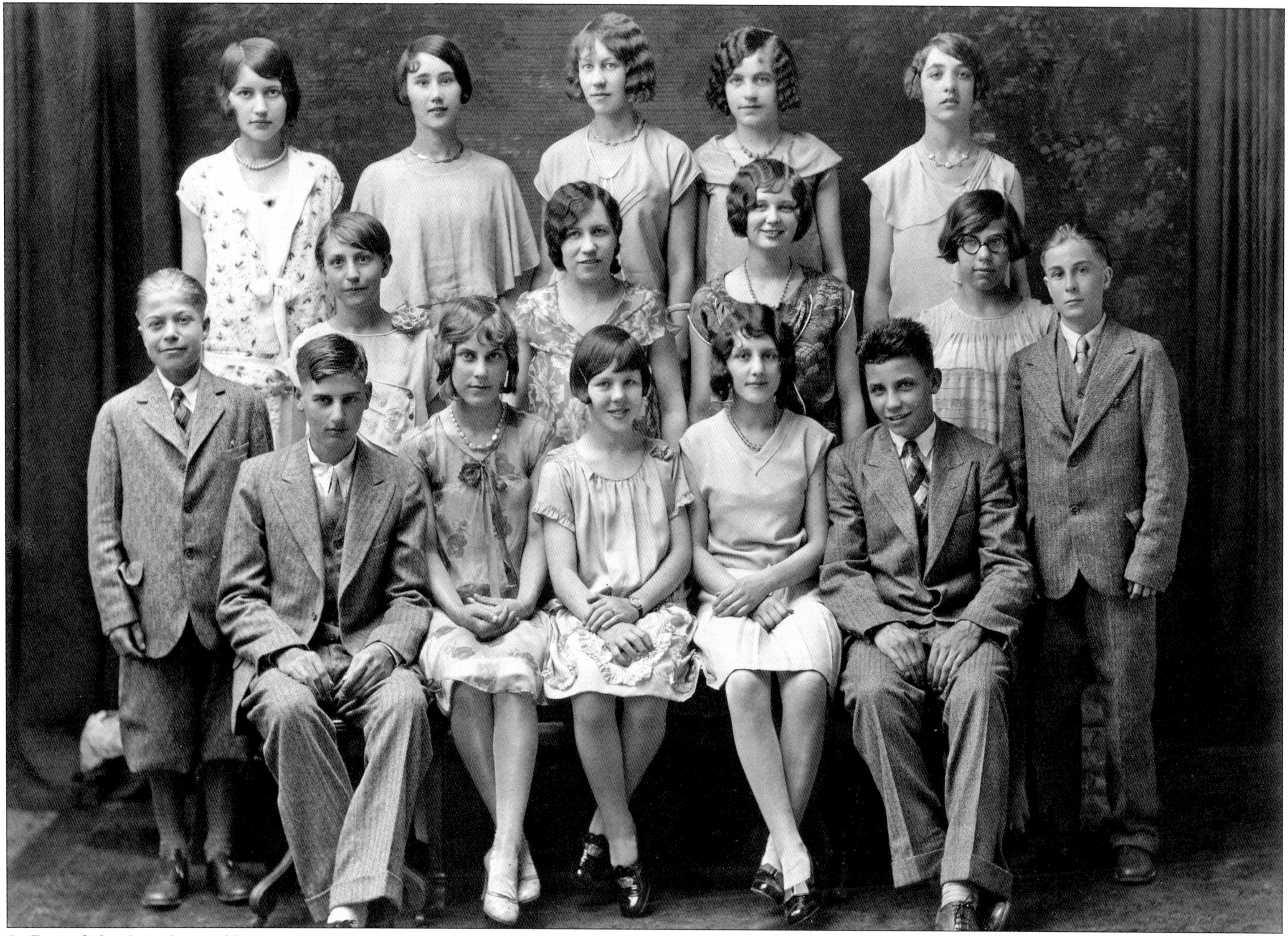

LaPorte School students of Ingersoll Township, circa 1925. Front row, left to right: Walter Schlader, Pauline Delong, Helen Parker, Mary Palfy and Leonard Merrill. Second row: Chancey DeLong, Virginia Harding, teacher Axcy Weineke, Juanita Spyker, Mable Schlader and Robert Anger. Back row: Arlene Chamberlain, Eledene Maier, Madeline Wehner, Clara Munger and Lucille Cook. *Courtesy of Janet Rice*

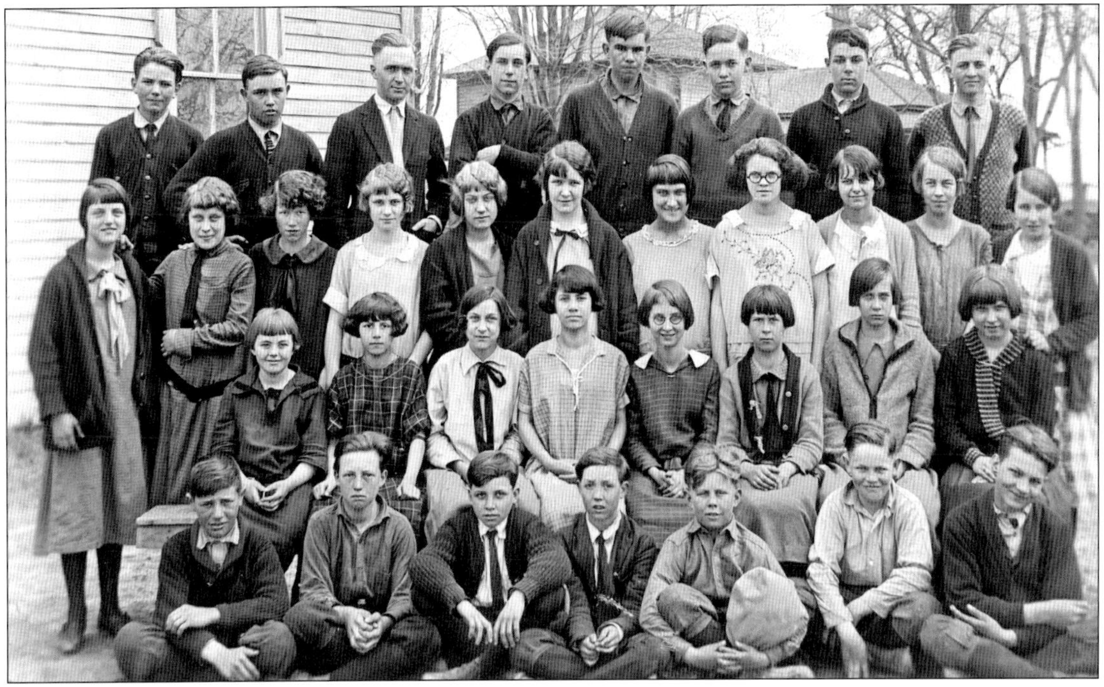

Students in front of the LaPorte School in Ingersoll Township, 1925. Front row, left to right: Clarence Schlader, Henry Beem, Leonard Merrill, Melvin Maier, Vernon Chamberlain, Ernest Chamberlain and Wesley Krapohl. Second row: Zona Reinhart, Mary Palfy, Marion Johnson, Hilda Palfy, Irene Maier, Lottie Anger, Fanny Anger and Natalie Delong. Third row: Bernice Beam, Norma Gifford, Dorothy Gould, Beatrice Cook, Dorothy Delong, Neola Townsend, Helen Atchinson, Nova Keel, Grace Schlader, Madeline Wehner and Thursa Brugge. Fourth row: Ray Garrett, Clifford McNett, teacher Melvin Chamberlain, Edward Wickman, Roland Krapohl, Otis Chamberlain, William Schlader and Bernard Winslow.
Courtesy of Janet Rice

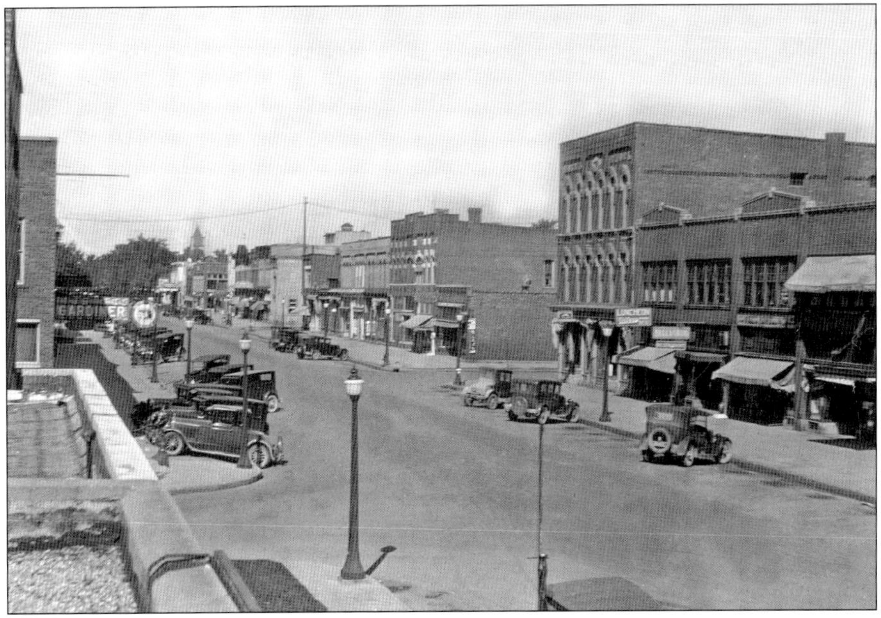

Looking at the northeast side of Main Street in Midland, 1925.
Courtesy of Midland County Historical Society

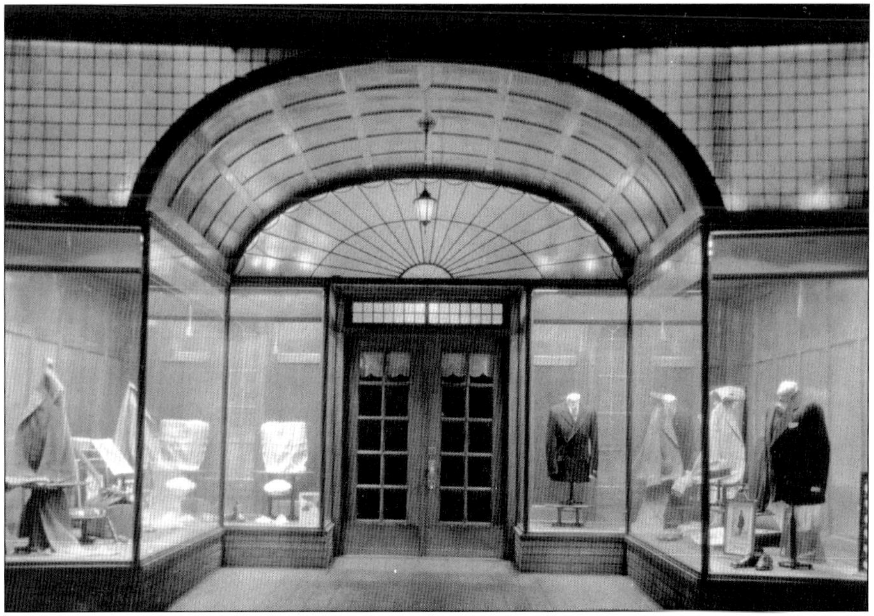

Display windows at McCann and Sons Clothing store, West Main Street, Nov. 1, 1926. *Courtesy of Midland County Historical Society*

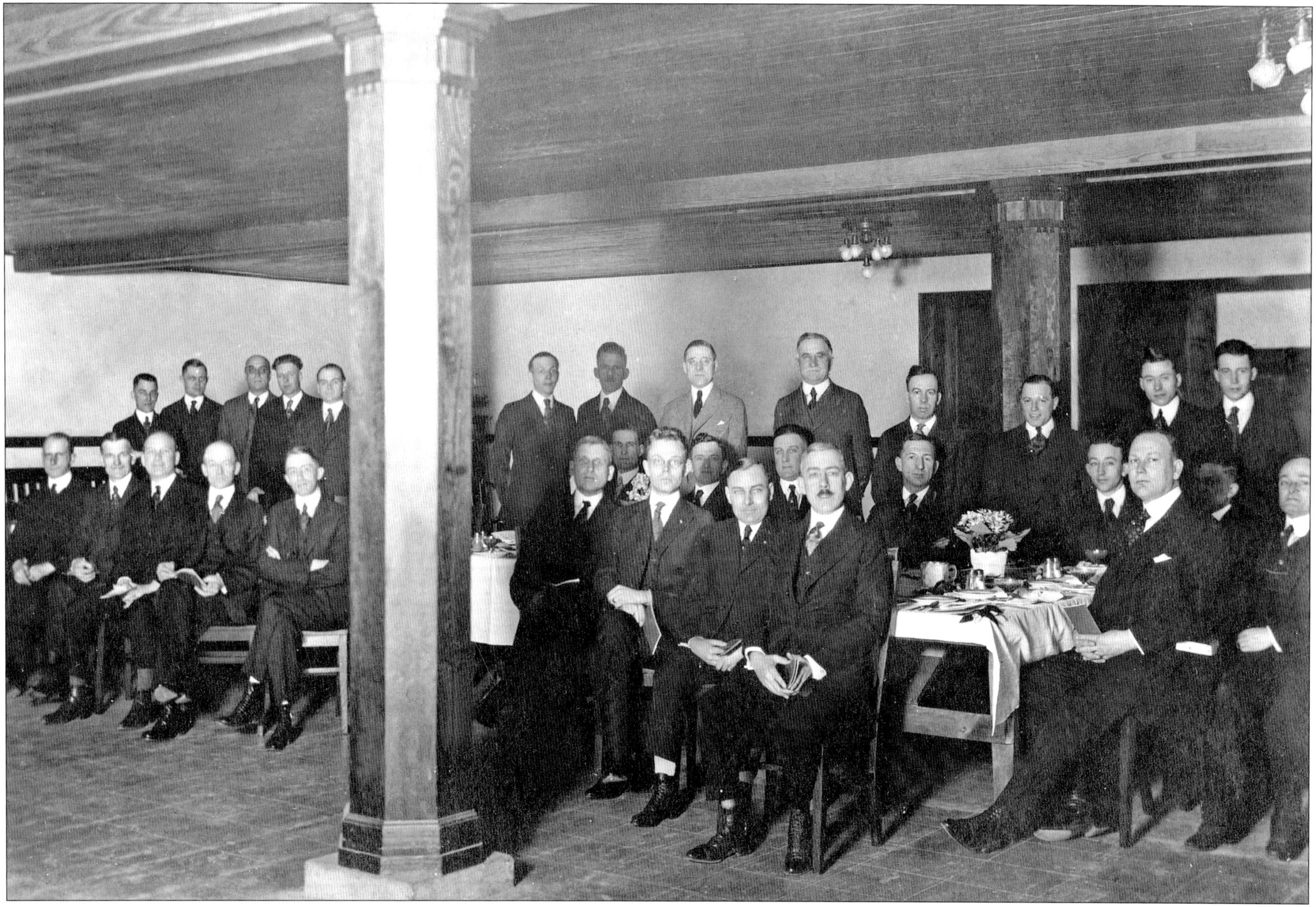

The Dow Chemical Company employees, 1925. Front row, left to right: Joseph E. LeFevre, Thomas Griswold Jr., Oscar C. Diehl, Fred N. Lowry, Roy Osmun, E. O. Barstow, Sherman Putnam, Roy Fleming, Dr. Ralph E. Darland, G. Lee Camp and Earl W. Bennett. Second row, seated: Lou Chichester, George Good, Joseph A. Cavanagh, Charles J. Strosacker, Leland I. Doan and Ivan F. Harlow. Third row, standing: R. K. Snow, Mark E. Putnam, Frank Allen, Fred Osborn, Carl E. Barnes, Hira D. Anderson, Arthur Newland, John A. Panter, Herbert H. Dow, unidentified, Grover Serenbetz, unidentified and unidentified.

Courtesy of Midland County Historical Society

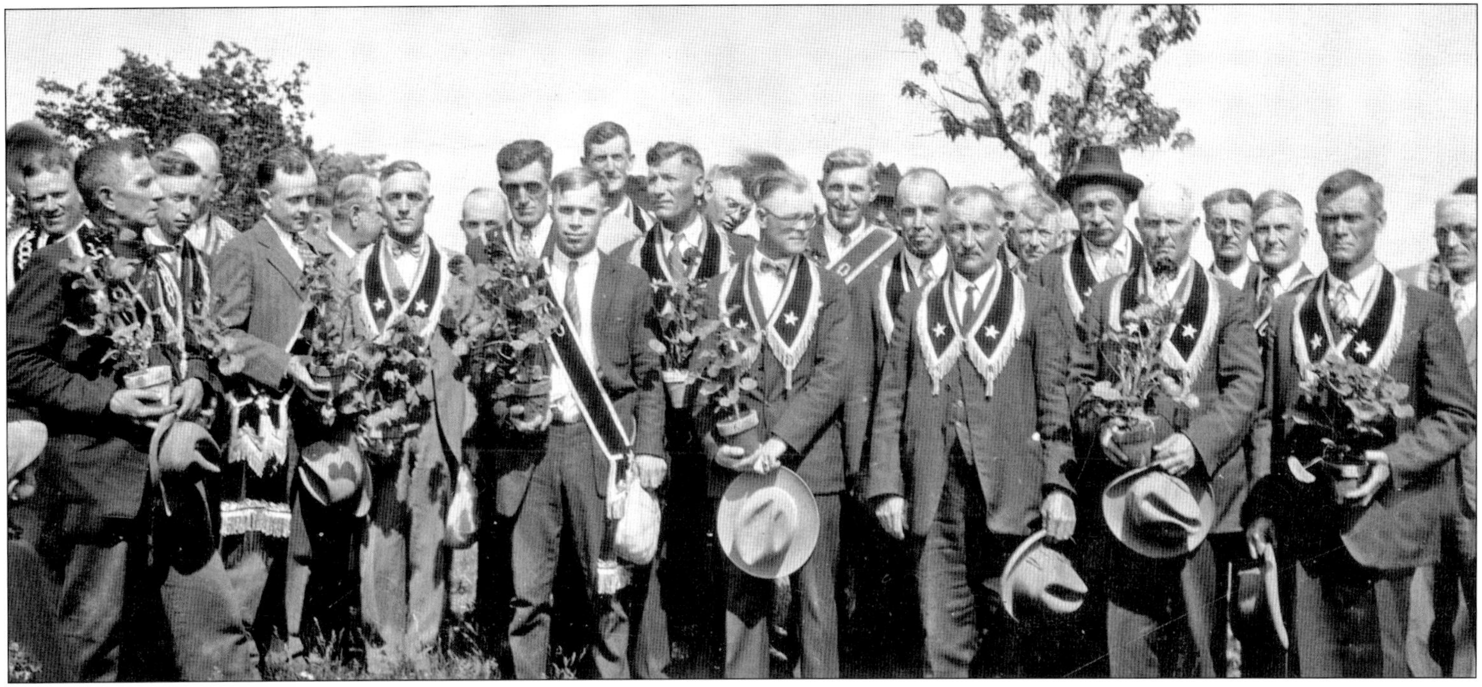

The Odd Fellows at LaPorte in Ingersoll Township, June, 1927. *Courtesy of Janet Rice*

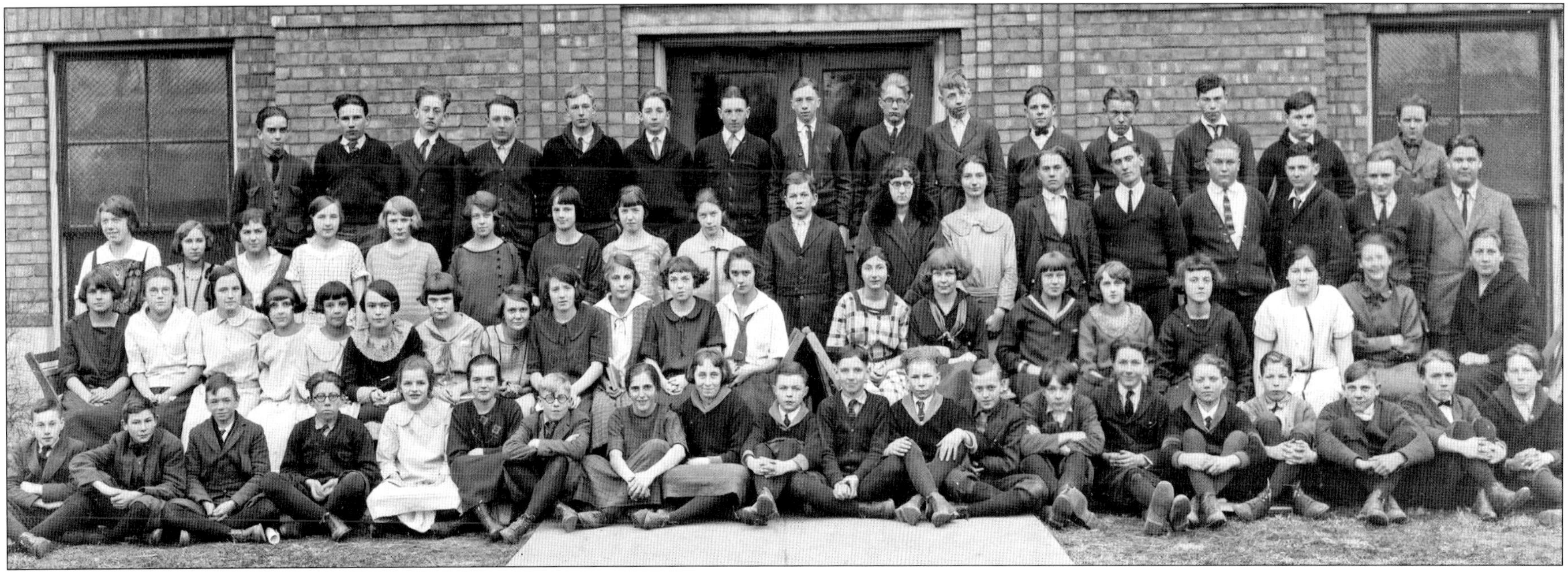

Midland High School freshman class, 1924. *Courtesy of Midland County Historical Society*

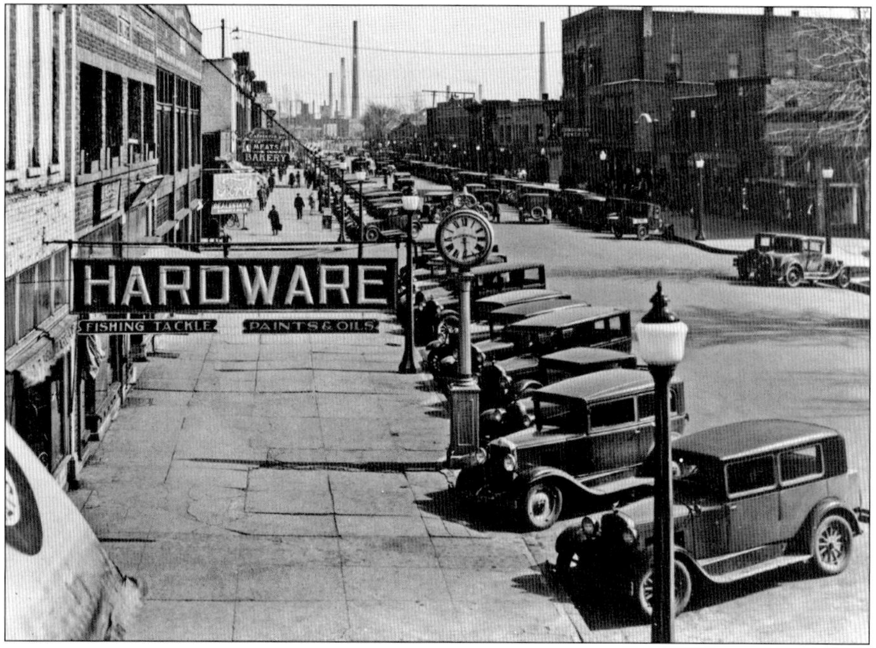

Main Street in Midland, 1929. *Courtesy of Midland County Historical Society*

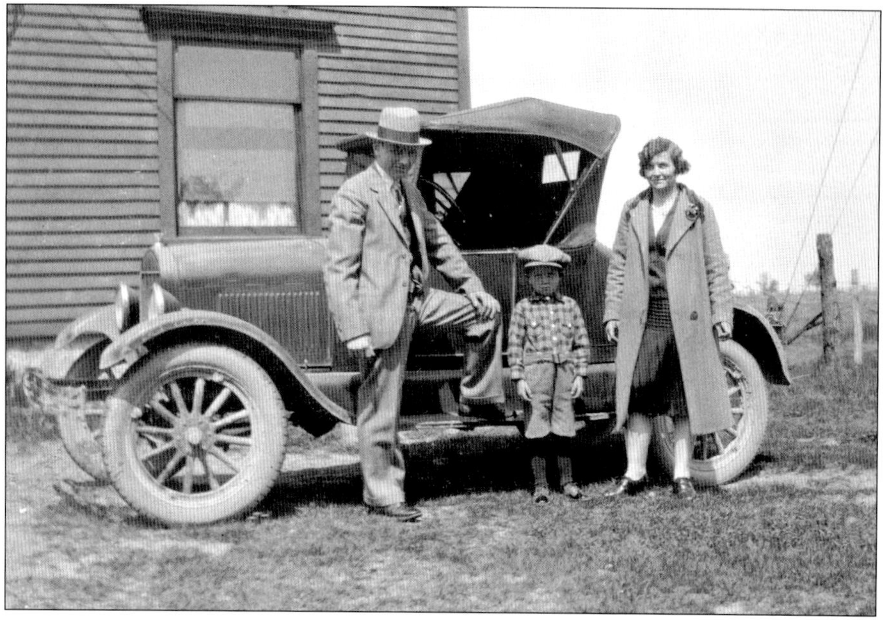

Willard, Rolin and Verna Moore ready to leave Coleman to travel to Ohio, circa 1928. *Courtesy of Don and Sandy Methner Moore*

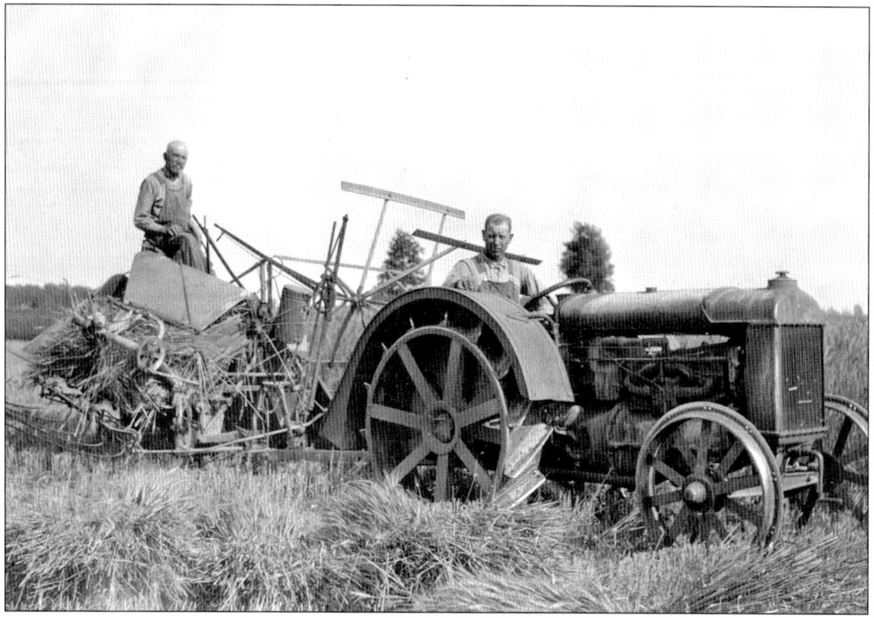

Byron Ostrander, left, and George Schlader harvesting wheat at 3830 Smith Crossing Rd., 1929. *Courtesy of Janet Rice*

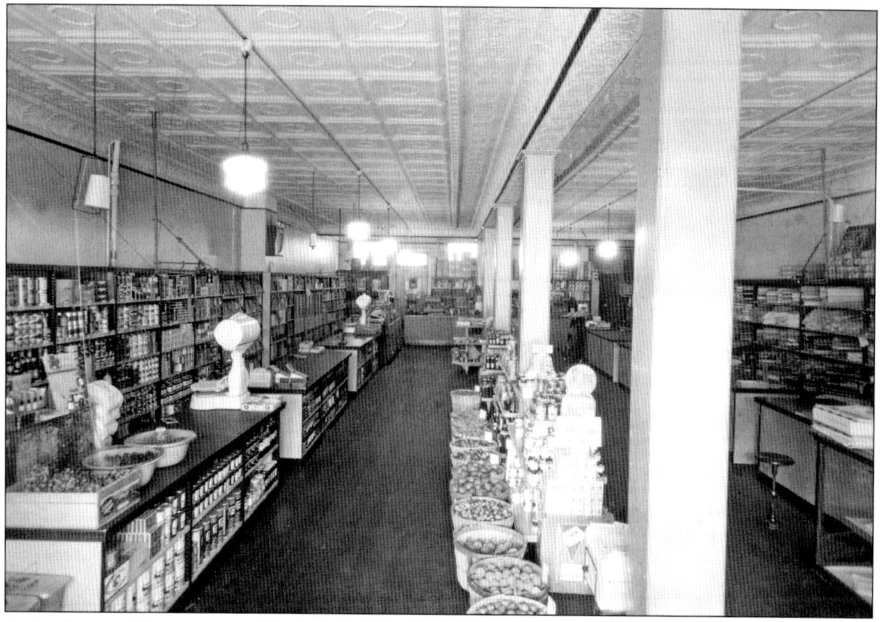

Interior of Thompson Mercantile, circa 1925.
Courtesy of Midland County Historical Society

The 1930s

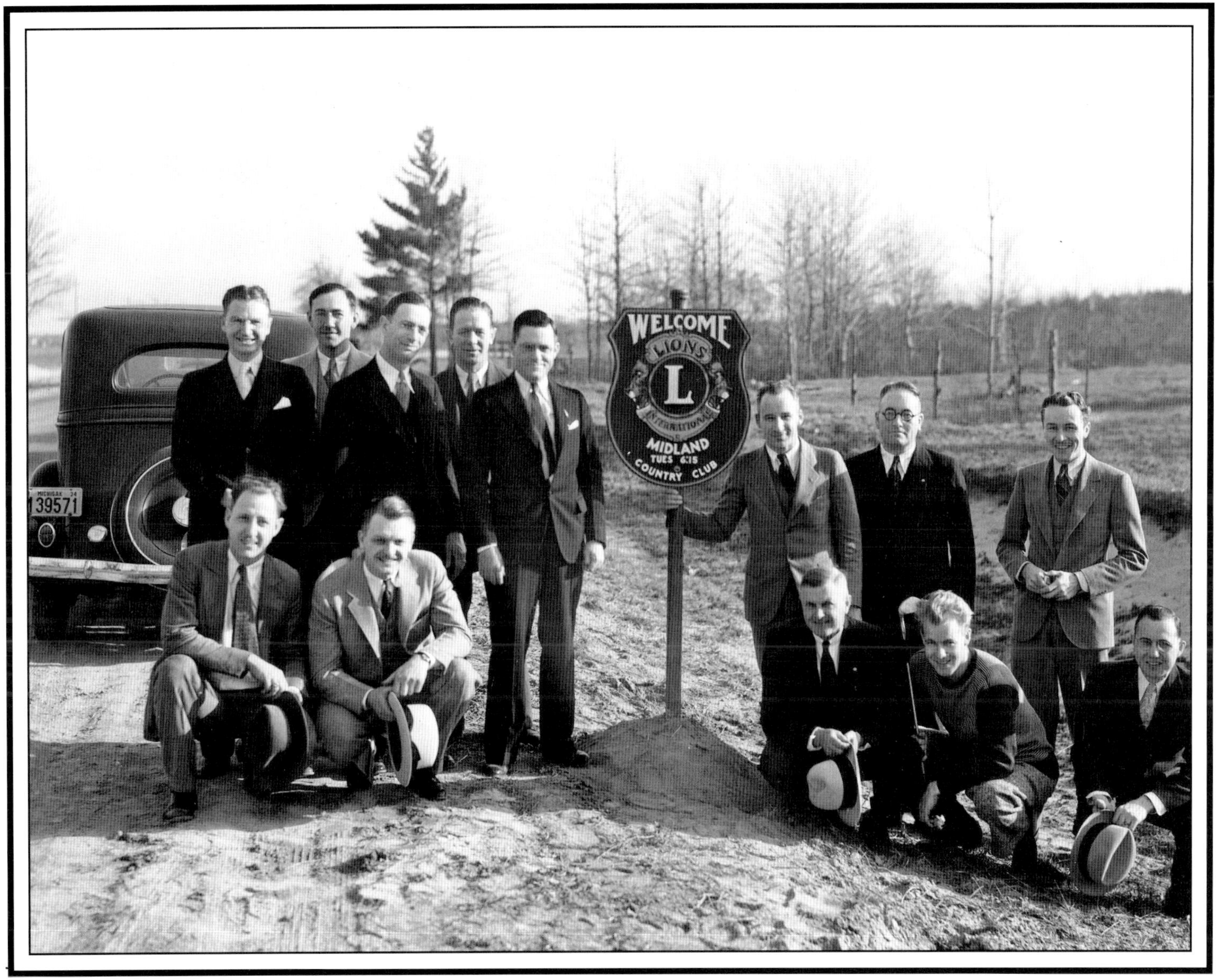

Members of the Midland Lions Club set a welcome sign, 1934. *Courtesy of Midland County Historical Society*

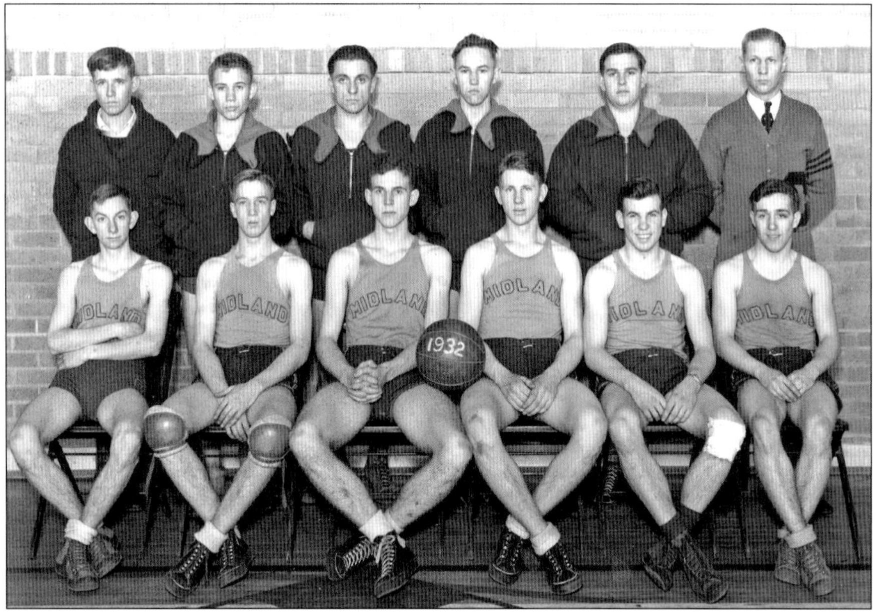

Midland High School basketball team, 1932.
Courtesy of Midland County Historical Society

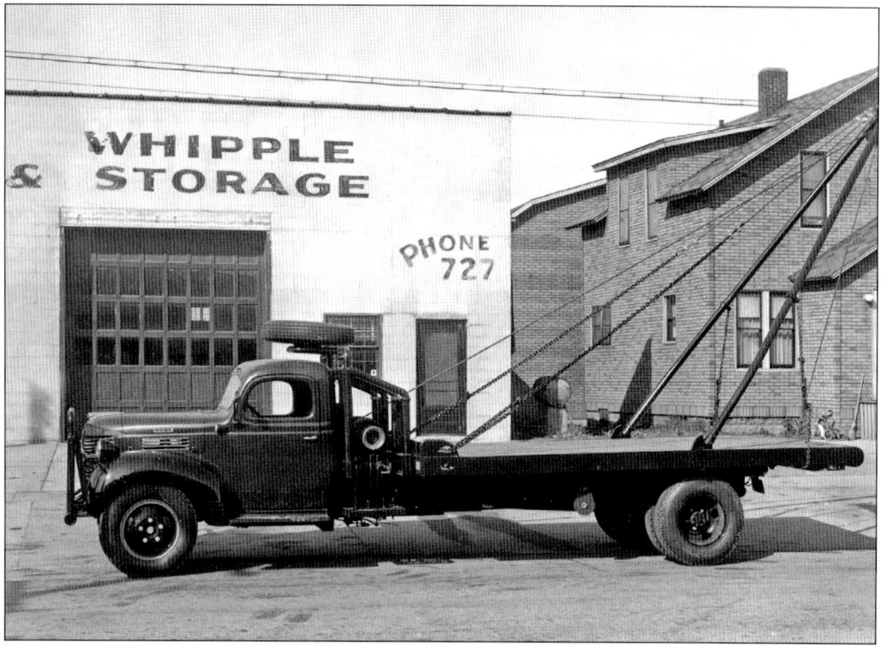

Whipple Storage, 1109 E. Buttles St., circa 1930. *Courtesy of Bernadette K. Herkner*

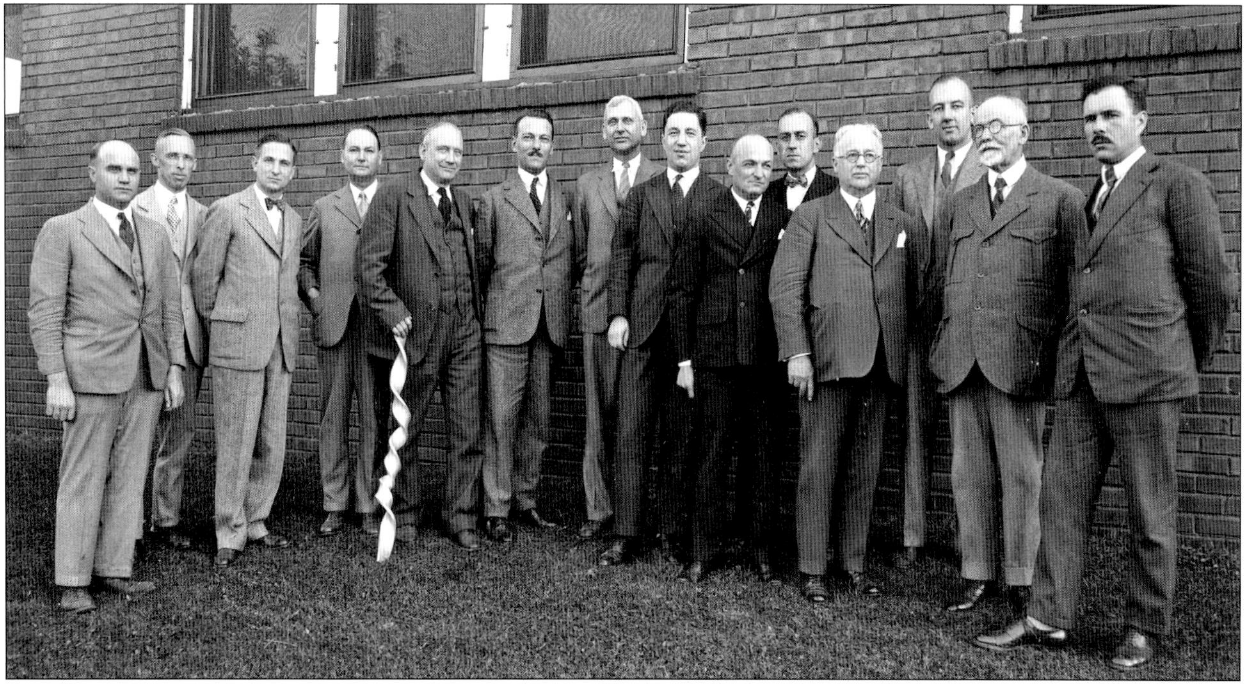

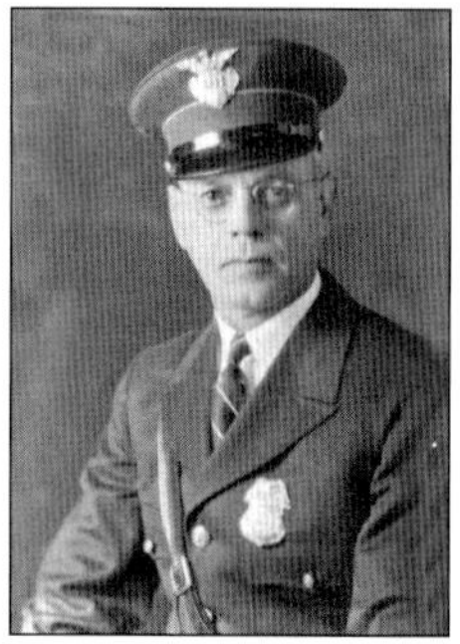

Fred V. Sayles, Midland's first Chief of Police, 1930.
Courtesy of Joyce and Dee Olds

The Dow Chemical Company's management group with men from France who came to learn about magnesium, 1930. Included are Lew Ward, John Gann, Willard Dow, William Hale, Oscar Diehl, Mons. Penard, E. O. Barstow, Earl Bennet, Ralph Hunter, (unknown) Parker, Jed Heath, Mons. Hubine and unidentified.
Courtesy of Midland County Historical Society

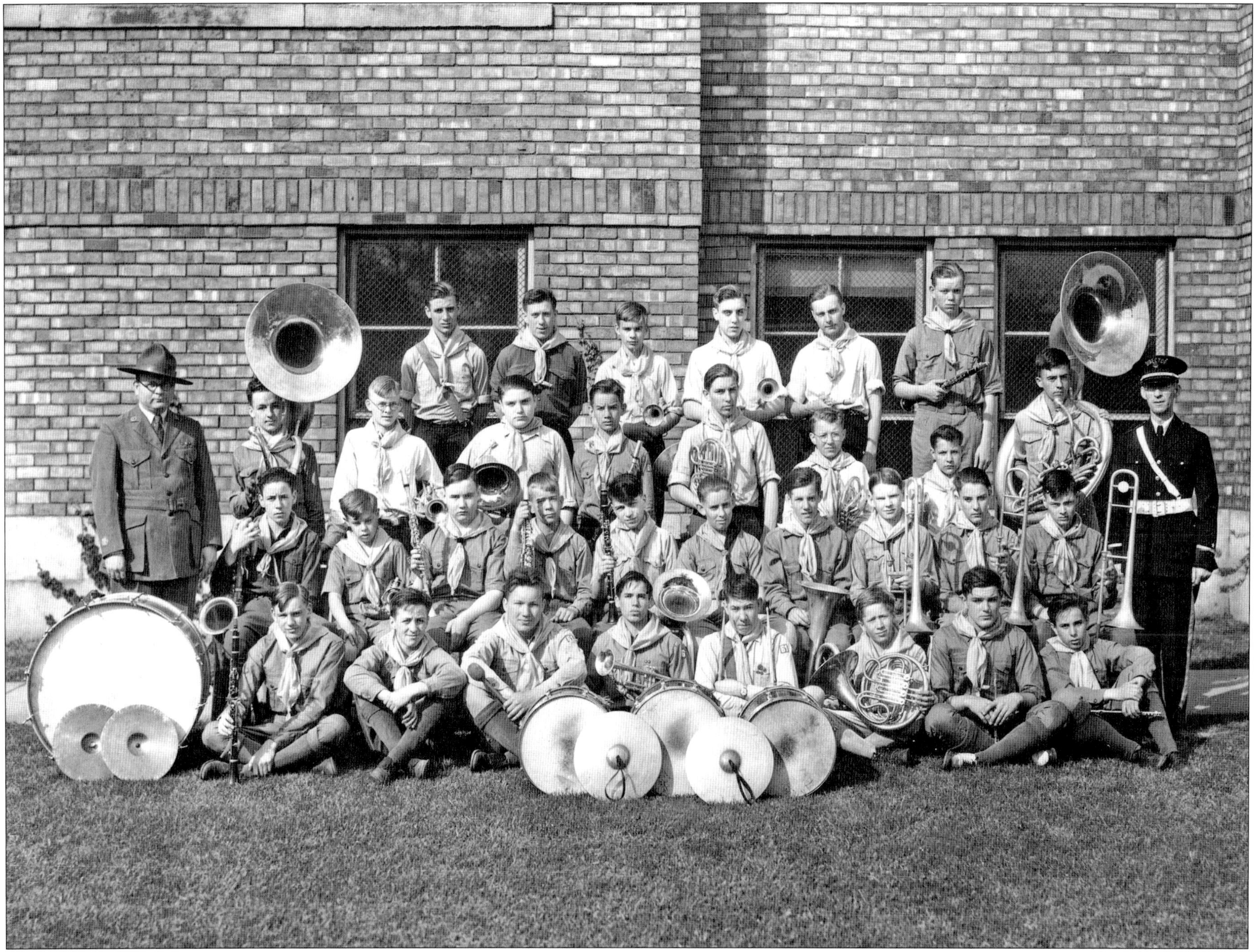

Boy Scout Band behind Midland High School on Grove Street, circa 1930. *Courtesy of Midland County Historical Society*

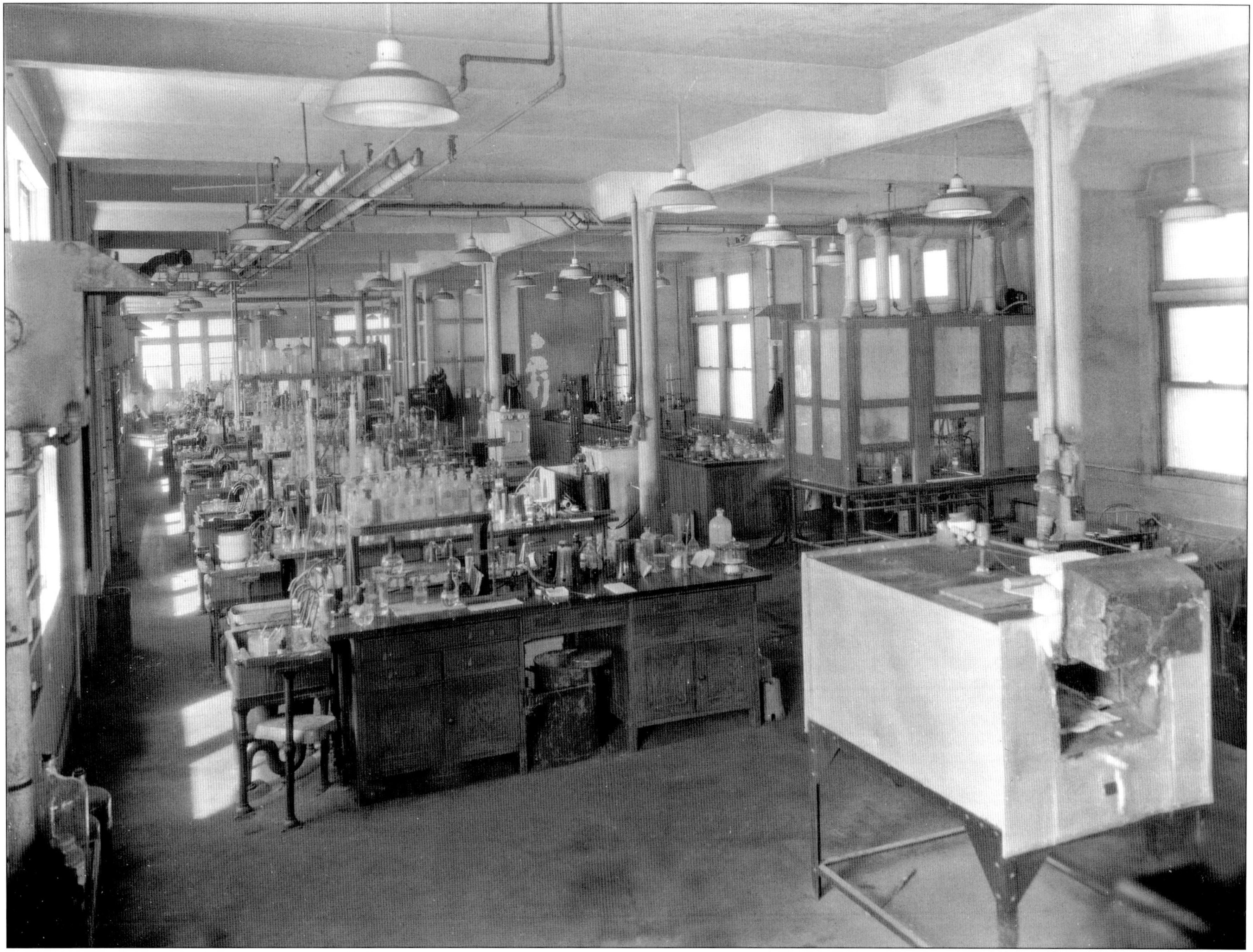

Inside The Dow Chemical Company, circa 1930. *Courtesy of Midland County Historical Society*

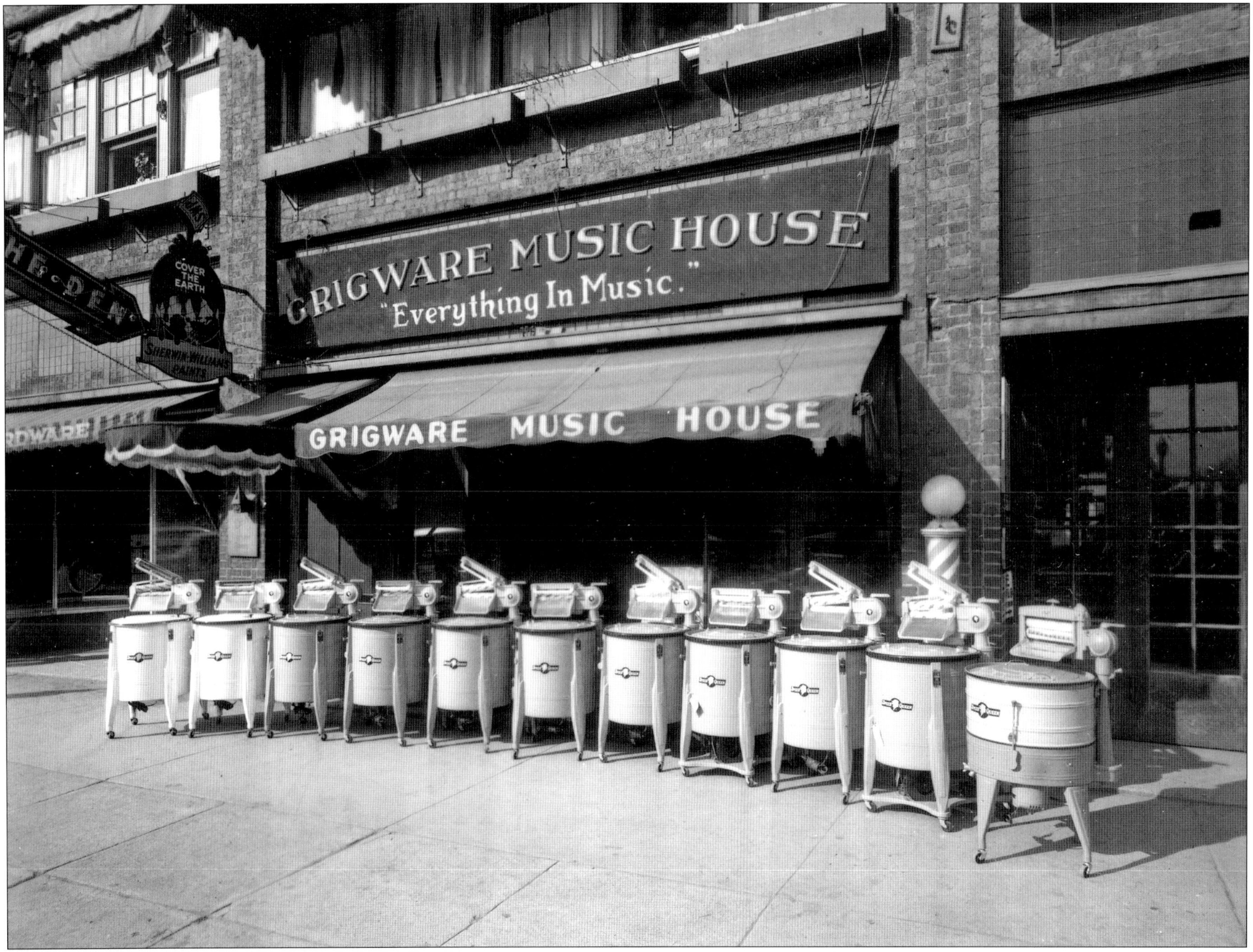

Grigware Music Store, circa 1930. *Courtesy of Midland County Historical Society*

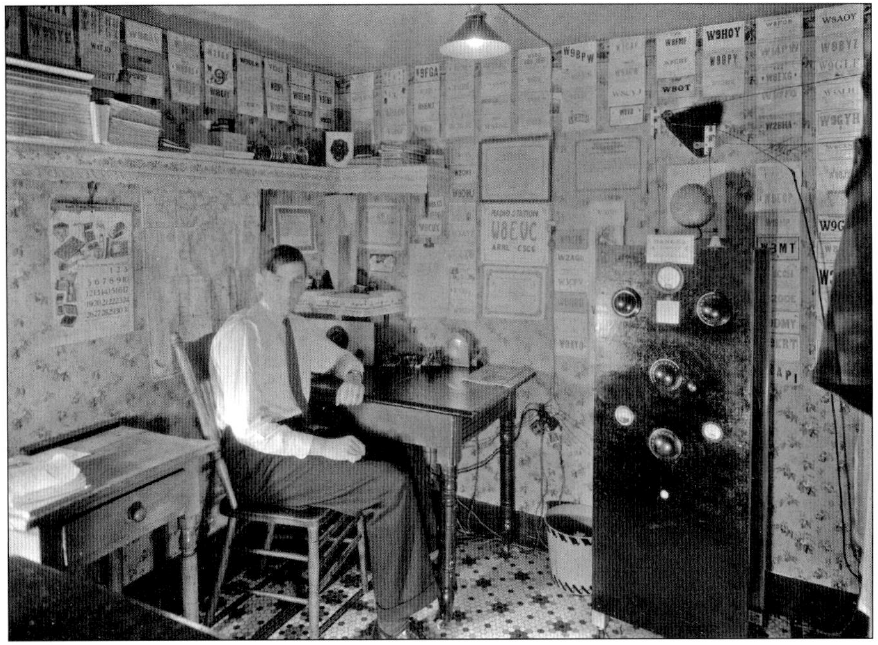

Ham radio operator in Midland, 1932. *Courtesy of Midland County Historical Society*

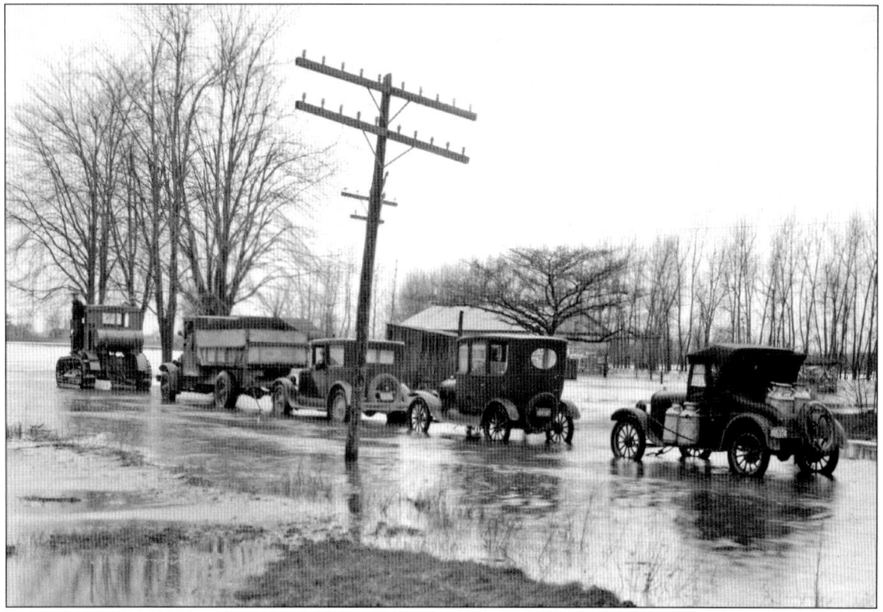

Flood scene on Benson Street near Poseyville, 1934.
Courtesy of Midland County Historical Society

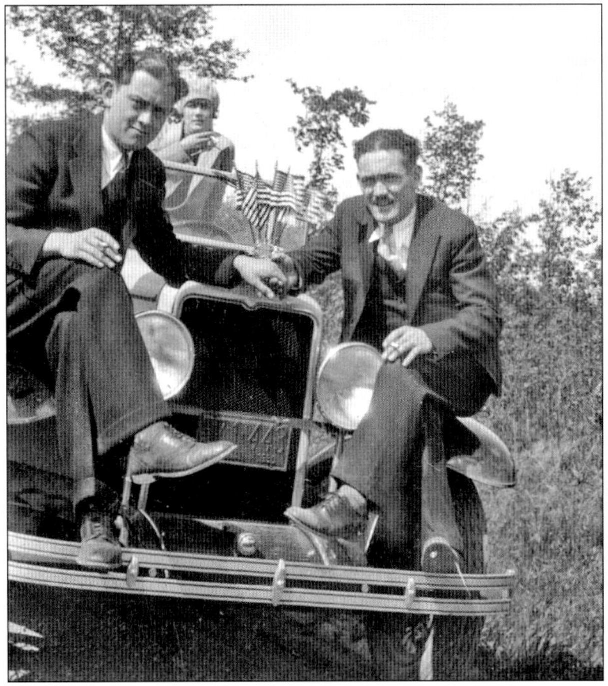

Elden Rice and friends with a car decorated for a parade in the 1930s.
Courtesy of Barbara Rice

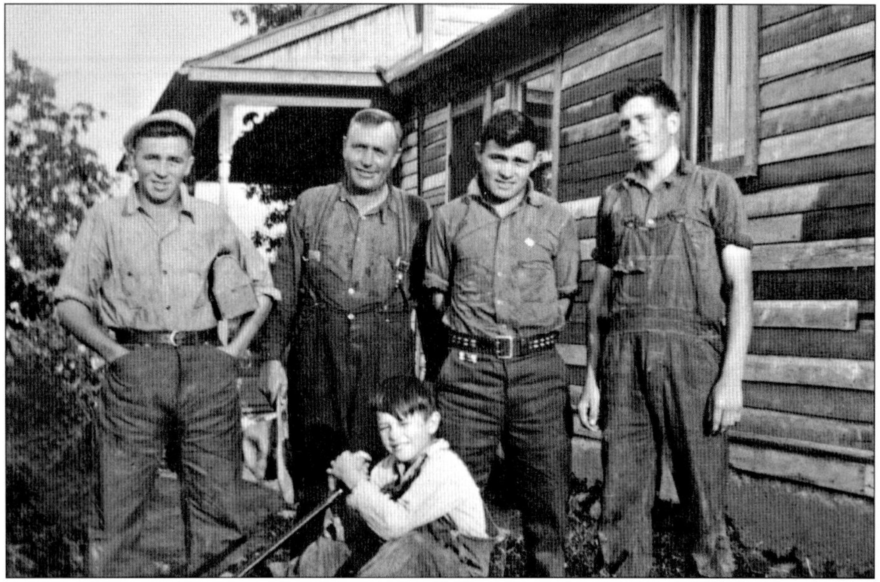

On the Valliere farm in Mount Haley Township, 1934, standing left to right: Arthur, Eugene, Laurence and Cyrille Valliere. Henry is in the wagon.
Courtesy of Linda Harbron

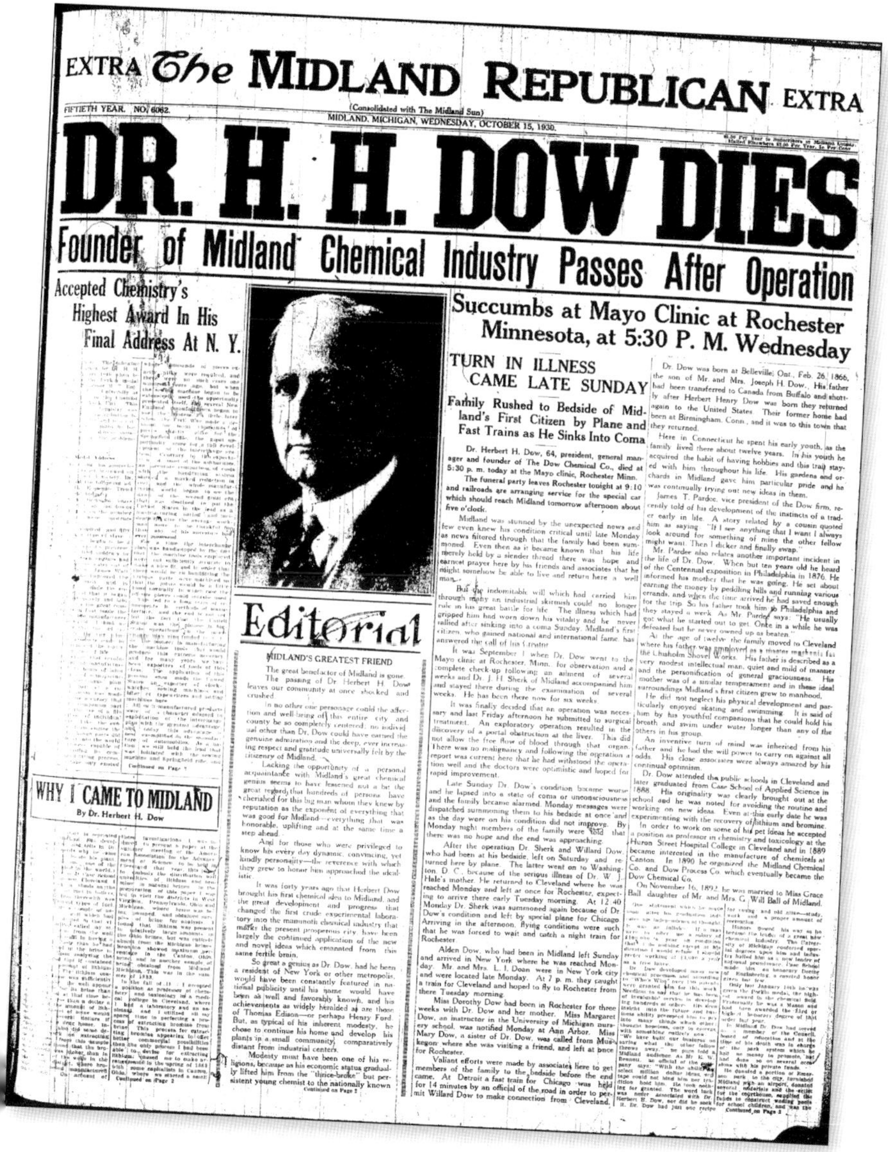

EXTRA The MIDLAND REPUBLICAN EXTRA

(Consolidated with The Midland Sun)

FIFTIETH YEAR. NO. 6062. MIDLAND, MICHIGAN, WEDNESDAY, OCTOBER 15, 1930.

DR. H. H. DOW DIES

Founder of Midland Chemical Industry Passes After Operation

Accepted Chemistry's Highest Award In His Final Address At N. Y.

Succumbs at Mayo Clinic at Rochester Minnesota, at 5:30 P. M. Wednesday

TURN IN ILLNESS CAME LATE SUNDAY

Family Rushed to Bedside of Midland's First Citizen by Plane and Fast Trains as He Sinks Into Coma

Dr. Herbert H. Dow, 64, president, general manager and founder of The Dow Chemical Co., died at 5:30 p. m. today at the Mayo clinic, Rochester Minn.

The funeral party leaves Rochester tonight at 9:10 and railroads are arranging service for the special car which should reach Midland tomorrow afternoon about five o'clock.

Midland was stunned by the unexpected news and few even knew his condition critical until late Monday as news filtered through that the family had been summoned. Even then as it became known that his life merely held by a slender thread there was hope and earnest prayer here by his friends and associates that he might somehow be able to live and return here a well man.

But the indomitable will which had carried him through many an industrial skirmish could no longer rule in his great battle for life. The illness which had gripped him had worn down his vitality and he never rallied after sinking into a coma Sunday. Midland's first citizen, who gained national and international fame, has answered the call of his Creator.

It was September 1 when Dr. Dow went to the Mayo clinic at Rochester, Minn., for observation and a complete check-up following an ailment of several weeks and Dr. J. H. Sherk of Midland accompanied him and stayed there during the examination of several weeks. He has been there now for six weeks.

It was finally decided that an operation was necessary and last Friday afternoon he submitted to surgical treatment. An exploratory operation resulted in the discovery of a portal obstruction at the liver. This did not allow the free flow of blood through that organ. There was no malignancy and following the operation a report was current here that he had withstood the operation well and the doctors were optimistic and hoped for rapid improvement.

Late Sunday Dr. Dow's condition became worse and he lapsed into a state of coma or unconsciousness and the family became alarmed. Monday messages were dispatched summoning them to his bedside at once and as the day wore on his condition did not improve. By Monday night members of the family were told that there was no hope and the end was approaching.

After the operation Dr. Sherk and Willard Dow, who had been at his bedside, left on Saturday and returned here by plane. The latter went on to Washington, D. C., because of the serious illness of Dr. W. J. Hale's mother. He returned to Cleveland where he was reached Monday and left at once for Rochester, expecting to arrive there early Tuesday morning. At 12:40 Monday Dr. Sherk was summoned again because of Dr. Dow's condition and left by special plane for Chicago. Arriving in the afternoon, flying conditions were such that he was forced to wait and catch a night train for Rochester.

Alden Dow, who had been in Midland left Sunday and arrived in New York where he was reached Monday. Mr. and Mrs. L. I. Doan were in New York city and were located late Monday. At 7 p. m. they caught a train for Cleveland and hoped to fly to Rochester from there Tuesday morning.

Miss Dorothy Dow had been in Rochester for three weeks with Dr. Dow and her mother. Miss Margaret Dow, an instructor in the University of Michigan nursery school, was notified Monday at Ann Arbor. Miss Mary Dow, a sister of Dr. Dow, was called from Muskegon where she was visiting a friend, and left at once for Rochester.

Valiant efforts were made by associates here to get members of the family to the bedside before the end came. At Detroit a fast train for Chicago was held for 14 minutes by an official of the road in order to permit Willard Dow to make connection from Cleveland.

Dr. Dow was born at Belleville, Ont., Feb. 26, 1866, the son of Mr. and Mrs. Joseph H. Dow. His father had been transferred to Canada from Buffalo and shortly after Herbert Henry Dow was born they returned again to the United States. Their former home had been at Birmingham, Conn., and it was to this town that they returned.

Here in Connecticut he spent his early youth, as the family lived there about twelve years. In his youth he acquired the habit of having hobbies and this trait stayed with him throughout his life. His gardens and orchards in Midland gave him particular pride and he was continually trying out new ideas in them.

James T. Pardee, vice president of the Dow firm, recently told of his development of the instincts of a trader early in life. A story related by a cousin quoted him as saying: "If I see anything that I want I always look around for something of mine the other fellow might want. Then I dicker and finally swap."

Mr. Pardee also relates another important incident in the life of Dr. Dow. When but ten years old he heard of the Centennial exposition in Philadelphia in 1876. He informed his mother that he was going. He set about earning the money by peddling bills and running various errands, and when the time arrived he had saved enough for the trip. So his father took him to Philadelphia and they stayed a week. As Mr. Pardee says: "He usually got what he started out to get. Once in a while he was defeated but he never owned up as beaten."

At the age of twelve the family moved to Cleveland where his father was employed as a master mechanic for the Chisholm Shovel Works. His father is described as a very modest intellectual man, quiet and mild of manner and the personification of general graciousness. His mother was of a similar temperament and in these ideal surroundings Midland's first citizen grew to manhood.

He did not neglect his physical development and particularly enjoyed skating and swimming. It is said of him by his youthful companions that he could hold his breath and swim under water longer than any of the others in his group.

An inventive turn of mind was inherited from his father and he had the will power to carry on against all odds. His close associates were always amazed by his continual optimism.

Dr. Dow attended the public schools in Cleveland and later graduated from Case School of Applied Science in 1888. His originality was clearly brought out at the school and he was noted for avoiding the routine and working on new ideas. Even at this early date he was experimenting with the recovery of lithium and bromine.

In order to work on some of his pet ideas he accepted a position as professor in chemistry and toxicology at the Huron Street Hospital College in Cleveland and in 1889 became interested in the manufacture of chemicals at Canton. In 1890 he organized the Midland Chemical Co. and Dow Process Co. which eventually became the Dow Chemical Co.

On November 16, 1892, he was married to Miss Grace Ball, daughter of Mr. and Mrs. G. Will Ball of Midland.

Editorial

MIDLAND'S GREATEST FRIEND

The great benefactor of Midland is gone.

The passing of Dr. Herbert H. Dow leaves our community at once shocked and crushed.

In no other one personage could the affection and well-being of this entire city and county be so completely centered; no individual other than Dr. Dow could have earned the genuine admiration and the deep, ever increasing respect and gratitude universally felt by the citizenry of Midland.

Lacking the opportunity of a personal acquaintance with Midland's great chemical genius seems to have lessened not a bit the great regard that hundreds of persons have cherished for this big man whom they knew by reputation as the exponent of everything that was good for Midland—everything that was honorable, uplifting and at the same time a step ahead.

And for those who were privileged to know his every day dynamic, convincing, yet kindly personality—the reverence with which they grew to honor him approached the idealistic.

It was forty years ago that Herbert Dow brought his first chemical idea to Midland, and the great development and progress that changed the first crude experimental laboratory into the mammoth chemical industry that marks the present prosperous city, have been largely the continued application of the new and novel ideas which emanated from this same fertile brain.

So great a genius as Dr. Dow, had he been a resident of New York or other metropolis, would have been constantly featured in national publicity until his name would have been as well and favorably known, and his achievements as widely heralded as are those of Thomas Edison—or perhaps Henry Ford. But, as typical of his inherent modesty, he chose to continue his home and develop his plants in a small community, comparatively distant from industrial centers.

Modesty must have been one of his religions, because as his economic status gradually lifted him from the "thrice-broke" but persistent young chemist to the nationally known

Continued on Page 2

WHY I CAME TO MIDLAND

By Dr. Herbert H. Dow

The Midland Republican reporting the death of Dr. H. H. Dow, Oct. 15, 1930. *Courtesy of Midland Daily News*

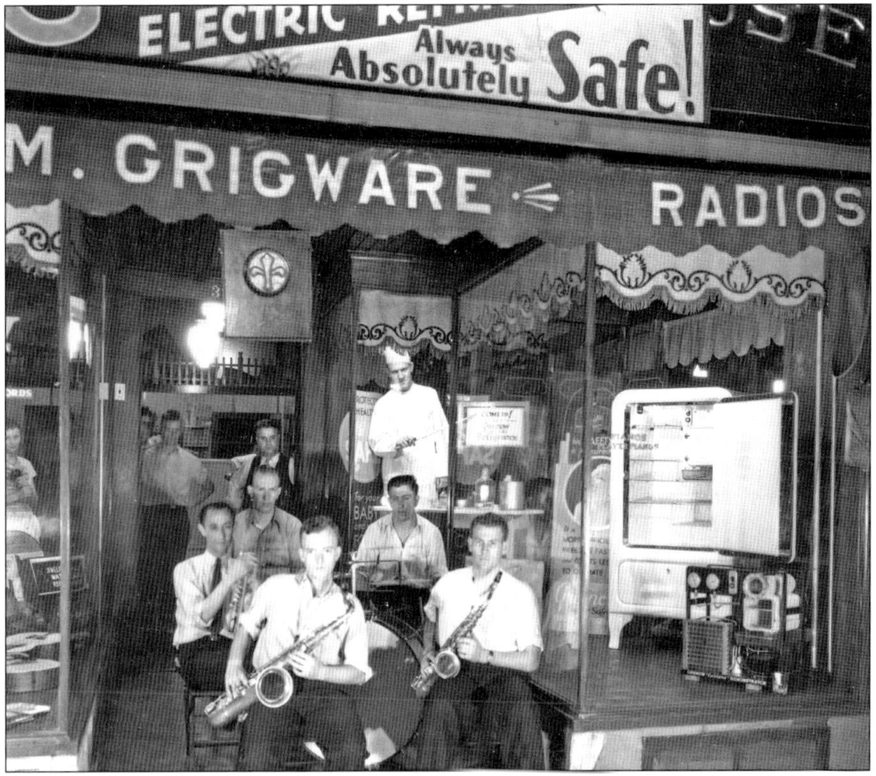

Grigware Appliance Store, circa 1932. *Courtesy of Midland County Historical Society*

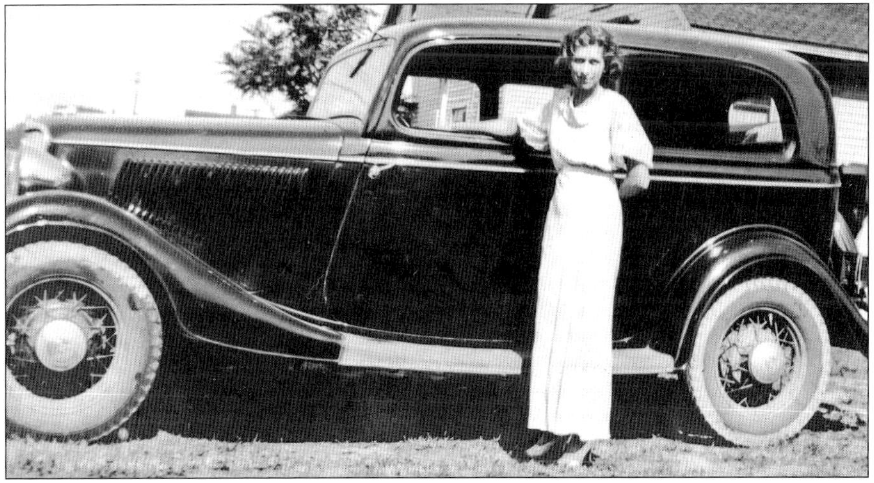

Anne Grotkowski Pnacek in front of the car parked at their home in Midland, June 1934. *Courtesy of Barbara Rice*

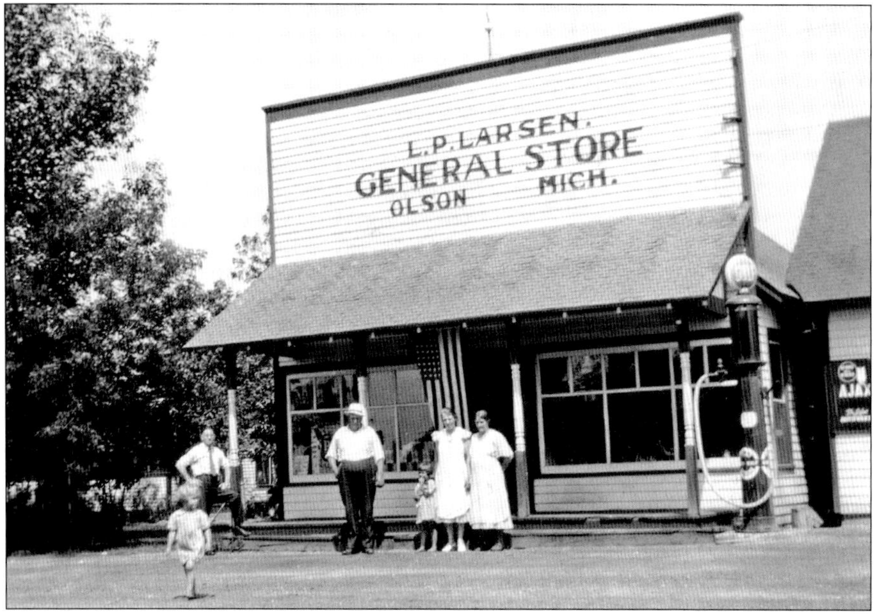

L. P. Larsen General Store, Lee Township, Olson, 1935. L. P. Larsen is in the center. *Courtesy of Naomi Haebler*

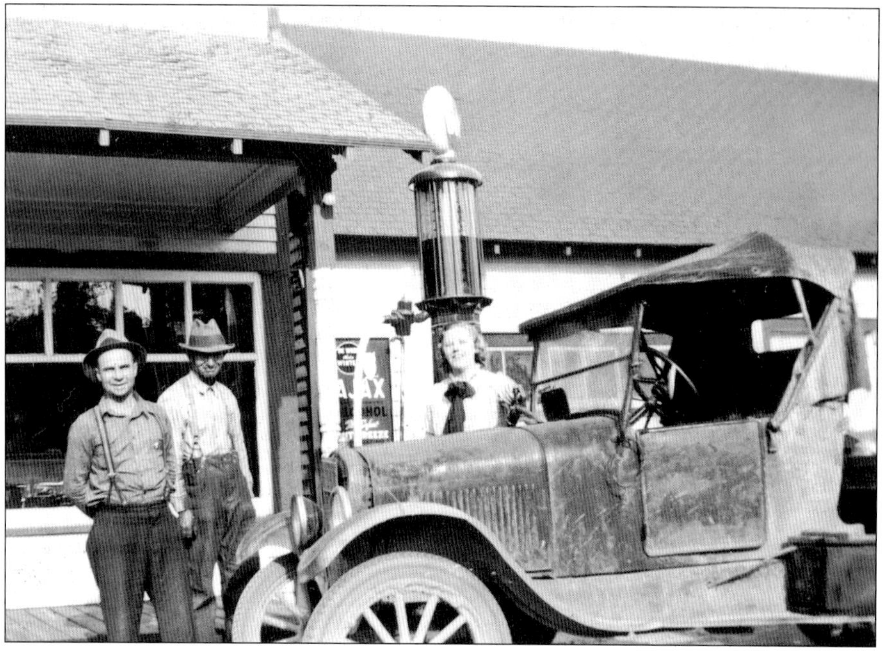

Olson Store in Lee Township June 13, 1935. *Courtesy of Naomi Haebler*

The Board of Supervisors, 1932. Front row, left to right: Floyd Cade, William Kuehlman, Dexter Fales, Michael Saiko, Herbert Hardy, John Smith, William E. Ryan, James W. Driver and L. P. Larsen. Second row: Edward Blackhurst, Charles Farnsworth, Aaron T. Bliss and Al Thorsberg. Back row: Andrew S. Arbury, William Woodcock, Henry W. Harrison, Arthur Clarke, William Nobbs, John Vincent, Glenn Brown, Arthur Reiss, Andrew L. Mullet, Chester E. Morris, Roy Sias and William Day. *Courtesy of Midland County Historical Society*

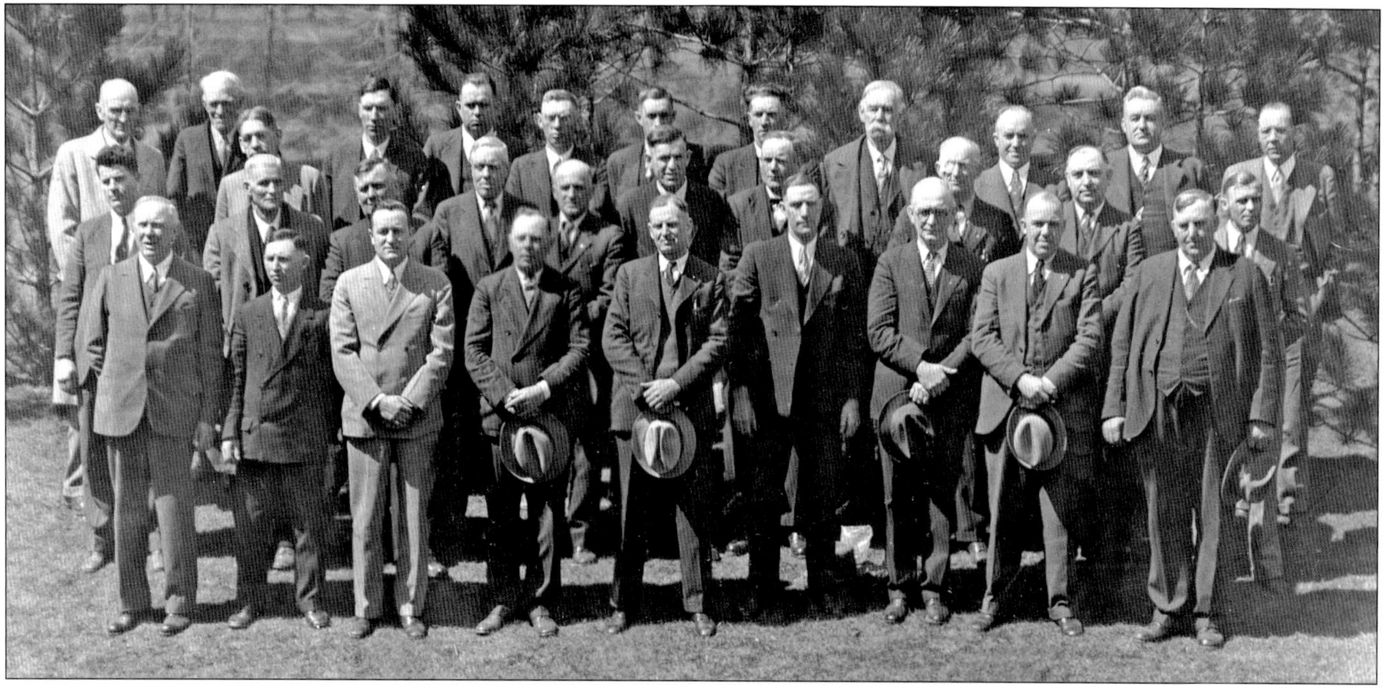

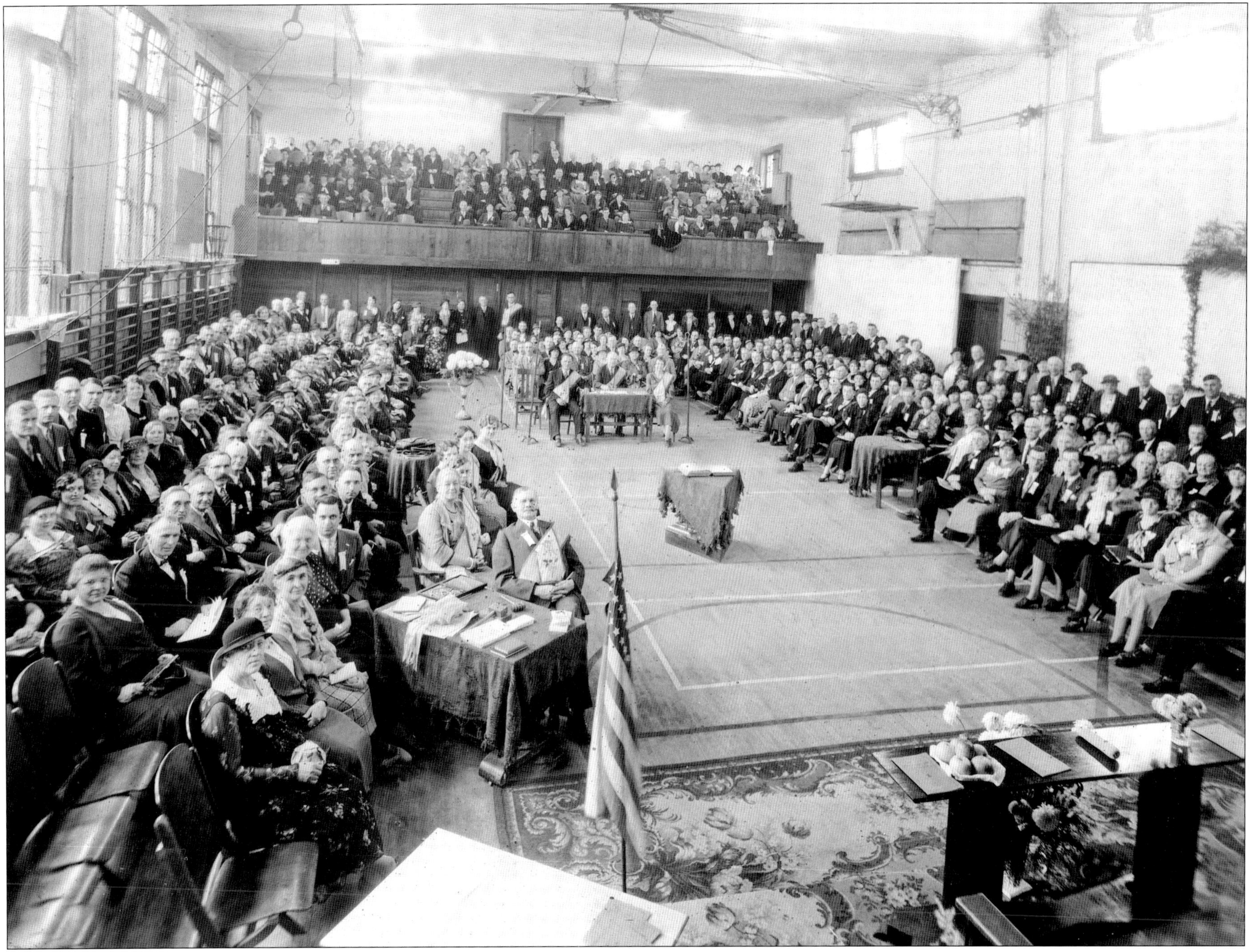

State Grange meeting at the Midland Community Center, 1934. The meeting lasted from October 29 to November 3. *Courtesy of Midland County Historical Society*

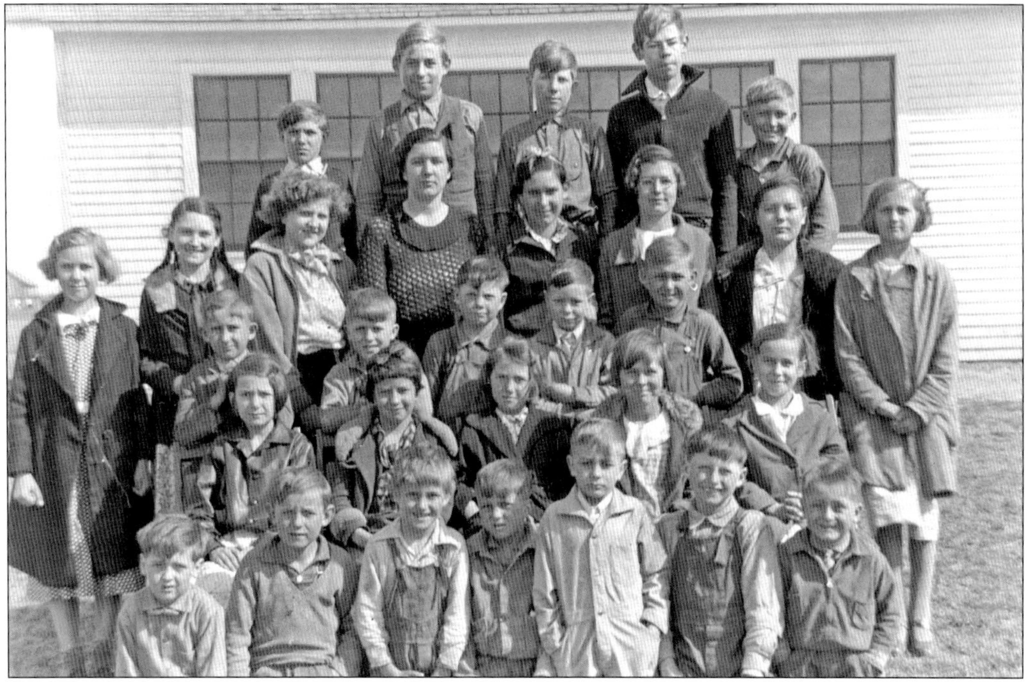

Waldo School in Larkin Township, circa 1936. First row, left to right: Melvin Hocricke, Norman Westphal, Ed Zondlak, Earl Gerstacker, Detrick Krentz, John Wontorick and Carl Schoenbine. Second row: Frieda Westphal, Julia Westphal, Emma Westphal, Joan Zondlak and Augusta Sereck. Third row: Leo Wontorick, Don Zondlak, Wilber Krentz, Clair Gerstacker and Gust Wontorick. Fourth row: Josephine Serveck, unidentified, Leona Andrews, teacher Mrs. Van Meter, Helen Wontorick, Anna Zondlak, unidentified and Luella Schoebine. Fifth row: Gordon Hitchcock, Fred Hoenicke, Martin Westphal, Ed Hoenicke and Henry Wontorick. *Courtesy of Jean Griebe Baker*

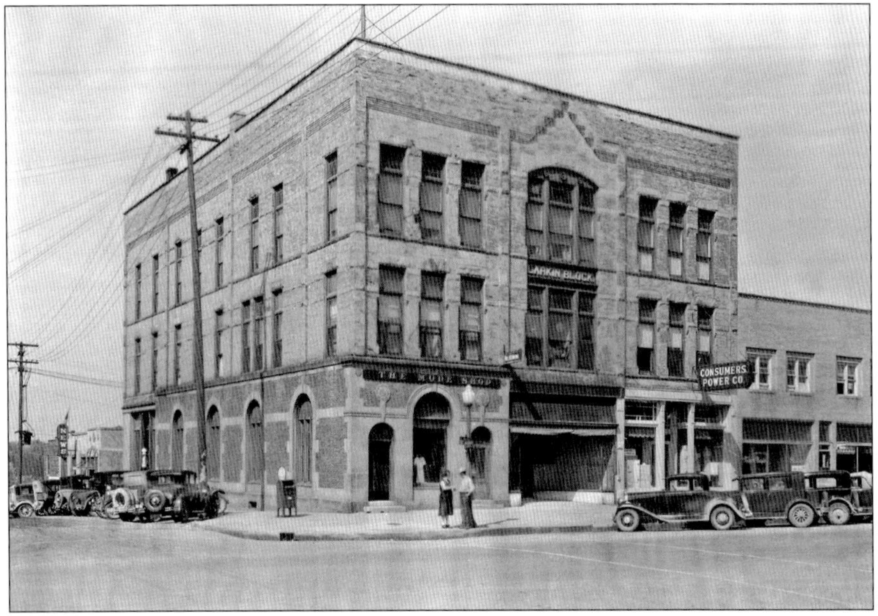

Larkin Block on Main Street in Midland, 1935.
Courtesy of Midland County Historical Society

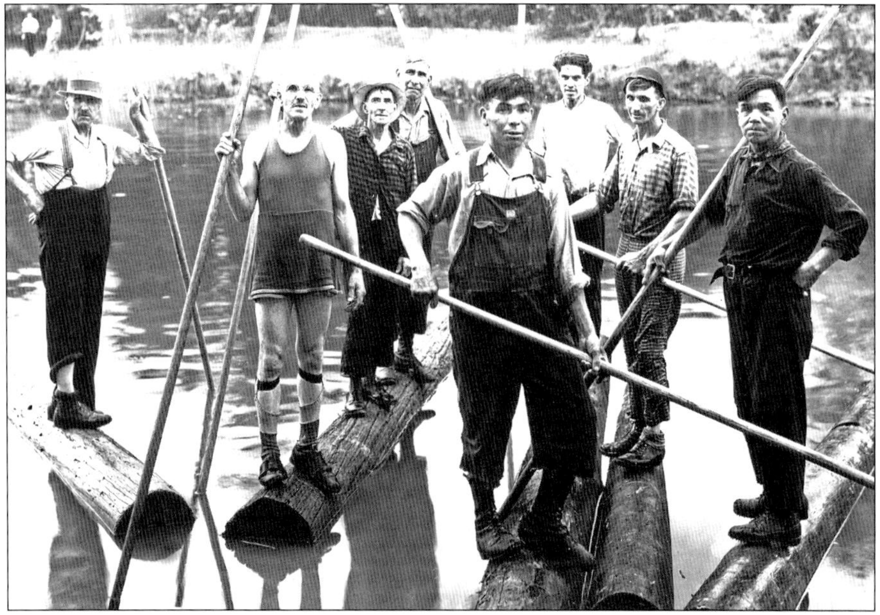

"River hogs" at Lumberjack Days in Edenville, 1936. Frank Wixom organized this annual event. *Courtesy of Midland County Historical Society*

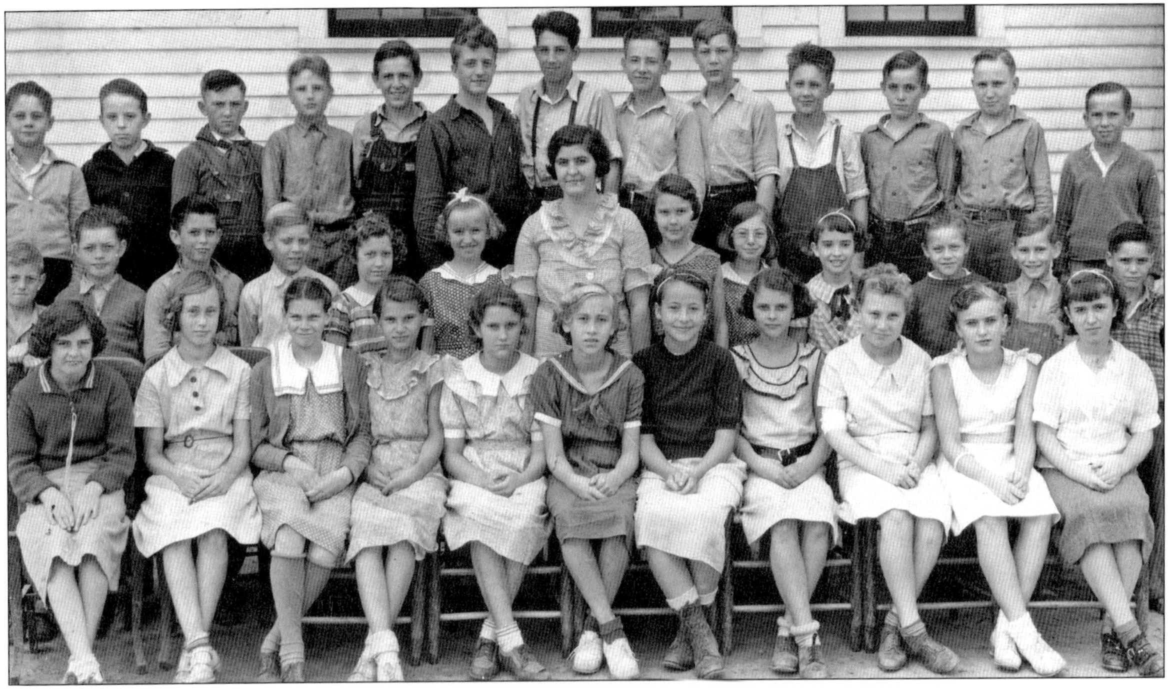

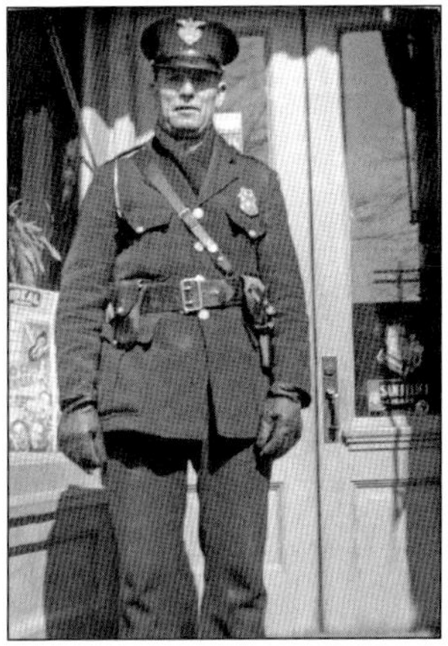

Marshall George E. Moore on Main Street, 1938.
Courtesy of Don and Sandy Methner Moore

McGill School, 1937. In the front row, the second girl from the left is Katherine Koenders and the sixth girl is Helen Draves. In the second row, the sixth person is Dorothy Draves and the seventh person is teacher Mrs. Hauri. In the back row, the seventh person is Harvey Ropp. *Courtesy of Carol Gillespie*

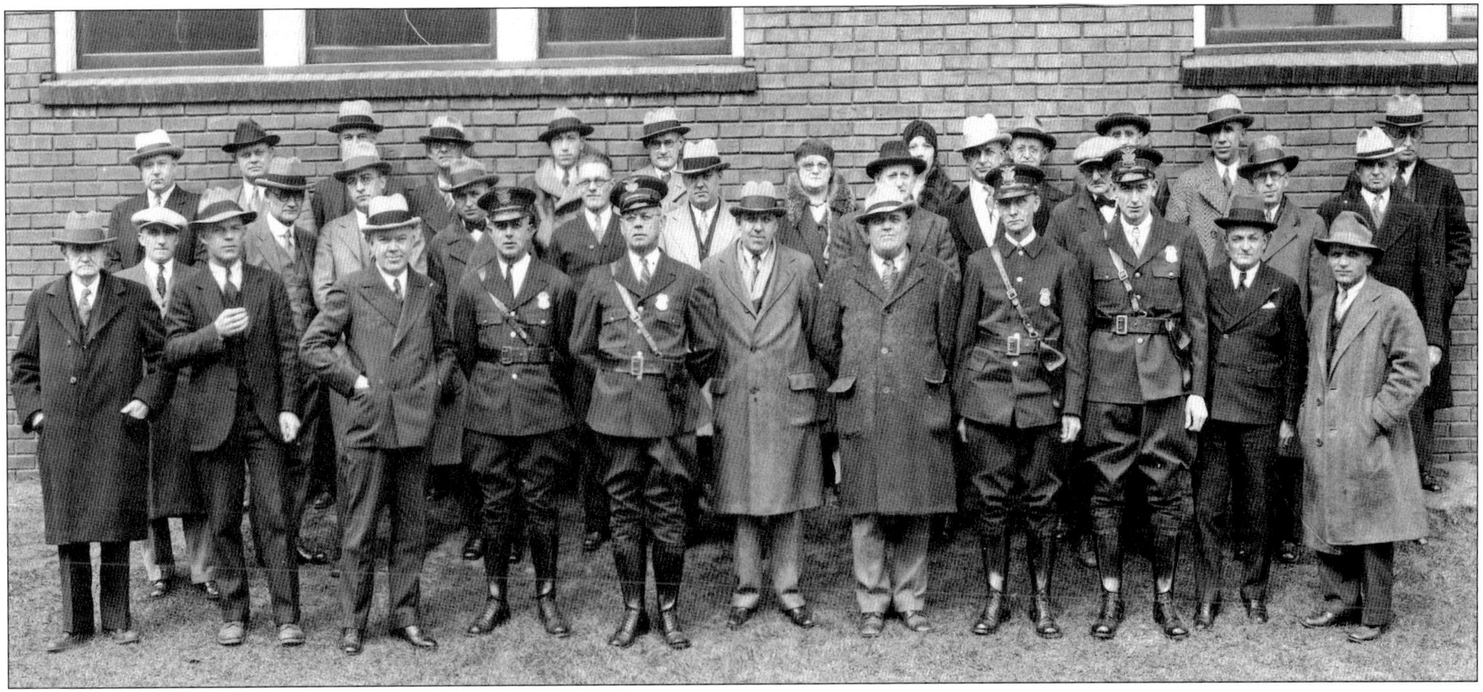

Policemen and Midland County officials, circa 1935. Included in the front row: George Metcalf, Carl Branson, G. A. Currie, Heine Ross, Fred Sales, Jim Drum, E. W. Bennett and Dutch Buctel. E. R. McLaughlen is in the second row.
Courtesy of Midland County Historical Society

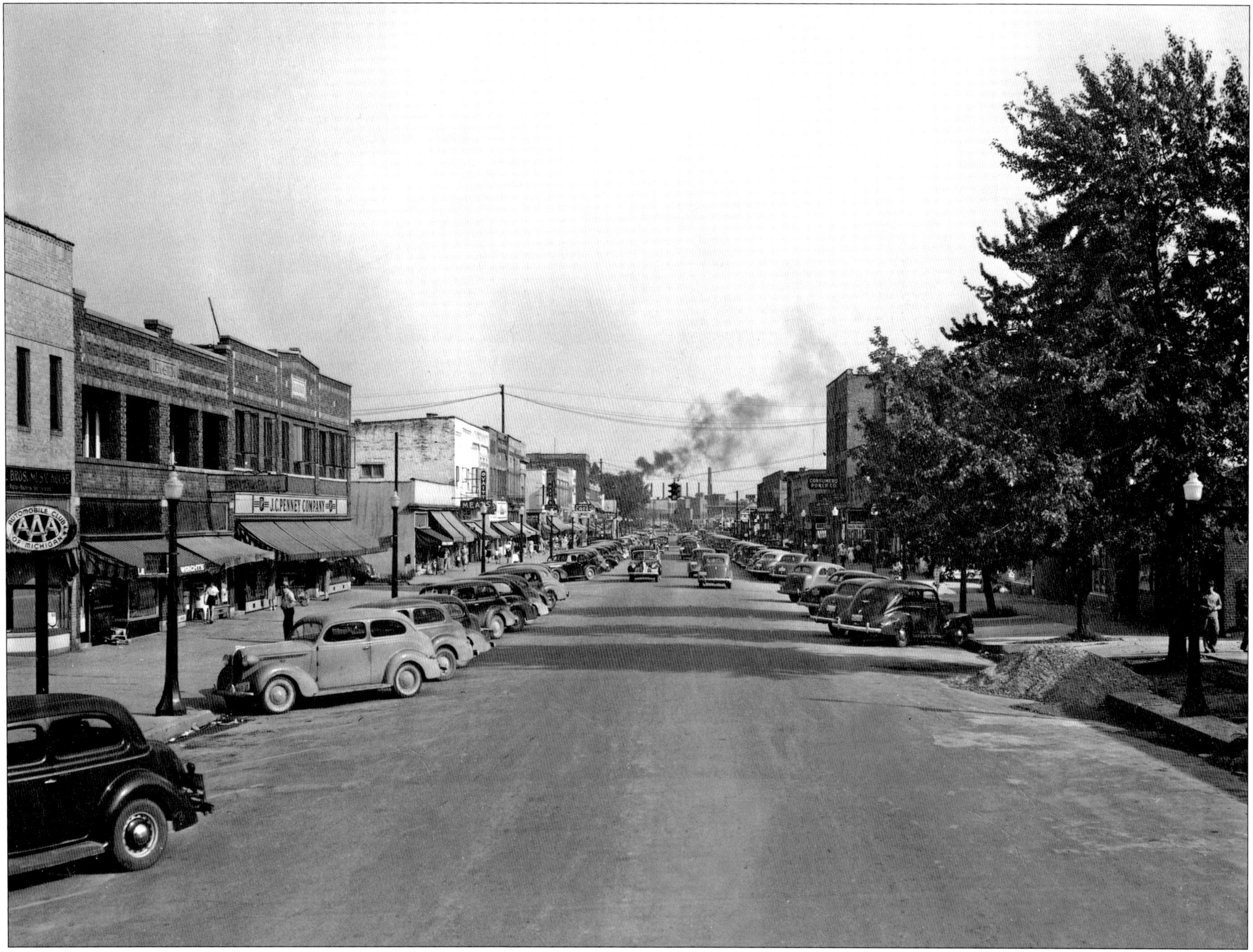

Main Street in Midland, 1936. *Courtesy of Midland County Historical Society*

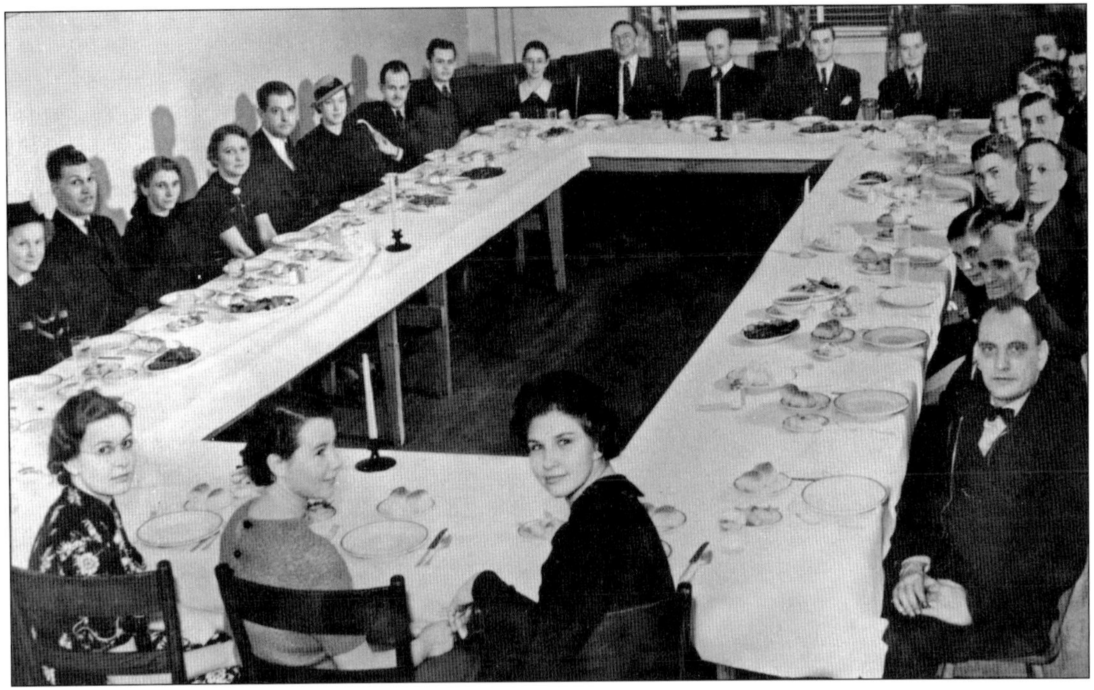

Employees of the *Midland Daily News* at a venison dinner, November 1937. Clockwise from upper left corner: Dorothy Langdon Yates, Arthur Johnstone, Claire Morrill, Margaret Vanest, Clarence Turner Vanest, Jean Warner, Elmer James, Curtis Layman, Helen Cox, Jack Hinkle, Alanson Sherwood, Earl Ervans, Marshall Dooley Hyde, Ervin Helmey, unidentified, Norman Slim Rumple, Florence Parker, Gordon Phillips, Robert Gildart, Philip T. Rich, Marie Helmey, Frank Feighner, unidentified, Clara Mills, Eleanor Lee and Margaret Albee.
Courtesy of Midland Daily News

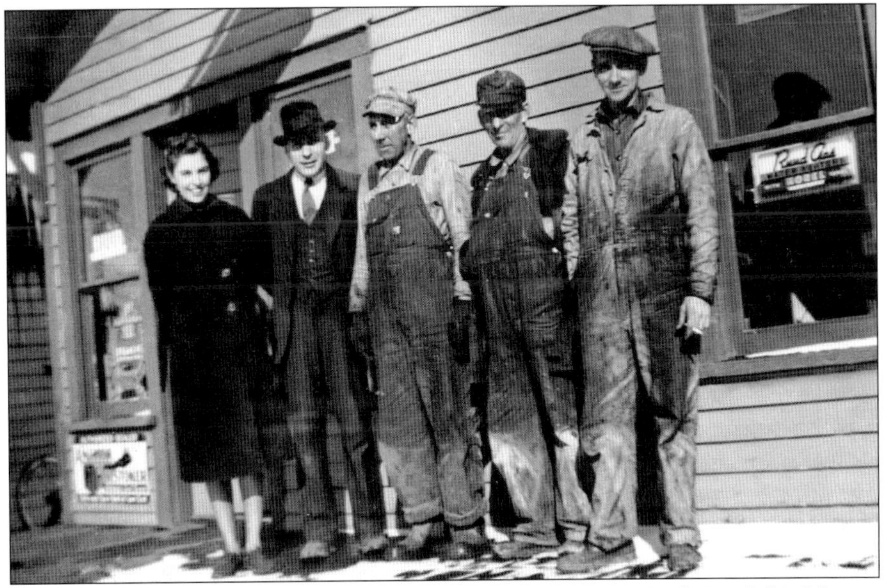

E. L. Modders Plumbing shop at 419 E. Main St., 1937. Left to right: Marge Milner, Ernest L. Modders, Bill Maddern, John Moored and Bill Lape.
Courtesy of Donna Modders Goodwin

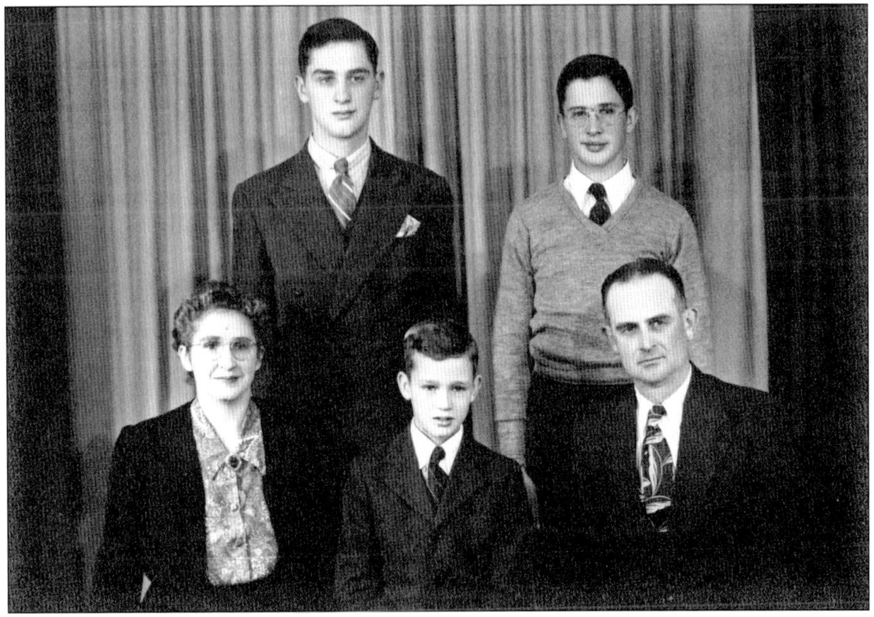

Courtney, Dewitt, Wilma, Tom and Cecil Fillmore at Wright Studio in Midland, 1937. *Courtesy of Sally Stanford*

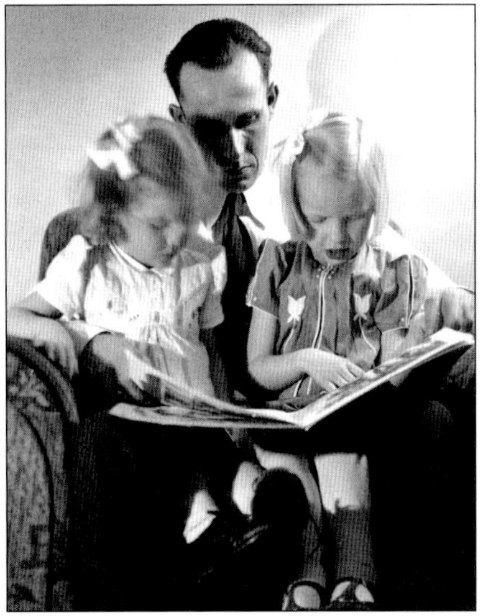

Russell Green reading to his daughters, Janet, left, and Lois, at their home at 111 E. Harold St., circa 1938. *Courtesy of Janet Rice*

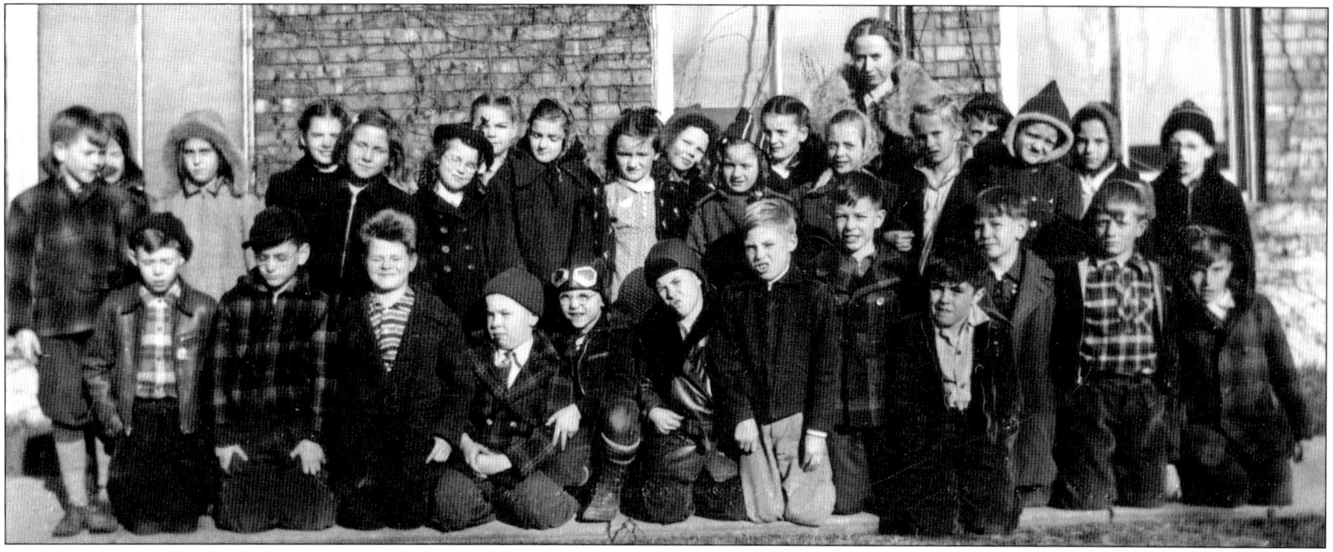

Third-grade class at the Second Ward School on Grove and Ashman streets, 1939. Included are Gene Thurston, Keith Kemmer, Lee Neeb, Jerry Green, Jim Moutsatson, Dee Olds, Herb Hagle, Skip Jackson, Joe Hickerson, Gene Wilson, Gary Loebrick, Joan Wenzel, Rosalind Beamish, Doris Frizzle, Marjean Eastman, Joyce Sayles, teacher Miss Ritchi, Carol Inman, Pat Weinberg and Buddy Fields. *Courtesy of Joyce and Dee Olds*

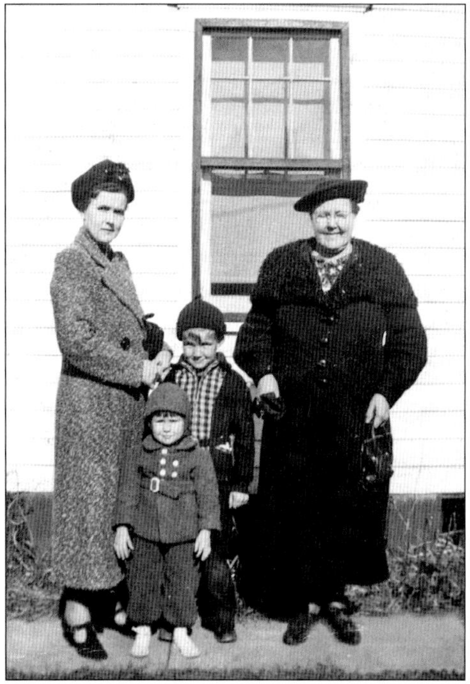

Standing in front of their home in Midland are Lafey Leuenberger, Edna Maxwell, Ray Leuenberger and Sally Leuenberger, 1939.
Courtesy of Sally Stanford

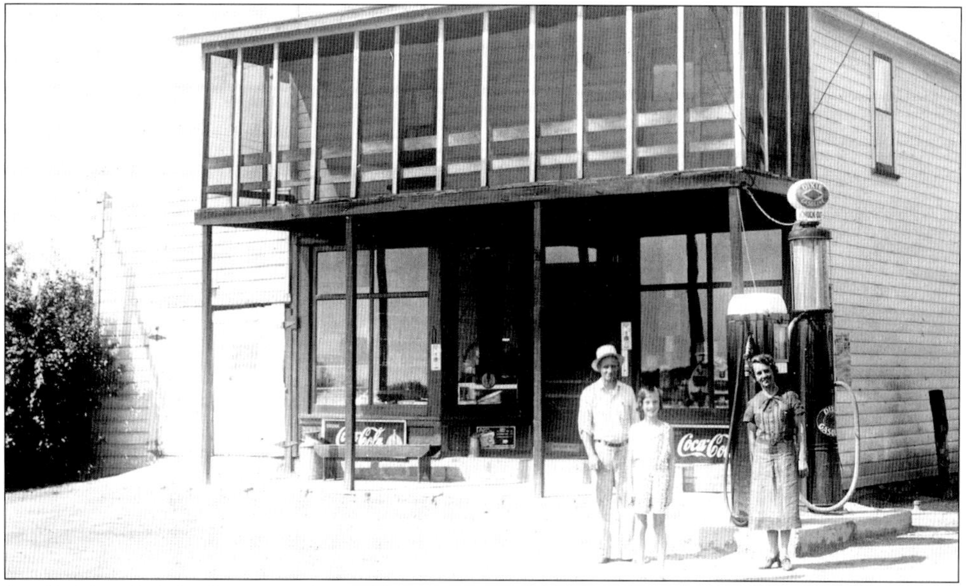

O. G. Franklin's General Store on the corner of Poseyville and Freeland roads, August 1938. Standing in front of the store are Oliver, Jean and May Franklin.
Courtesy of James J. Dion

The 1940s

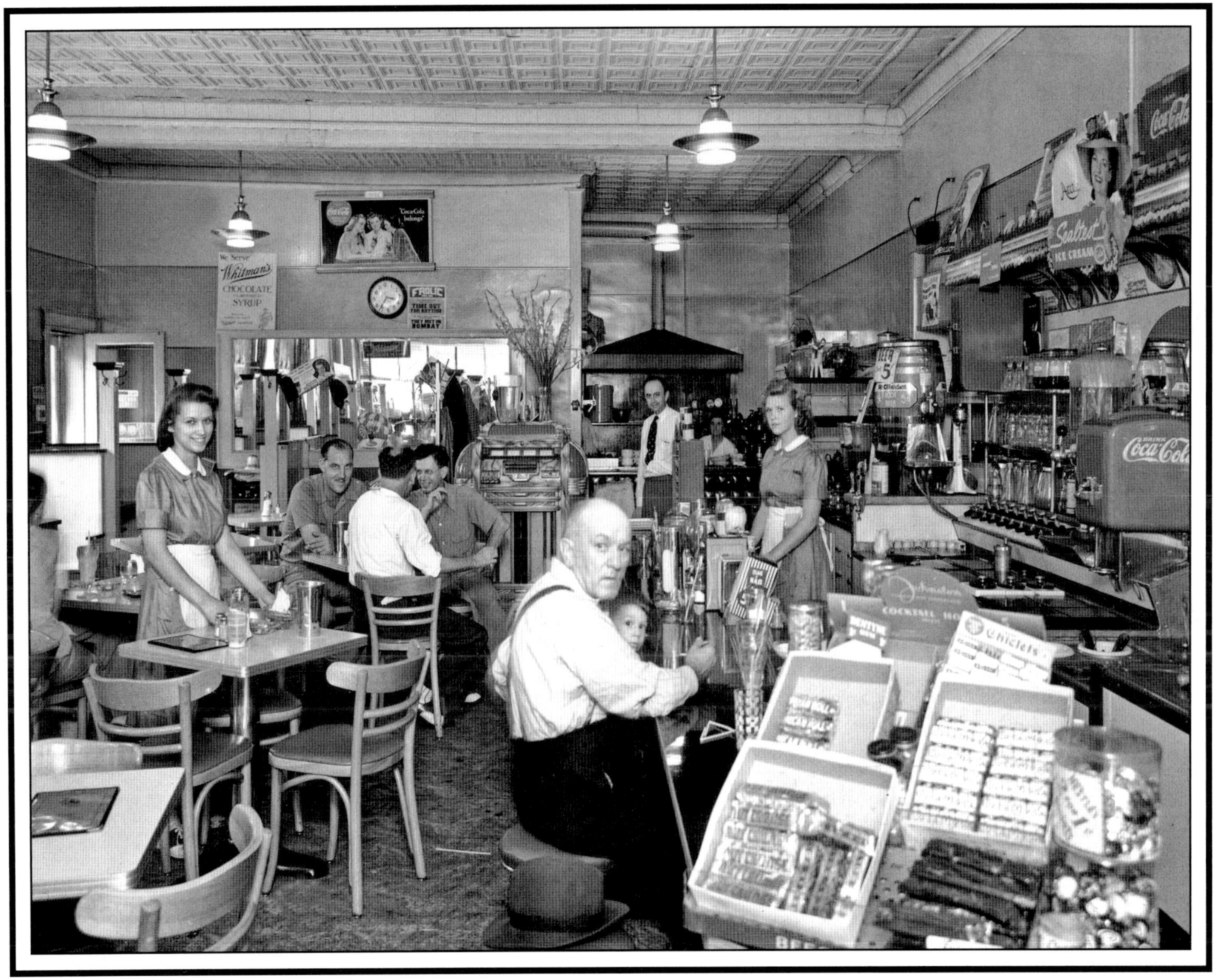

The Frolic Sweet Shop on Main Street, 1943. Wilfred Cox is standing in the back. *Courtesy of Thomas J. Cox*

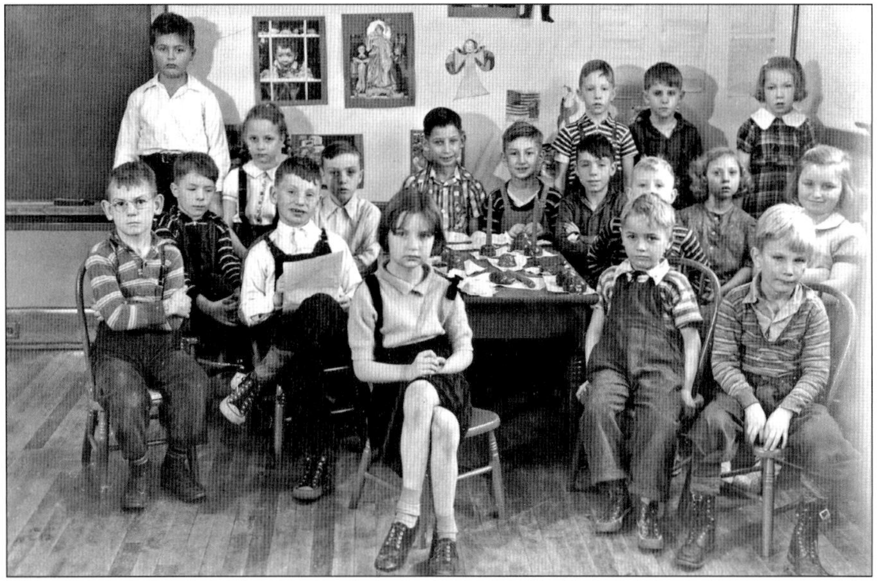
State Street Elementary School classroom, 1940. Russell Stanford is second from the left in the back row. In the second row, Jim Wade is third from the right. *Courtesy of Sally Stanford*

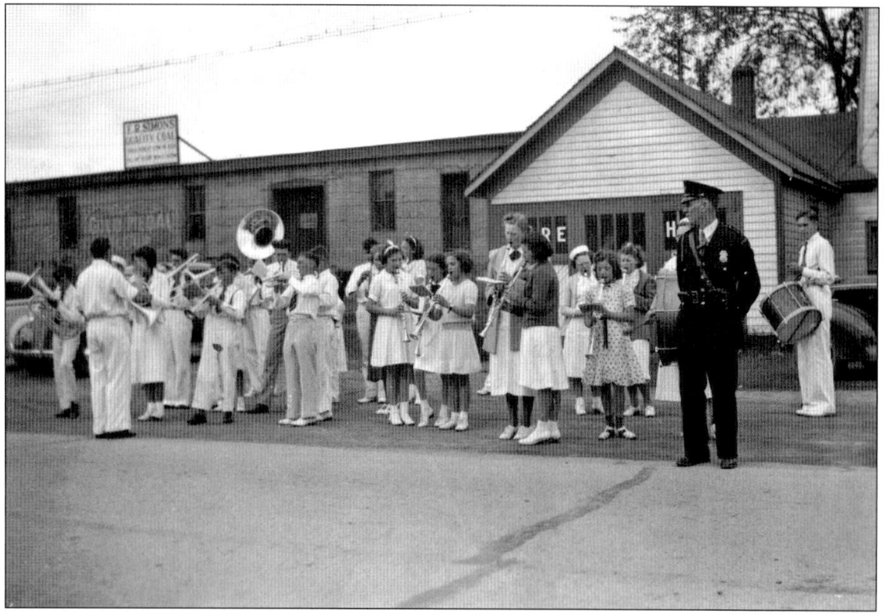
Coleman School Band with Marshall George E. Moore on Coleman's Main Street by the old firehouse, circa 1940. *Courtesy of Don and Sandy Methner Moore*

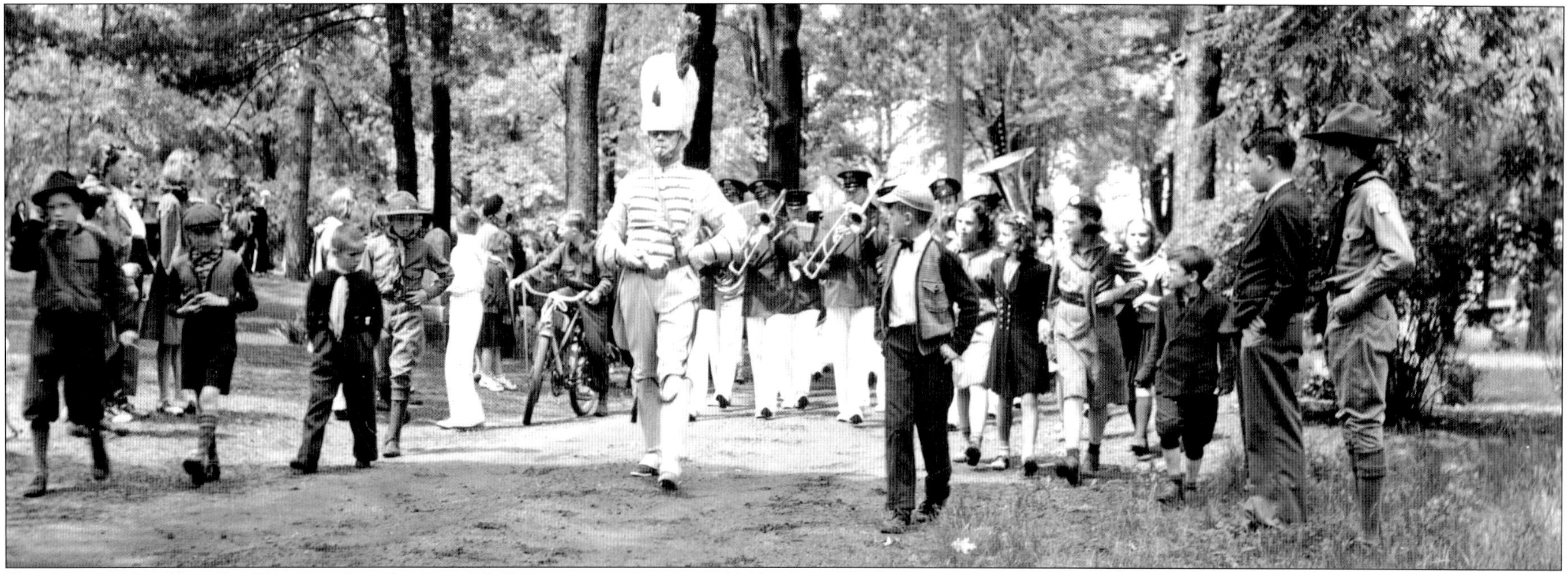
Fred Sayles leading the City Band in the Dow Field Days Parade, circa 1940. *Courtesy of Joyce and Dee Olds*

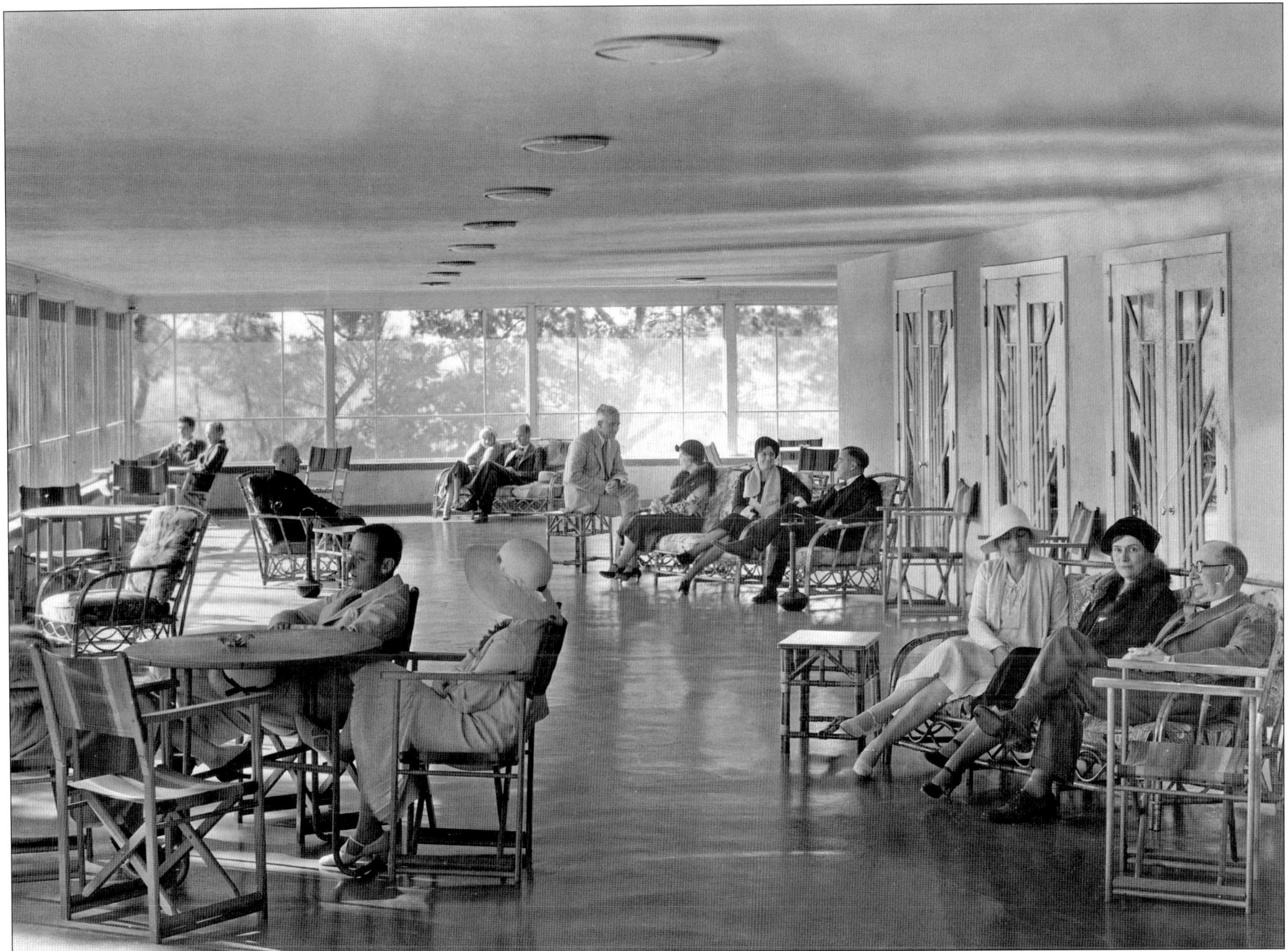

Porch at the Midland Country Club, circa 1940. It later became a dining room. The building was designed by Alden B. Dow.

Courtesy of Midland County Historical Society

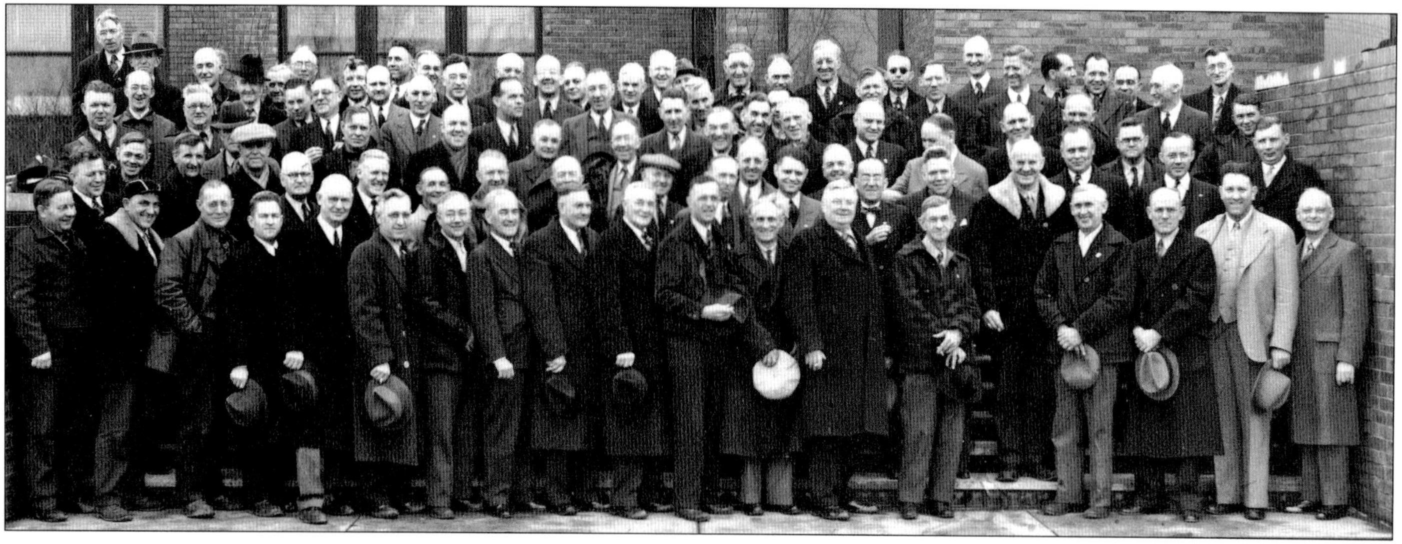

The Dow Chemical Company employees in the 1940s. In the front row, fourth from the left is Al Beshgetoor. In the second row, first is E. C. Brown, seventh is Earl Pelton and starting in the thirteenth position: John Garm, Garfield Brown, (unknown) Kendall, unidentified, Ralph Hunter and Mark Thorsberg. In the third row, starting in the sixth position: Al Armstrong, (unknown) Rich, Max Kohls, Les Richang, (unknown) Stark, E. R. McLoughlin, Carl Pranson, Rex Ward and Guy Sharp. In the fourth row, starting in the seventh position: Morrison (unknown), unidentified, Earl Stein, Lee Draves, unidentified and C. C. Kennedy. In the fourth row, the twenty-first person is L. A. Chechester, and the twenty-seventh person is E. C. Burdick. *Courtesy of Midland County Historical Society*

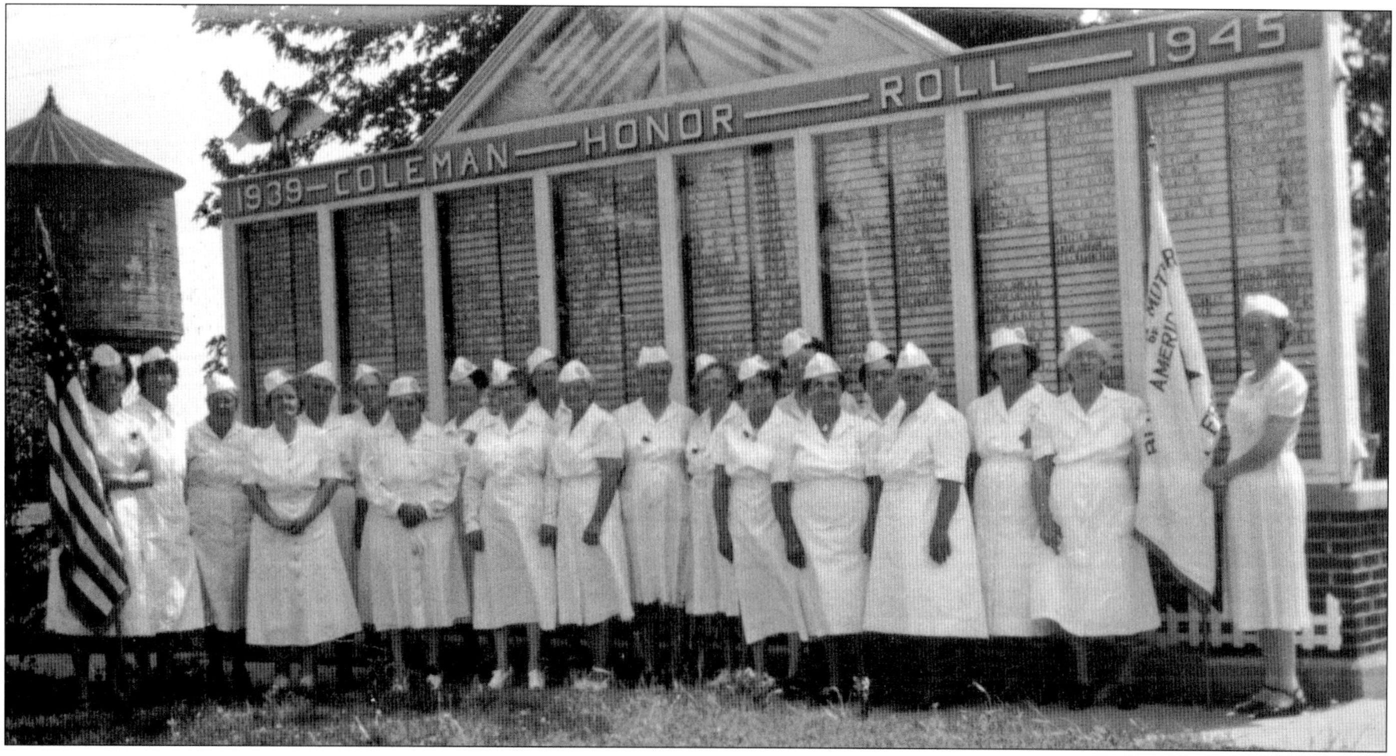

Blue Star Mothers Honor Roll 1939 to 1945. Left to right: Cecil Johnson, Minnie Lyness, Marrion Dennis, Aileen Herkel, Mary Brown, Alverda Jeffery, Grace Thering, Natie Potter, Wilma Paxton, unidientified, Verna Moore, Mrs. Mester, Florence Simons, Louise Wilson, Eva Vought, Sadie Relinger, Angie Shelby, Clara Callison, Emma Sentz, Angie Swan and Ruby Carrick. The Blue Star and Gold Star Mothers built the Honor Roll. *Courtesy of Don and Sandy Methner Moore*

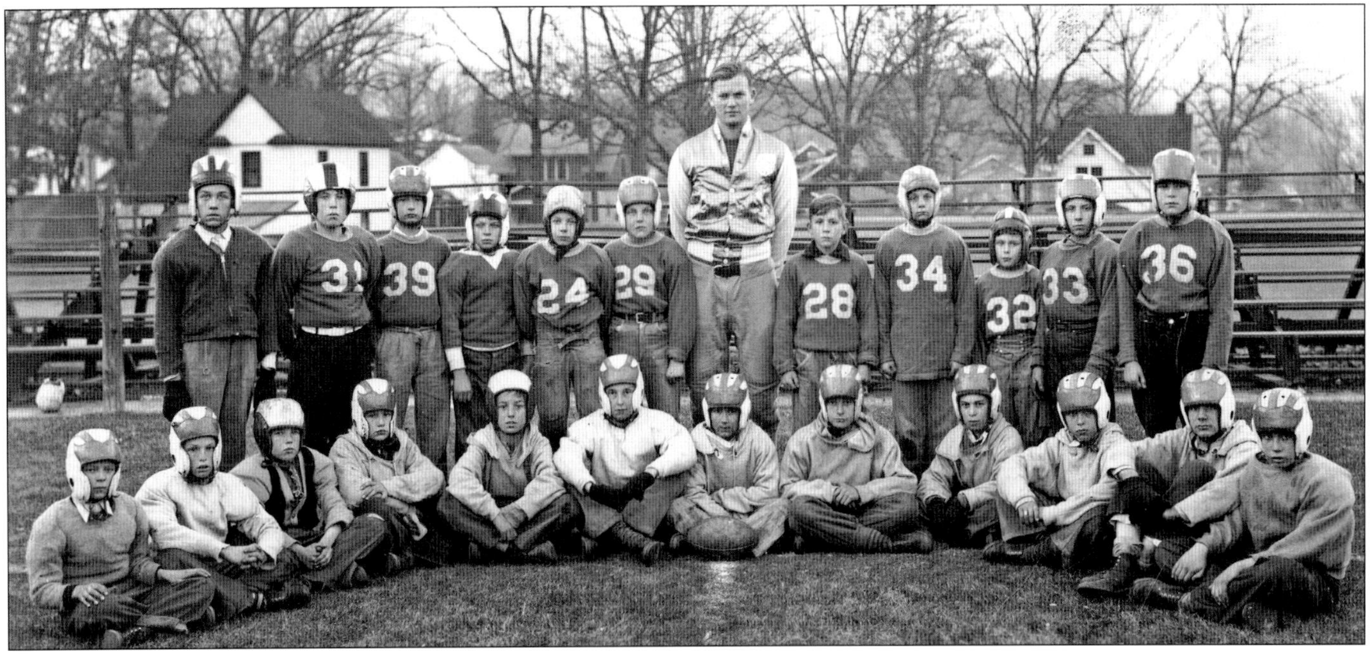

Midland football team, 1940. *Courtesy of Midland County Historical Society*

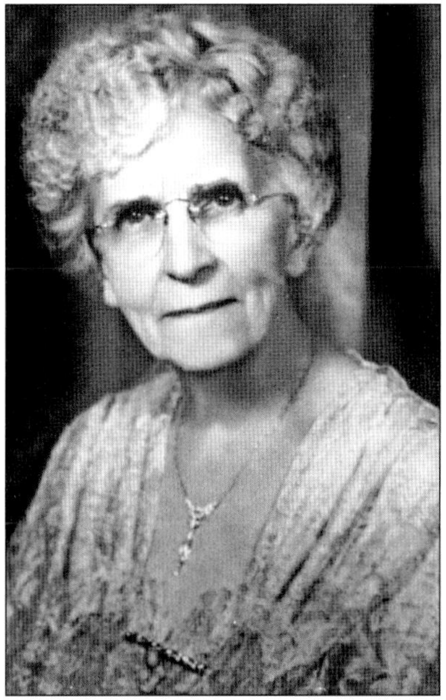

Grace A. Dow, 1943.
Courtesy of Post Street Archives

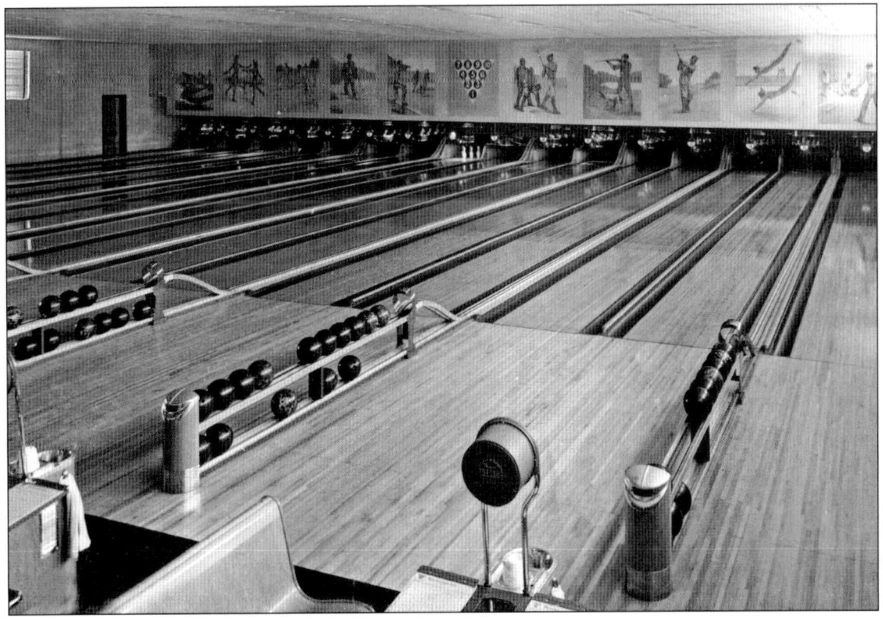

Midland Bowling, owned by Bill and Deloris Cassidy, 1940.
Courtesy of Thomas J. Cox

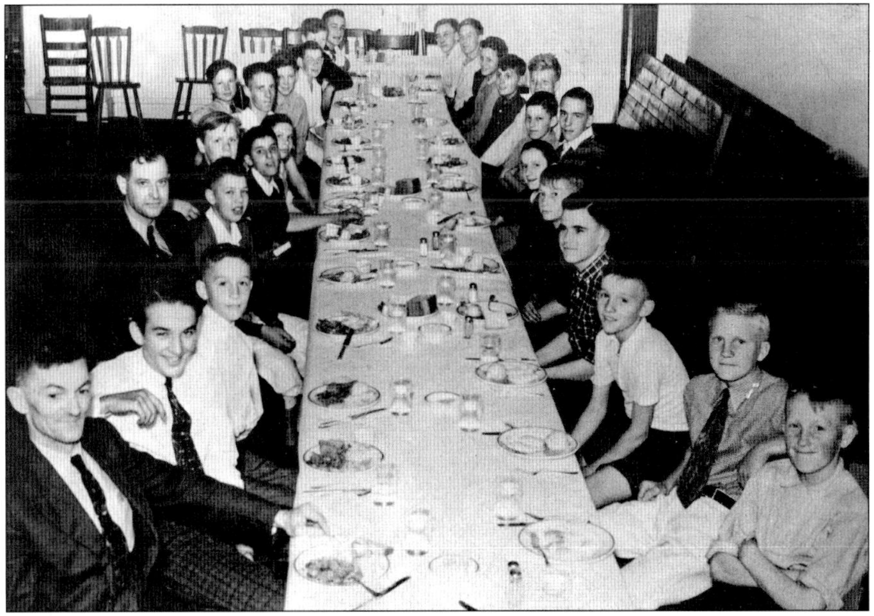

Event for the *Midland Daily News* carriers in the 1940s. The adults are Alex Thorpe and Clarence Vanest. *Courtesy of Midland Daily News*

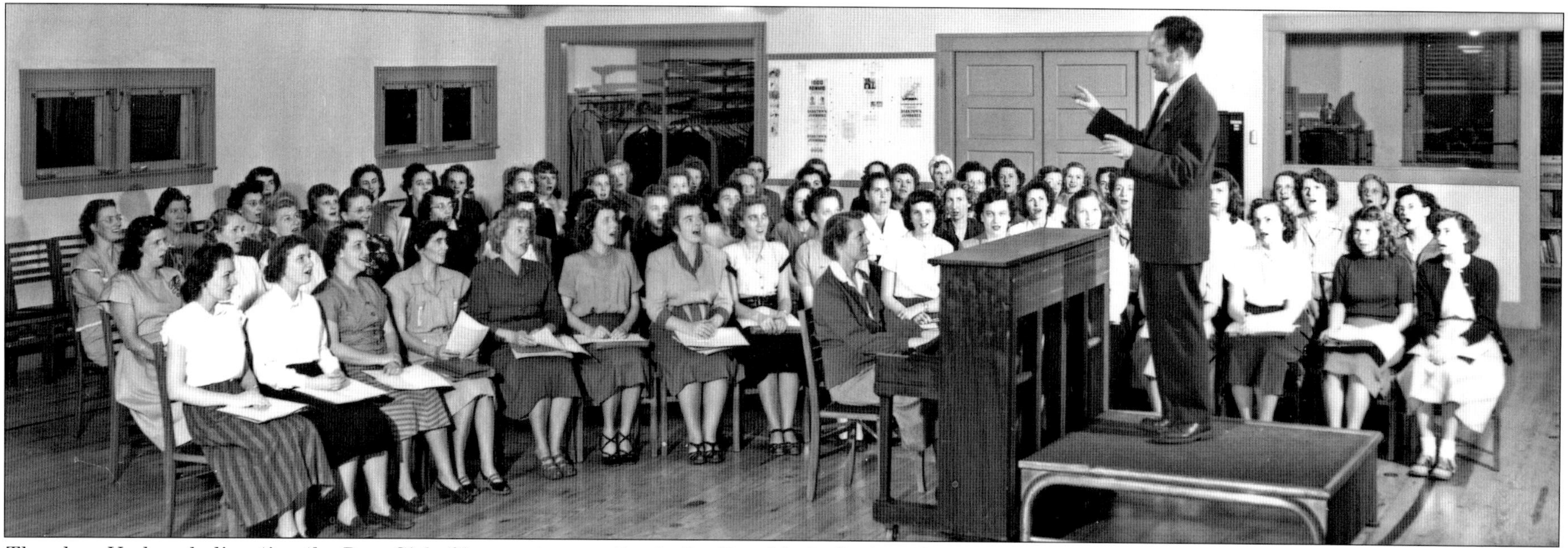

Theodore Vosburgh directing the Dow Girls Chorus at a practice in the Dow Music Center, 1940. The Center was at State and Ellsworth streets.

Courtesy of Midland County Historical Society

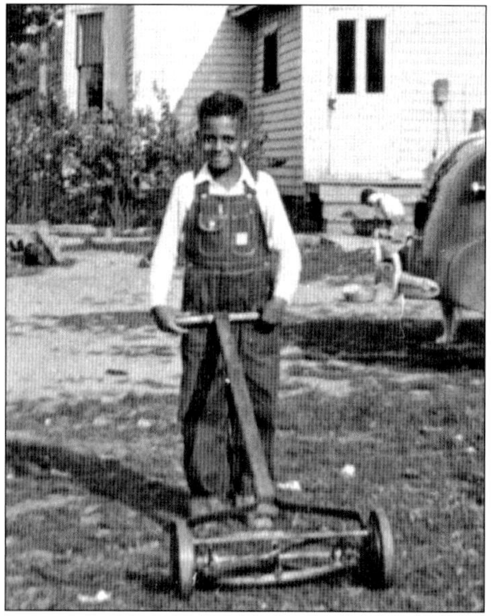

Tom Chatman at the Steve Farmer home in Midland, circa 1940.

Courtesy of Midland County Historical Society

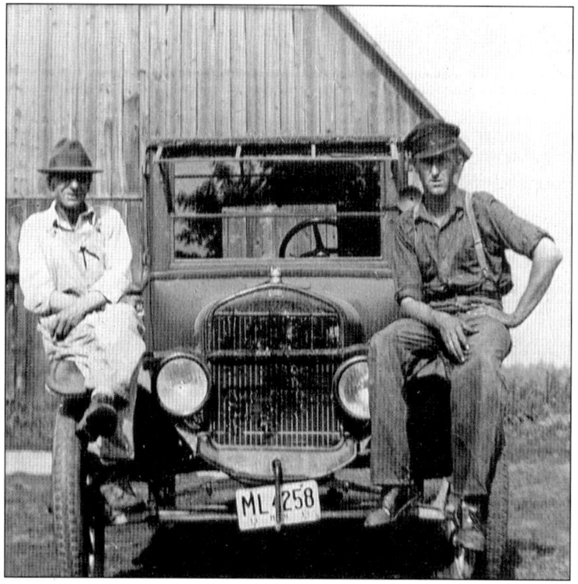

William Fisher, left, and Walter G. Fisher, sitting on a car at a Midland County farm, circa 1940.

Courtesy of Joann Lightfoot

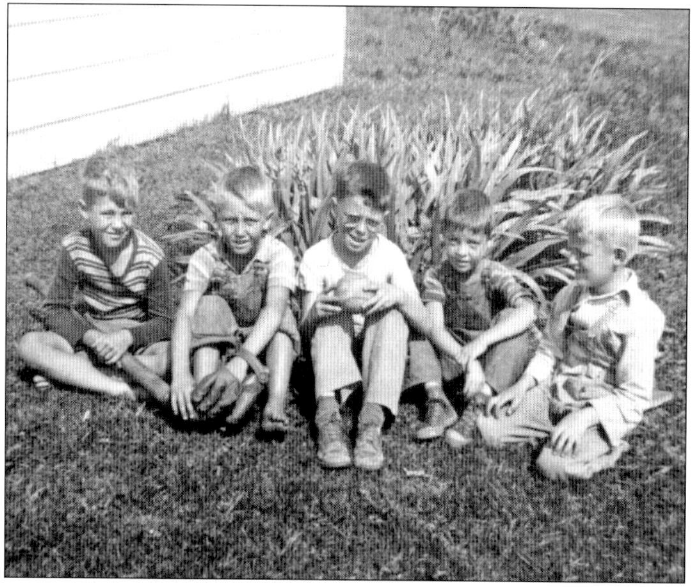

Dee Olds, Bill Horning, Del Copus, Nick Smith and Red Ostrander in the yard of a Midland home, 1942.

Courtesy of Joyce and Dee Olds

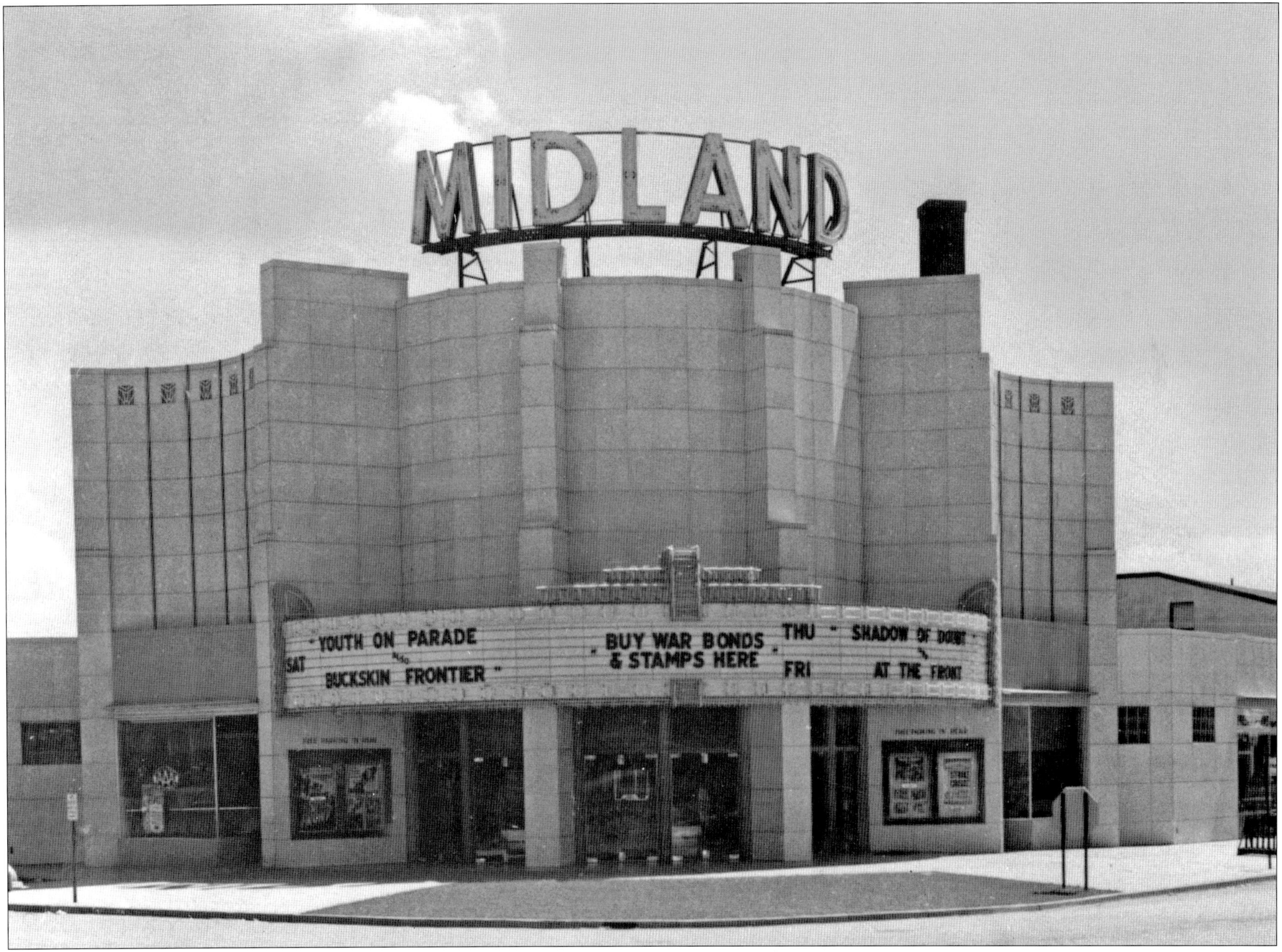

Midland Theater, circa 1943. Bill Cassidy, owner, opened the theater May 23, 1942, spending $300,000 on the building. He had previously owned the Mecca and Frolic theaters on Main Street. *Courtesy of Midland County Historical Society*

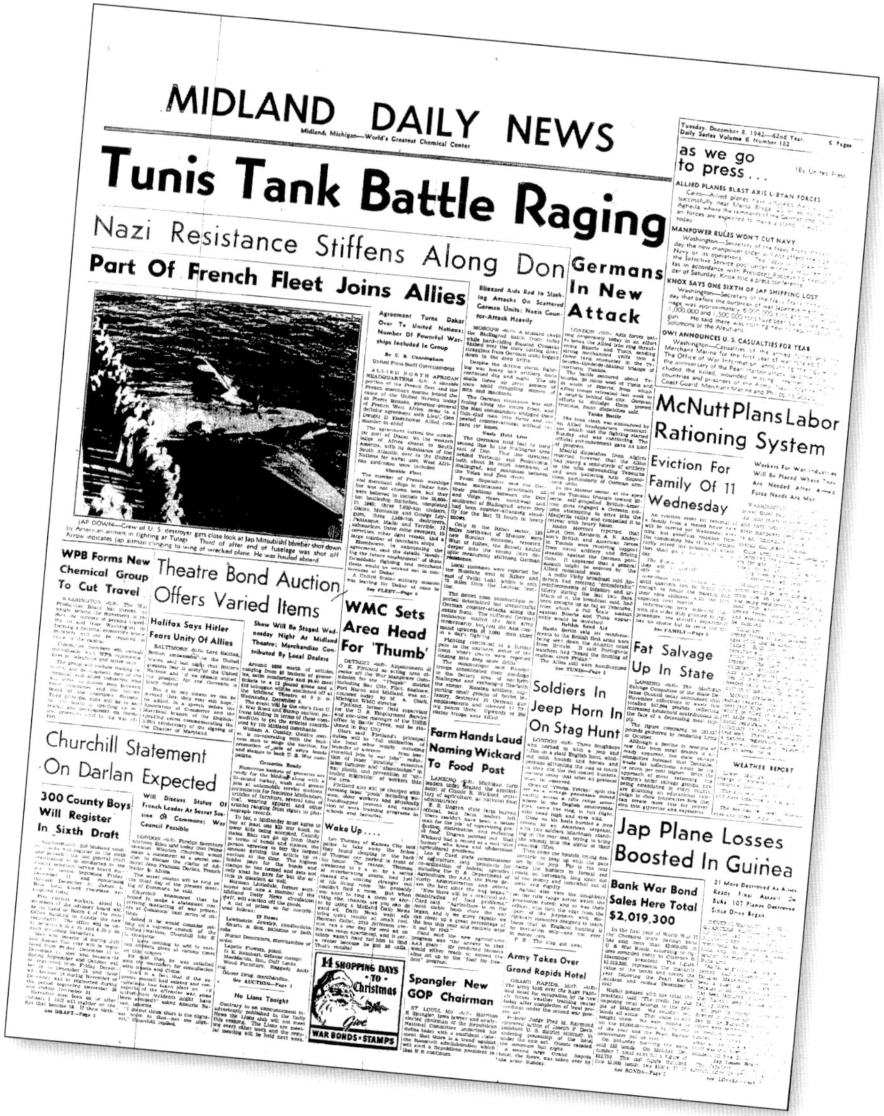

MIDLAND DAILY NEWS

Midland, Michigan—World's Greatest Chemical Center

Tuesday, December 8, 1942

Tunis Tank Battle Raging

Nazi Resistance Stiffens Along Don

Part Of French Fleet Joins Allies

Germans In New Attack

as we go to press . . .

McNutt Plans Labor Rationing System

Eviction For Family Of 11 Wednesday

WPB Forms New Chemical Group To Cut Travel

Theatre Bond Auction Offers Varied Items

Halifax Says Hitler Fears Unity Of Allies

WMC Sets Area Head For 'Thumb'

Fat Salvage Up In State

Soldiers In Jeep Horn In On Stag Hunt

Churchill Statement On Darlan Expected

300 County Boys Will Register In Sixth Draft

Farm Hands Laud Naming Wickard To Food Post

Wake Up . . .

Jap Plane Losses Boosted In Guinea

Bank War Bond Sales Here Total $2,019,300

Army Takes Over Grand Rapids Hotel

Spangler New GOP Chairman

14 SHOPPING DAYS TO Christmas — Give WAR BONDS • STAMPS

The front page of *Midland Daily News* reporting the latest news from the front during World War II, Dec. 8, 1942. *Courtesy of Midland Daily News*

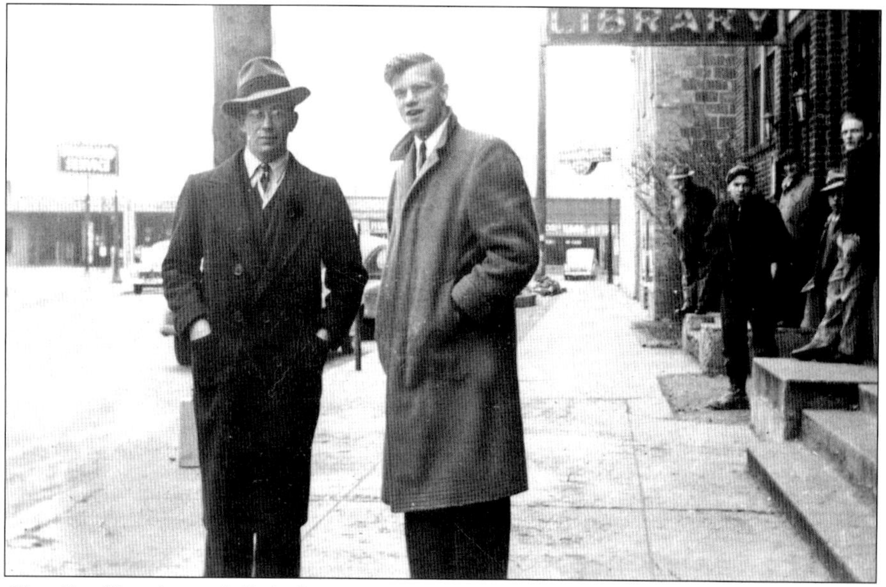

Charlie Chapin and Pete Larson in front of Midland Community Center on Townsend Street awaiting the bus to leave for the Army, circa 1942.
Courtesy of Naomi Haebler

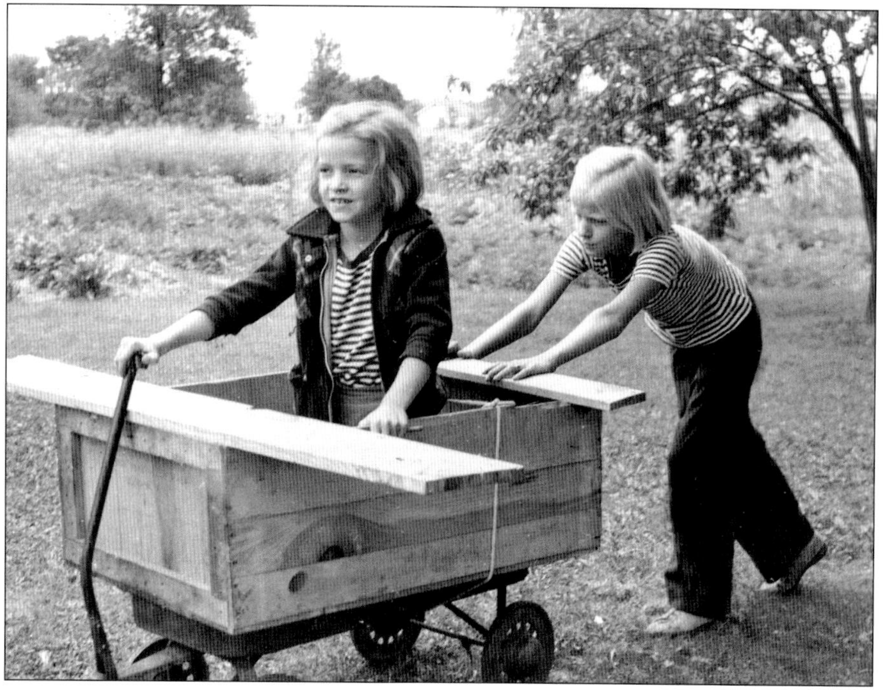

Lois Green pushing Janet Green at 111 E. Harold St. in a makeshift airplane made from a packing box from their father's business, Russell Green's Plumbing & Heating, circa 1944. *Courtesy of Janet Rice*

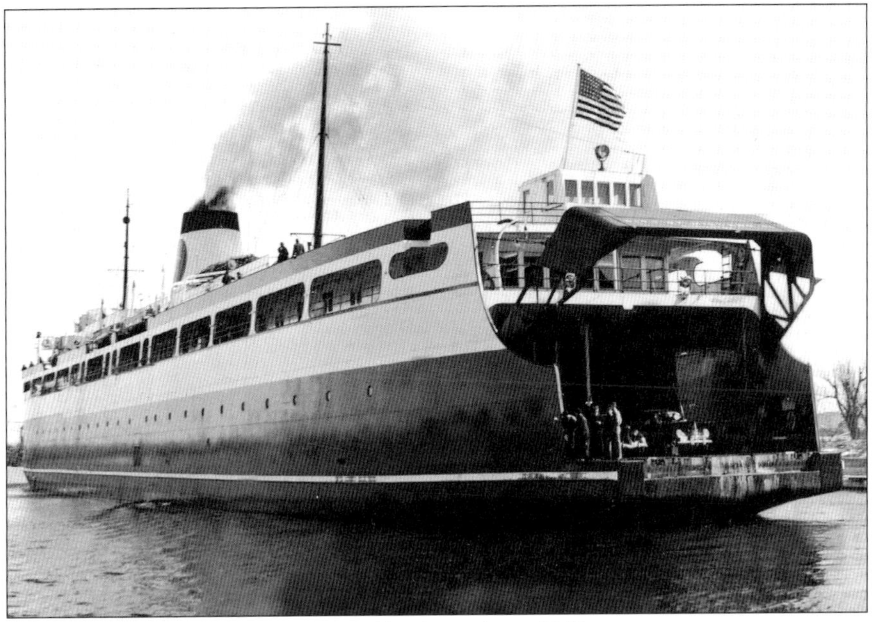

City of Midland car ferry in Ludington, circa 1945.

Courtesy of Joyce and Dee Olds

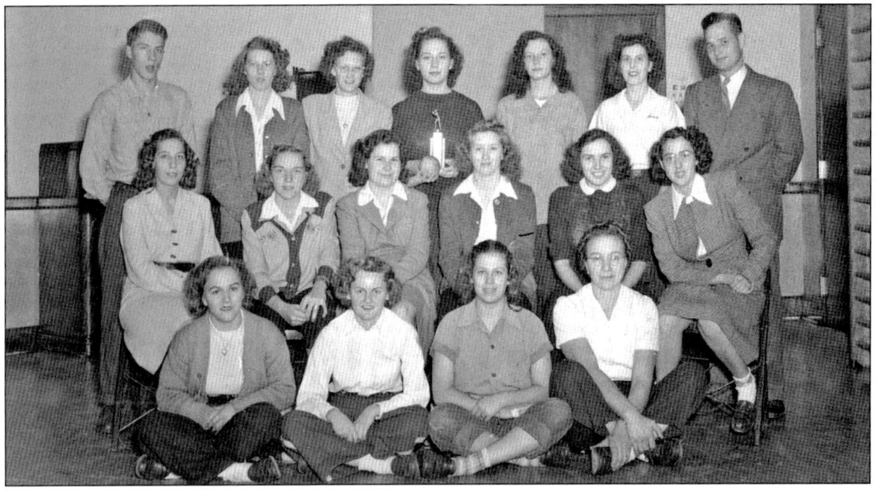

The 1946 Michigan State Class C hi-speed girls' champion softball team. First row, left to right: Donna Fenske, Lois Sackrider, Jane Engwis and Ann Hanson. Second row: Ila Heath, Donna Modders, Arlene Reger, Betty Davis, Lois Tisdale and Pat Phemister. Third row: co-manager Hal Purves, Kay Purves, Virginia Hayden, Jean Weidenmier, Bonnie Heiser, Madeline Dunn and sponsor Walt Palmer. *Courtesy of Donna Modders Goodwin*

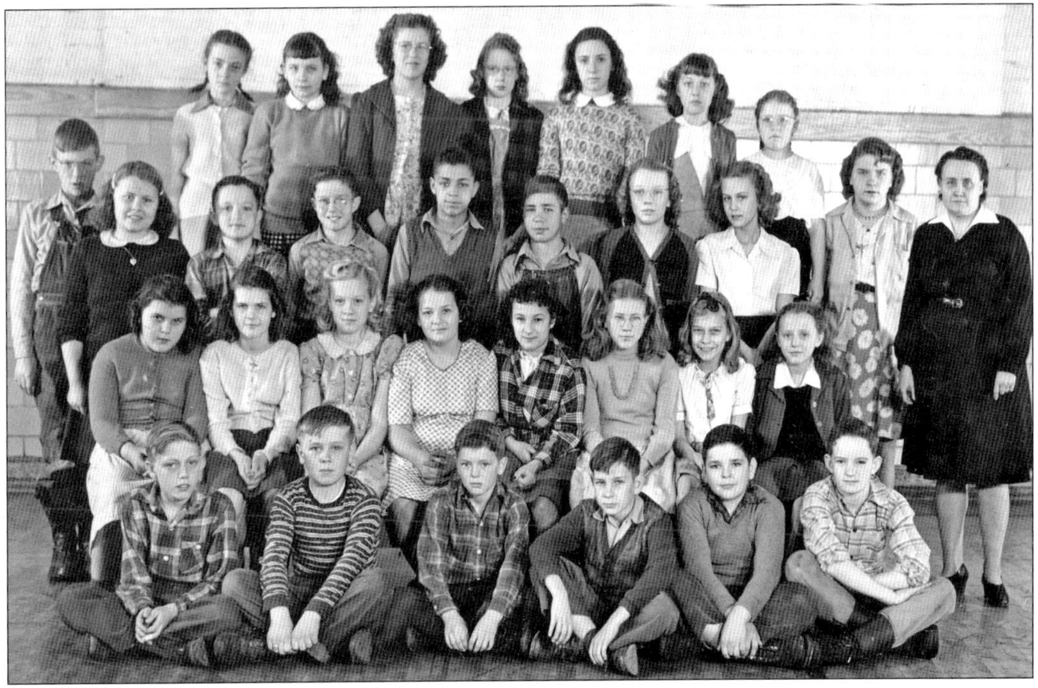

Class of 1947 at Coleman School. Front row, left to right: Ken Little, Jack Schrader, Don Foreman, Bill Haggerty, Ed Mester and Jarvis Jones. Second row: Bernice Seaman, Juanita Burke, Donna Allison, Elizabeth Cozat, Mary Lou Eagley, Leila Woodbury, Lillian Bauder and Vera Nobbs. Third row: Shirley Searight, Pat O'Laughlin, Don Moore, Wayne Brown, Bergess Jenkins, Barbara Mac Donald and Luella Orr. Fourth row: Sherley Francis, Janet Bolin, Eleanor Klashek, Eileen Watson, Ruth Eagly, Barbara Kennedy, Mary Ruth Little, Lucy Curtis, Margaret Leauder and teacher Mrs. Baker.

Courtesy of Don and Sandy Methner Moore

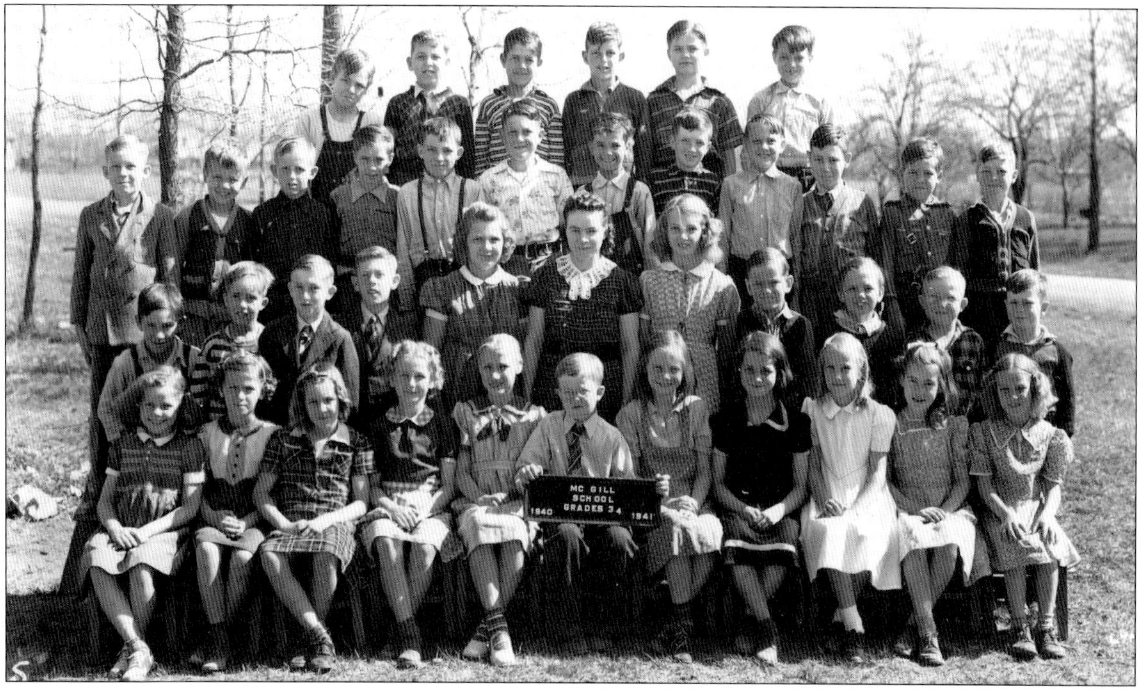

Third- and fourth-grade classes of McGill School, 1941–42. Front row, left to right: Doreen Church, Margaret Norak, Alice Maynard, Joyce Abbey, Rose Myors, Douglass Schultz, Nora Bell Jacobs, Helen Stilwell, Bettie Linton, Mary Mayes and Pauline Kazee. Second row: Harvey Mitchell, unidentified, Robert Schnell, Donald Schnell, Waunettah Martinski, teacher Wanda Erickson, Patricia Jardis, Vernon Berier, Lloyd Jewell, Albert Mitchell and Orie Dean Church. Third row: Buddy "Orville" Mapes, Kenneth Dowker, Earl Coltson, Dale Muir, Ernest Trombley, Bill Beck, Gerald Miner, Dale Anderson, Kenneth Parsons, Ivan Church, Albert Case, Bruce Wray and unidentified. Fourth row: William Maynard, Norman Carter, Donald Miner, Jimmie Wray, Calvin Jones and Maynard Parsons. Those not included are Rosalie Miner, Beverly Thompson, Mable Trombley, Duana Lalone, Charlie Reisner and Joyce Smith. *Courtesy of Midland County Historical Society*

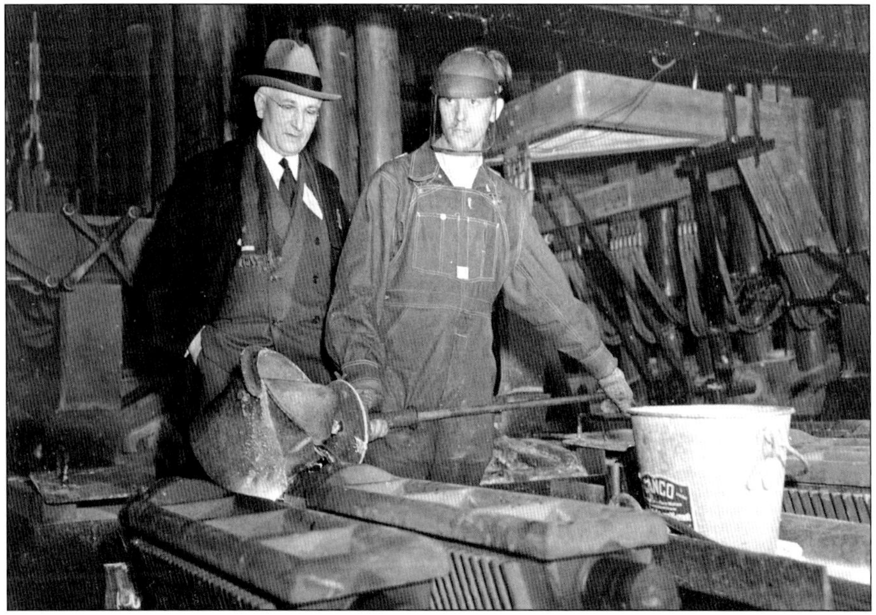

Willard Dow and an employee, circa 1945.

Courtesy of Midland County Historical Society

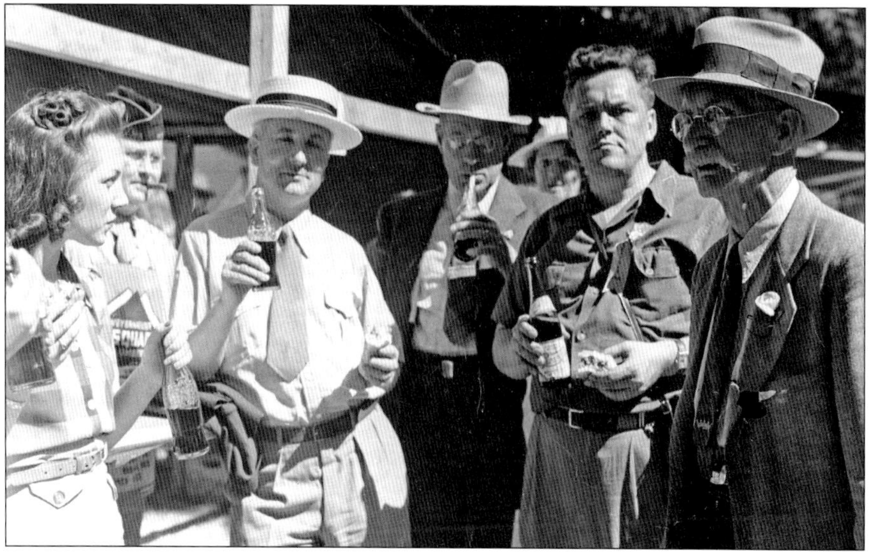

Sharing soft drinks at The Dow Chemical Company's Field Day, 1945, left to right: Catherine Laebrich Sinclair, George Metcalfe, Willard Dow, Walter Beckwith, Helen Beckwith and Chet Wright.

Courtesy of Midland County Historical Society

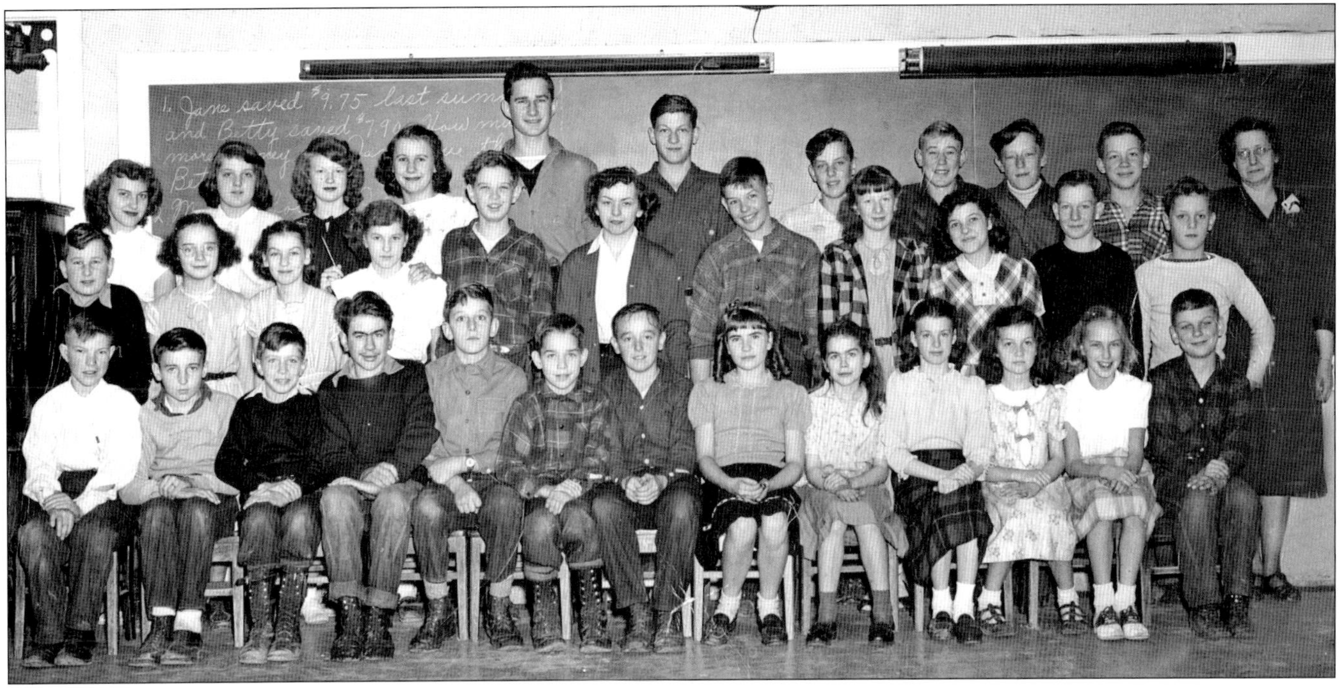

Students of Fulmer School, circa 1946. The teacher is Cecelia Dean. Front row, left to right: Norm Ordiway, Jim Lambert, Denny Howard, James Lee, Virgil Zimmerman, Ray Ward, Stan Short, Gail Stowits, (unknown) Lee, Minnie Sian, Sally Martin, Janice Bernard and Bob Phillips. Second row: Rick Love, Patty Hoffman, Margaret Castley, Janice Hayes, Larry Ward, Marcelline Short, Dick Townsend, Ellamay Sian, Marilyn Martin, Bob Castley and Joe Richardson. Third row: Joyce Bernard, Sheila Richardson, Dolores Sian, Carol Love, Ray Love, Charles Langsdorf, Dave Richardson, Jay Arthur, Dale Phillips and Jerry Hoffman.

Courtesy of Midland County Historical Society

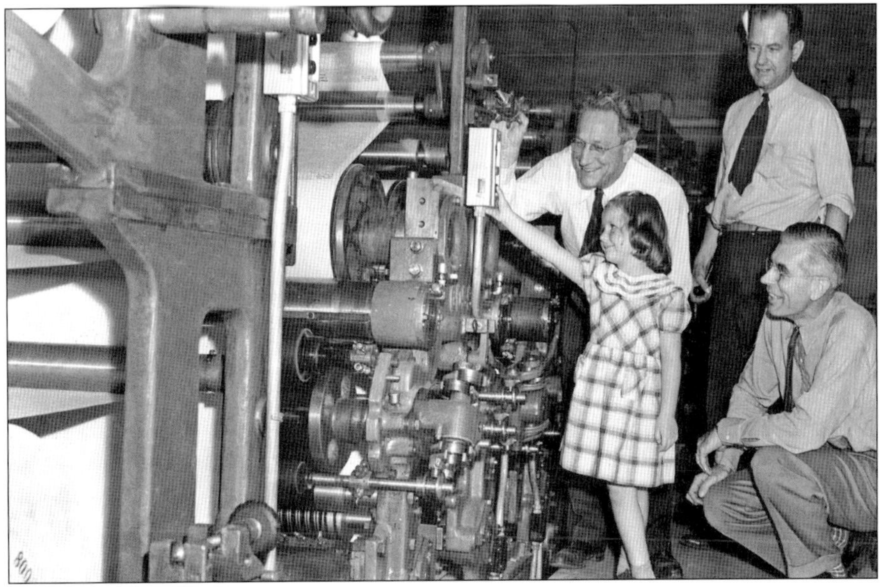

Inaugurating the new 16-page press at the *Midland Daily News*, 1947. Left to right: Linda Phillips, Philip T. Rich, Turner Vanest and Gordon F. Phillips.

Courtesy of Midland Daily News

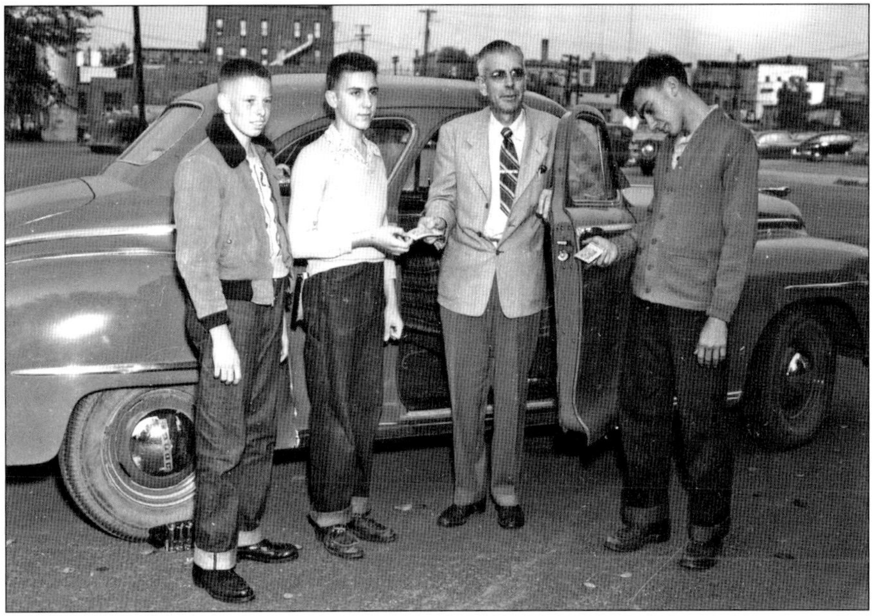

Gordon Phillips, in the tie, with *Midland Daily News* carriers, 1947.

Courtesy of Midland Daily News

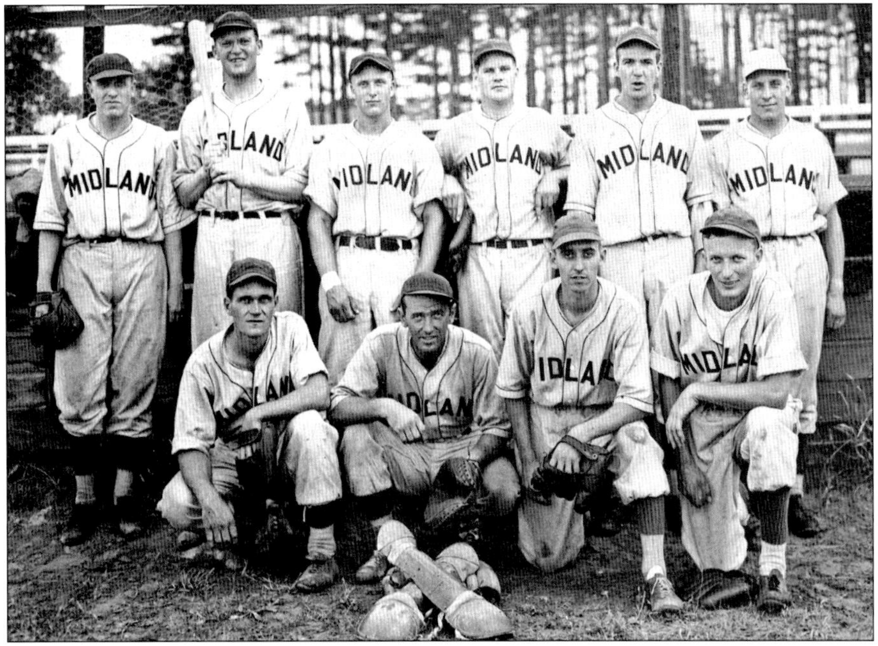

Community Center softball team, 1946. *Courtesy of Midland County Historical Society*

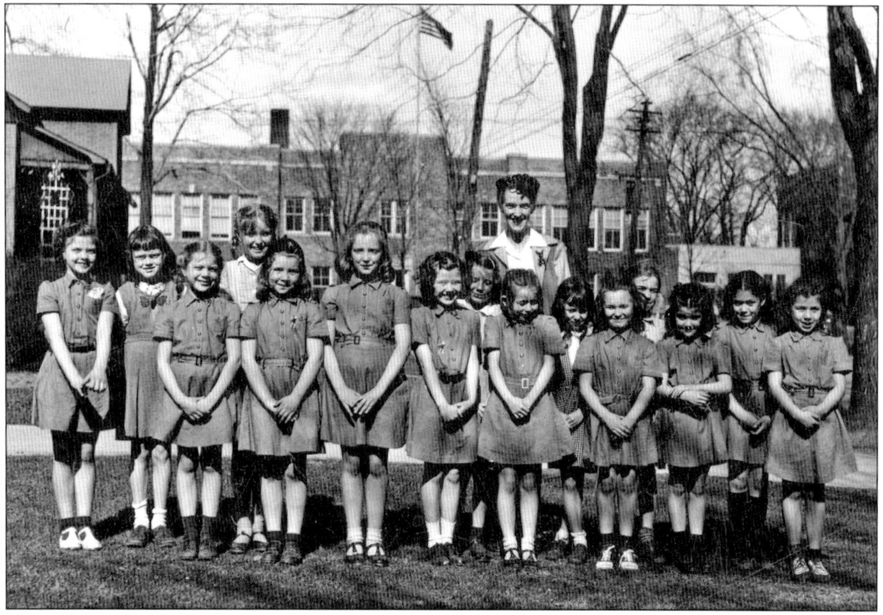

Brownie Troop in front of 505 McDonald St., 1947. The Thompson Elementary School is in the background. *Courtesy of Midland County Historical Society*

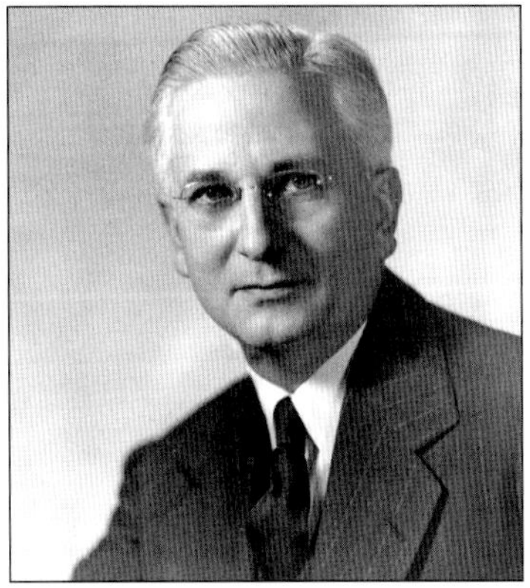

Willard Dow, 1947. He was killed in a plane crash in 1949. *Courtesy of Post Street Archives*

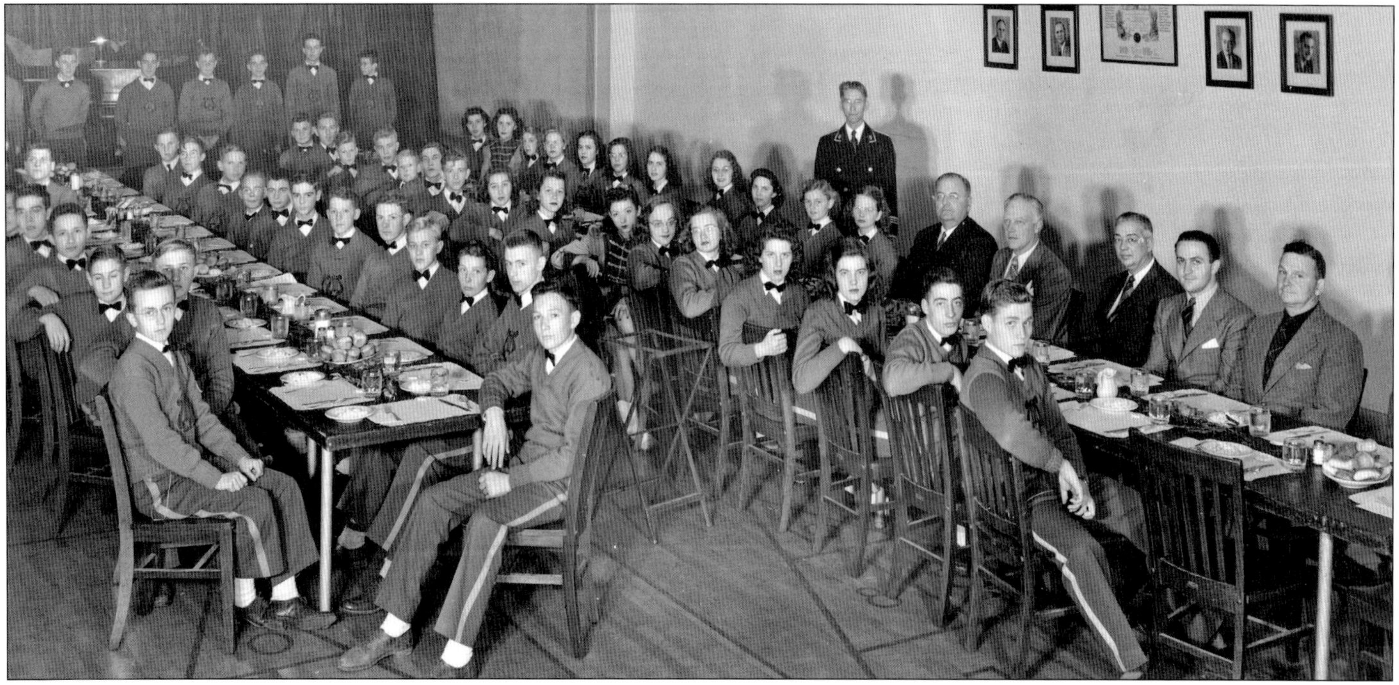

Midland High School Band and parents, circa 1947. Ted Nickolson is the director. *Courtesy of Midland County Historical Society*

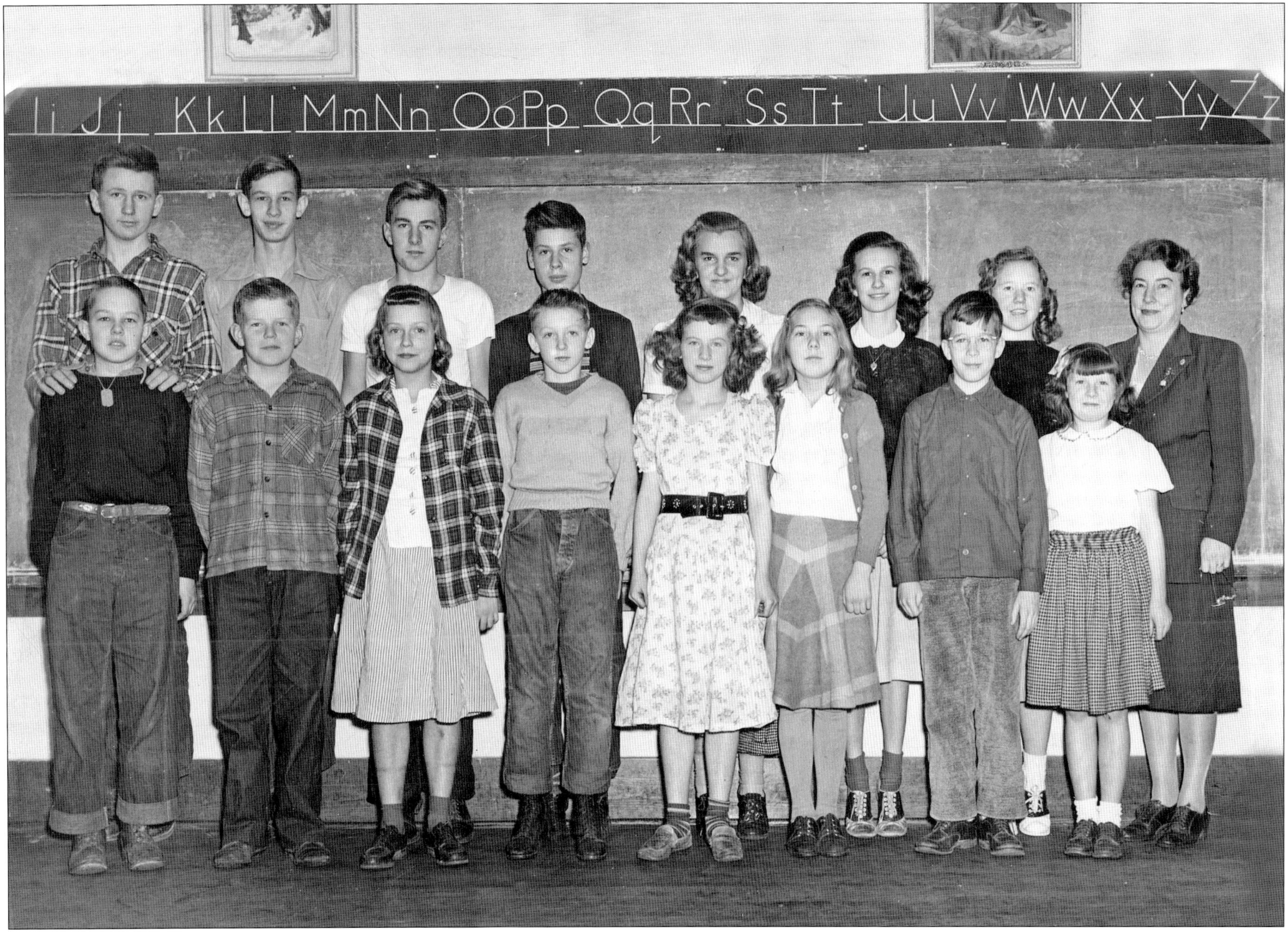

Hope Elementary School, 1947. Those included: Clessen Martin, Curt Maxwell, Lois Marsh, Bill Maxwell, Carol Keyes, (unknown) Lanfield, Ted Cumings, Carmelita Thomas, Jim Joynt, Gilbert Maxwell, Ted Wendt, Buddy Keyes, Bertha Wendt, Sally Leuenberger, Pauline Fillmore and teacher Clarisa Dean.

Courtesy of Sally Stanford

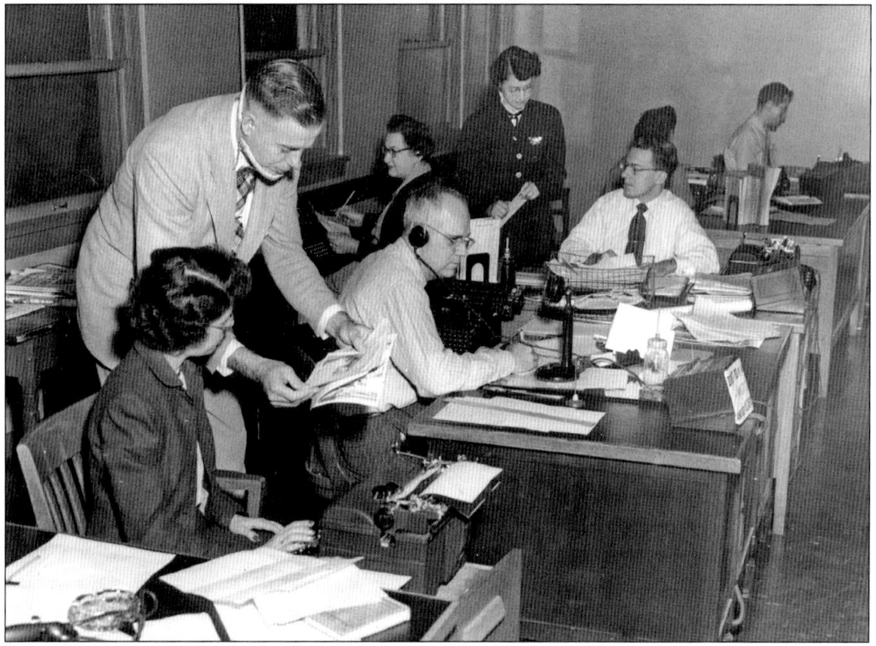

Newsroom at the *Midland Daily News*, circa 1947. *Courtesy of Midland Daily News*

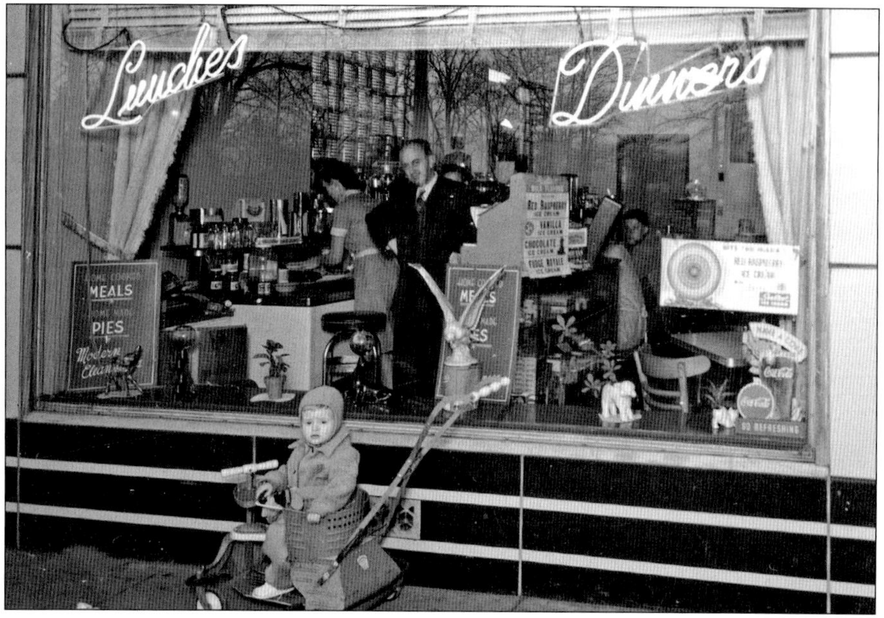

Frolic Sweet Shop on Main Street, 1947. Wilfred Cox is in the window with his son, Tom, in front of the shop. *Courtesy of Thomas J. Cox*

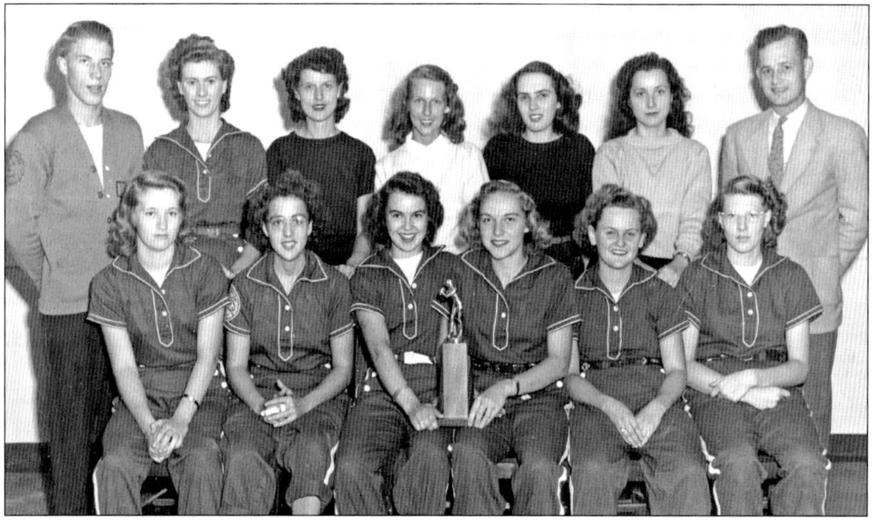

Walt Palmer's hi-speed girls' Michigan State Class B champion softball team, 1947. Front row, left to right: Betty Davis, Pat Phemister, Greta Yoder, Donna Modders, Lois Sackrider and Kay Purves. Back row: co-manager Hal Purves, Jane Boggs, Fran Sampson, Helen Gordon, Lois Tisdale, Jan Clark and sponsor Walt Palmer. *Courtesy of Donna Modders Goodwin*

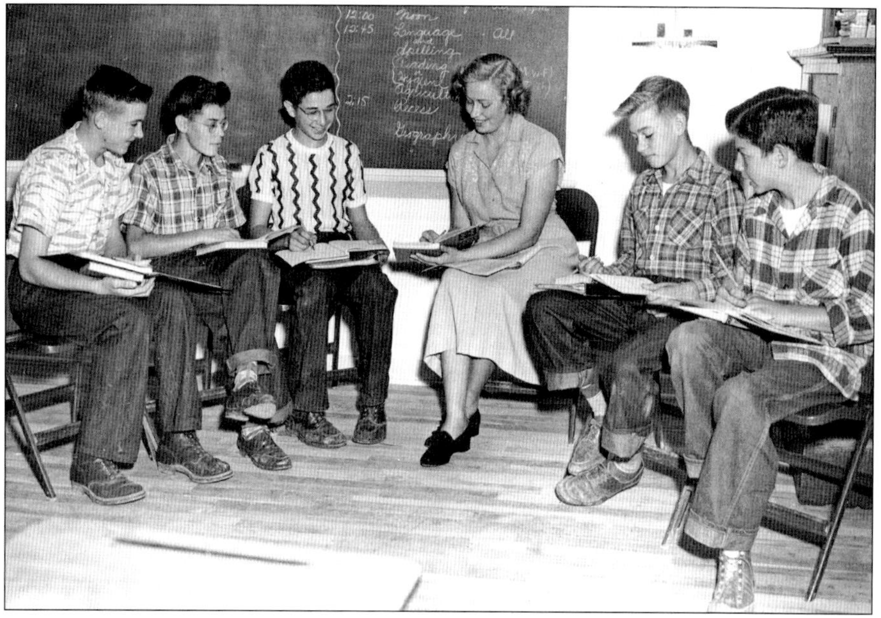

Miss Petrie and students at Poseyville School in Ingersoll Township, Sept. 13, 1949. *Courtesy of Midland County Historical Society*

The 1950s

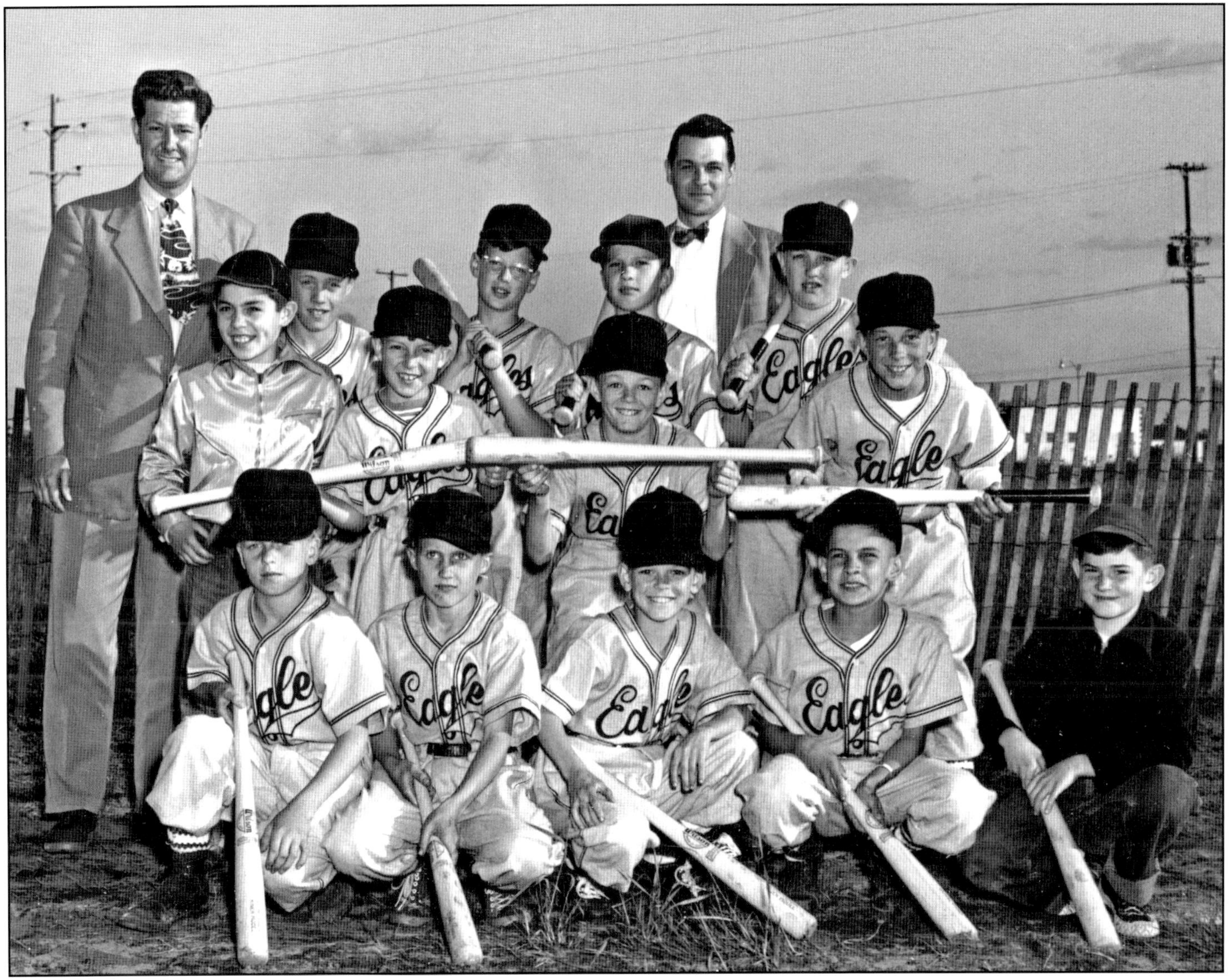

Eagle Little League softball team, 1951. *Courtesy of Midland County Historical Society*

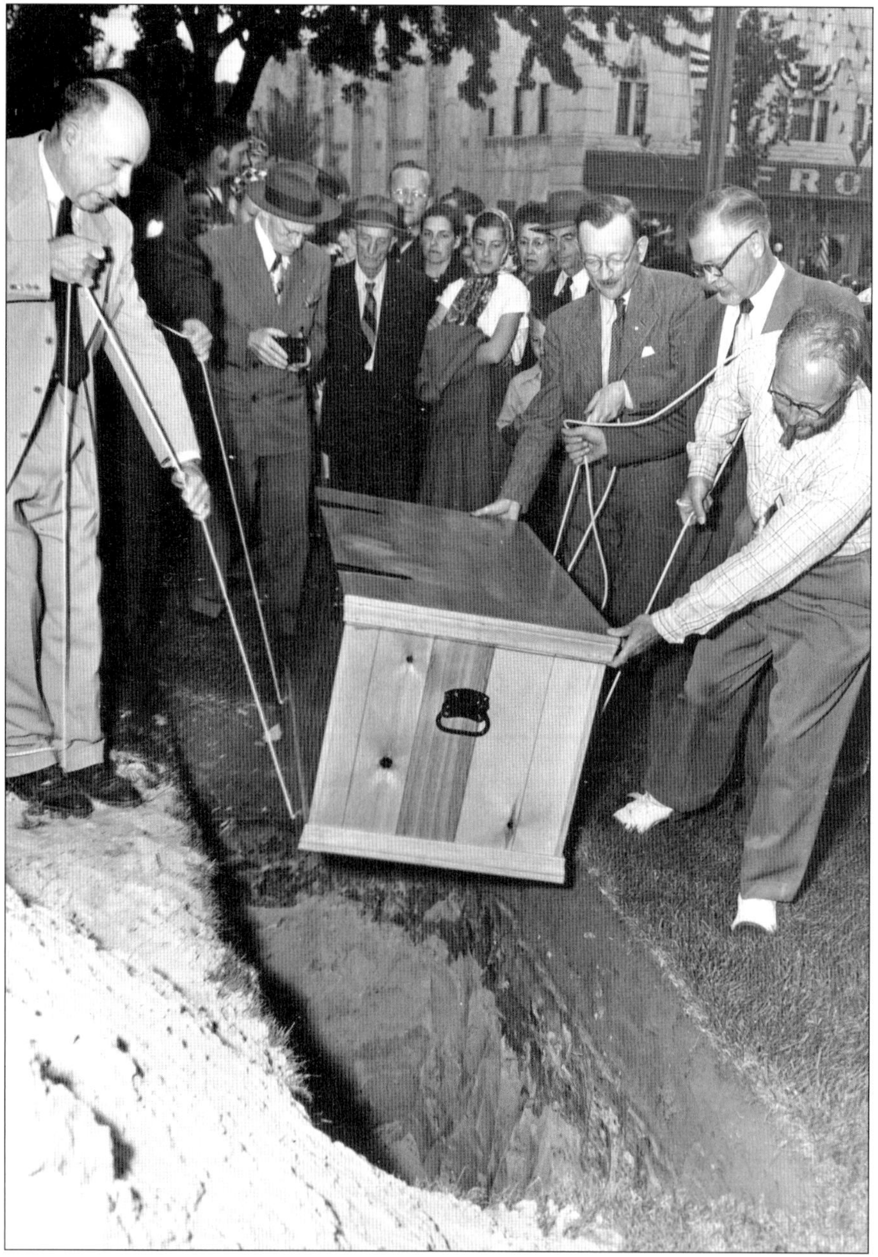

For Midland County's 1950 Centennial, mementos were put in a specially-treated box that would be buried and intact until 2000 A.D. Clockwise, left to right: Frank Whaley, John Strouss, J. Dale Madill, C. C. BeMent and B. F. Crocker. *Courtesy of Midland Daily News*

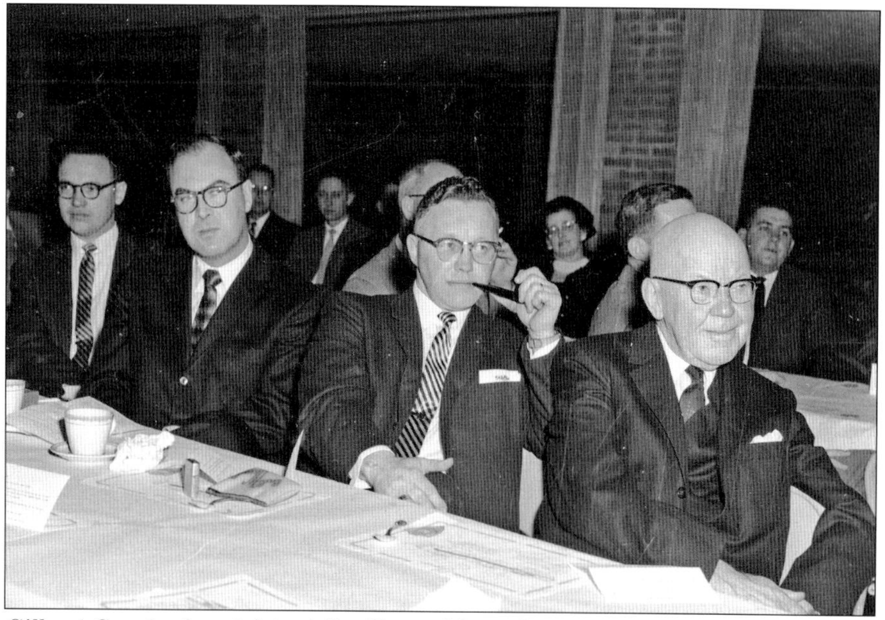

Gilbert Currie, far right, at the Young Man of the Year event at the Midland Country Club, circa 1950. *Courtesy of James J. Dion*

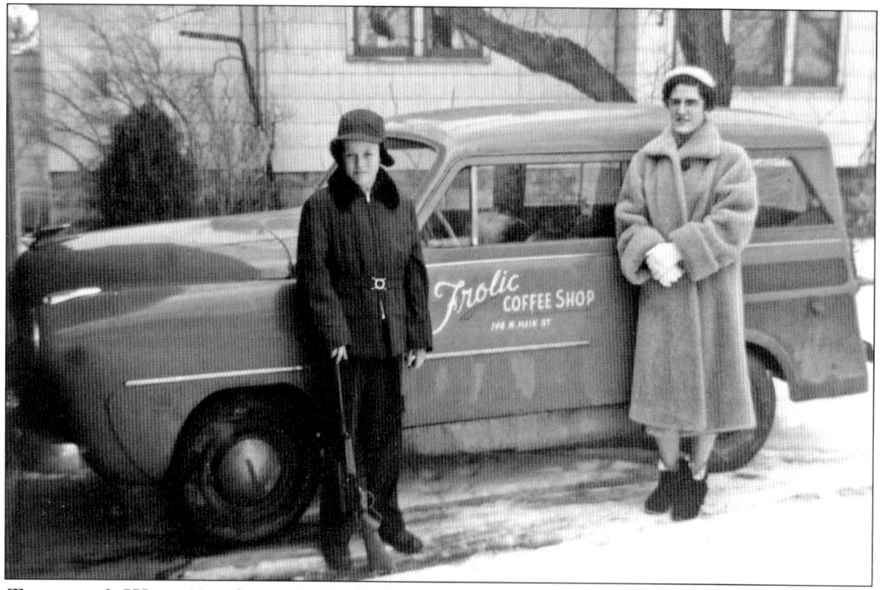

Tom and Wynette Cox at their home on Eastman Road, 1953. They are standing in front of the 1951 Crosley advertising Frolic Coffee Shop.
Courtesy of Thomas J. Cox

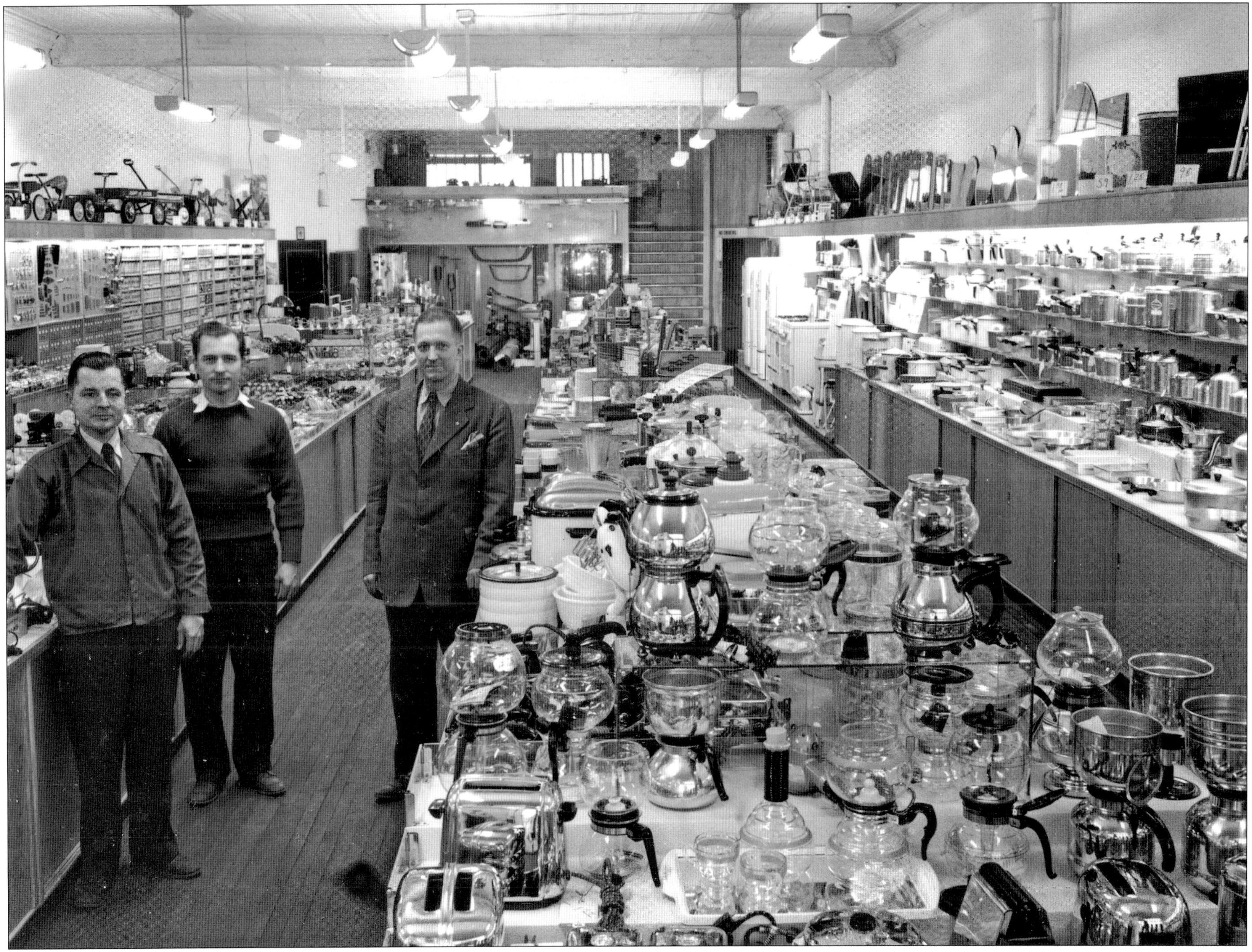

Wenzel's Hardware, circa 1950. *Courtesy of Midland County Historical Society*

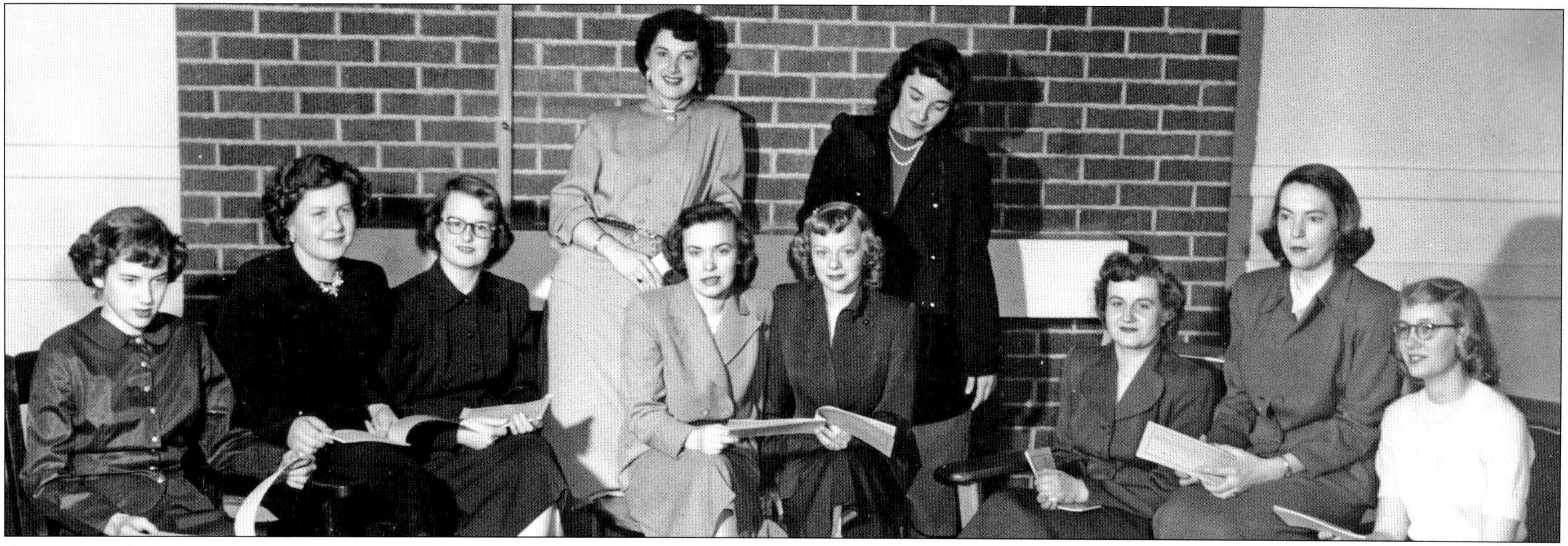

Centennial Queen contestants meet at the Community Center, 1950. Seated, left to right: Jan Whaley, Doreen Church, Sherron Reinsmith, Dorothy Burke, Pat Bliss, Allegra Wylie, Mary Sherriff and Donela Fales. Standing are Grace Ann Malinetz and Lois Graves. *Courtesy of Midland Daily News*

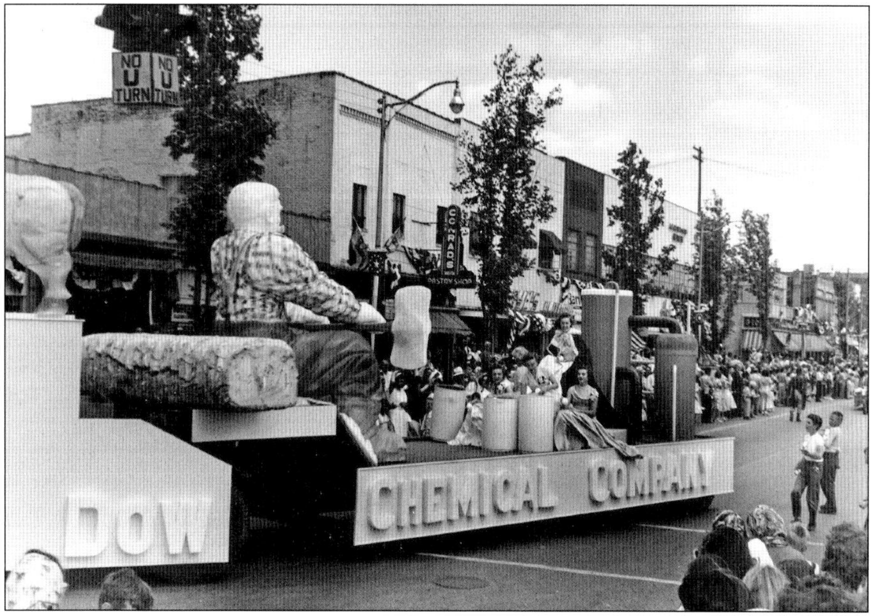

The Dow Chemical Company's float in Midland County's Centennial Parade, 1950. *Courtesy of Midland Daily News*

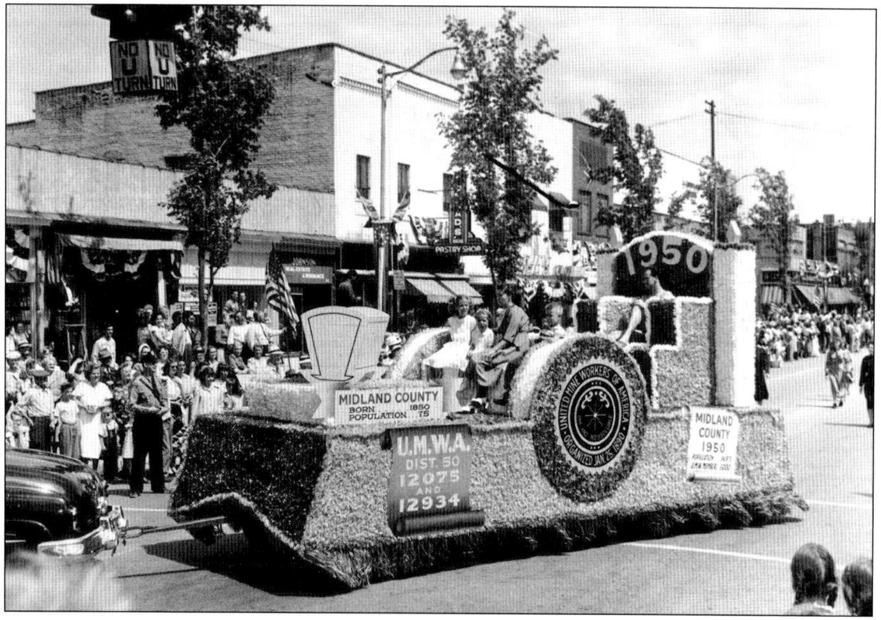

United Mine Workers of America float in the Midland County Centennial Parade, 1950. *Courtesy of Midland Daily News*

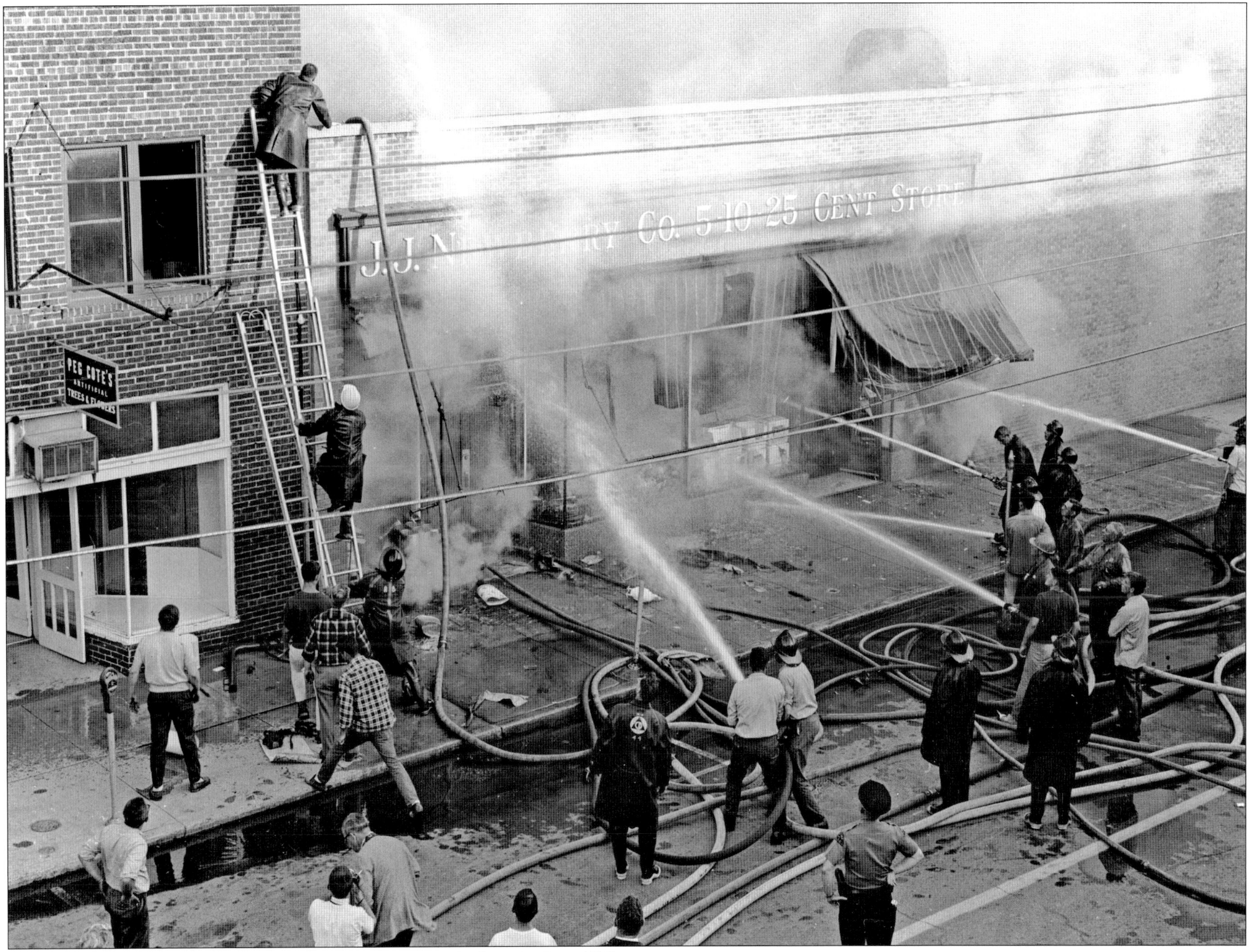

The fire at J. J. Newberry Co. 5–10–25 Cent Store on Main Street, circa 1950. *Courtesy of James J. Dion*

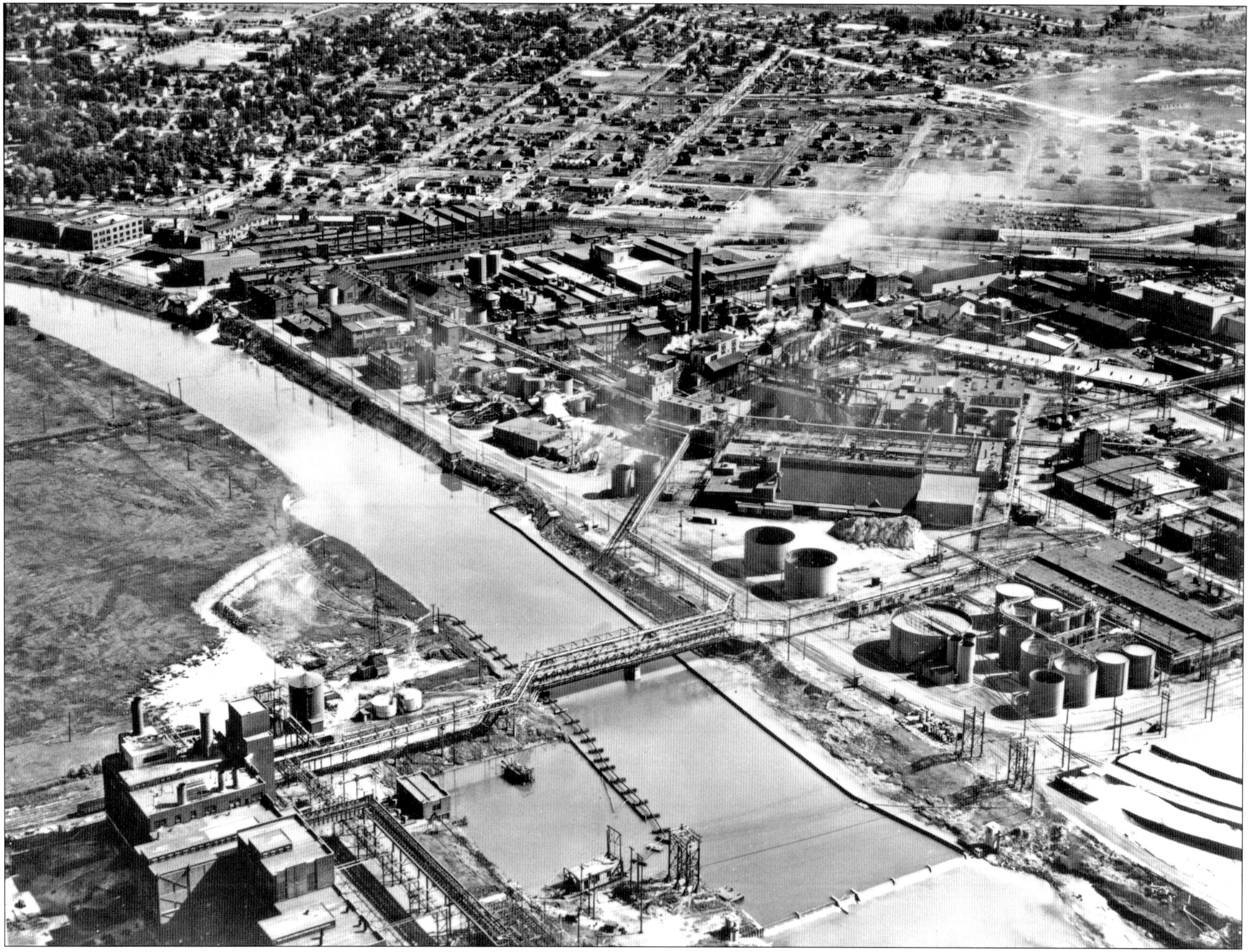

Aerial view of The Dow Chemical Company, circa 1950. *Courtesy of Midland County Historical Society*

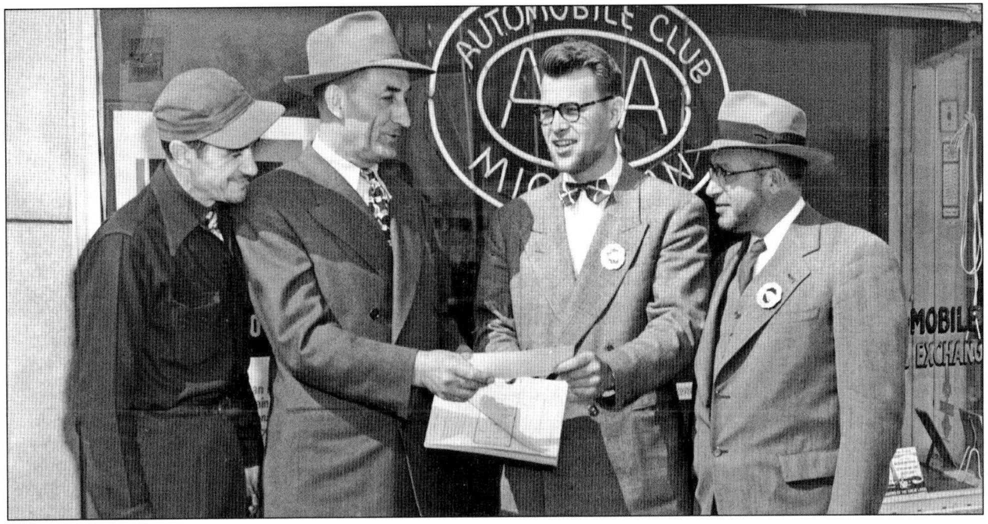

The purchase of $50 in Midland County Centennial membership certificates by Circle Businessmen's Association, May 3, 1950. Left to right: secretary-treasurer of the businessmen's association Roy Bergtold, president of the association Harvey Trombley, secretary-treasurer of the Centennial corporation John Collinson and member of the Centennial executive committee B. F. Crocker. *Courtesy of Midland Daily News*

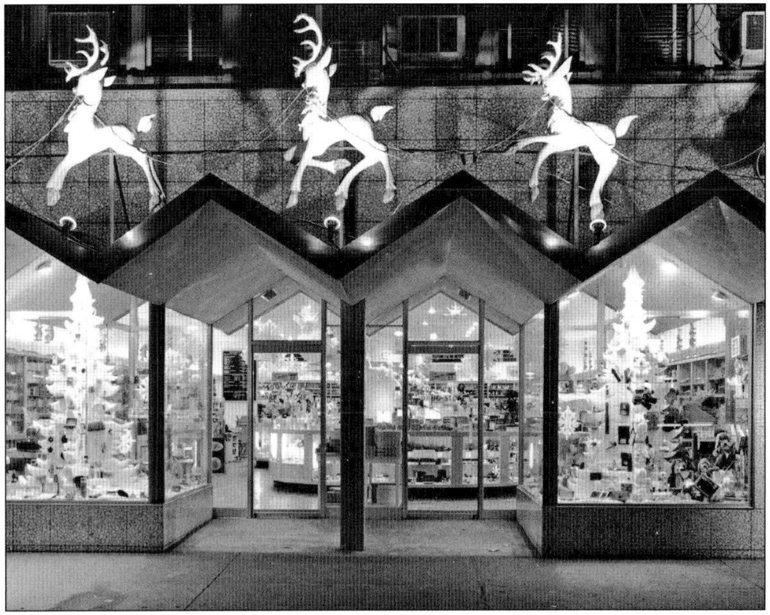

Community Drug Store on Main Street owned by the Bergstein family, circa 1950. *Courtesy of James J. Dion*

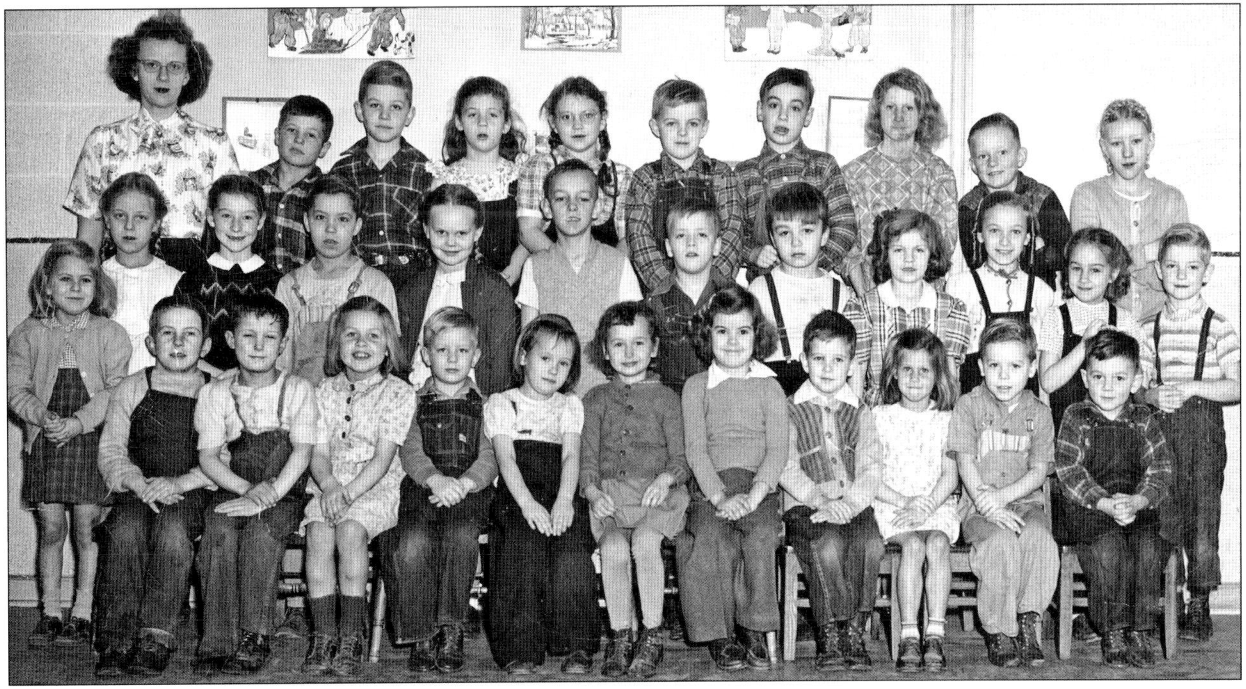

Kindergarten, first- and second-grade classes at Averill School in Lincoln Township, 1950. Seated in the front row, left to right: Martin Osburn, Burt Osburn, Mable Reger, Don Draves, Margie Deverics, Connie Varner, Ann Valentine, Gary Briggs, Jean Reger, Gerald Hatt and Roger Hackett. Standing in the second row: Paulette Peterson, Judy Draves, Jack Hatt, Ruth Richardson, Robert Seaman, Dave Draves, Philip Losey, Sue Sasse, Letha Suderman, Becky Bailey and Ernest Harman. Third row: teacher Mrs. Barbara Stoppard, Maurice Finney, Dale Varner, Carol Parks, Esther French, Lee Valentine, Russell Deverics, Violet Osburn, Jim Brown and Janke Lauack. *Courtesy of Connie Moe*

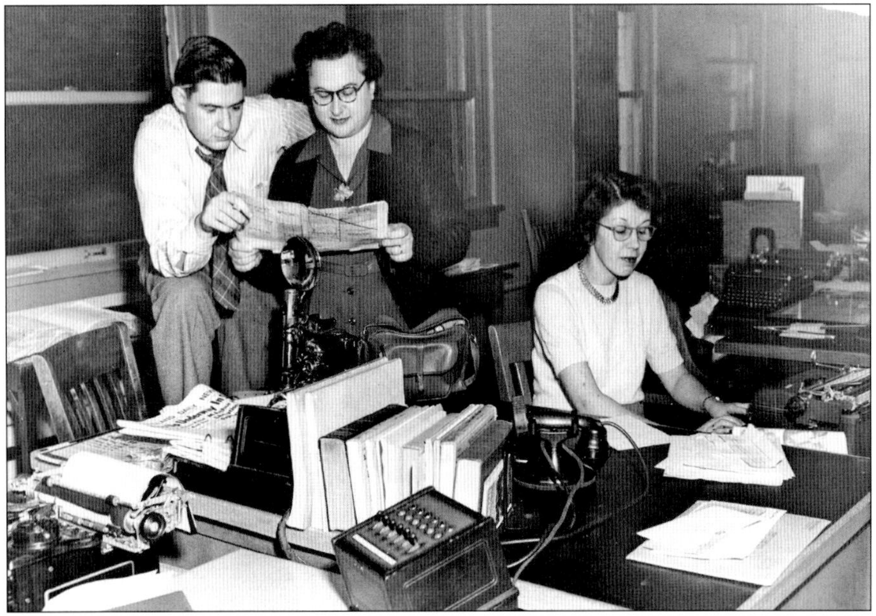

James Fessler, Marjorie Lefler and Kathryn Emmenecker in the newsroom at the *Midland Daily News*, circa 1950. *Courtesy of Midland Daily News*

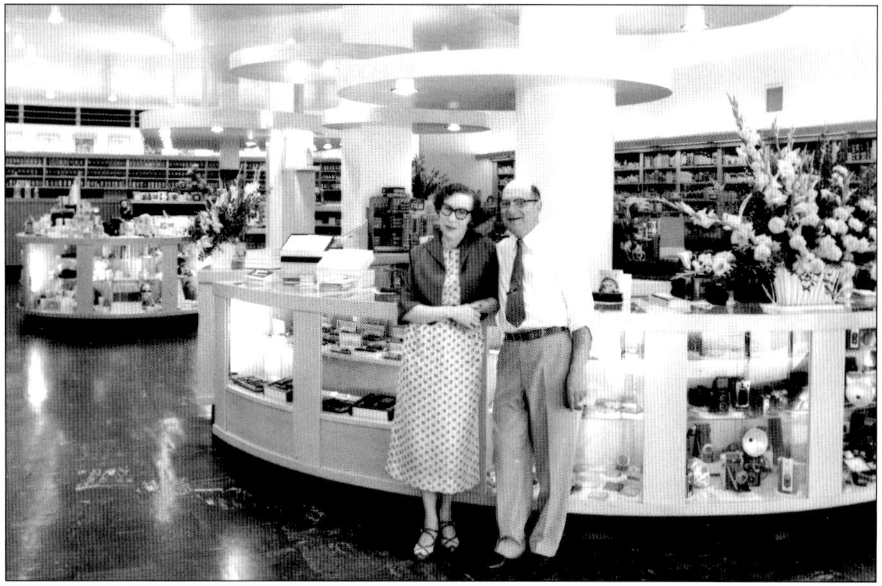

Leonard and Esther Bergstein at the grand re-opening of newly enlarged Community Drug, 311 S. Main St., downtown Midland, June 8, 1952. Their first grandson was born during the open house. *Courtesy of Stuart Bergstein.*

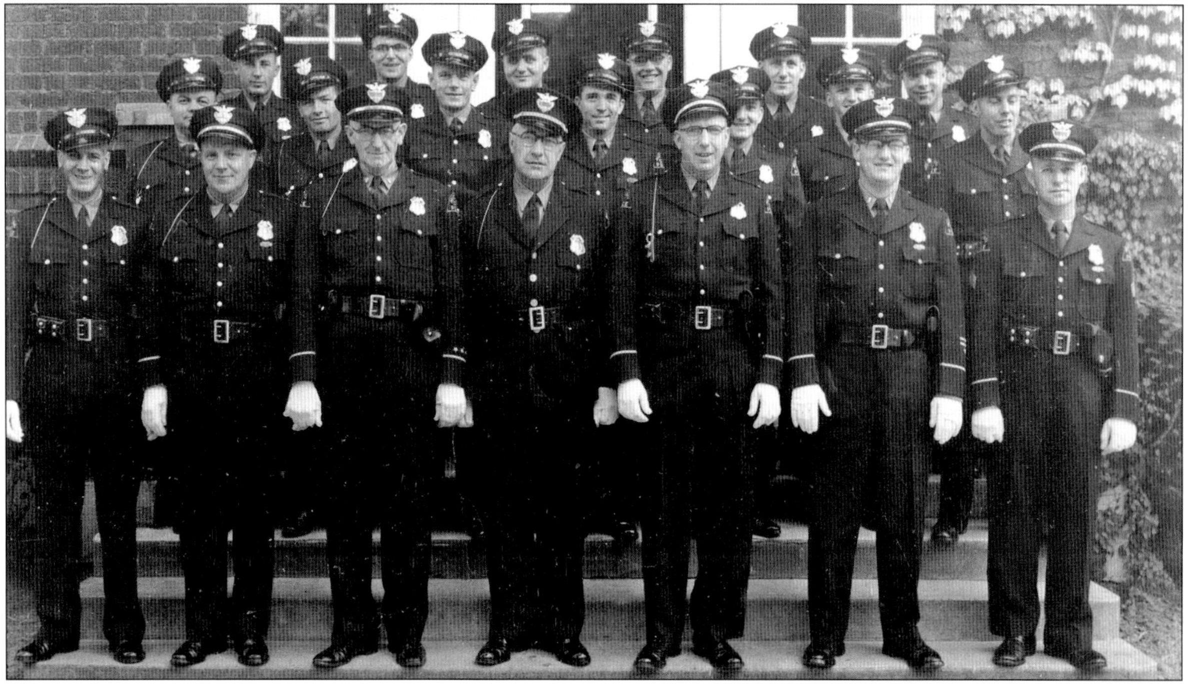

The Midland City Police Department, Memorial Day, 1952. Front row, left to right: Ray Rowe, Roger Briggs, Captain Stanley Sage, Chief Richard Rogers, Lt. Burr Corner, Douglas Craig and William Maxwell. Second row: H. L. Vern Miner, Lewis Church, Sheldon Rhodes, Edward Cherry, Herbert Carter, John Smallwood and Robert Rowe. Third row: Robert Brandt, Donald Brown, Calvin Haylie, Arlie Sage, Paul Bolander and Kenneth Bullenbacker.

Courtesy of Midland County Historical Society

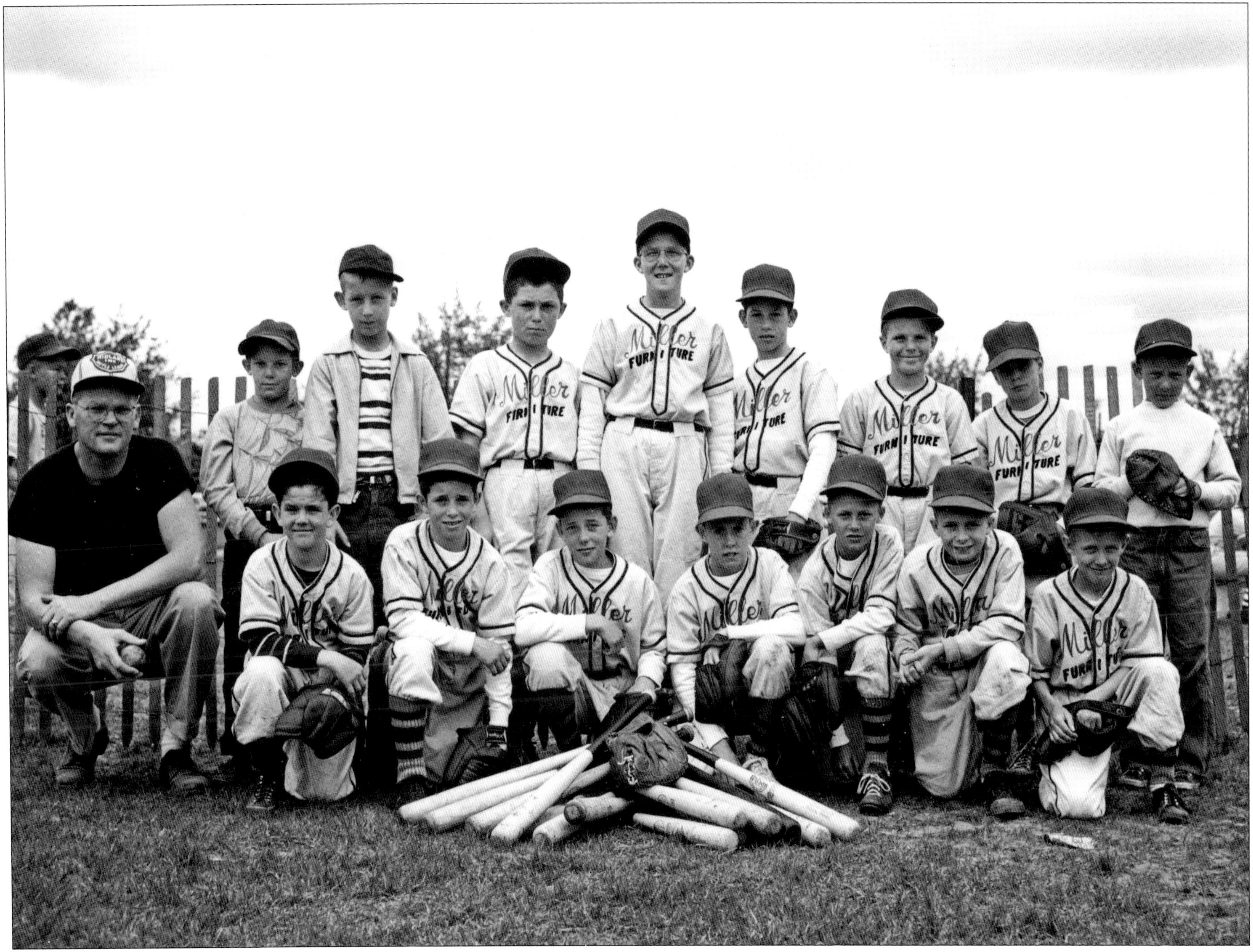

Miller Furniture Little League baseball team, 1952. *Courtesy of Midland County Historical Society*

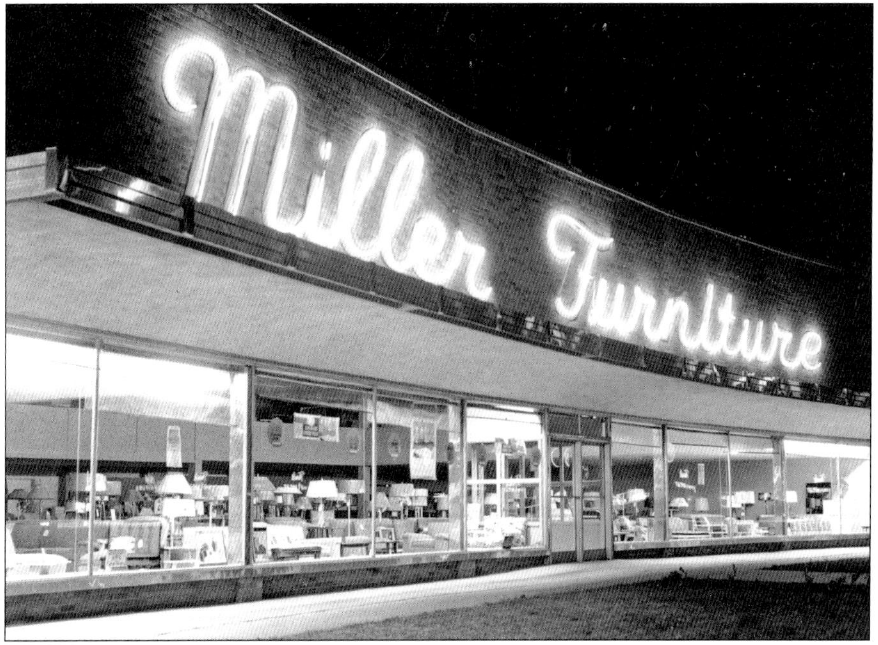

Miller Furniture on the Circle in 1953. *Courtesy of James J. Dion*

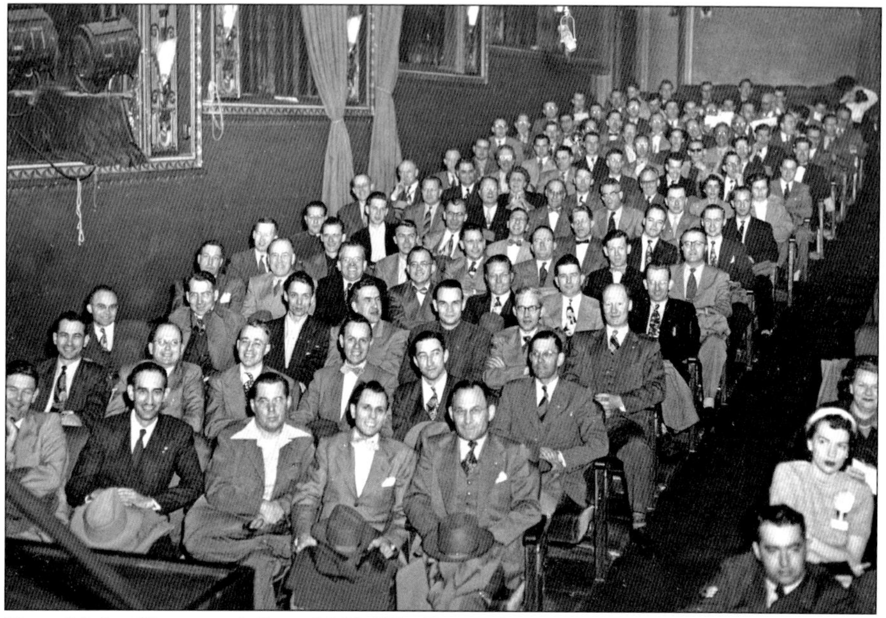

Dow Male Chorus at Don McNeill's Breakfast Club radio show in Chicago where the group performed, 1953. *Courtesy of Midland County Historical Society*

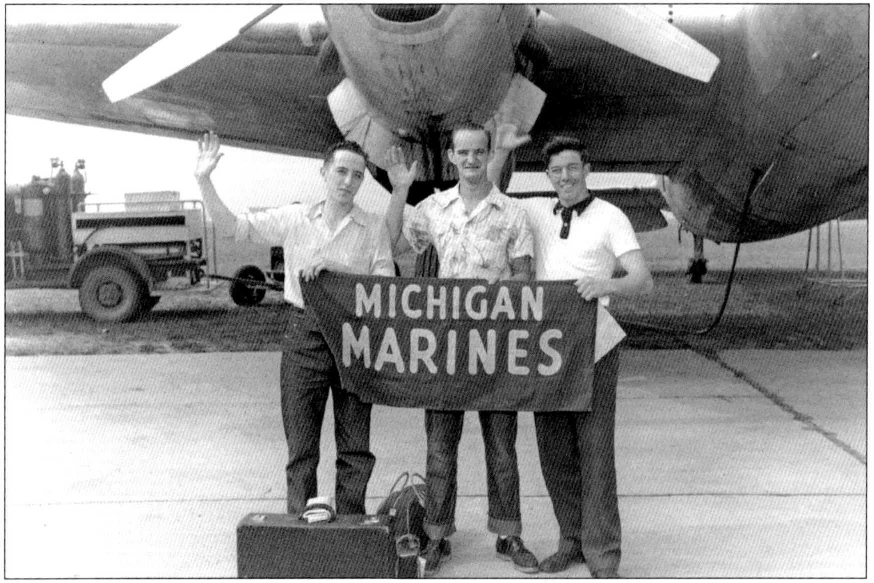

Colemen friends leaving from Detroit to go to California for boot camp and later to Korea, left to right: Patrick O'Laughlin, Jarvis Jones and Donald Moore, circa 1953. *Courtesy of Don and Sandy Methner Moore*

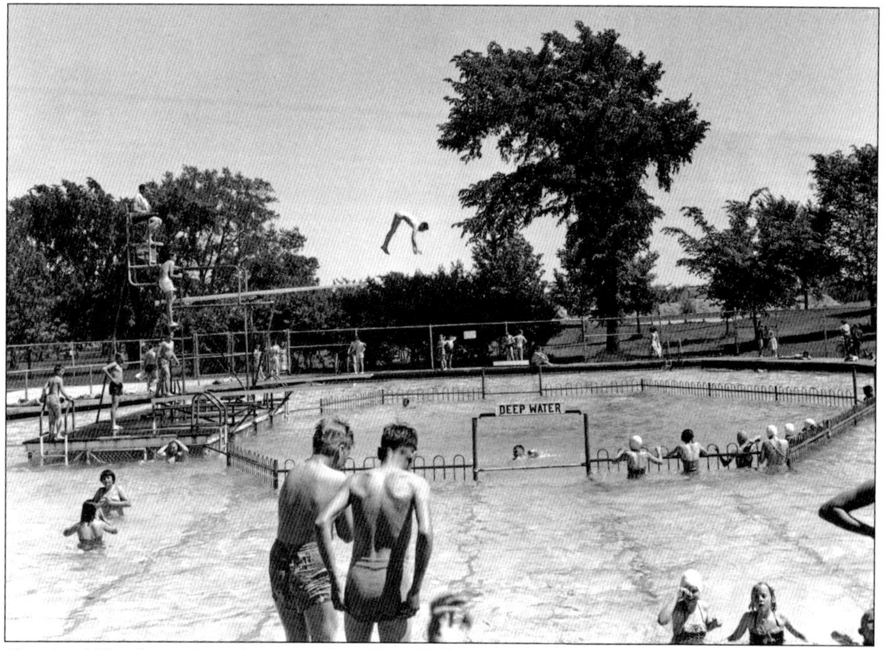

Central Park swimming pool on Rodd Street, 1953. *Courtesy of James J. Dion*

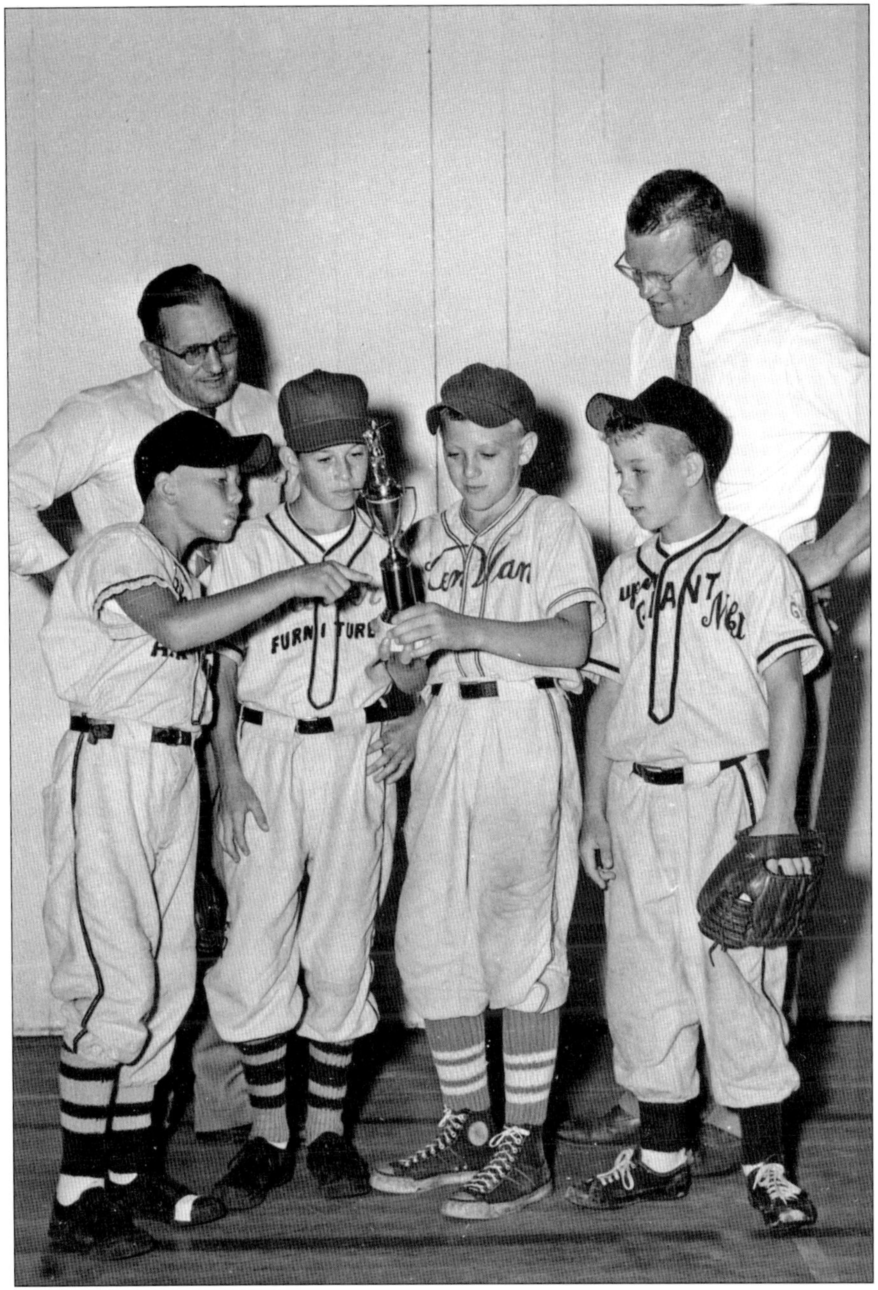

Midland Little League All-Stars, 1952. Front row, left to right: Ricky Ludwig, Marlin Ranger, Mike Westley and Mike Ivan. Standing in the back are Don Streder and Danny Smick. *Courtesy of Midland County Historical Society*

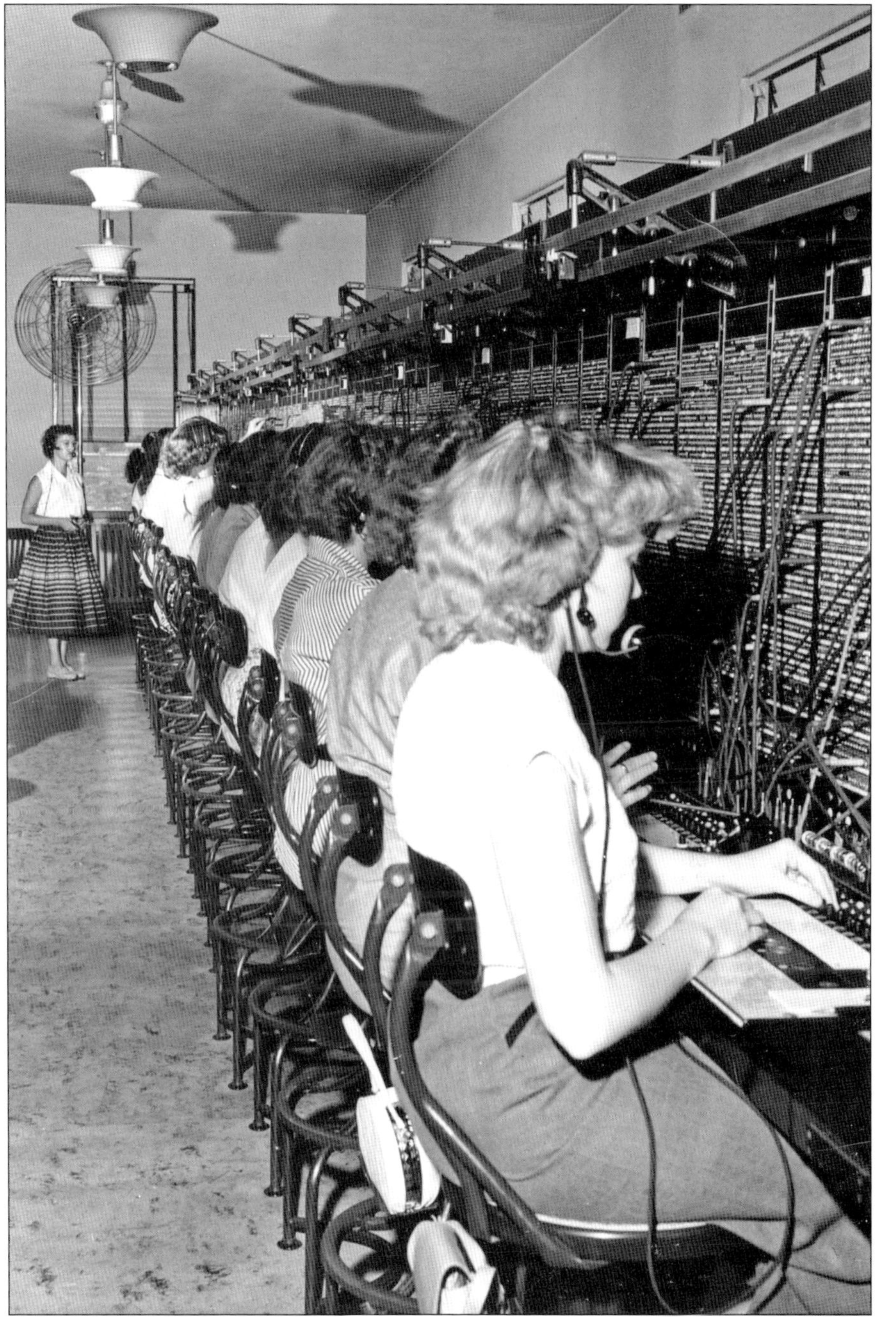

Operators at Michigan Bell Telephone Company in Midland, July 29, 1953. *Courtesy of Midland County Historical Society*

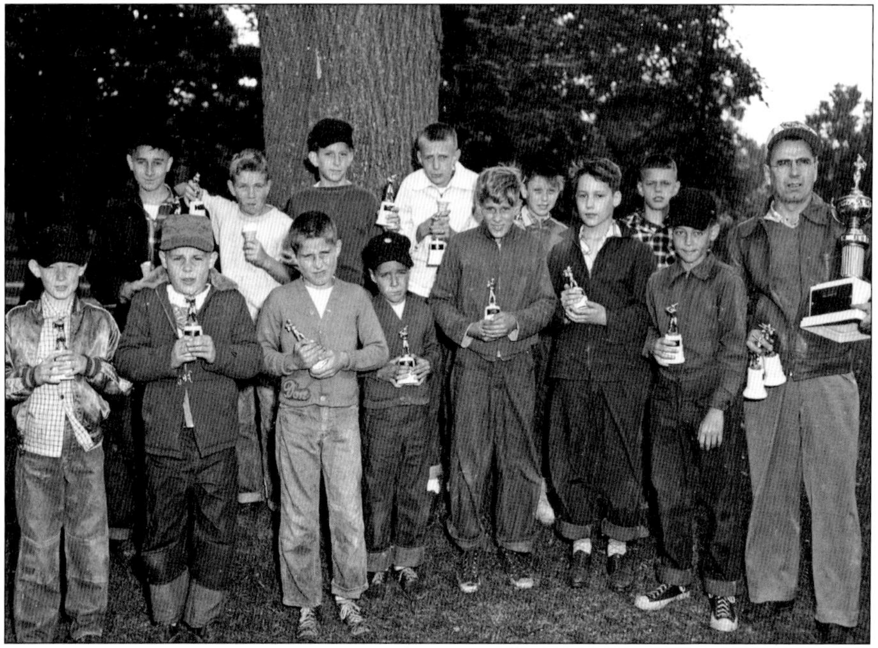

Moose Frat League champions, 1953. *Courtesy of Midland County Historical Society*

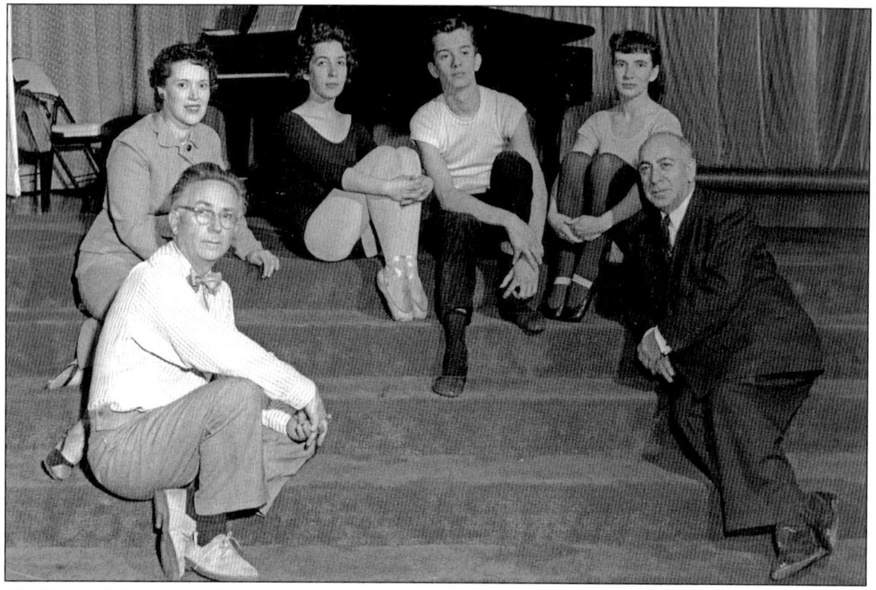

Gathered for a production using "Somnaphonics" at the Grace A. Dow Library Auditorium, March 27, 1956: Alden Dow, Jane Stark, Mary Lou Robinson, Mel Lazarevick, Ginger Cristy and Dr. L. Pedosky. *Courtesy of James J. Dion*

Kindergarten class at Eastlawn School Wheelock Park Annex in 1953. First row, left to right: Susan Dersnah, Linda Crow, Susan Sanders, Karen Harrington, Patty White, Libby Lipke, Tommy Wilcox, David Barrons, Steve Anderson, Patty Merrill and Jane VanHouten. Second row: Dan Whitman, Randy Carey, Dennie Dumos, Lana Fairbank, Myron Nelson, Wayne Simington, Reggie Long, Bobby Miller and Joe Harper. Third row: teacher Jean Nichols, George Mayer, Cathy Amos, Consuelo Johnson, Brenda Parkinson, Linda Wixon, Cindy Kelly, Kathy Cutting, Ken Anderson, Richard Stein and Greg Austin. Those not included are Steven Seeburger, Doug Smith, John Yack, Ricky Greenlee, Syd Anderson, Mary C. Collamer, Chrissi Hayhoe, Mary Jo Johnson and Jan West.

Courtesy of Jean N. Hillman

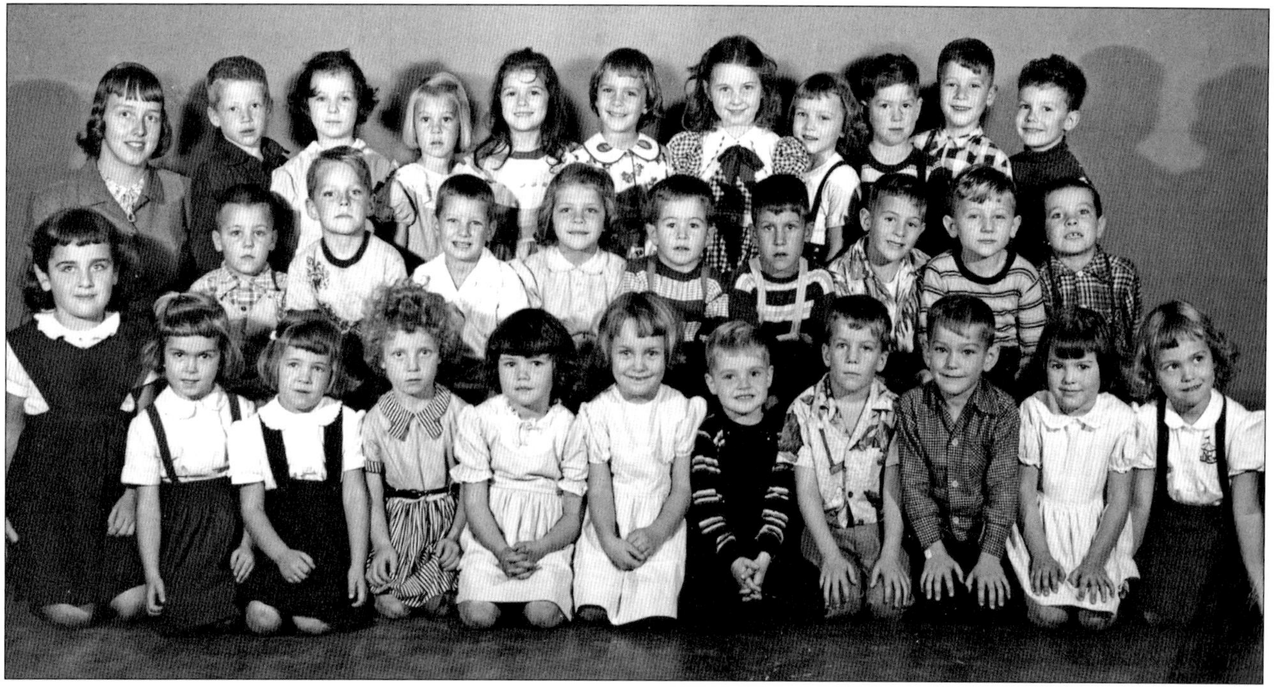

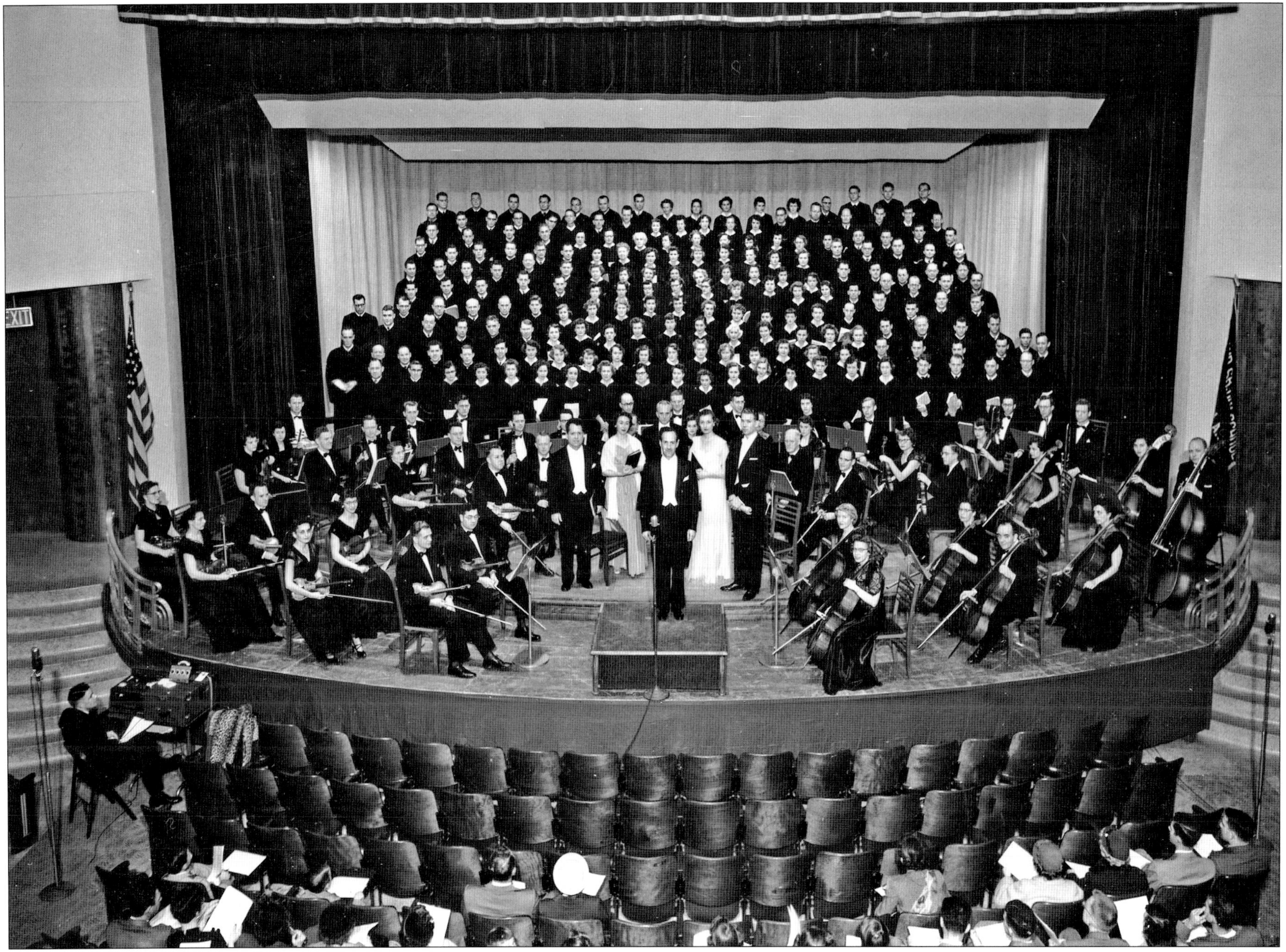

Dow Orchestra, Dow Women's Chorus and Dow Men's Glee Club at the Central High School Auditorium, December 1953. Dr. Theodore Vosburg is conducting "The Messiah." *Courtesy of Jean N. Hillman and Midland County Historical Society*

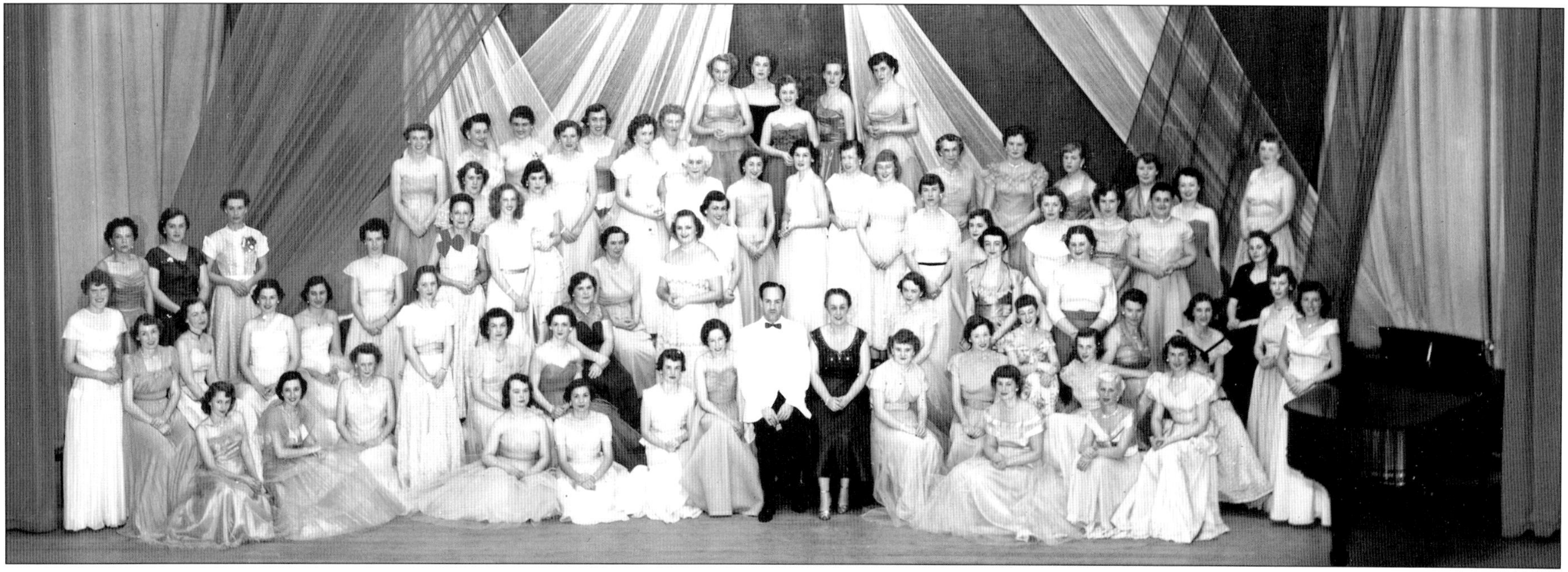

Dow Women's Chorus with Dr. Theodore Vosburg as director at the Central High School Auditorium, 1954. *Courtesy of Jean N. Hillman*

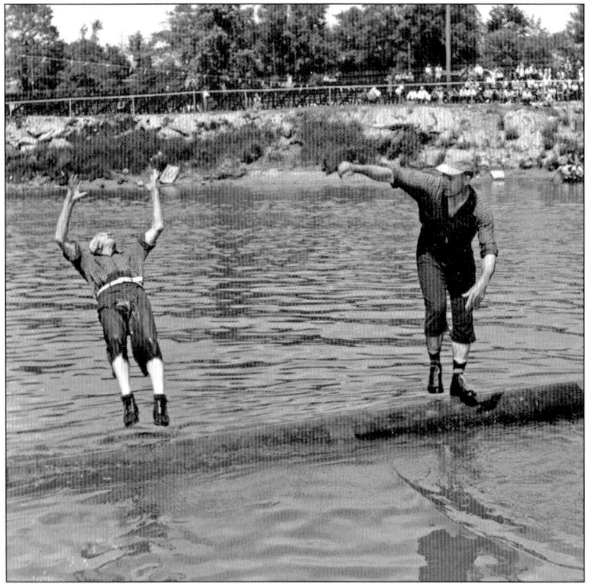

Log rolling during Riverdays on the Tittabawassee River in front of Emerson Park, June 13, 1953.
Courtesy of James J. Dion

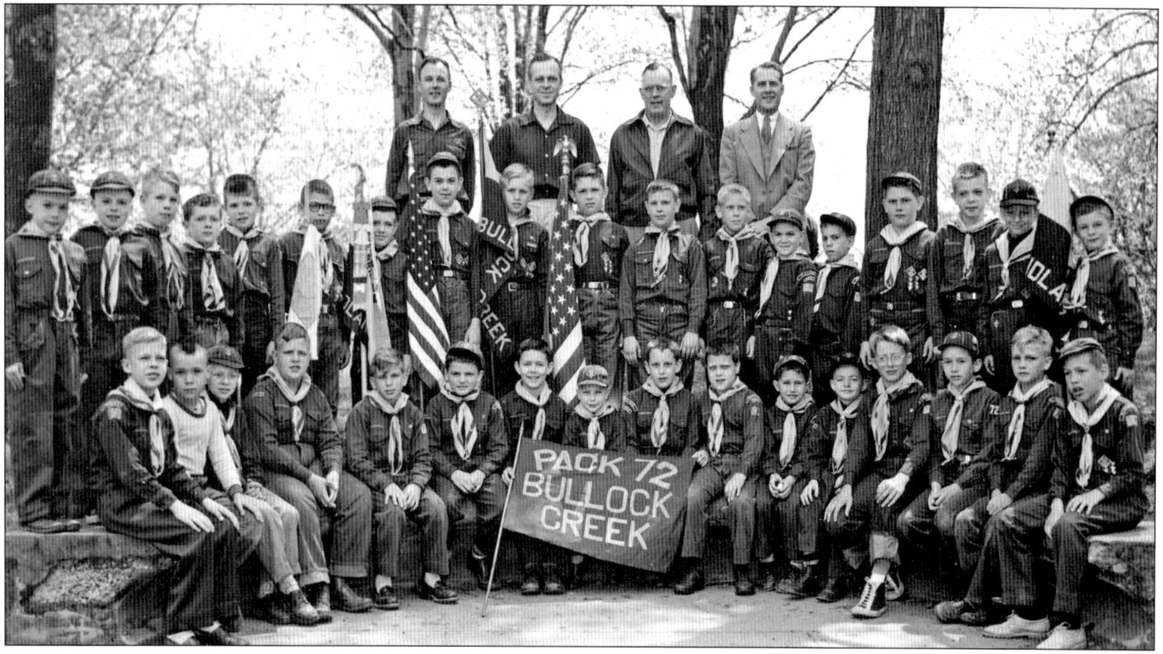

Bullock Creek Cub Scout Pack 72, 1954. *Courtesy of Midland County Historical Society*

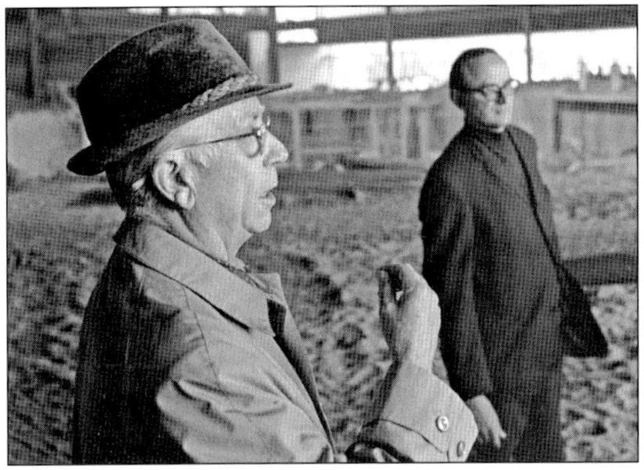

Architect Alden B. Dow and Robert Hammerschmidt discussing the construction of the Midland Center for the Arts, 1969. *Courtesy of Midland County Historical Society*

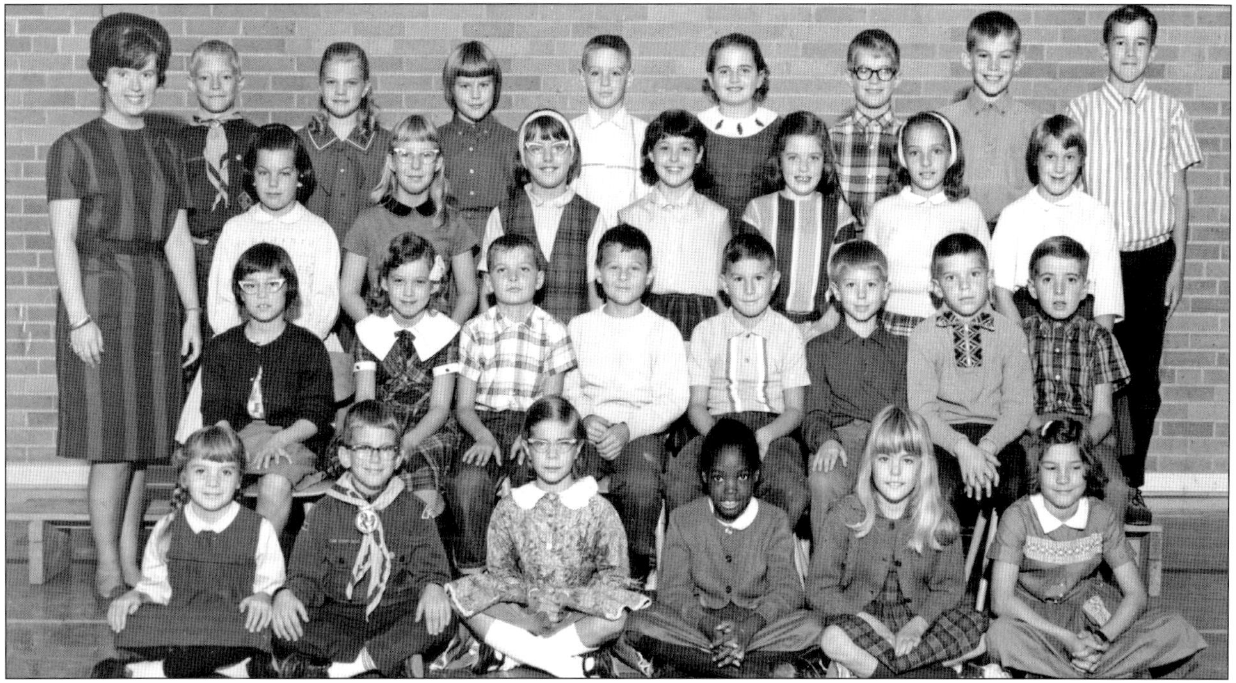

Fourth-grade class at Chestnut Hill Elementary, 1965. The teacher is Mrs. Dick Cross. In the second row, fifth from the left, is Greg Stanford. *Courtesy of Sally Stanford*

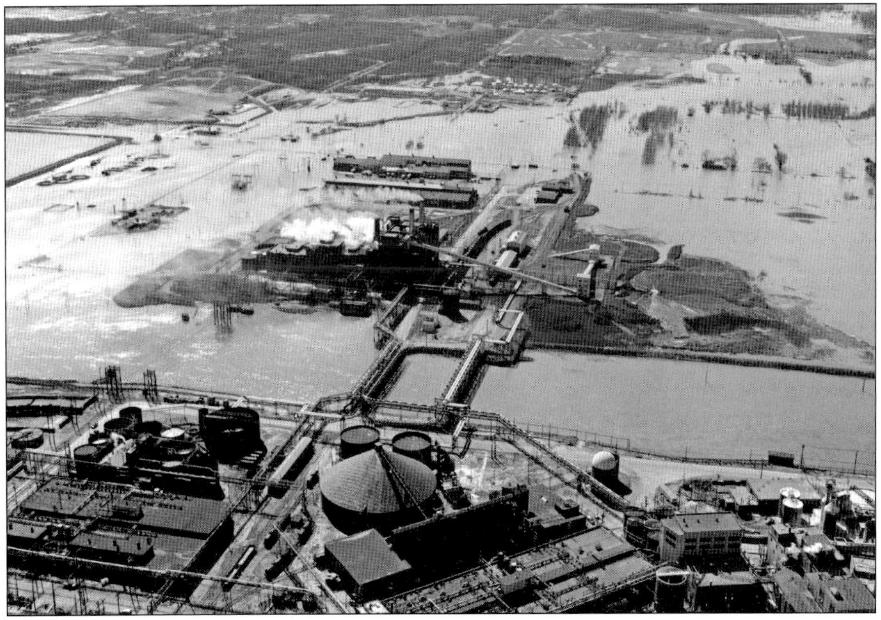

Aerial view of the west side of The Dow Chemical Company's powerhouse during the flood of 1965. *Courtesy of Midland County Historical Society*

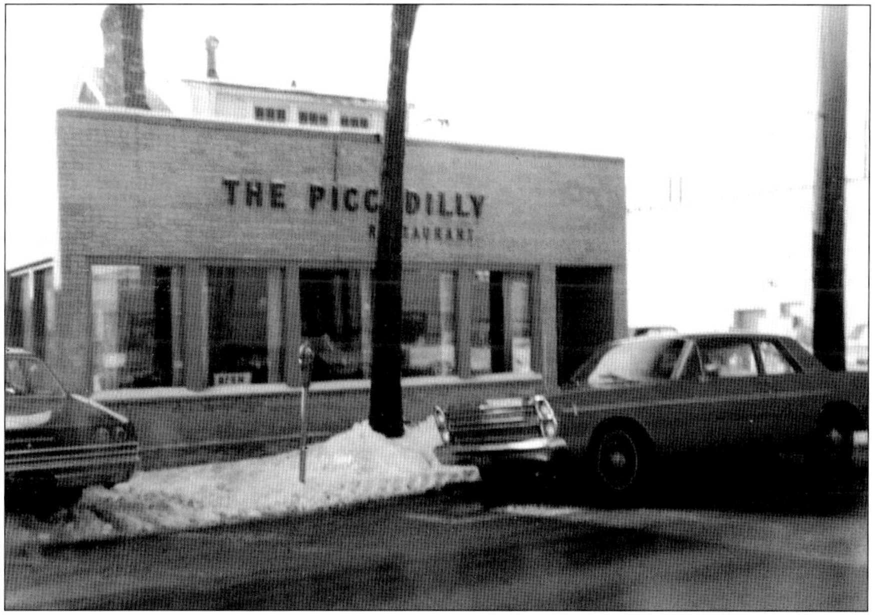

The Piccadilly Restaurant owned by Wilfrid and Wynette Cox on West Larkin Street, 1968. *Courtesy of Thomas J. Cox*

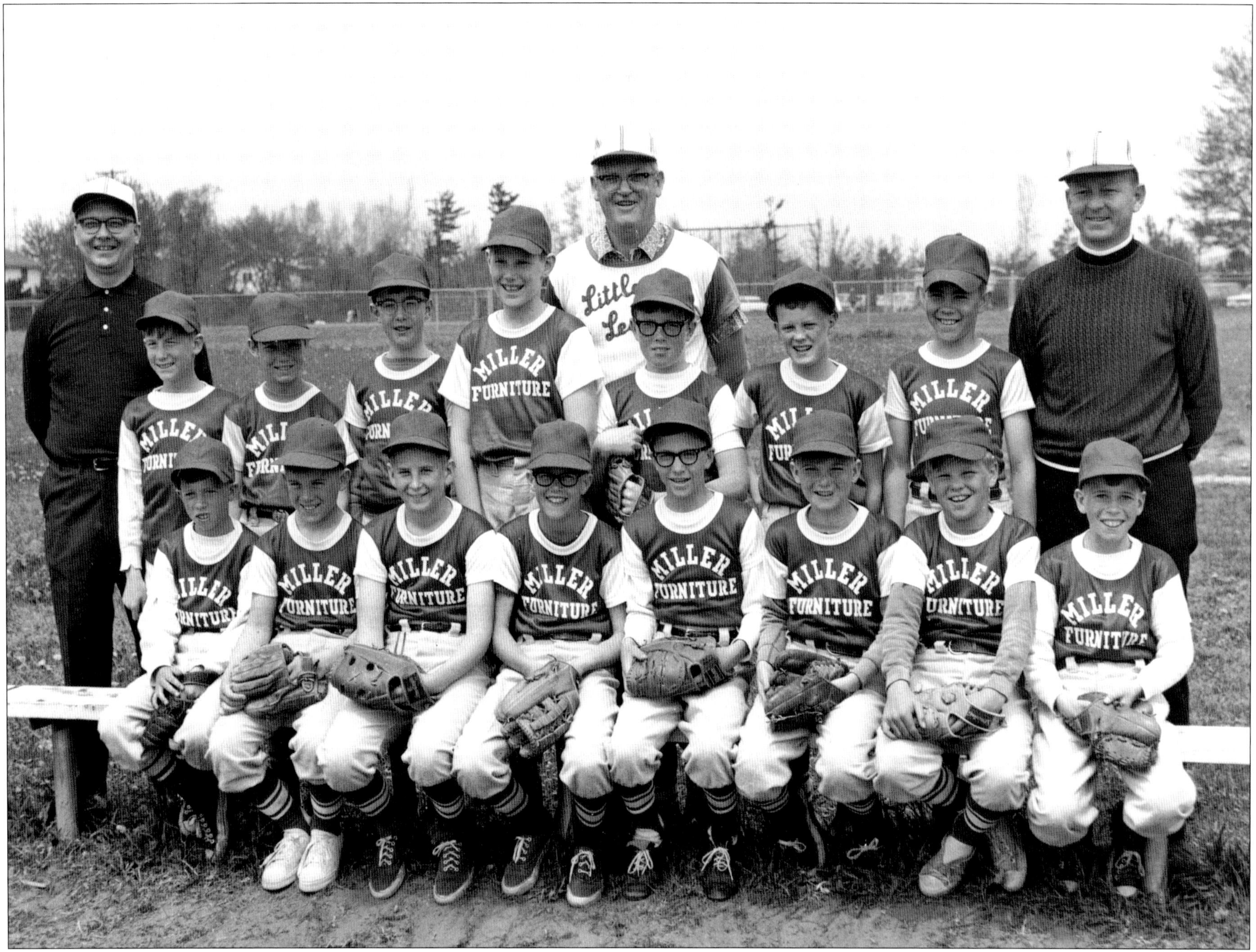

Miller Furniture Little League baseball team, 1967. *Courtesy of Midland County Historical Society*

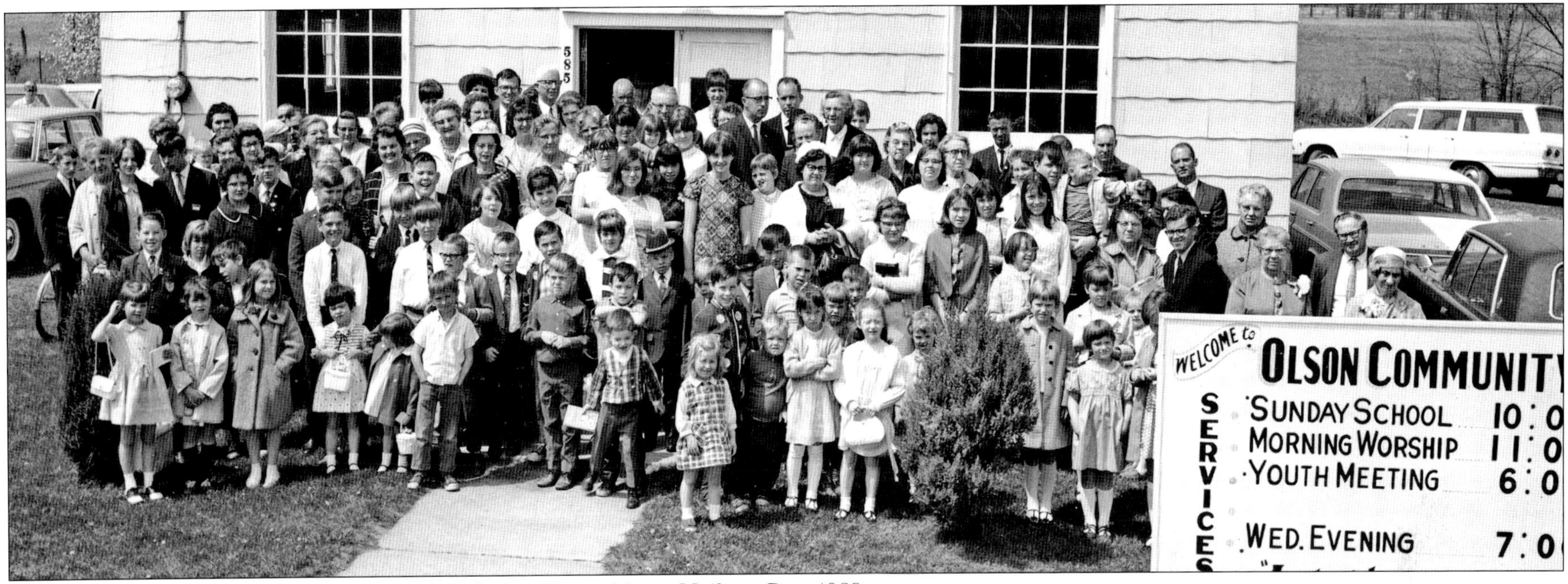

Congregation at the Olson Community Church in Lee Township on Mothers Day, 1968. *Courtesy of Naomi Haebler*

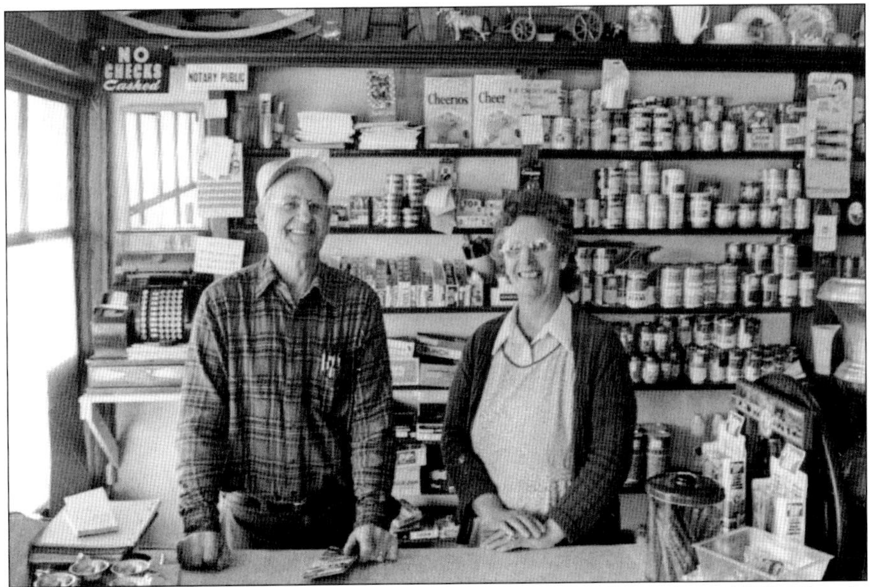

Ken and Elva Smith at the Olson Store in Lee Township, circa 1970. Elva is the daughter of L. P. Larsen who started the family store in 1904.

Courtesy of Naomi Haebler

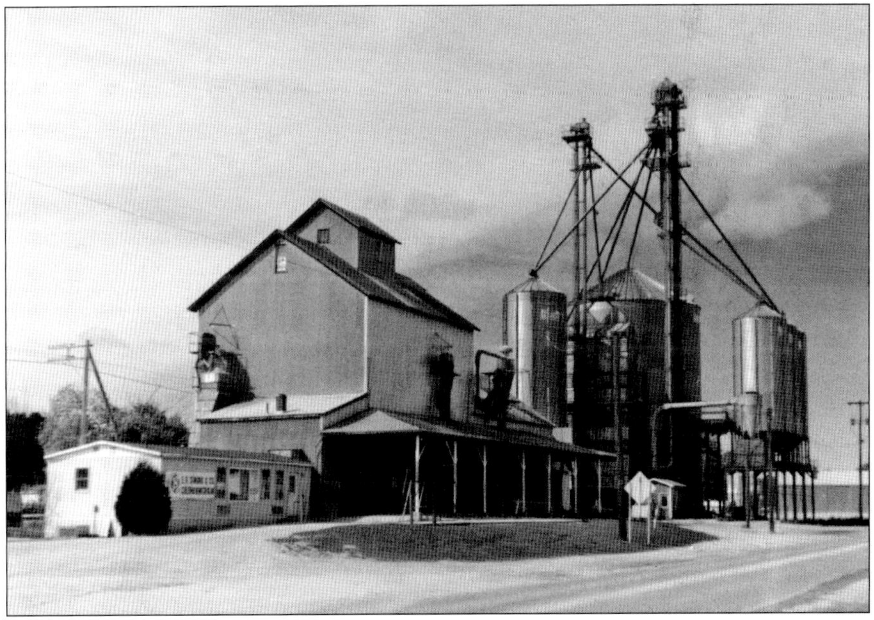

E. R. Simmons elevator in Coleman, circa 1975.

Courtesy of Midland County Historical Society

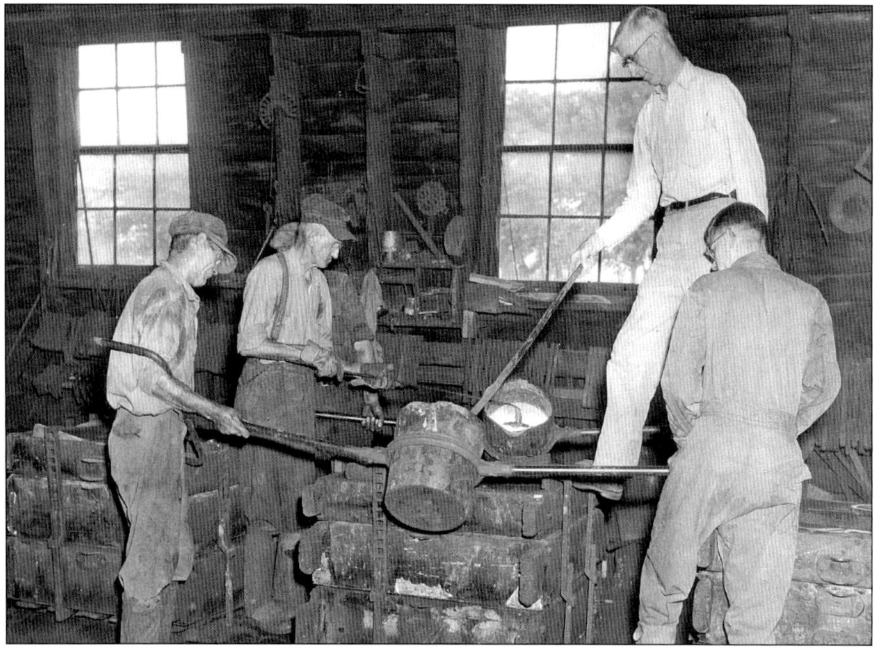

Midland Iron Works, 1978. *Courtesy of Midland County Historical Society*

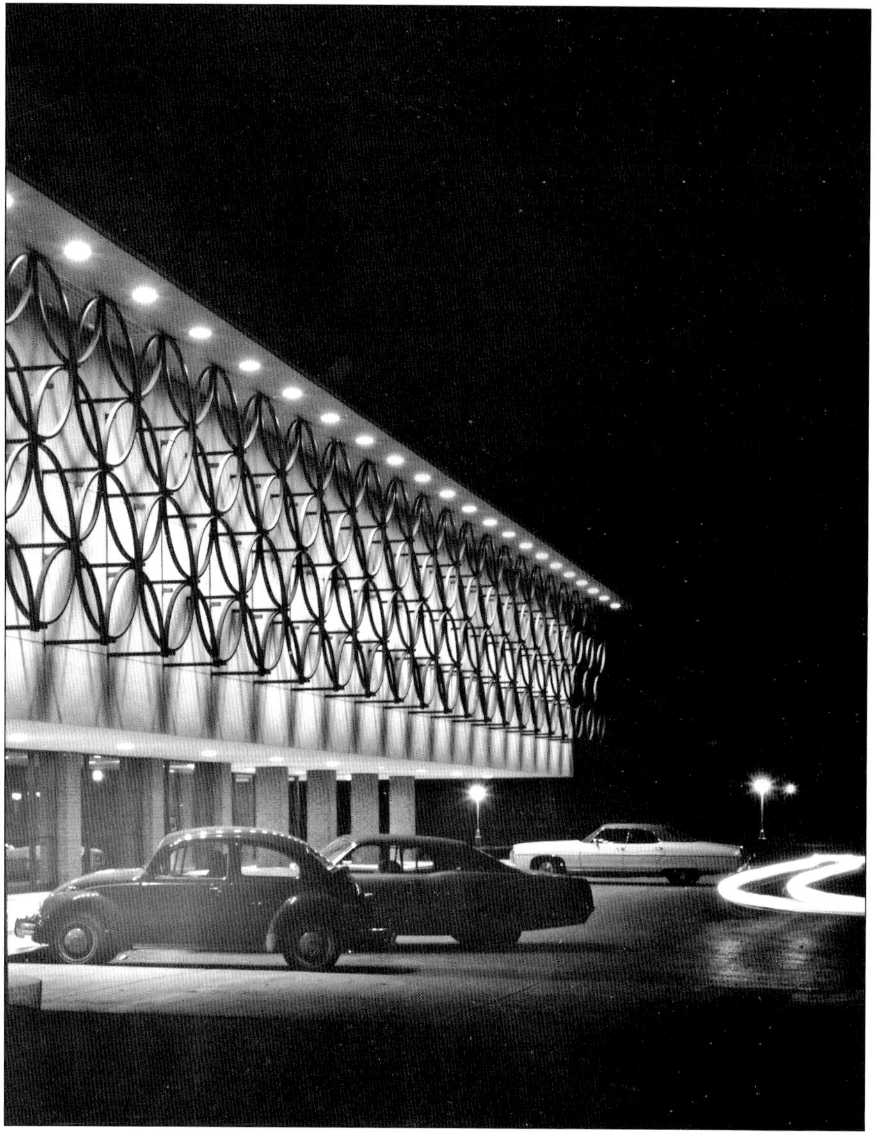

Midland Center for the Arts, 1971. The groundbreaking took place July 8, 1968, with funding from Alden and Vada B. Dow, Herbert H. and Grace A. Dow Foundation, Dow Foundation and public donations.
Courtesy of Midland Daily News

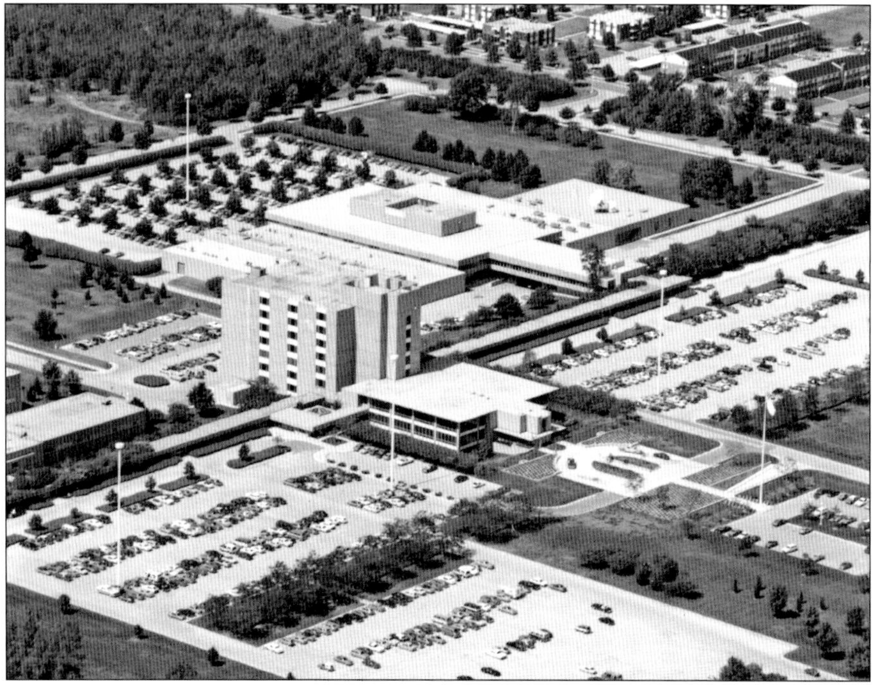

The Dow Chemical Company headquarters, circa 1975.
Courtesy of Midland County Historical Society

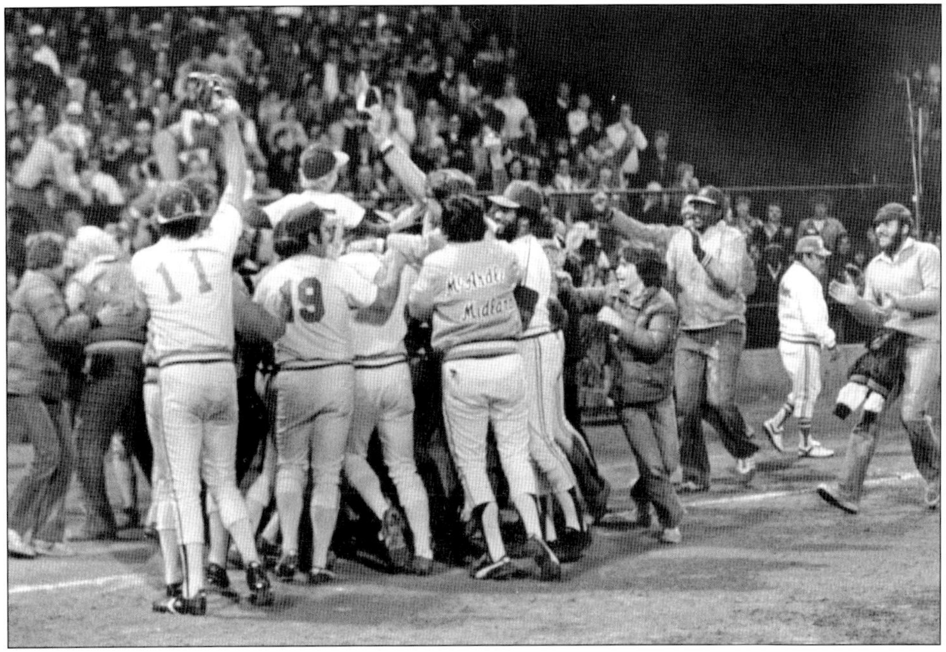

McArdle winning the softball championship, 1979. *Courtesy of Midland Daily News*

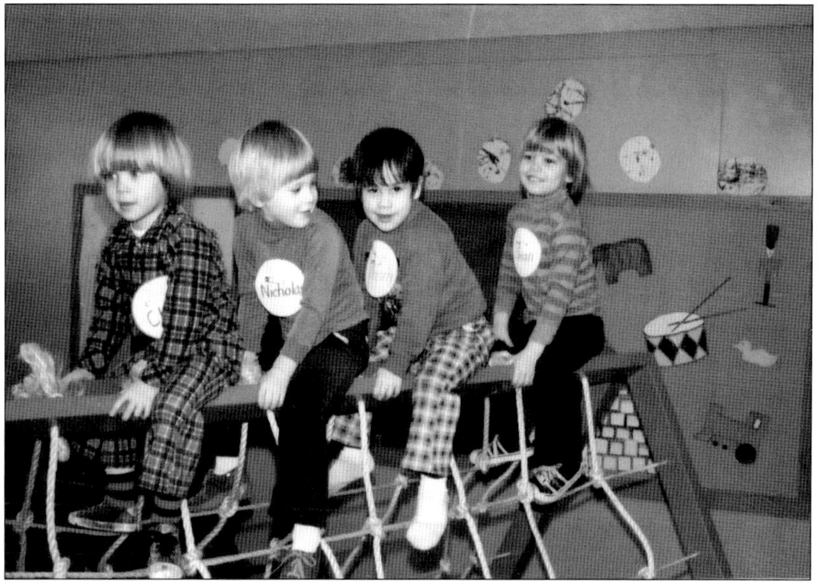

Chad Ignatowski, Nicolas (unknown), Danny (unknown) and Sean Lindsay at the St. John's Episcopal Nursery School, 1978.
Courtesy of William and Donna Lindsay

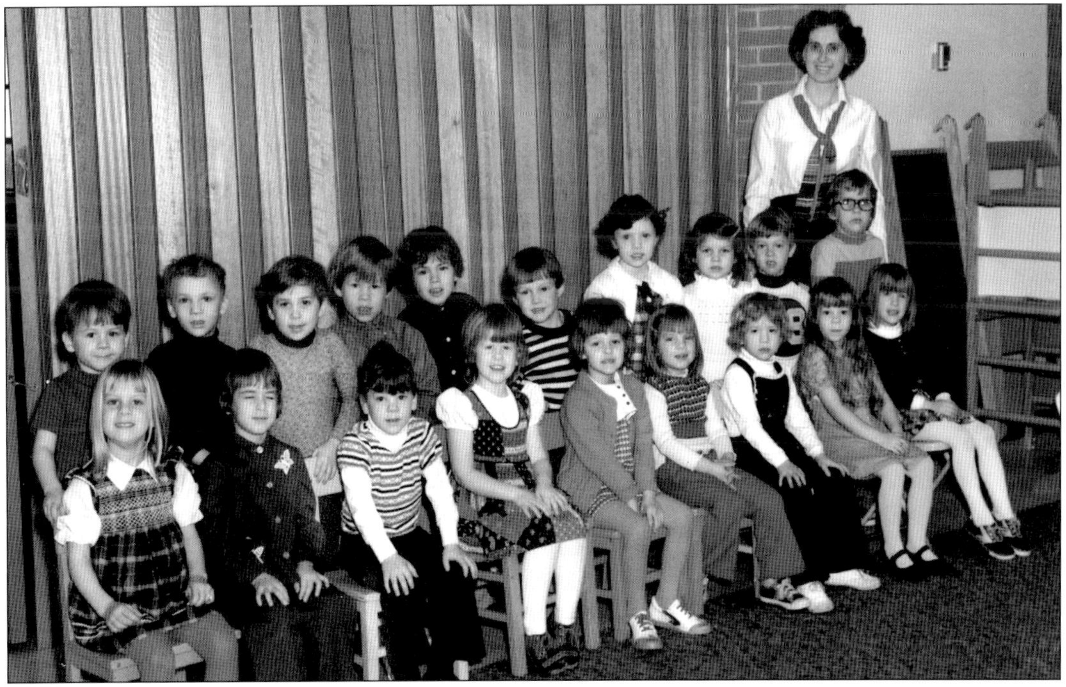

Kinder Keg Nursery School in Sanford, 1976. The teacher is Miss Marcia; in front of her is Craig Elliott. In the front row on the left is Amy Bailey Boxey. Sanford's Nursery School ran from 1975 to 2007. *Courtesy of Susan Francis Dexter*

The 1980s & 1990s

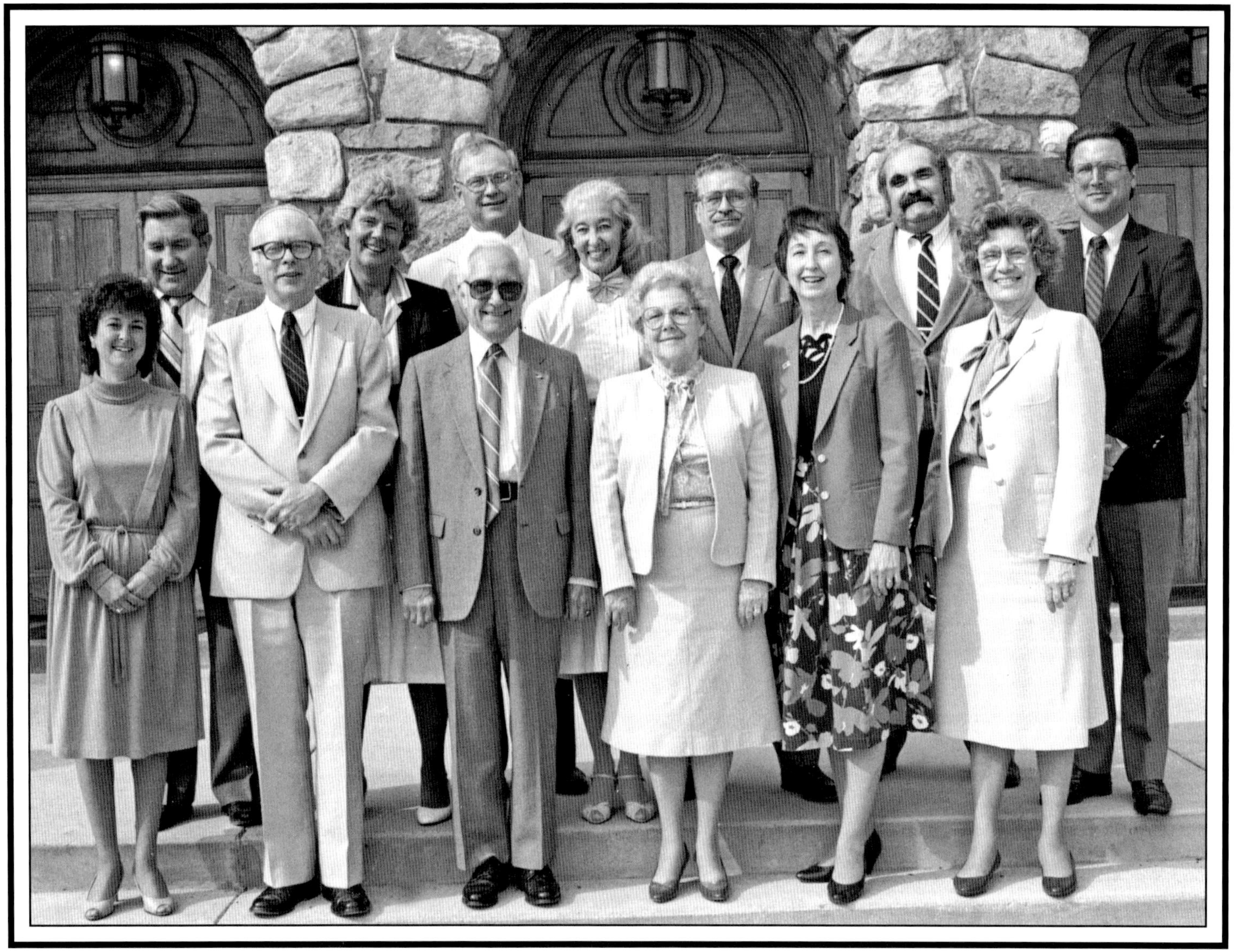

Midland County Commissioners, 1987. Front row, left to right: executive secretary for the board Mary Miller, Garth H. Beaver, A. Malcolm Gegenheimer, Leona Falkenstein, Betty Fillmore and chairman Anne Schilling. Back row: Roland R. Weaver, Anne Dever, Dale A. Wolfgang, Rose Marie McQuaid, Ronald L. Beech, Scott R. McDonald and county clerk Jeffrey P. Porter.

Courtesy of Midland County Historical Society

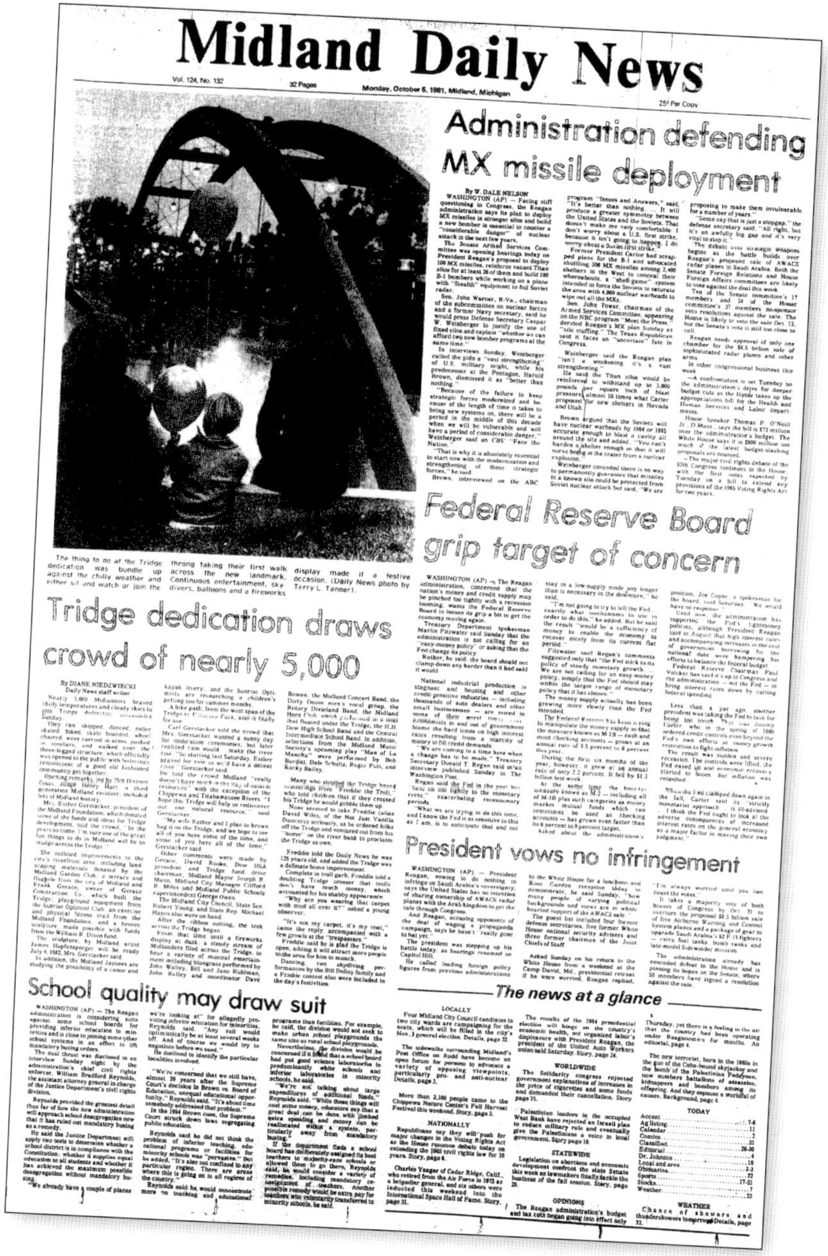

Midland Daily News

Vol. 124, No. 132 — 32 Pages — Monday, October 5, 1981, Midland, Michigan — 25¢ Per Copy

Administration defending MX missile deployment

By W. DALE NELSON

The thing to do at the Tridge dedication was bundle up against the chilly weather and either sit and watch or join the throng taking their first walk across the new landmark. Continuous entertainment, sky divers, balloons and a fireworks display made it a festive occasion. (Daily News photo by Terry L. Tanner)

Federal Reserve Board grip target of concern

Tridge dedication draws crowd of nearly 5,000

By DIANE NIEDZWIECKI

President vows no infringement

School quality may draw suit

The news at a glance

Midland Daily News reporting on the MX missile deployment and the Tridge dedication, Oct. 5, 1981. *Courtesy of Midland Daily News*

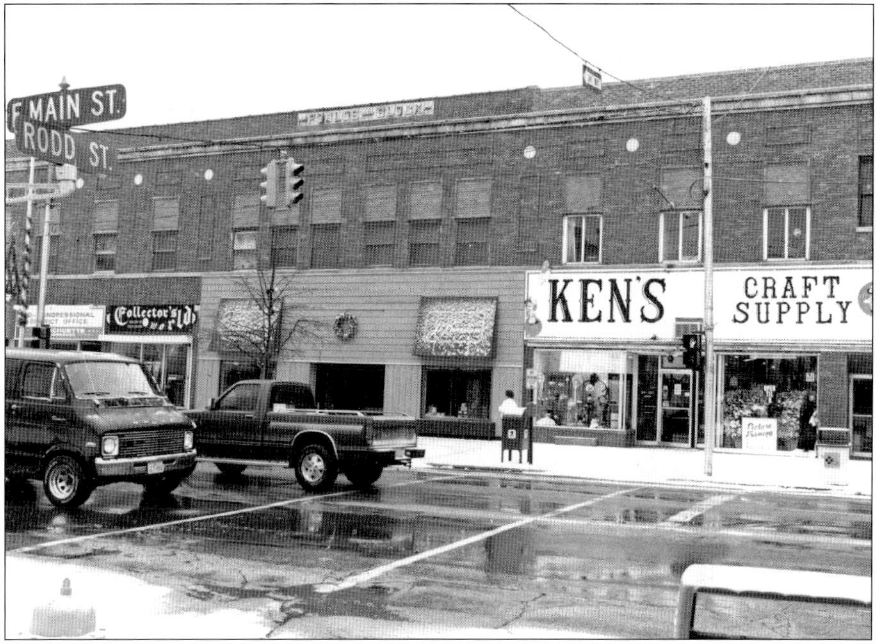

Main Street in Midland, 1981. *Courtesy of Midland County Historical Society*

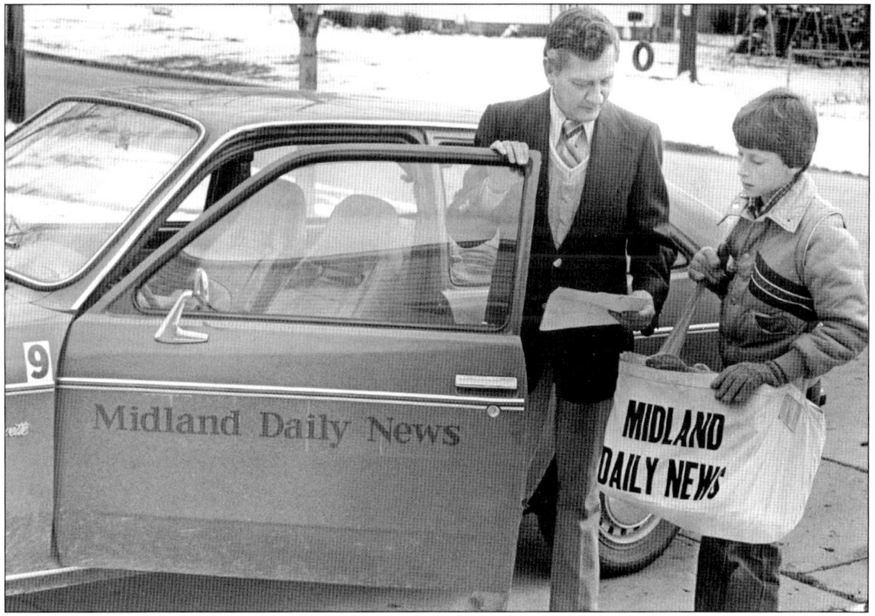

William D. Ducham, circulation manager at the *Midland Daily News*, with a newspaper carrier, November 1981. *Courtesy of Midland Daily News*

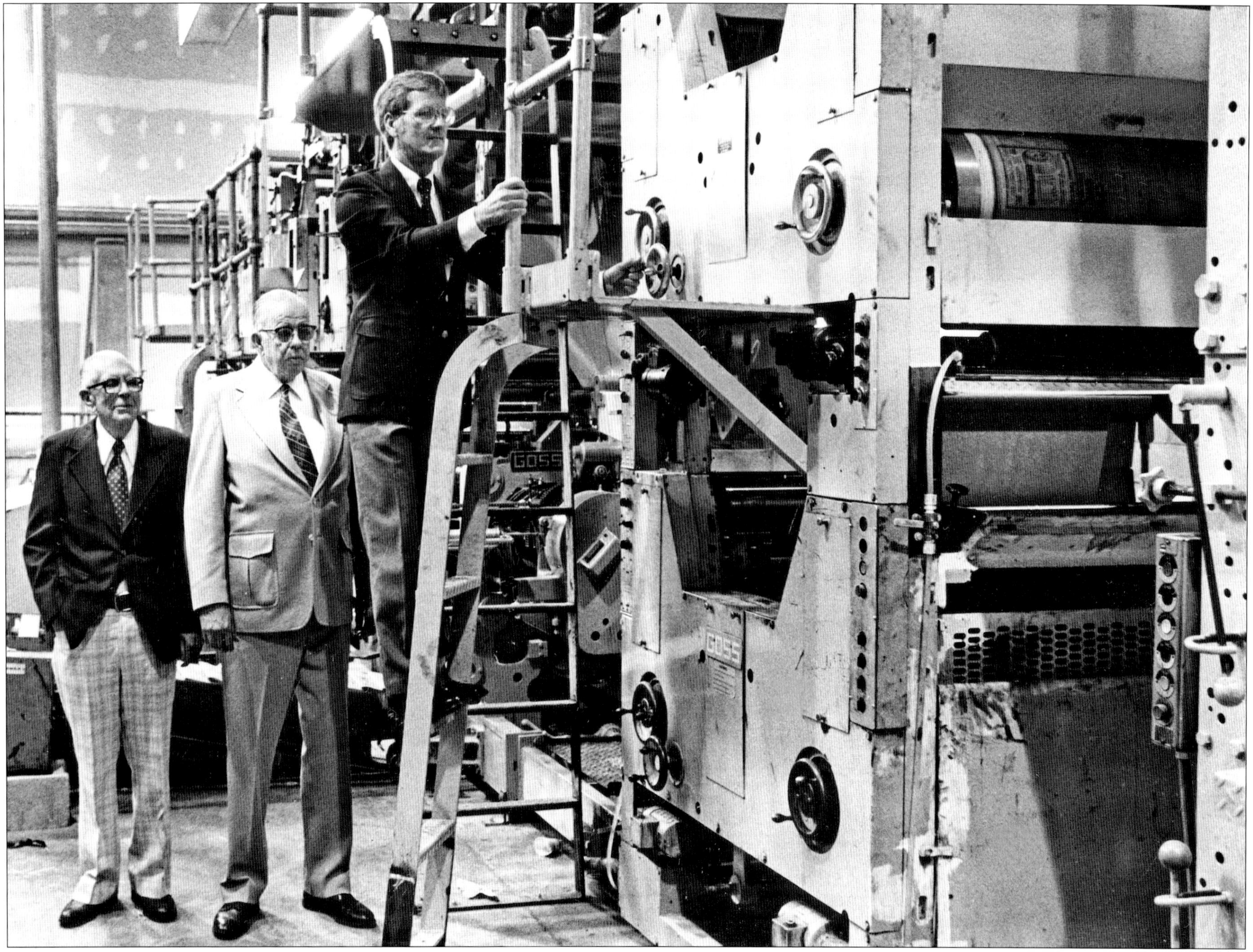

Surveying the newspaper's new Goss Urbanite press, 1984, left to right: Gordon F. Phillips, Norman Rumple and Charles Spence. *Courtesy of Midland Daily News*

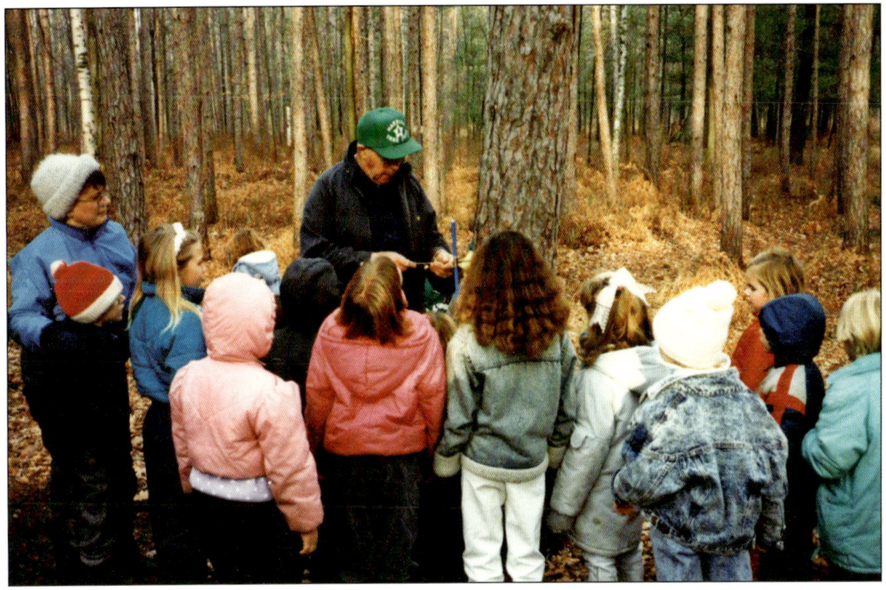

Ariel Haebler teaching students on a wood lot tour at Eight Mile Road, Jan. 15, 1986. School groups made regular field trips to his 64-acre tree farm. *Courtesy of Naomi Haebler*

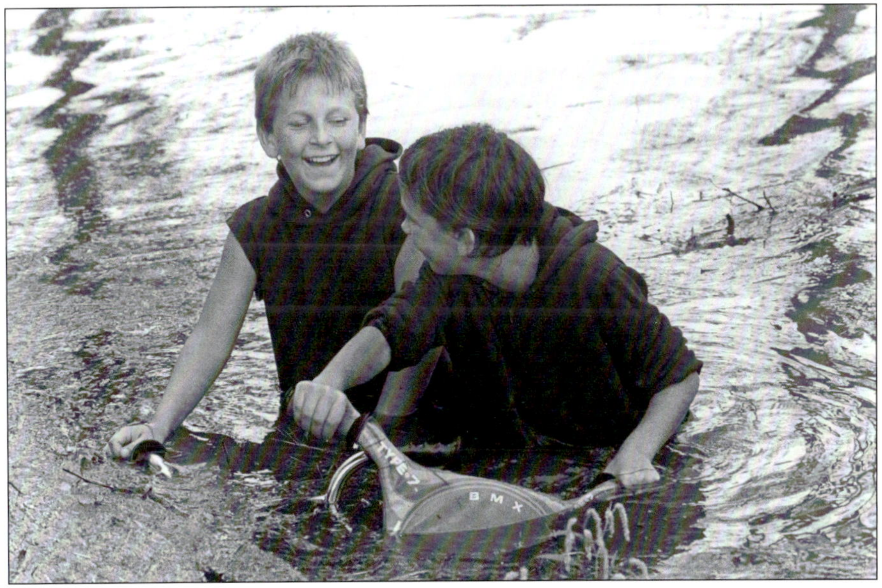

Ryan Steinka, age 10, on the left with Randy Peters, 11, at Sanford Senior Citizens Center playing in the flooded Sanford Park, 1986.
Courtesy of Midland Daily News

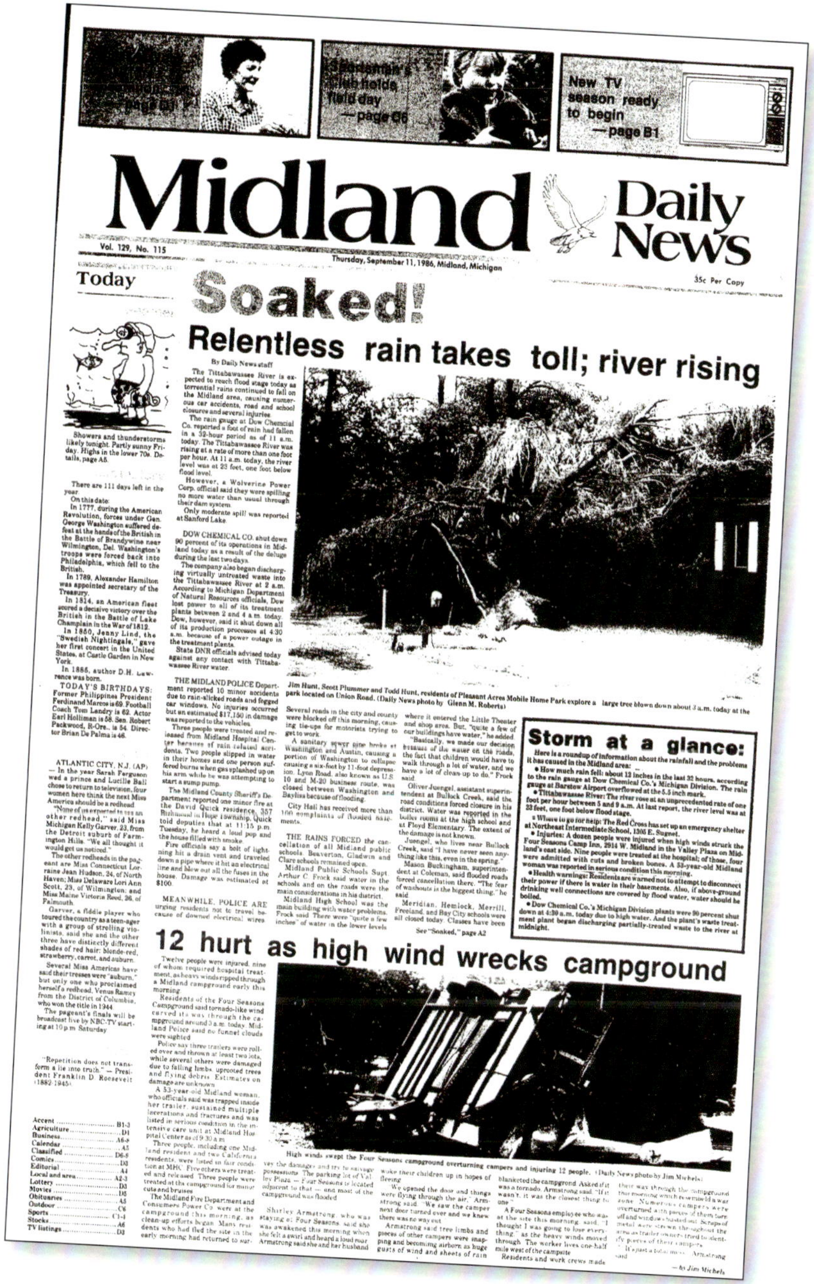

Sportsman's club holds field day —page C6

New TV season ready to begin —page B1

Midland Daily News

Vol. 129, No. 115

Thursday, September 11, 1986, Midland, Michigan

35¢ Per Copy

Today

Showers and thunderstorms likely tonight. Partly sunny Friday. Highs in the lower 70s. Details, page A5.

There are 111 days left in the year.

On this date:

In 1777, during the American Revolution, forces under Gen. George Washington suffered defeat at the hands of the British in the Battle of Brandywine near Wilmington, Del. Washington's troops were forced back into Philadelphia, which fell to the British.

In 1789, Alexander Hamilton was appointed secretary of the Treasury.

In 1814, an American fleet scored a decisive victory over the British in the Battle of Lake Champlain in the War of 1812.

In 1850, Jenny Lind, the "Swedish Nightingale," gave her first concert in the United States, at Castle Garden in New York.

In 1885, author D.H. Lawrence was born.

TODAY'S BIRTHDAYS: Former Philippines President Ferdinand Marcos is 69. Football Coach Tom Landry is 62. Actor Earl Holliman is 58. Sen. Robert Packwood, R-Ore., is 54. Director Brian De Palma is 46.

ATLANTIC CITY, N.J. (AP) — In the year Sarah Ferguson wed a prince and Lucille Ball chose to return to television, four women here think the next Miss America should be a redhead.

"None of us expected to see another redhead," said Miss Michigan Kelly Garver, 23, from the Detroit suburb of Farmington Hills. "We all thought it would get us noticed."

The other redheads in the pageant are Miss Connecticut Lorraine Jean Hudson, 24, of North Haven; Miss Delaware Lori Ann Scott, 23, of Wilmington; and Miss Maine Victoria Reed, 26, of Falmouth.

Garver, a fiddle player who toured the country as a teen-ager with a group of strolling violinists, said she and the other three have distinctly different shades of red hair: blonde-red, strawberry, carrot, and auburn.

Several Miss Americas have said their tresses were "auburn," but only one who proclaimed herself a redhead, Venus Ramey from the District of Columbia, who won the title in 1944.

The pageant's finals will be broadcast live by NBC-TV starting at 10 p.m. Saturday.

"Repetition does not transform a lie into truth." — President Franklin D. Roosevelt (1882-1945)

Soaked!

Relentless rain takes toll; river rising

By Daily News staff

The Tittabawassee River is expected to reach flood stage today as torrential rains continued to fall on the Midland area, causing numerous car accidents, road and school closures and several injuries.

The rain gauge at Dow Chemcial Co. reported a foot of rain had fallen in a 32-hour period as of 11 a.m. today. The Tittabawassee River was rising at a rate of more than one foot per hour. At 11 a.m. today, the river level was at 23 feet, one foot below flood level.

However, a Wolverine Power Corp. official said they were spilling no more water than usual through their dam system.

Only moderate spill was reported at Sanford Lake.

DOW CHEMICAL CO. shut down 90 percent of its operations in Midland today as a result of the deluge during the last two days.

The company also began discharging virtually untreated waste into the Tittabawassee River at 2 a.m. According to Michigan Department of Natural Resources officials, Dow lost power to all of its treatment plants between 2 and 4 a.m. today. Dow, however, said it shut down all of its production processes at 4:30 a.m. because of a power outage in the treatment plants.

State DNR officials advised today against any contact with Tittabawassee River water.

THE MIDLAND POLICE Department reported 10 minor accidents due to rain-slicked roads and fogged car windows. No injuries occurred but an estimated $17,150 in damage was reported to the vehicles.

Three people were treated and released from Midland Hospital Center because of rain-related accidents. Two people slipped in water in their homes and one person suffered burns when gas splashed up on his arm while he was attempting to start a sump pump.

The Midland County Sheriff's Department reported one minor fire at the David Quick residence, 357 Richmond in Hope township. Quick told deputies that at 11:15 p.m. Tuesday, he heard a loud pop and the house filled with smoke.

Fire officials say a bolt of lightning hit a drain vent and traveled down a pipe where it hit an electrical line and blew out all the fuses in the house. Damage was estimated at $100.

MEANWHILE, POLICE ARE urging residents not to travel because of downed electrical wires.

Jim Hunt, Scott Plummer and Todd Hunt, residents of Pleasant Acres Mobile Home Park explore a large tree blown down about 3 a.m. today at the park located on Union Road. (Daily News photo by Glenn M. Roberts)

Several roads in the city and county were blocked off this morning, causing tie-ups for motorists trying to get to work.

A sanitary sewer pipe broke at Washington and Austin, causing a portion of Washington to collapse causing a six-foot by 11-foot depression. Lyon Road, also known as U.S. 10 and M-20 business route, was closed between Washington and Bayliss because of flooding.

City Hall has received more than 100 complaints of flooded basements.

THE RAINS FORCED the cancellation of all Midland public schools. Beaverton, Gladwin and Clare schools remained open.

Midland Public Schools Supt. Arthur C. Frock said water in the schools and on the roads were the main considerations in his district.

Midland High School was the main building with water problems, Frock said. There were "quite a few inches" of water in the lower levels where it entered the Little Theater and shop area. But, "quite a few of our buildings have water," he added.

"Basically, we made our decision because of the water on the roads, the fact that children would have to walk through a lot of water, and we have a lot of clean-up to do," Frock said.

Oliver Juengel, assistant superintendent at Bullock Creek, said the road conditions forced closure in his district. Water was reported in the boiler rooms at the high school and at Floyd Elementary. The extent of the damage is not known.

Juengel, who lives near Bullock Creek, said "I have never seen anything like this, even in the spring."

Mason Buckingham, superintendent at Coleman, said flooded roads forced cancellation there. "The fear of washouts is the biggest thing," he said.

Meridian, Hemlock, Merrill, Freeland, and Bay City schools were all closed today. Classes have been

See "Soaked," page A2

Storm at a glance:

Here is a roundup of information about the rainfall and the problems it has caused in the Midland area:

- **How much rain fell:** about 12 inches in the last 32 hours, according to the rain gauge at Dow Chemical Co.'s Michigan Division. The rain gauge at Barstow Airport overflowed at the 5.5 inch mark.
- **Tittabawassee River:** The river rose at an unprecedented rate of one foot per hour between 5 and 9 a.m. At last report, the river level was at 23 feet, one foot below flood stage.
- **Where to go for help:** The Red Cross has set up an emergency shelter at Northeast Intermediate School, 1305 E. Sugnet.
- **Injuries:** A dozen people were injured when high winds struck the Four Seasons Camp Inn, 2914 W. Midland in the Valley Plaza on Midland's east side. Nine people were treated at the hospital; of those, four were admitted with cuts and broken bones. A 53-year-old Midland woman was reported in serious condition this morning.
- **Health warnings:** Residents are warned not to attempt to disconnect their power if there is water in their basements. Also, if above-ground drinking well connections are covered by flood water, water should be boiled.
- **Dow Chemical Co.'s Michigan Division plants** were 90 percent shut down at 4:30 a.m. today due to high water. And the plant's waste treatment plant began discharging partially-treated waste to the river at midnight.

12 hurt as high wind wrecks campground

Twelve people were injured, nine of whom required hospital treatment, as heavy winds ripped through a Midland campground early this morning.

Residents of the Four Seasons Campground said tornado-like wind carved its way through the campground around 3 a.m. today. Midland Police said no funnel clouds were sighted.

Police say three trailers were rolled over and thrown at least two lots, while several others were damaged due to falling limbs, uprooted trees and flying debris. Estimates on damage are unknown.

A 53-year-old Midland woman, who officials said was trapped inside her trailer, sustained multiple lacerations and fractures and was listed in serious condition in the intensive care unit at Midland Hospital Center as of 9:30 a.m.

Three people, including one Midland resident and two California residents, were listed in fair condition at MHC. Five others were treated and released. Three people were treated at the campground for minor cuts and bruises.

The Midland Fire Department and Consumers Power Co. were at the campground this morning, as clean-up efforts began. Many residents who had fled the site in the early morning had returned to survey the damages and try to salvage possessions. The parking lot of Valley Plaza — Four Seasons is located adjacent to that — and most of the campground was flooded.

High winds swept the Four Seasons campground overturning campers and injuring 12 people. (Daily News photo by Jim Michels)

Shirley Armstrong, who was staying at Four Seasons, said she was awakened this morning when she felt a swirl and heard a loud roar. Armstrong said she and her husband woke their children up in hopes of fleeing.

"We opened the door and things were flying through the air," Armstrong said. "We saw the camper next door turned over and we knew there was no way out."

Armstrong said tree limbs and pieces of other campers were snapping and becoming airborn as huge gusts of wind and sheets of rain blanketed the campgrond. Asked if it was a tornado, Armstrong said, "If it wasn't, it was the closest thing to one."

A Four Seasons employee who was at the site this morning, said, "I thought I was going to lose everything," as the heavy winds moved through. The worker lives one-half mile west of the campsite.

Residents and work crews made their way through the campground this morning which resembled a war zone. Numerous campers were overturned with pieces of them torn off and windows busted out. Scraps of metal were strewn throughout the area as trailer owners tried to identify pieces of their campers.

"It's just a total mess," Armstrong said.

— by Jim Michels

Midland Daily News reporting on the Tittabawassee River rising, Sept. 11, 1986. *Courtesy of Midland Daily News*

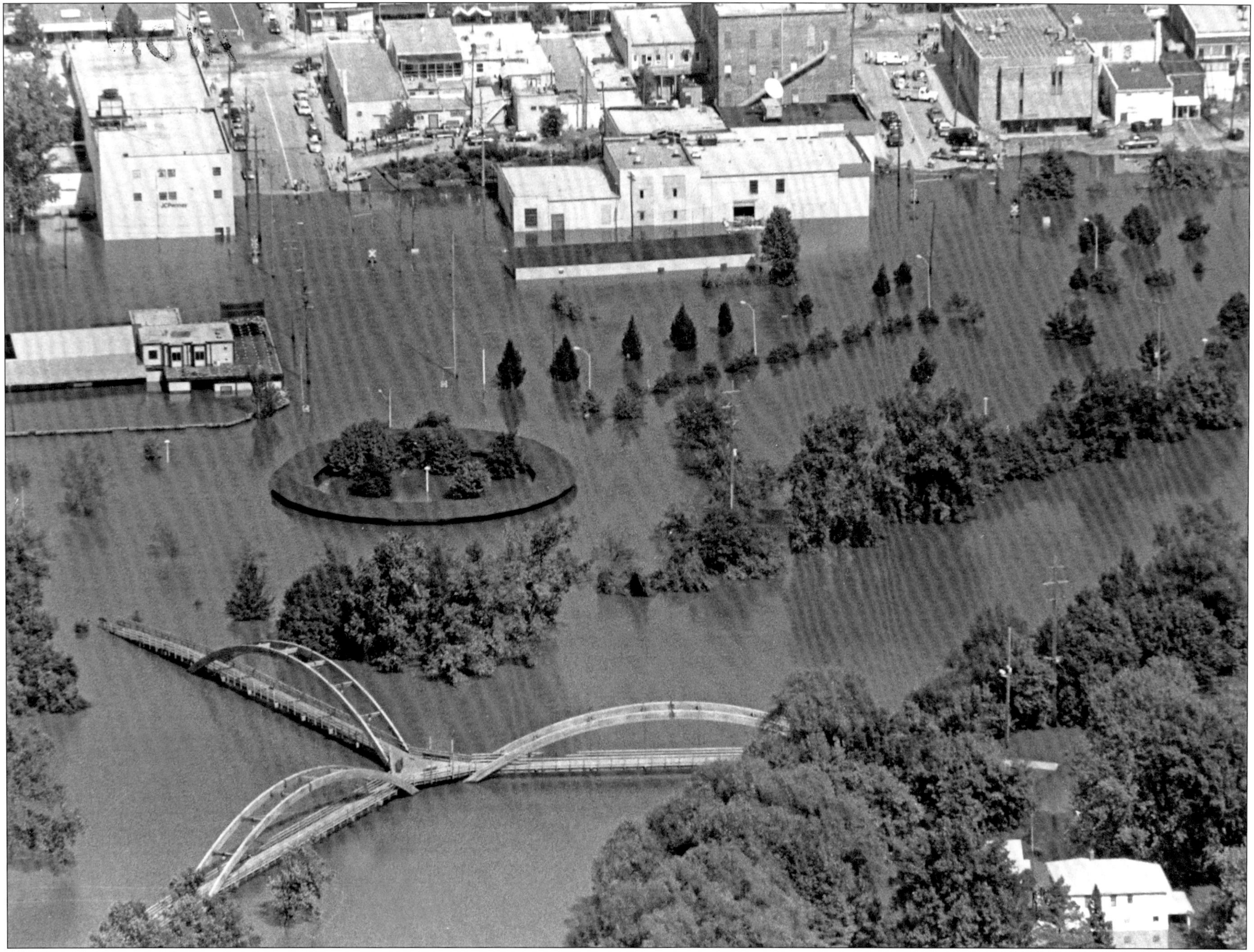

Flood in Midland, 1986. *Courtesy of Midland Daily News*

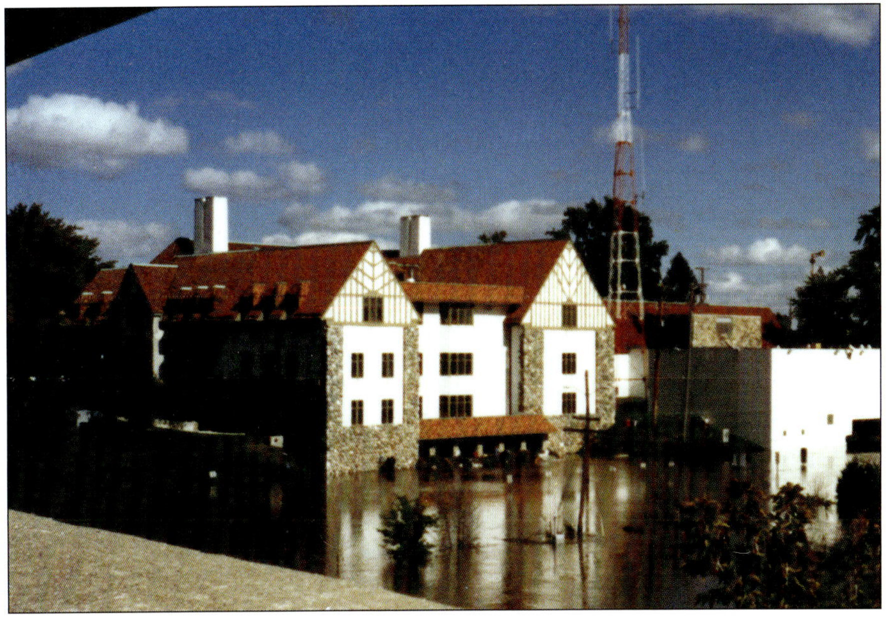

The courthouse on Sept. 13, 1986, in the aftermath of flooding downtown. *Courtesy of Connie Pound*

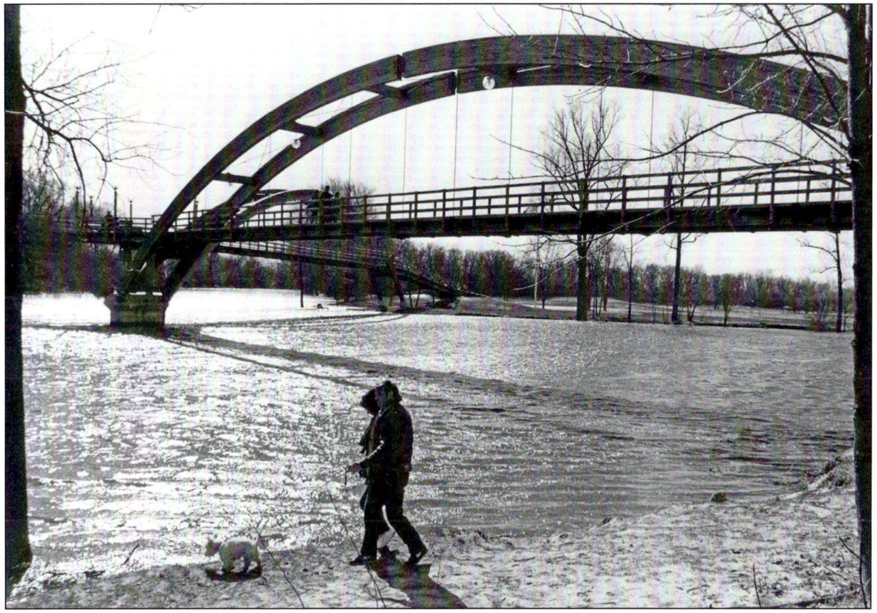

Bob and Marilyn DeNooyer taking their dog, Snuggles, for a walk along Tittabawassee River, March 24, 1986. *Courtesy of Midland Daily News*

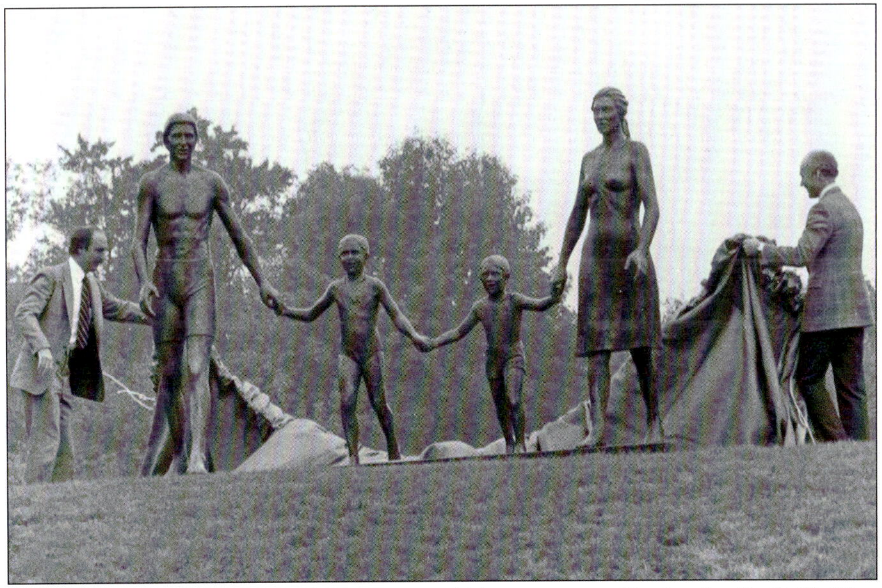

Unveiling of the bronze sculpture in Chippewassee Park, April 1987. The sculpture was created by art teacher Jim Hopfensperger and commissioned by the William R. Dixon Memorial Fund. *Courtesy of Midland Daily News*

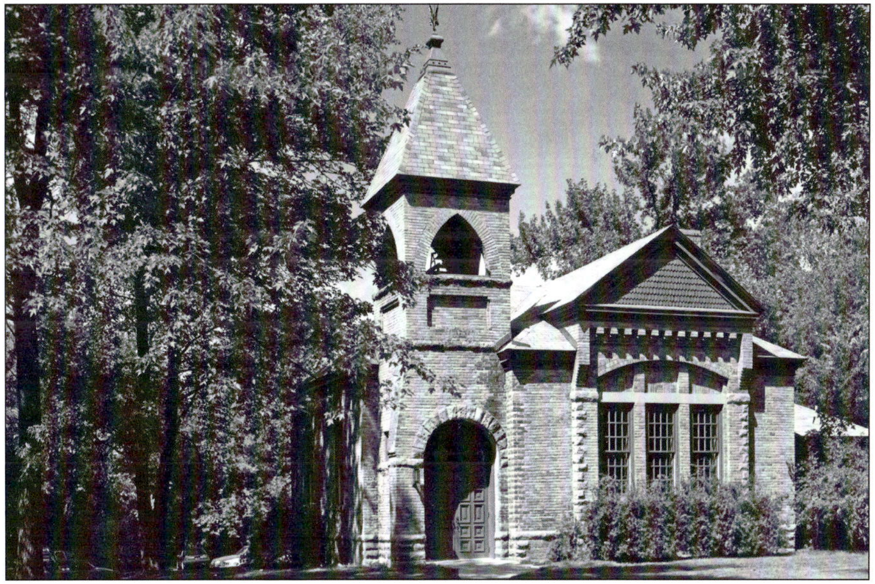

Post Street Archives, 1988. The building, built in 1888, was the Post Street School. Grace Ball was teaching at the school when she met H. H. Dow. They later married. *Courtesy of Midland County Historical Society*

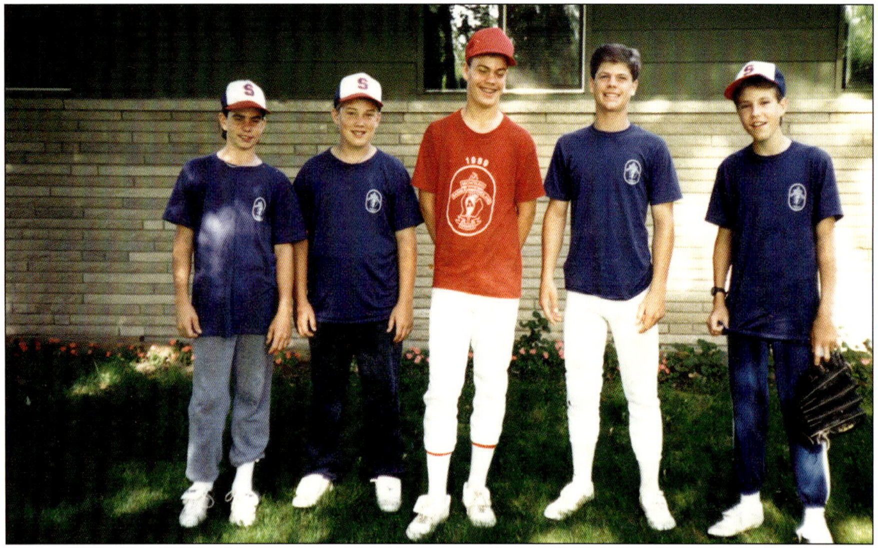

Players in the Michitario Games, 1989. Left to right: Dave Murray, Brian Watson, Sean Lindsay, Greg Armitage and Jason Smith. The four boys in blue shirts were from Sarnia, Ontario, and stayed at the Lindsay home as guests from Canada during the games. *Courtesy of William and Donna Lindsay*

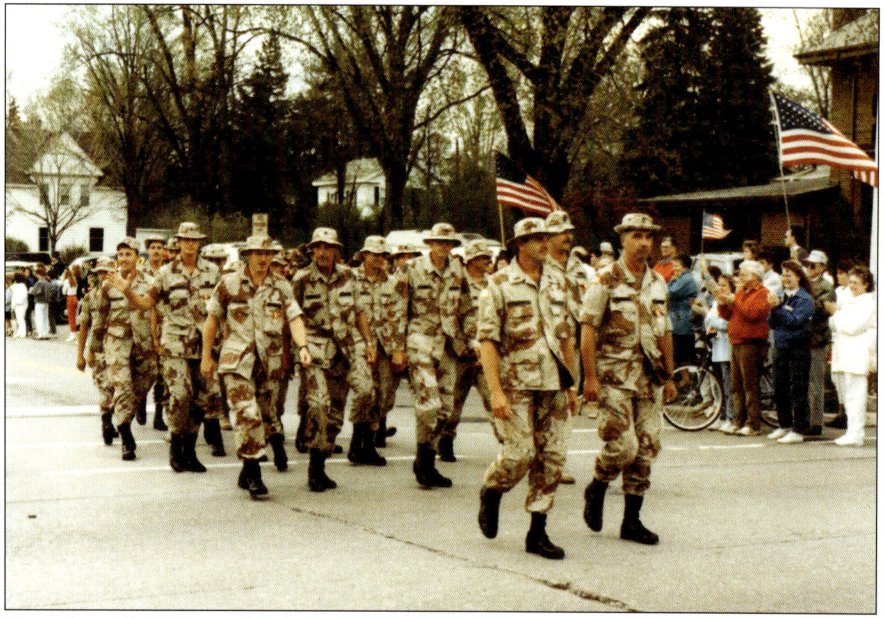

Parade of Michigan National Guard Midland Unit soldiers returning from Operation Desert Storm, 1991. *Courtesy of Midland County Historical Society*

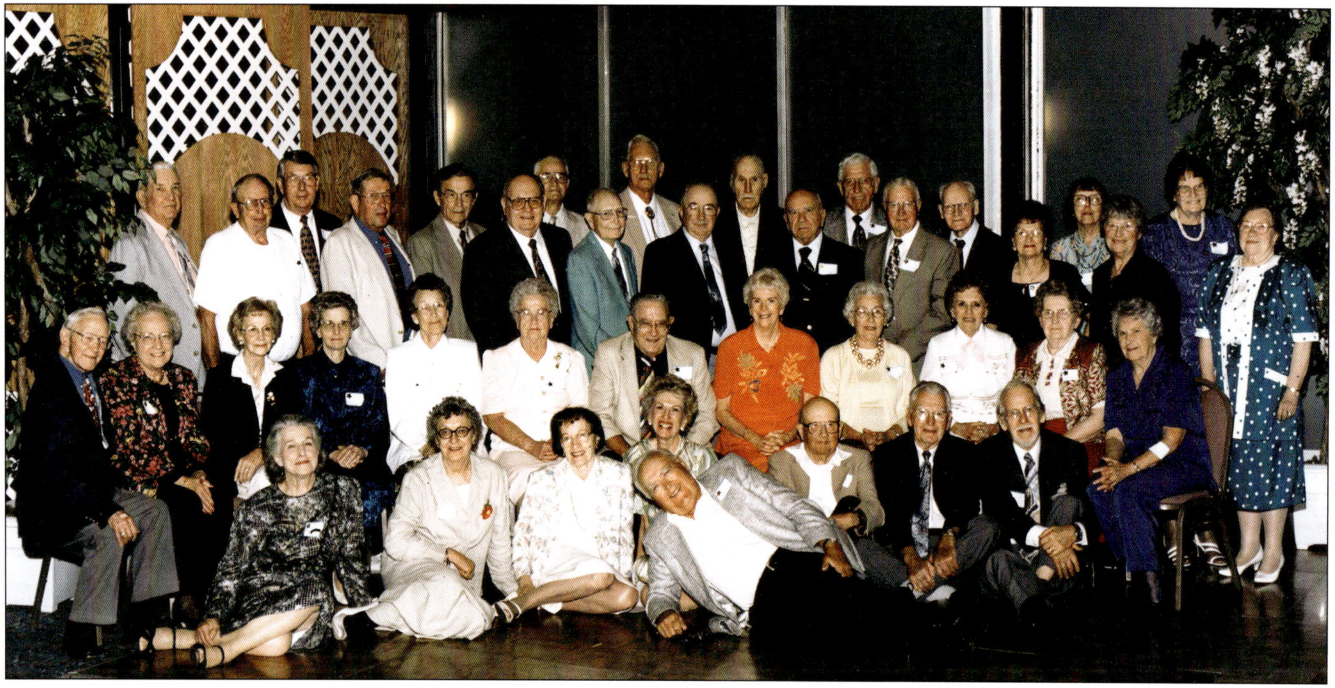

Fiftieth reunion of the Midland High School class of 1939.
Courtesy of Midland County Historical Society

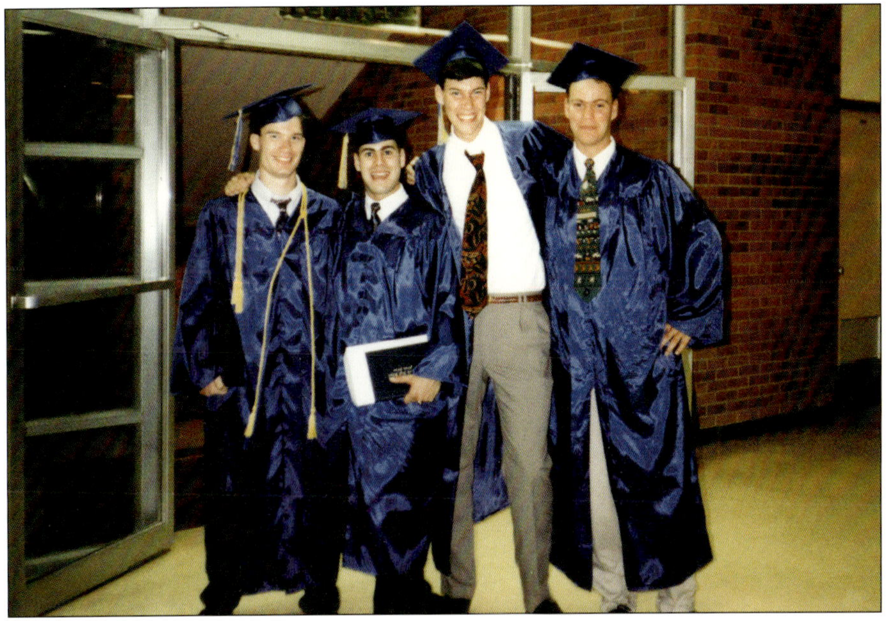

Midland High School graduation, 1993. Left to right: Joe Klesney, Eric Dean, Cory Deborsky and Sean Lindsay. *Courtesy of William and Donna Lindsay*

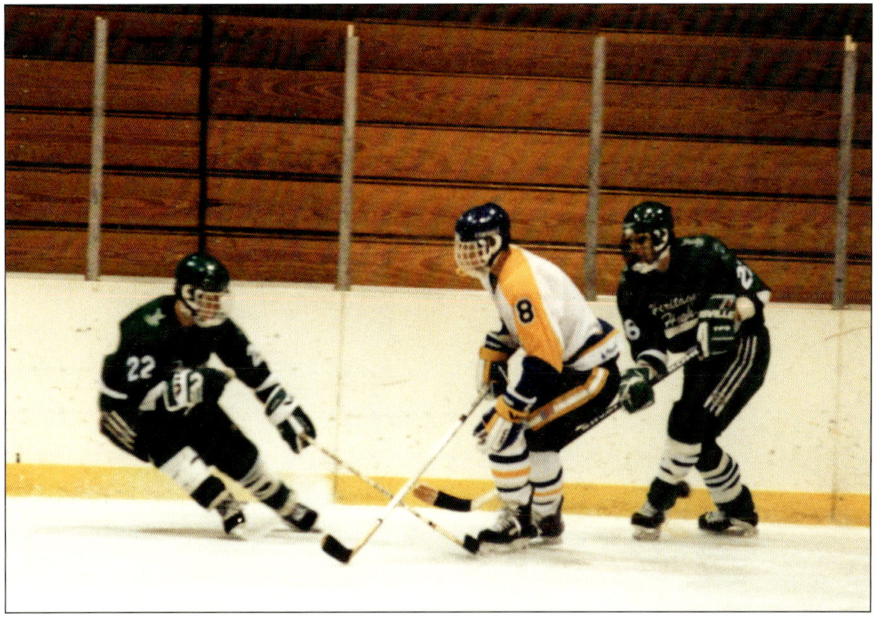

Sean Lindsay, center, playing in the Midland High School vs. Dow High School hockey game in the winter of 1993. *Courtesy of William and Donna Lindsay*

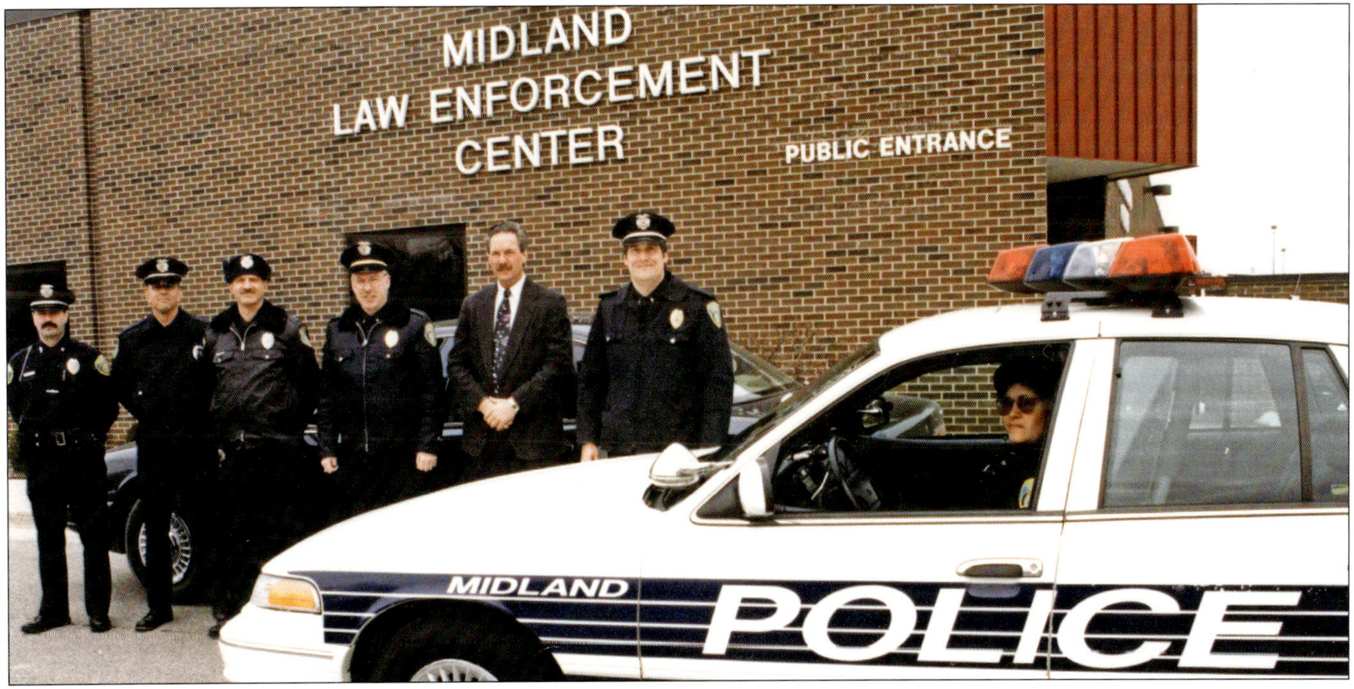

Midland policemen in front of the Law Enforcement Center, circa 1997.
Courtesy of Midland County Historical Society

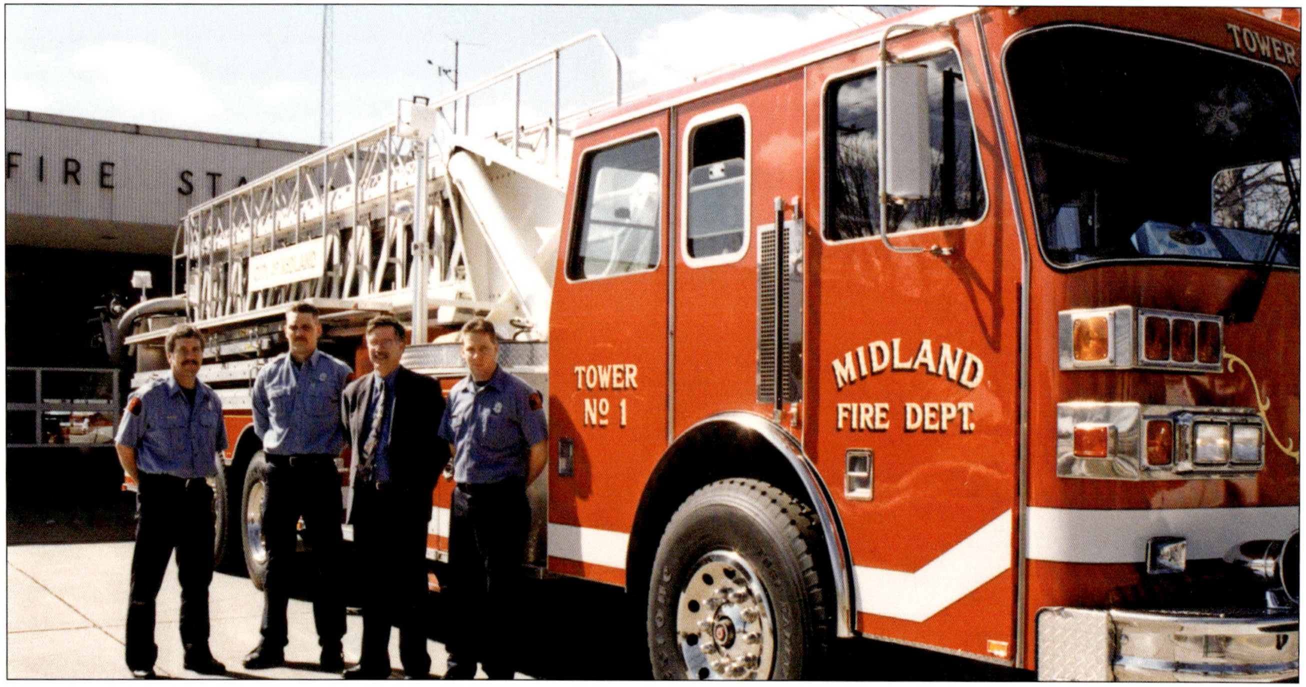

Midland firemen in front of Tower No. 1 truck, 1997: in-truck operator Michael Fletcher, firefighter Mark Kloha, fire chief Daniel Harsarten and firefighter Steven Makowski.

Courtesy of Midland County Historical Society

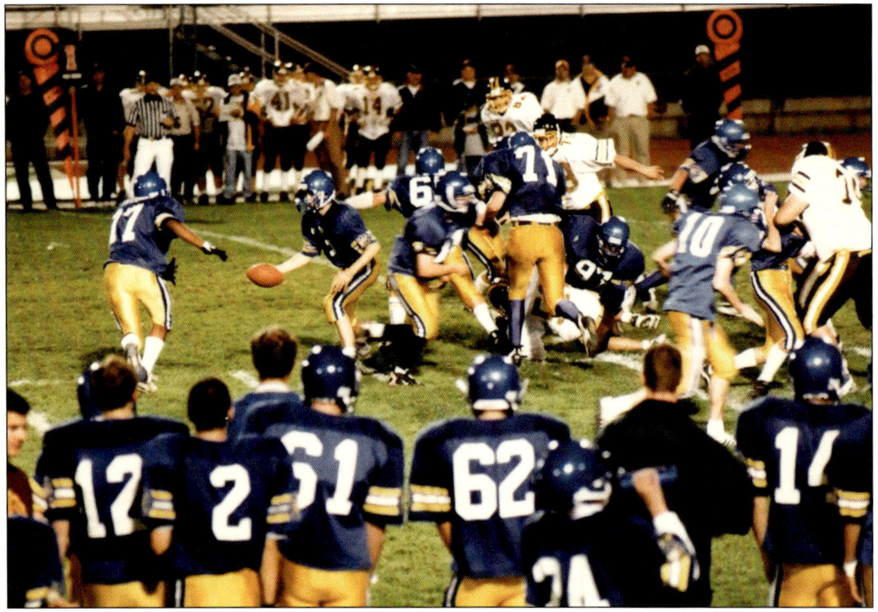

Midland High School football game, 1996.

Courtesy of Midland County Historical Society

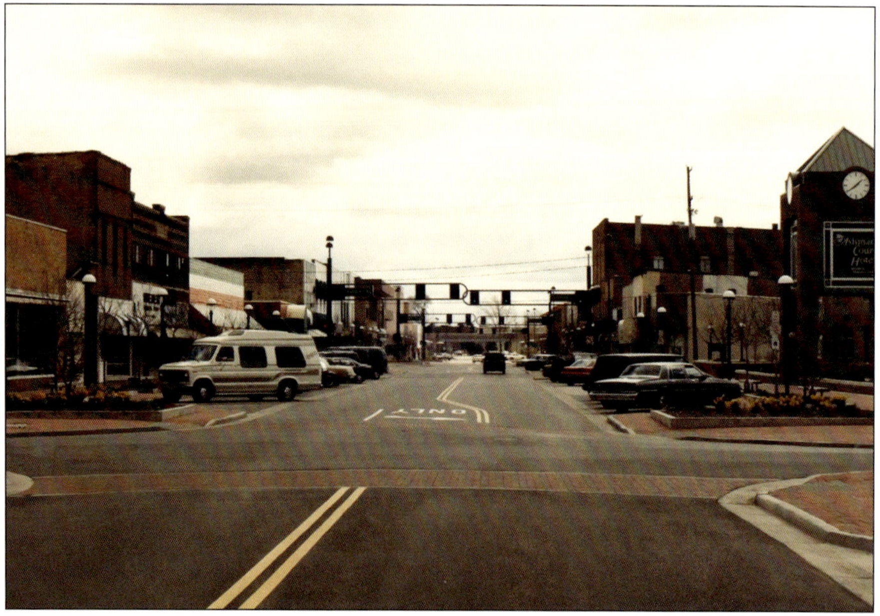

Main Street in Midland looking east from Gordon Street, circa 1995.

Courtesy of Midland County Historical Society

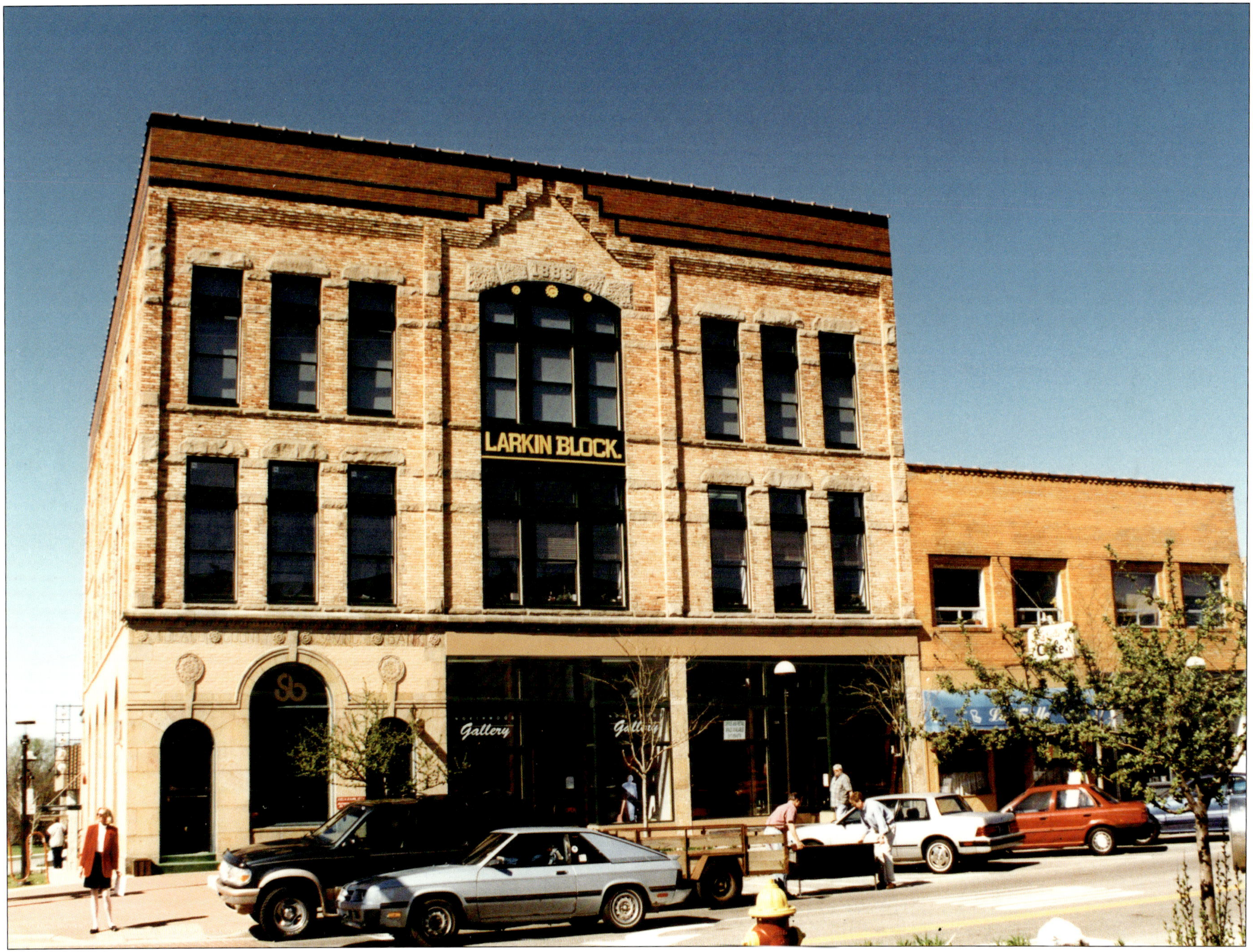

Larkin Block building on Main Street in Midland, 1997. *Courtesy of Midland County Historical Society*

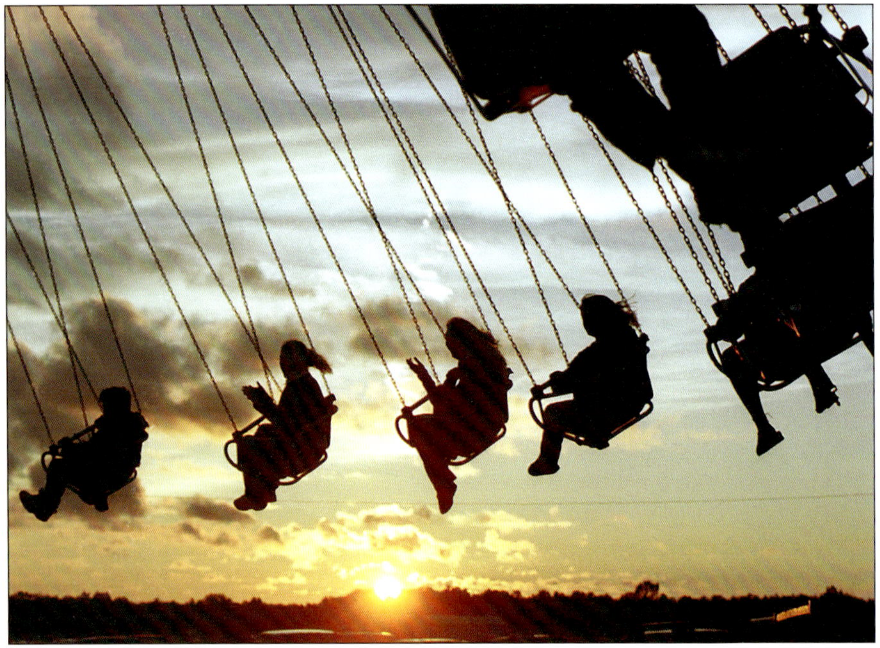

Carnival riders at the Midland County Fair, 1997. *Courtesy of Midland Daily News*

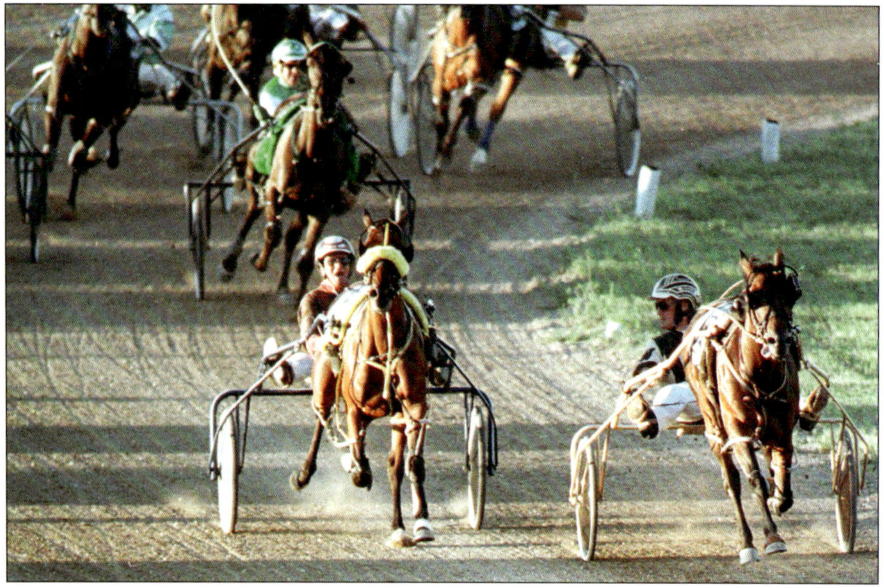

G I Jill, left, overtakes Brittster in the stretch run to win the spartan futurity two-year-old filly pace at the Midland County Fair, 1999. G I Jill, owned by Midland's Doak Stolz, was in ninth and last place for more than half of the race. *Courtesy of Midland Daily News*

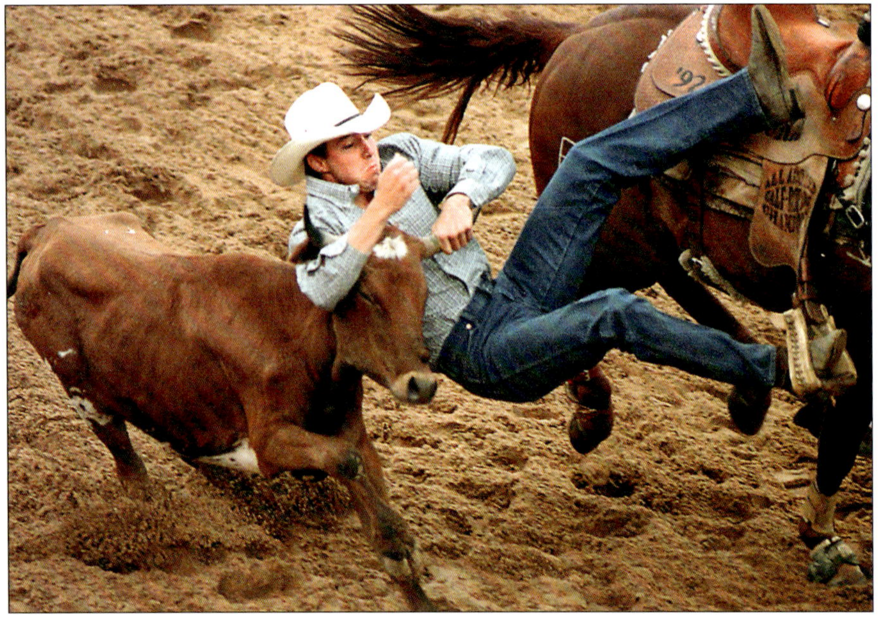

Jim Griffin of Lennon tries to subdue a steer during a rodeo at the Midland County Fair, 1997. *Courtesy of Midland Daily News*

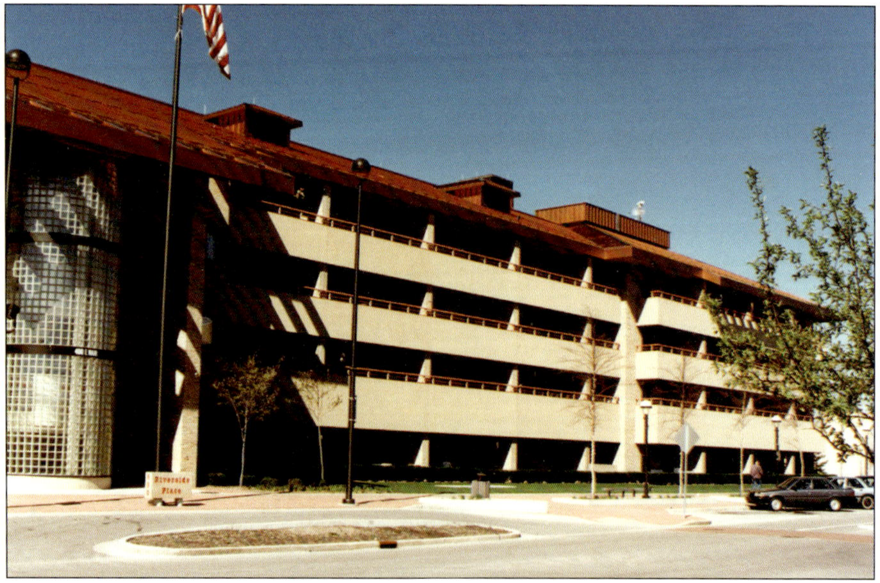

Riverside Place on Main Street, circa 1997.
Courtesy of Midland County Historical Society

A New Century

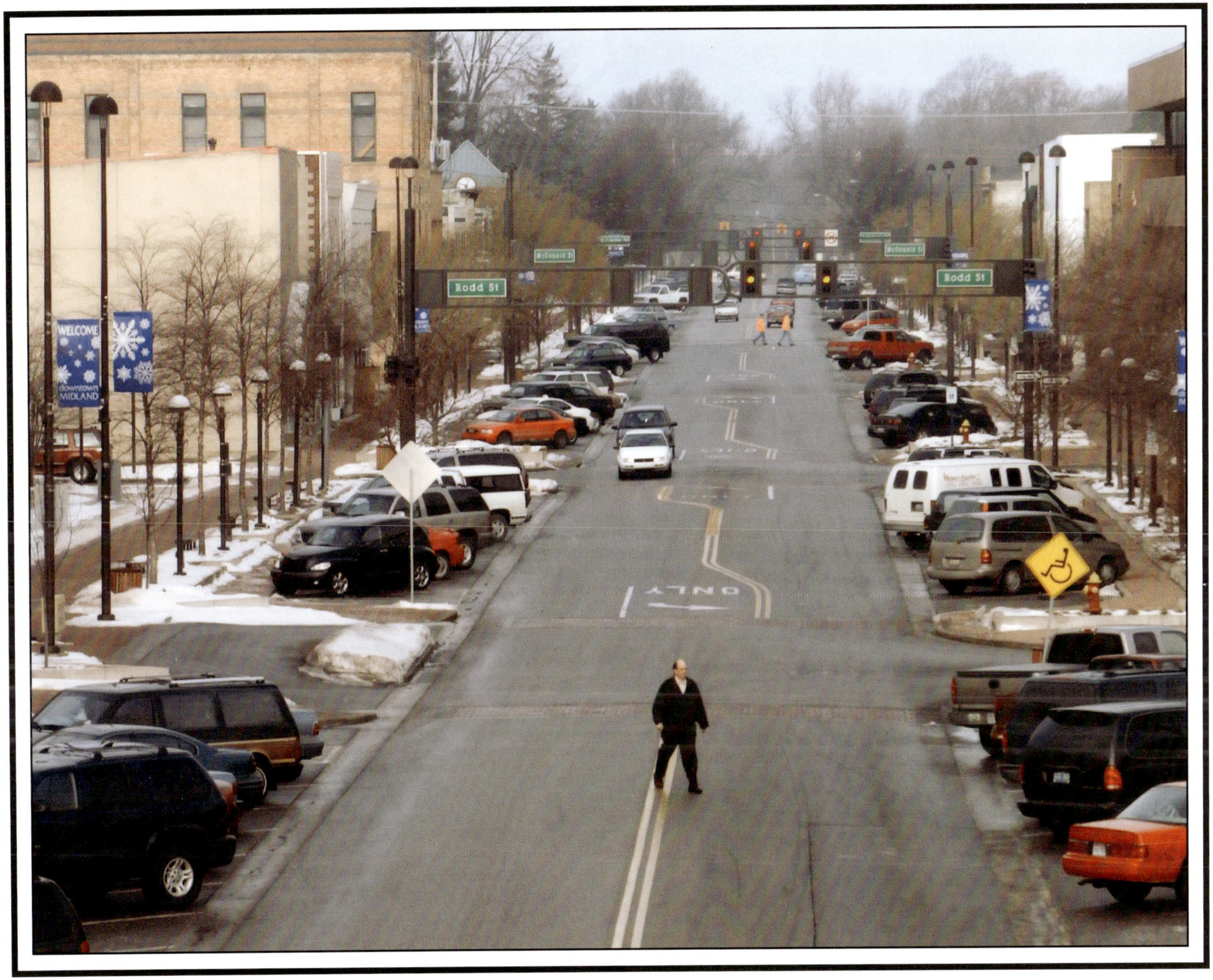

Downtown Midland looking northwest from the top of the Mark Putnam Bridge, February 2002.

Courtesy of Midland County Historical Society

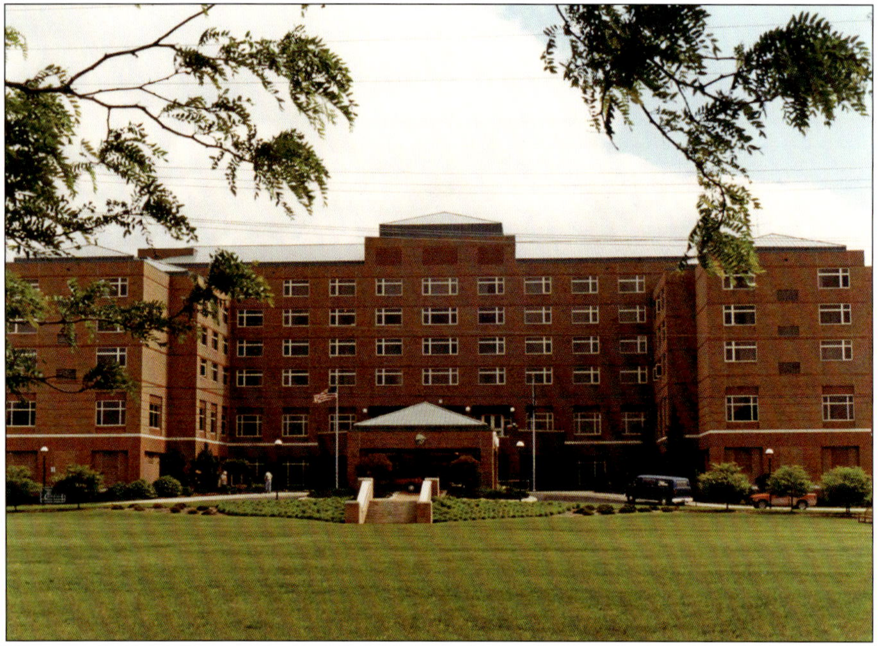

Ashman Court Hotel, 2000. *Courtesy of Midland County Historical Society*

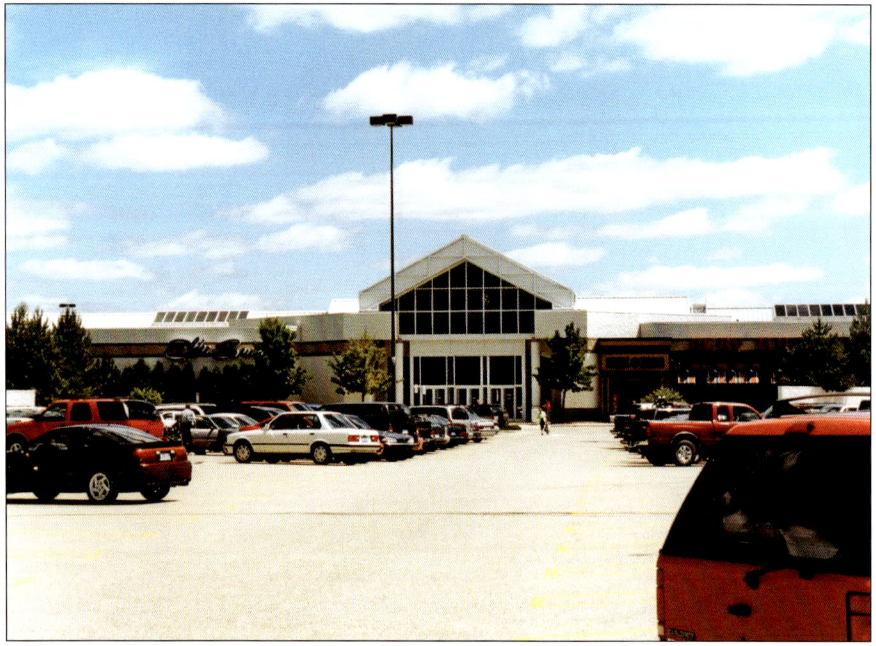

Midland Mall, 2000. *Courtesy of Midland County Historical Society*

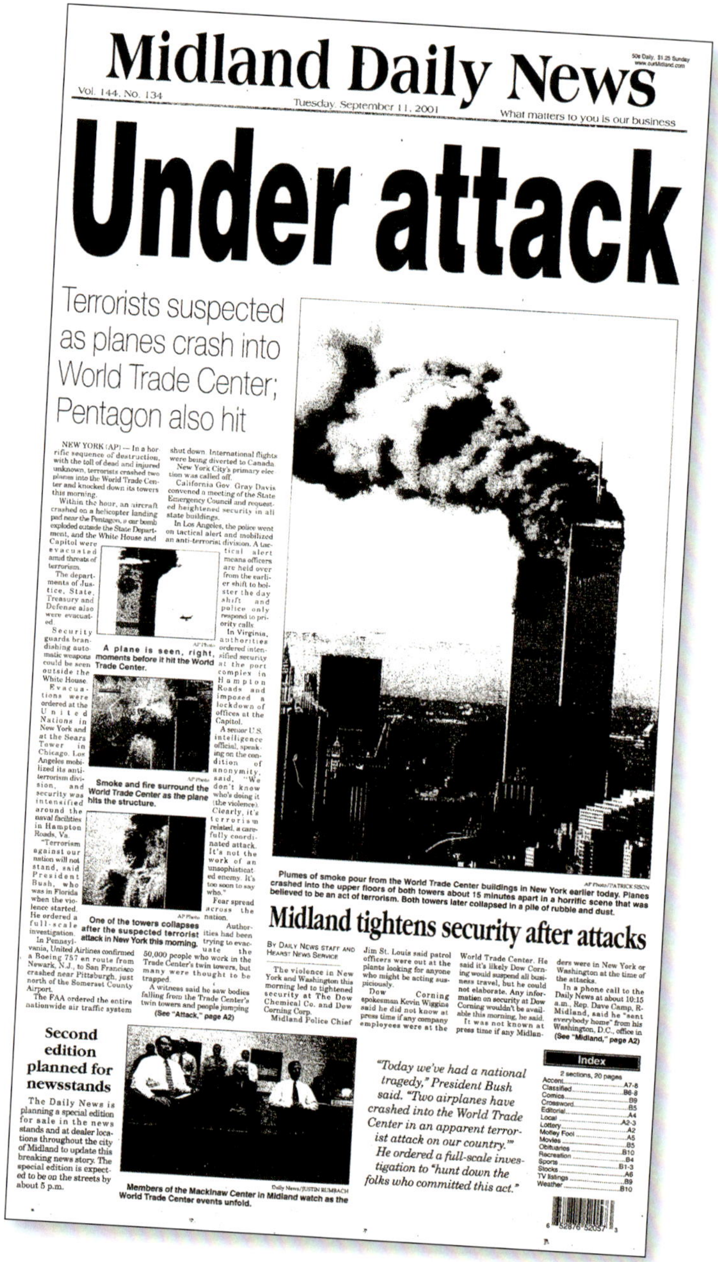

Midland Daily News

50¢ Daily, $1.25 Sunday
www.ourMidland.com

Vol. 144, No. 134 — Tuesday, September 11, 2001 — What matters to you is our business

Under attack

Terrorists suspected as planes crash into World Trade Center; Pentagon also hit

NEW YORK (AP) — In a horrific sequence of destruction, with the toll of dead and injured unknown, terrorists crashed two planes into the World Trade Center and knocked down its towers this morning.

Within the hour, an aircraft crashed on a helicopter landing pad near the Pentagon, a car bomb exploded outside the State Department, and the White House and Capitol were evacuated amid threats of terrorism.

The departments of Justice, State, Treasury and Defense also were evacuated.

Security guards brandishing automatic weapons could be seen outside the White House.

Evacuations were ordered at the United Nations in New York and at the Sears Tower in Chicago. Los Angeles mobilized its anti-terrorism division, and security was intensified around the naval facilities in Hampton Roads, Va.

"Terrorism against our nation will not stand, said President Bush, who was in Florida when the violence started. He ordered a full-scale investigation.

In Pennsylvania, United Airlines confirmed a Boeing 757 en route from Newark, N.J., to San Francisco crashed near Pittsburgh, just north of the Somerset County Airport.

The FAA ordered the entire nationwide air traffic system shut down. International flights were being diverted to Canada.

New York City's primary election was called off.

California Gov. Gray Davis convened a meeting of the State Emergency Council and requested heightened security in all state buildings.

In Los Angeles, the police went on tactical alert and mobilized an anti-terrorist division. A tactical alert means officers are held over from the earlier shift to bolster the day shift and police only respond to priority calls.

In Virginia, authorities ordered intensified security at the port complex in Hampton Roads and imposed a lockdown of offices at the Capitol.

A senior U.S. intelligence official, speaking on the condition of anonymity, said, "We don't know who's doing it (the violence). Clearly, it's terrorism related, a carefully coordinated attack. It's not the work of an unsophisticated enemy. It's too soon to say who."

Fear spread across the nation.

Authorities had been trying to evacuate the 50,000 people who work in the Trade Center's twin towers, but many were thought to be trapped.

A witness said he saw bodies falling from the Trade Center's twin towers and people jumping

(See "Attack," page A2)

AP Photo

A plane is seen, right, moments before it hit the World Trade Center.

AP Photo

Smoke and fire surround the World Trade Center as the plane hits the structure.

AP Photo

One of the towers collapses after the suspected terrorist attack in New York this morning.

AP Photo/PATRICK SISON

Plumes of smoke pour from the World Trade Center buildings in New York earlier today. Planes crashed into the upper floors of both towers about 15 minutes apart in a horrific scene that was believed to be an act of terrorism. Both towers later collapsed in a pile of rubble and dust.

Midland tightens security after attacks

By Daily News staff and Hearst News Service

The violence in New York and Washington this morning led to tightened security at The Dow Chemical Co. and Dow Corning Corp.

Midland Police Chief Jim St. Louis said patrol officers were out at the plants looking for anyone who might be acting suspiciously.

Dow Corning spokesman Kevin Wiggins said he did not know at press time if any company employees were at the World Trade Center. He said it's likely Dow Corning would suspend all business travel, but he could not elaborate. Any information on security at Dow Corning wouldn't be available this morning, he said.

It was not known at press time if any Midlanders were in New York or Washington at the time of the attacks.

In a phone call to the Daily News at about 10:15 a.m., Rep. Dave Camp, R-Midland, said he "sent everybody home" from his Washington, D.C., office in

(See "Midland," page A2)

Second edition planned for newsstands

The Daily News is planning a special edition for sale in the news stands and at dealer locations throughout the city of Midland to update this breaking news story. The special edition is expected to be on the streets by about 5 p.m.

Daily News/JUSTIN RUMBACH

Members of the Mackinaw Center in Midland watch as the World Trade Center events unfold.

"Today we've had a national tragedy," President Bush said. "Two airplanes have crashed into the World Trade Center in an apparent terrorist attack on our country." He ordered a full-scale investigation to "hunt down the folks who committed this act."

Index

2 sections, 20 pages

6 52876 52057 3

Midland Daily News reports the terrorist attacks on the World Trade Center and Pentagon, Sept. 11, 2001. *Courtesy of Midland Daily News*

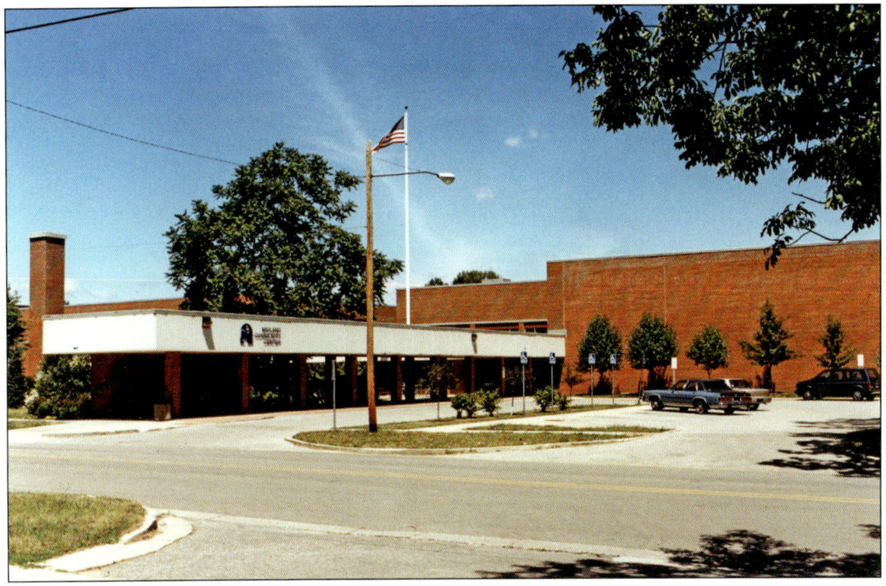

Midland Community Center, 2000. The Center opened Sept. 6, 1955, with The Dow Chemical Company funding the $1.5 million project.
Courtesy of Midland County Historical Society

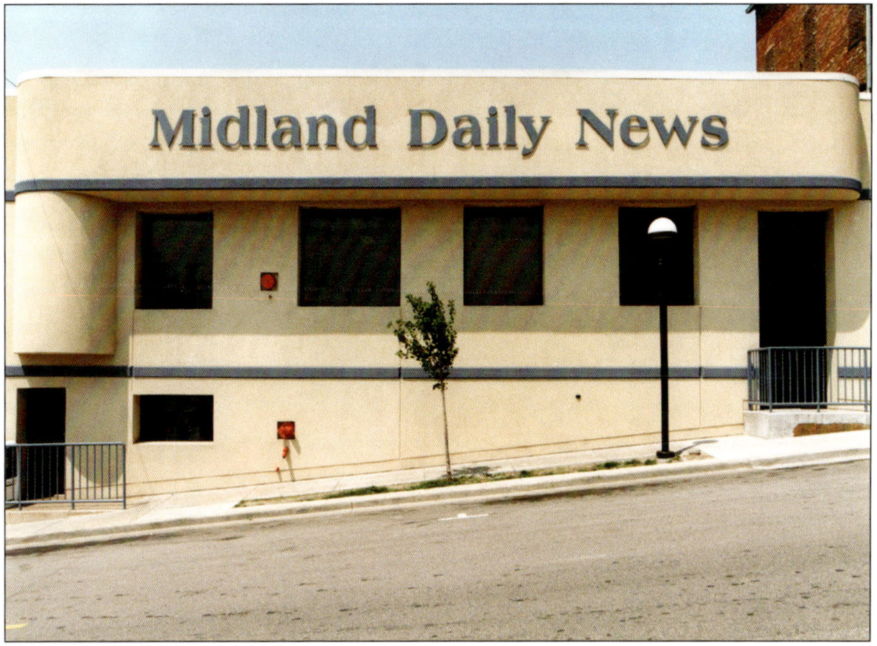

Midland Daily News building, 2002. *Courtesy of Midland Daily News*

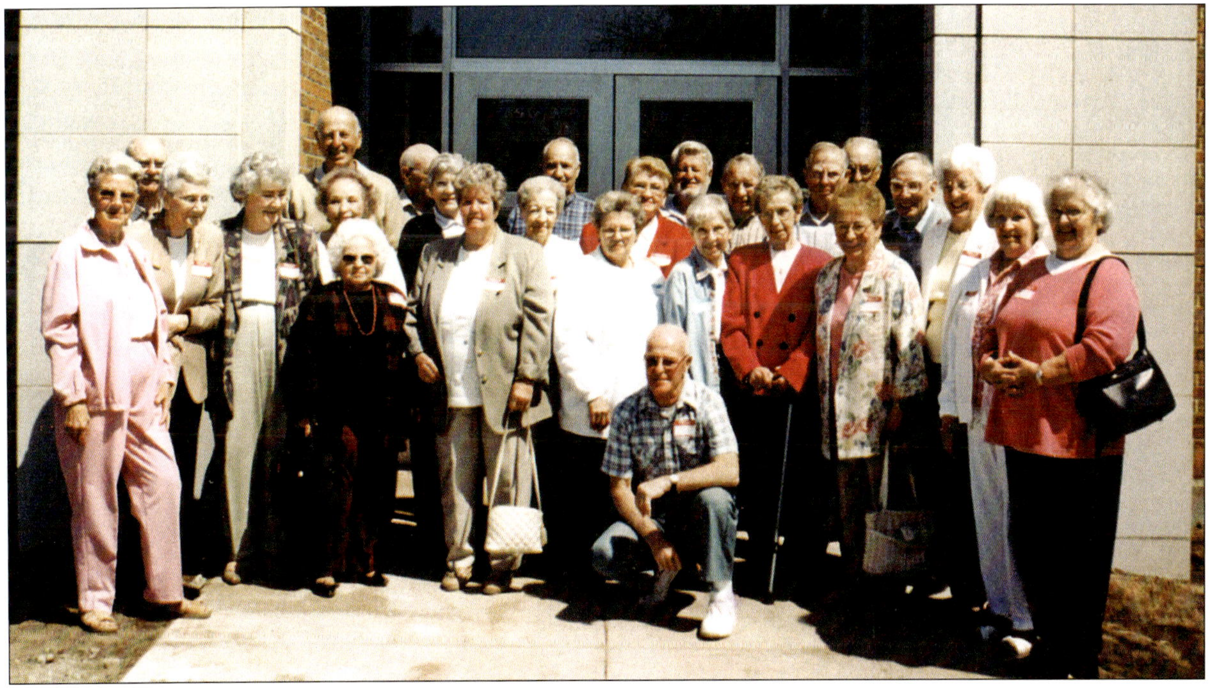

Former students and spouses celebrating the seventieth anniversary of Bullock Creek School in Homer Township, 2002. Kneeling in the front is Bob Moe. Second row, left to right: Ruby Woods, Mildred Moe, Joyce Hagle, Jackie Tisdale, Clara Moe Penny, Betty Burch Titus, Geraldine Buckey Smokoska and Lillian Buckey Richardson. Third row: Elaine Varner Kastl, Mary Hlavacek Allen, Naaomi Crawford Neuman, Phyliss Price Kuchek, Mrs. Melvin VanMeter, Mrs. Donald Bloomfield, Goldie Gyory Spann, Ed Penny, Mike Hagle, Nelson Tisdale and Betty Sweebe Jacobs. Fourth row: Leonard Kuchek, Melvin VanMeter, Donald Bloomfield, Kenneth Neirholzer and James Fisher.
Courtesy of Midland County Historical Society

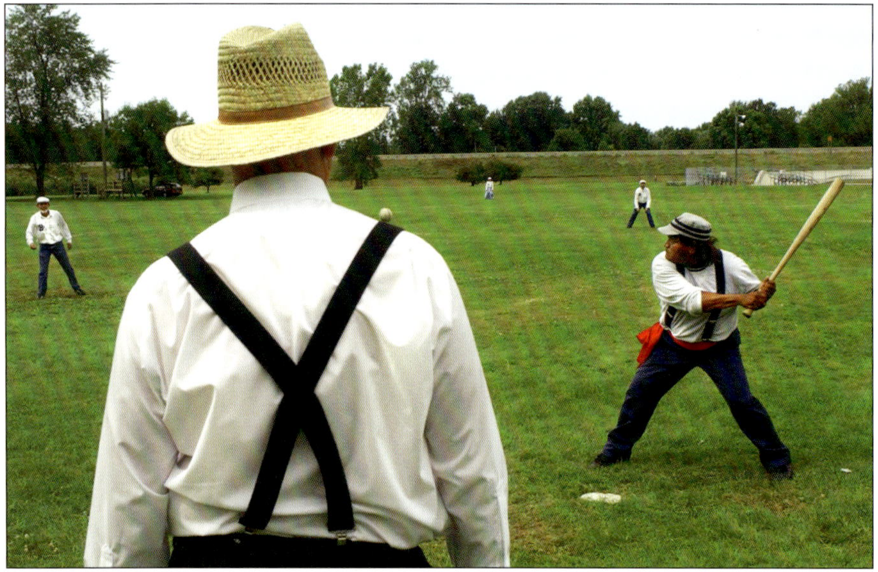

Umpire Dennis Wolf watches Midland player Steven "Geronimo" Rocha swing at Ray Pritchett's pitch in a vintage baseball game between the Mighty River Hogs of Midland County and the House of David of Benton Harbor at Chippewassee Park, 2002. The "gentleman's" game is played by 1861 rules which means no gloves, no sliding and no spitting or swearing. *Courtesy of Midland Daily News*

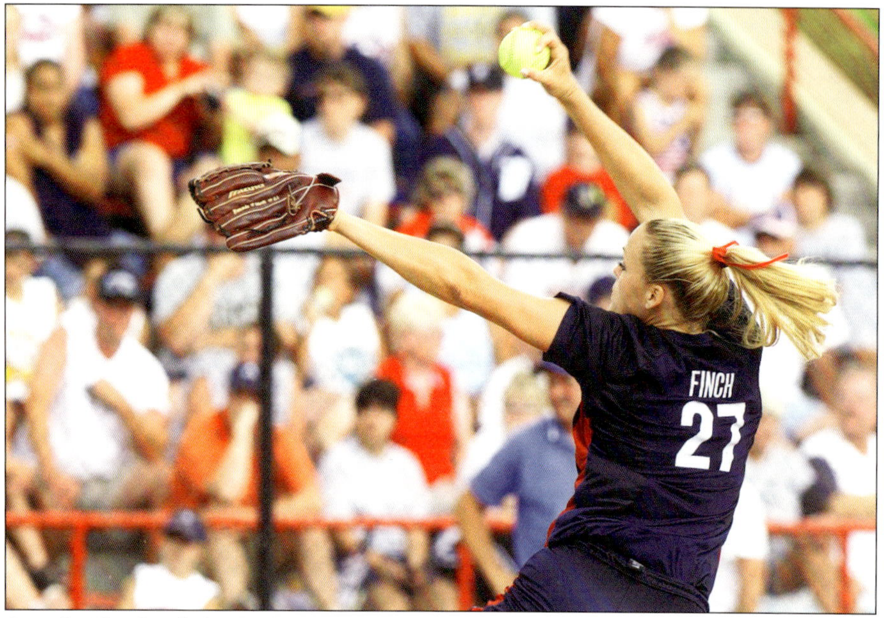

Jennie Finch of the U.S.A. Olympic Women's Softball team pitches against the Lady Explorers, 2003. *Courtesy of Midland Daily News*

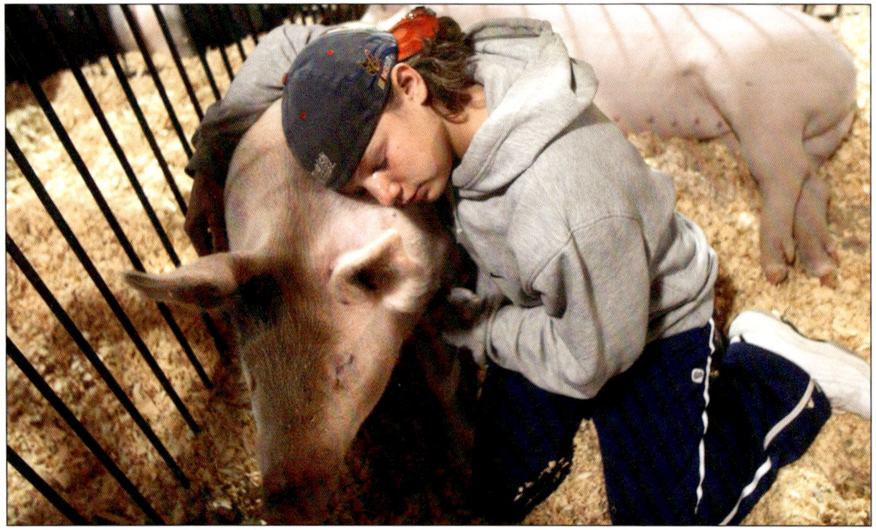

Lyndsey Beaubien, 14-year-old 4-H member, says goodbye to her pig, Smyes, during the Midland County Fair, 2004. *Courtesy of Midland Daily News*

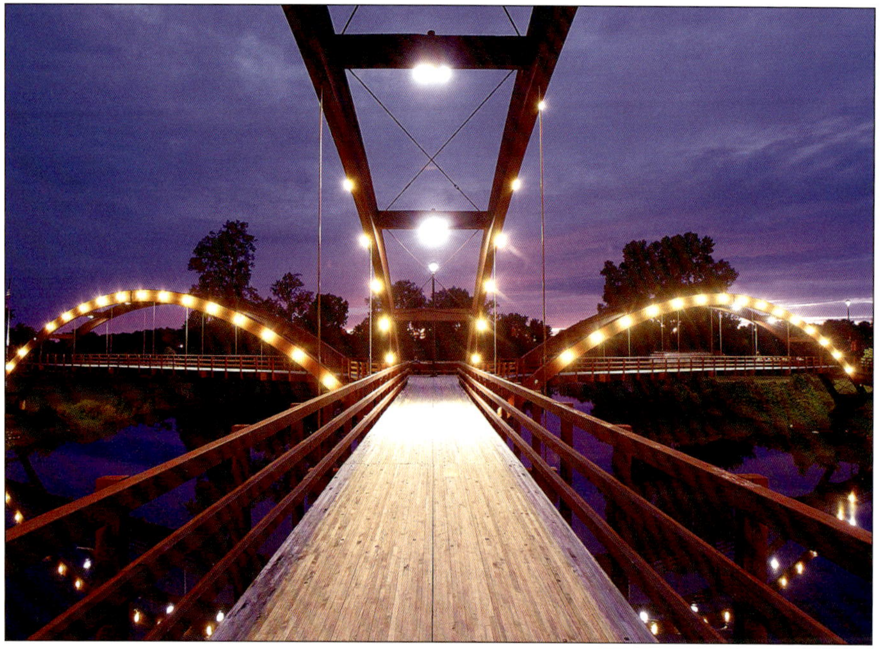

The Tridge, 2003. *Courtesy of Midland Daily News*

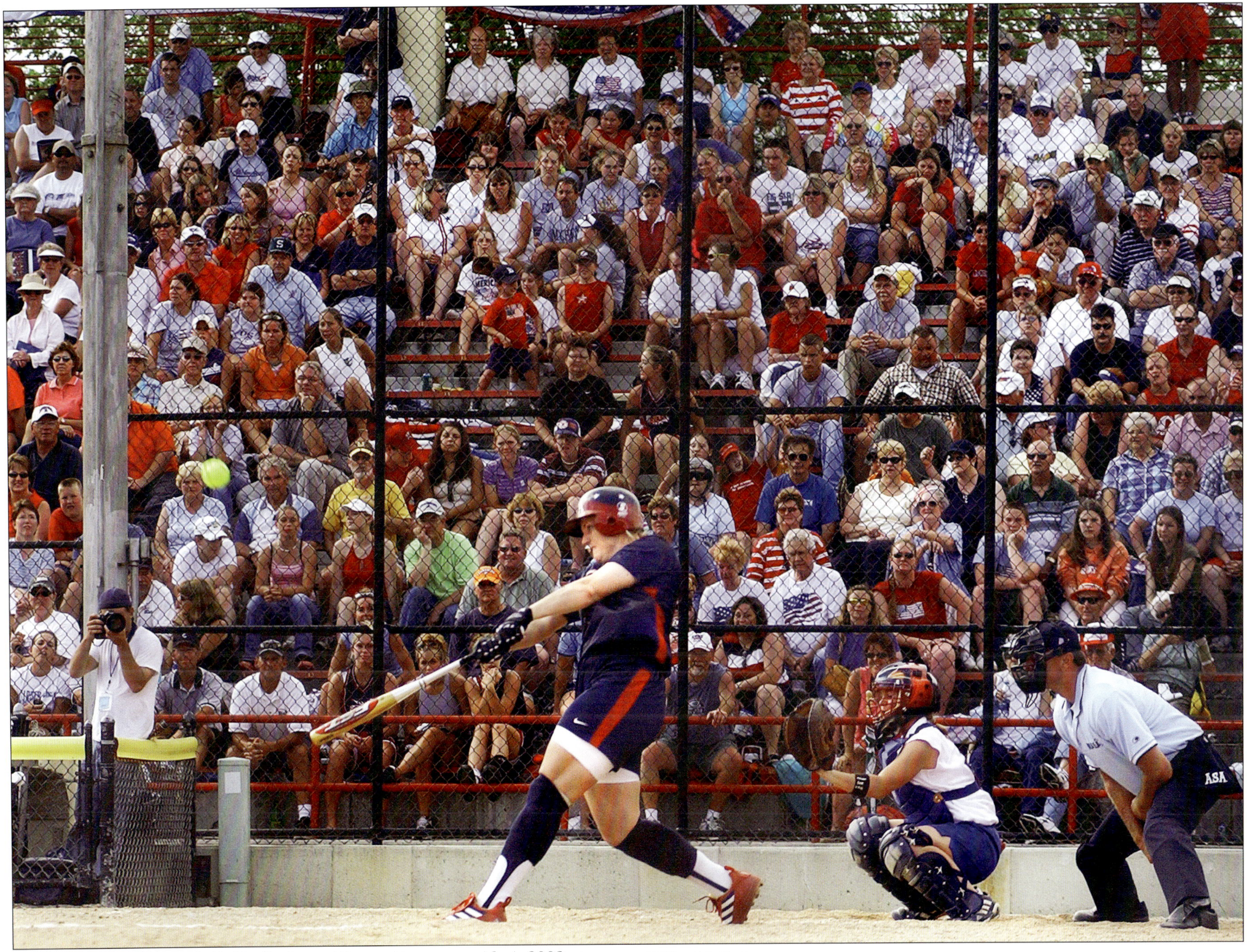

U.S.A. Olympic Women's Softball player Stacey Nuveman at bat, 2003. *Courtesy of Midland Daily News*

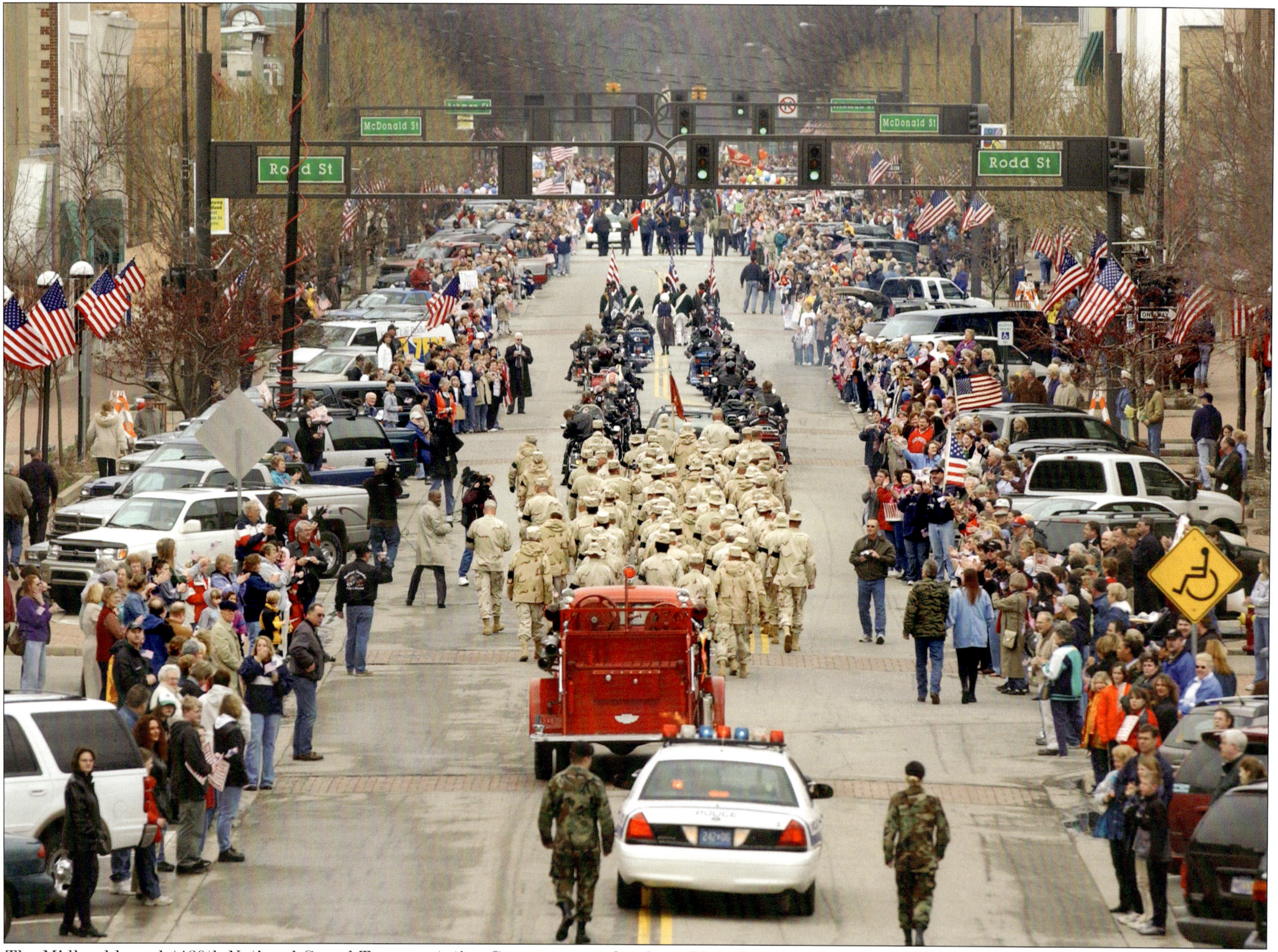

The Midland-based 1460th National Guard Transportation Company parades down Main Street in downtown Midland, 2004. The company returned after serving 14 months on deployment. *Courtesy of Midland Daily News*

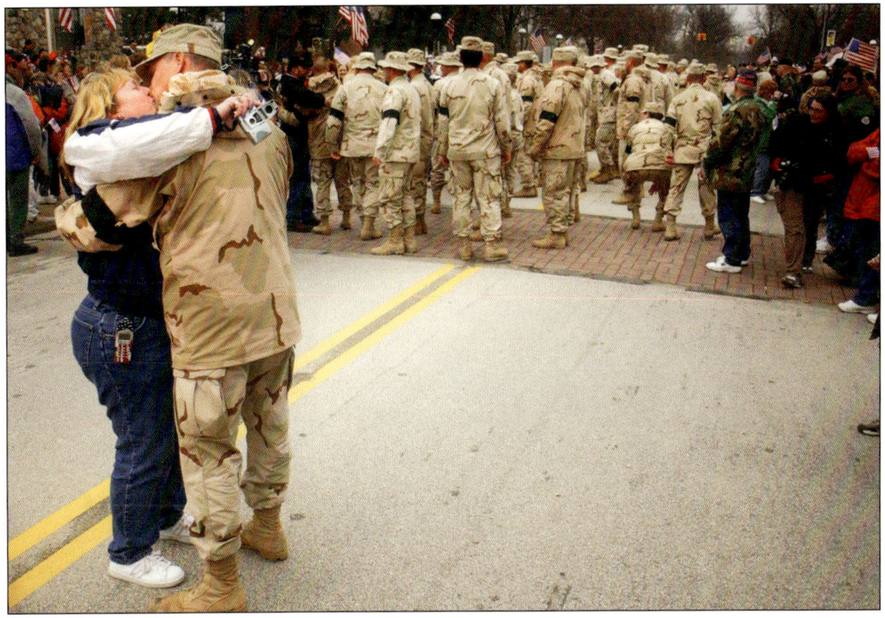

Cindy Asakevich of Rhodes gives her husband, Greg, a kiss after running out onto Main Street during the parade welcoming home the Midland-based 1460th National Guard Transportation Company, April 2004.

Courtesy of Midland Daily News

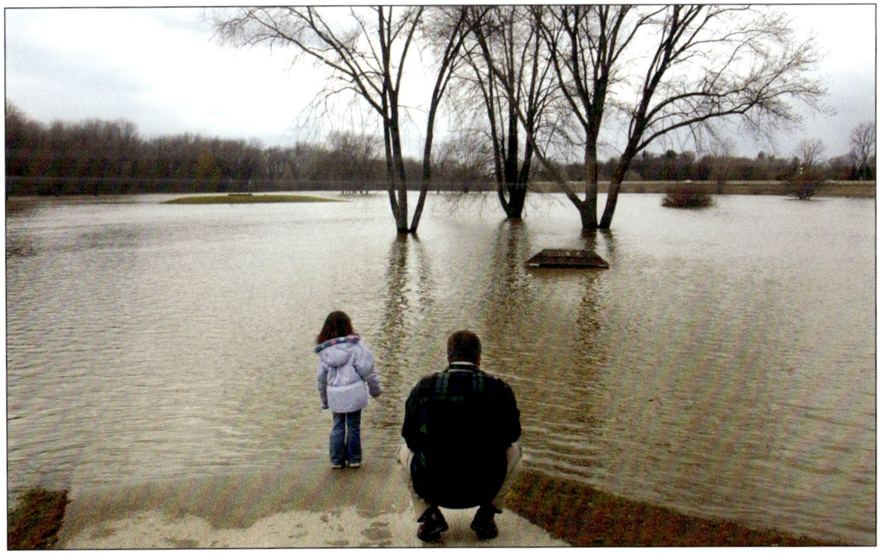

Emily Rice, 5, and Dave Rice look at the Chippewassee Park flood, 2004.

Courtesy of Midland Daily News

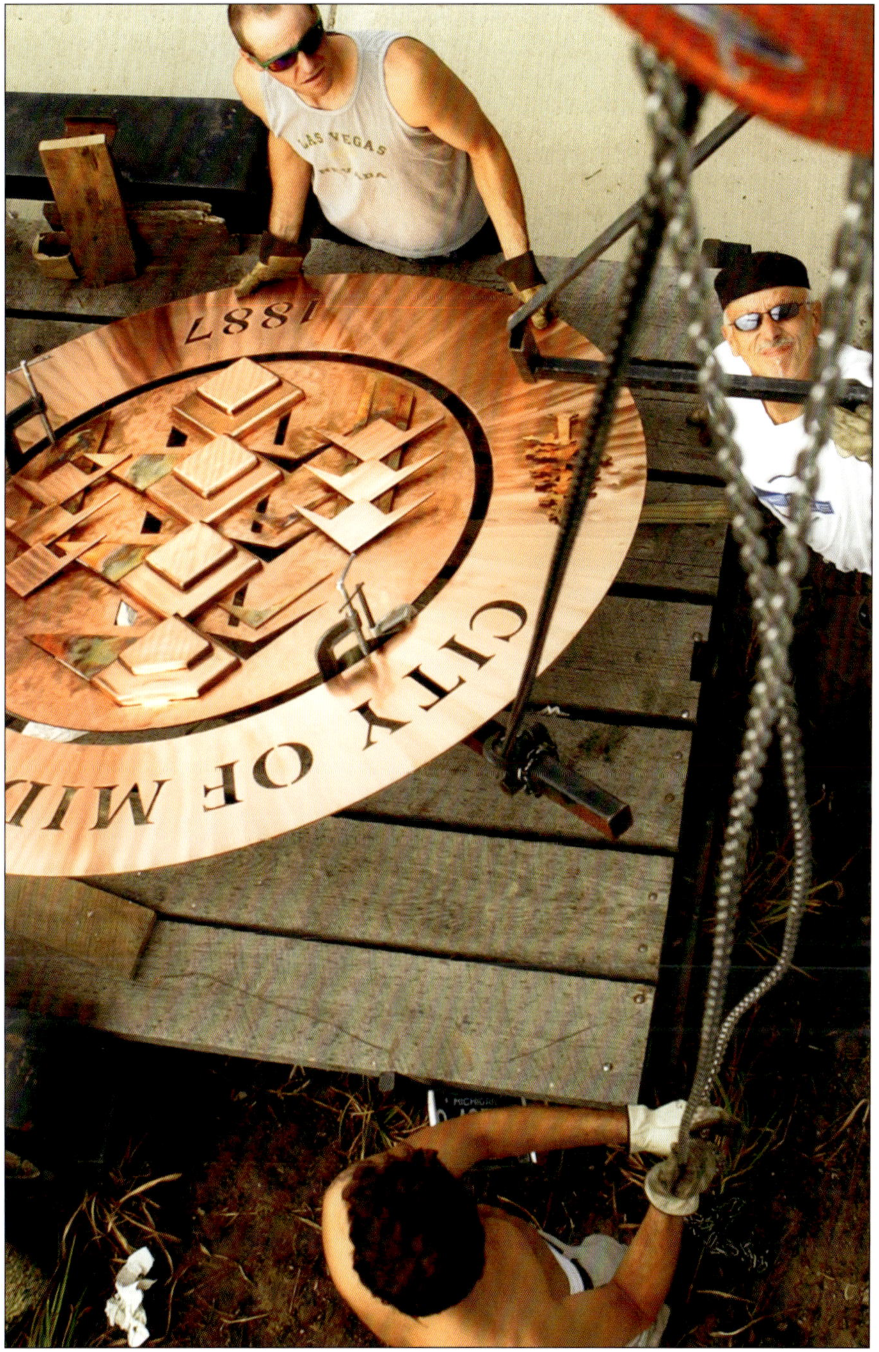

City emblem, 2004. *Courtesy of Midland Daily News*

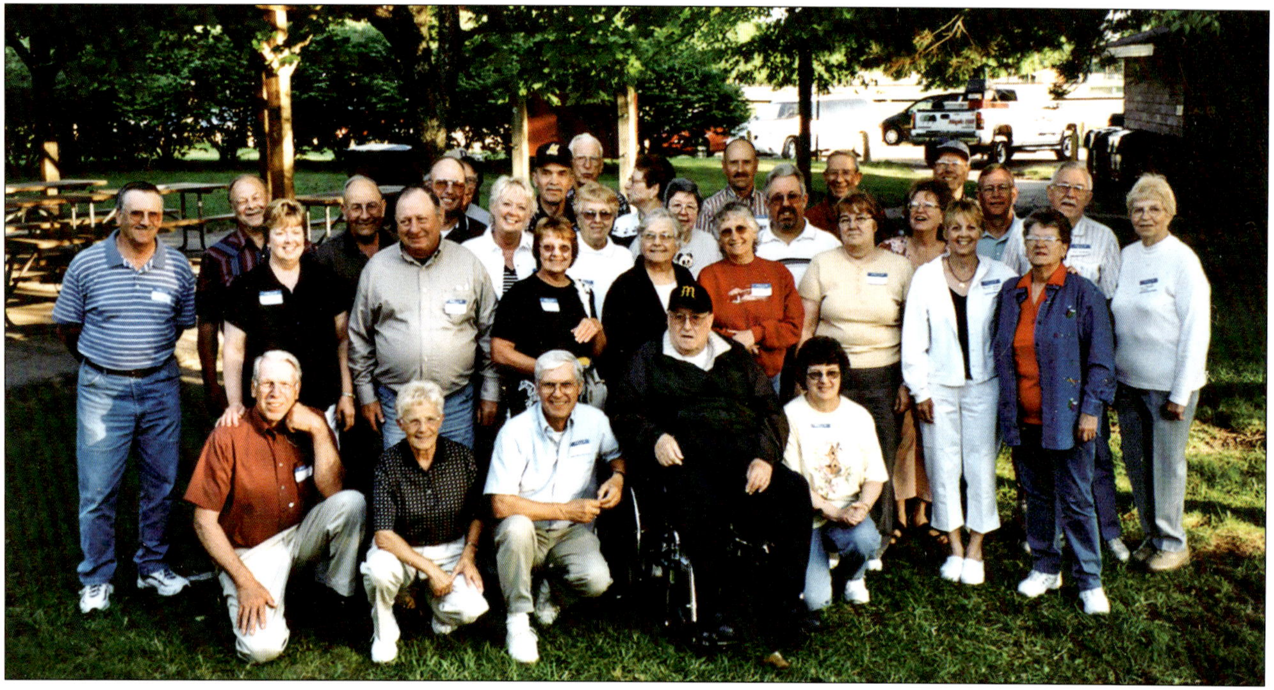

Former students of Waldo School gathered for a reunion in Plymouth Park, June 29, 2004. The school on Waldo Road closed in 1957. Front row, left to right: Kenneth Hoenicke, Donna Knight, Host Spittka, Carl Schonebine and Joyce Rabe. Second row: Barbara Miller, Oren Mieske, Pat Rhoades, Rose Lincoln, Kate Matthews, Jean Baker, Phyllis Koenig and Shirley Naples. Third row: Leonard Servinski, Ken Waskevich, Earl Gerstacker, Roger Mieske, Beverly Hughes, Joann Chartrand, Marge Fox, Ron St. John, Barb Bartos, Julia Retzloff, Hat Reiny Spittka, David Hitchcock, Eleanor Coggin, Joe Servinski, Clair Gerstacker, John Servinski and John Miller. *Courtesy of Jean Griebe Baker*

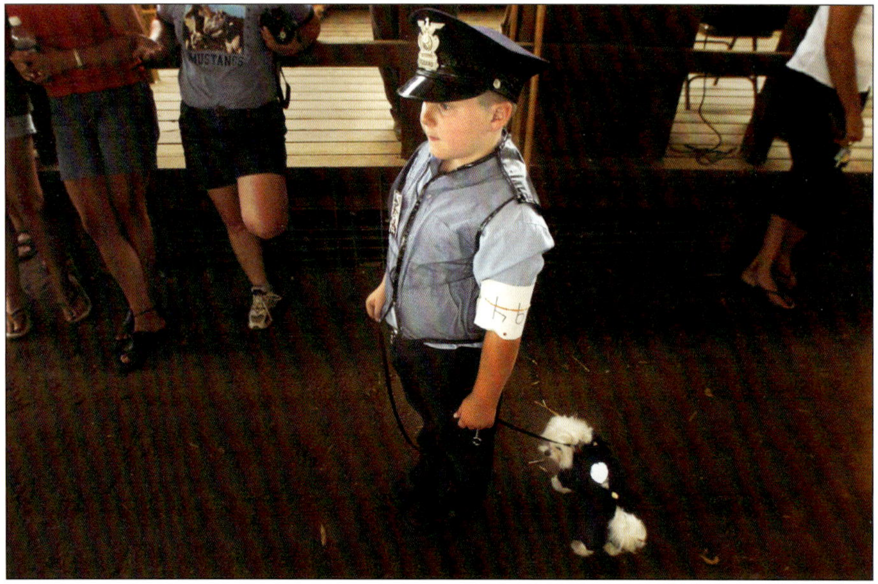

Nathan Bartosek, 8, stands with his Maltese, Bear, at the Midland County Fairgrounds during costume judging of the dog show, 2005. Nathan received first place honors for the police outfits. *Courtesy of Midland Daily News*

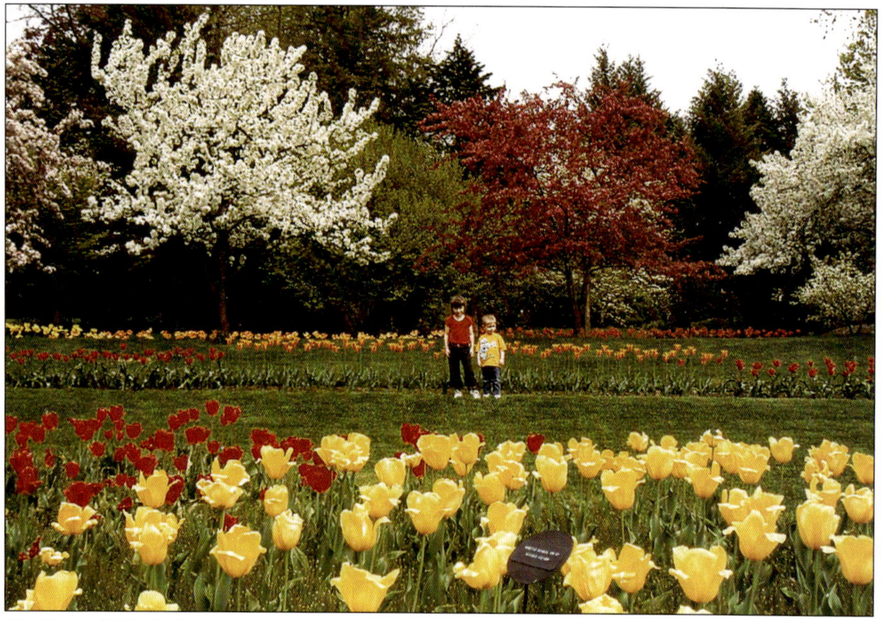

Codi and Nicholas Pound in Dow Gardens on May 18, 2005.
Courtesy of Connie Pound

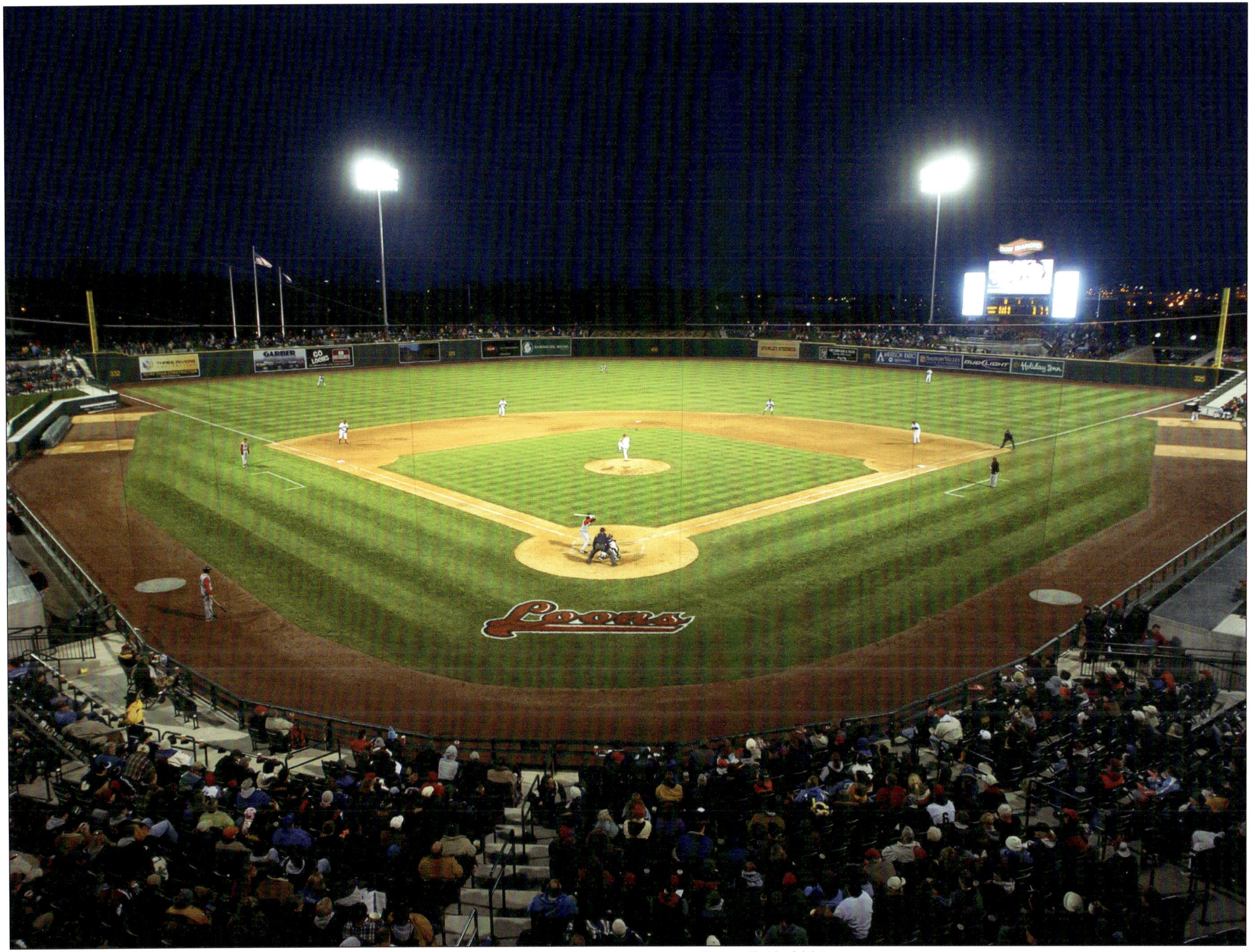

The Great Lakes Loons take on the Lansing Lugnuts in the first game at Dow Diamond, April 13, 2007. *Courtesy of Midland Daily News*

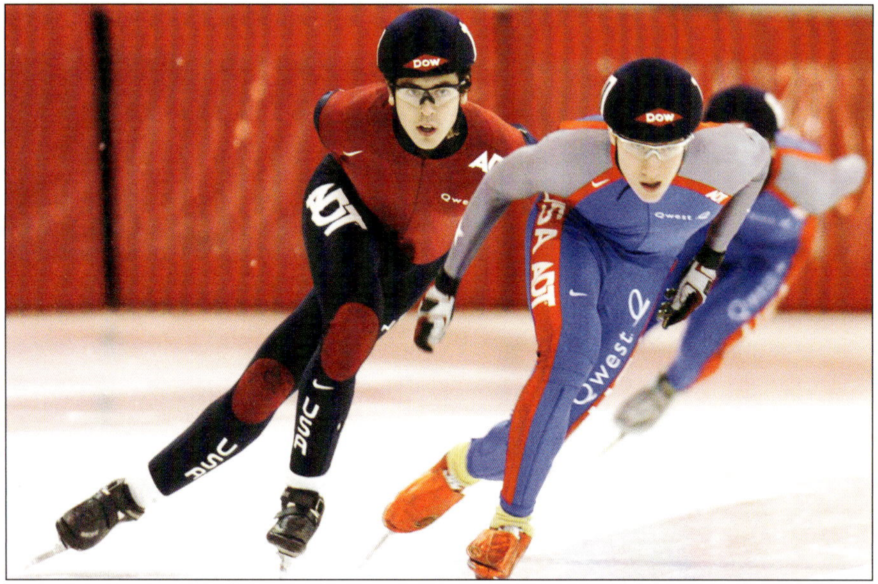

Ryan Bedford, left and Brent Aussprung compete in the 1500-meter qualifying heat at the 2006 U.S. Junior Short Track Speedskating Championships held at the Midland Civic Arena. *Courtesy of Midland Daily News*

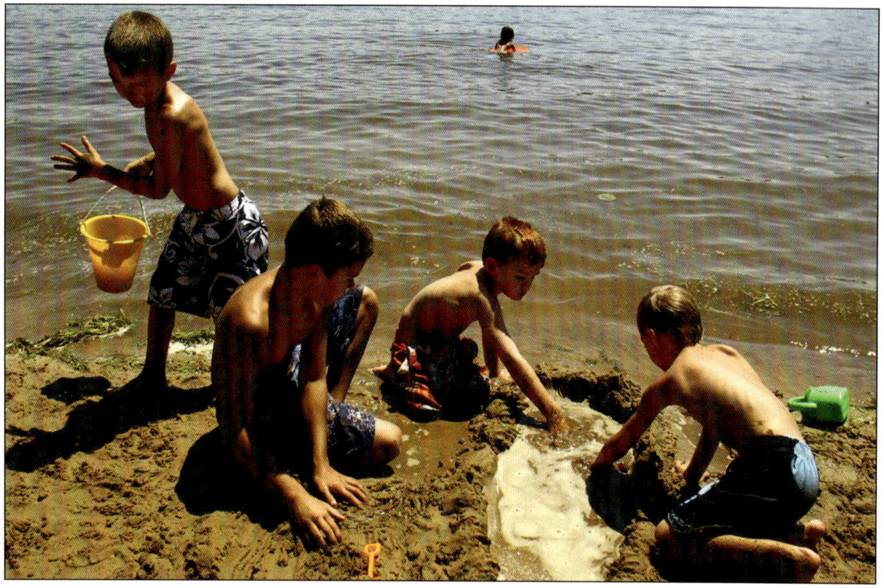

A day at the beach at Sanford Lake Park, 2007, left to right: Jack Doyle, 7, Blake Sorensen, 9, Michael Hall, 6, and Ethan Concannon, 7. They are from Saginaw Township. *Courtesy of Midland Daily News*

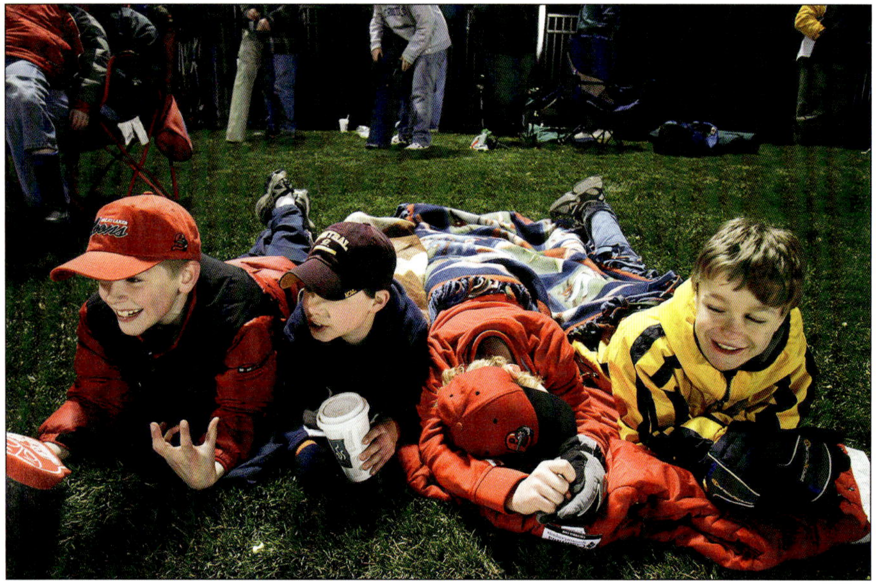

At the Great Lakes Loons first home game against the Lansing Lugnuts at Dow Diamond, 2007, left to right: Andrew Wells, 9, Conner Zaia, 9, Matthew Brennan, 10, and Jared Lane, 9. *Courtesy of Midland Daily News*

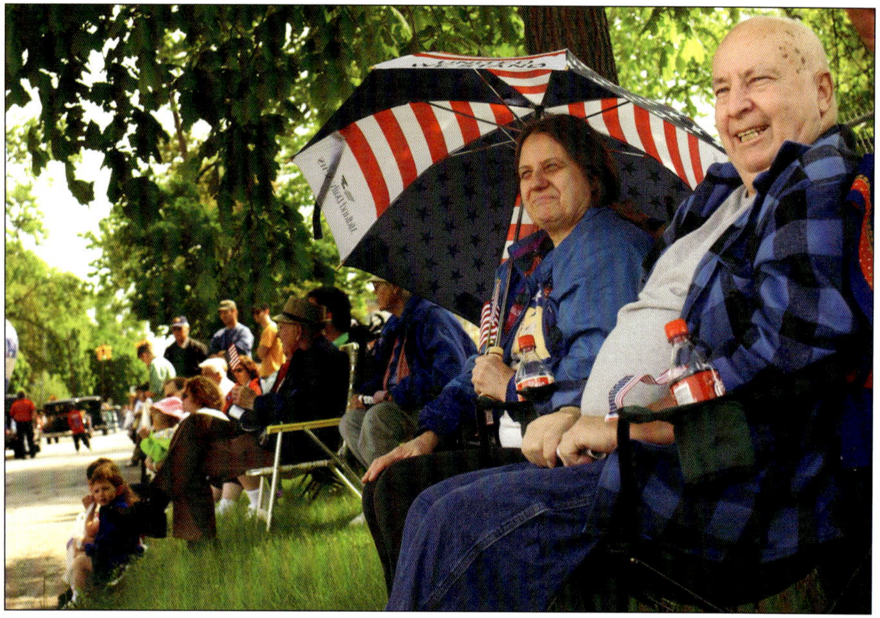

Marilene and James Merillot sit alongside Rodd Street during the Memorial Day parade, 2008. *Courtesy of Midland Daily News*

Featured Businesses

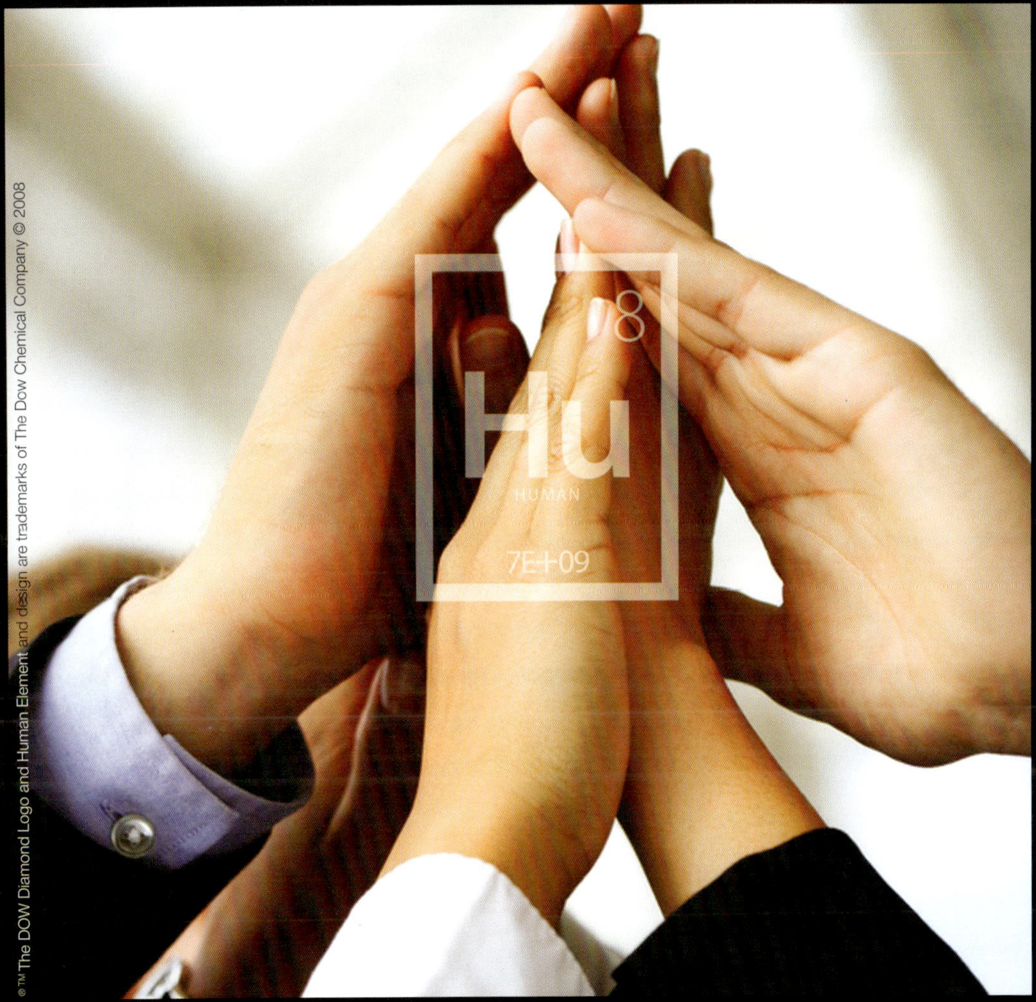

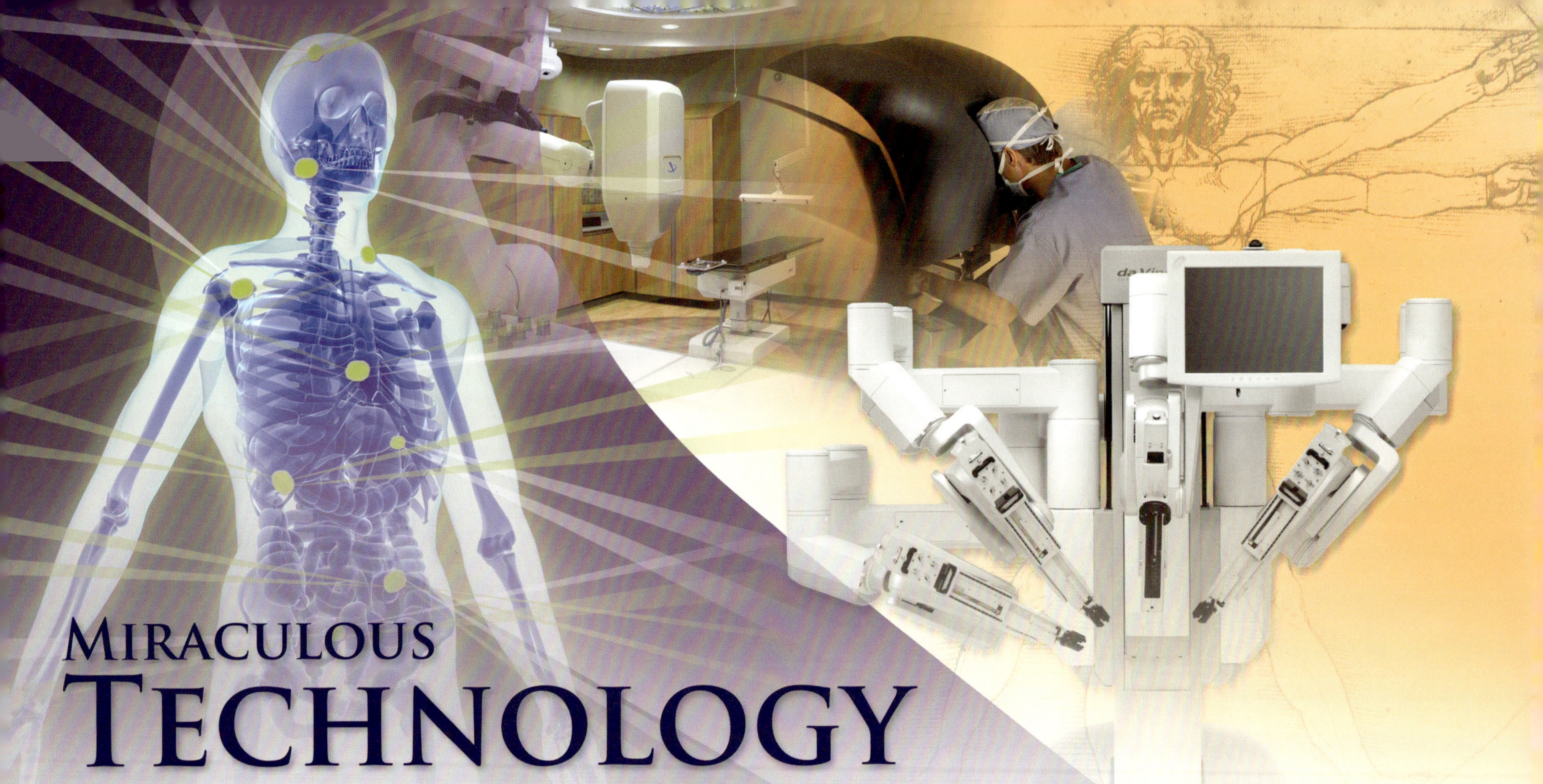

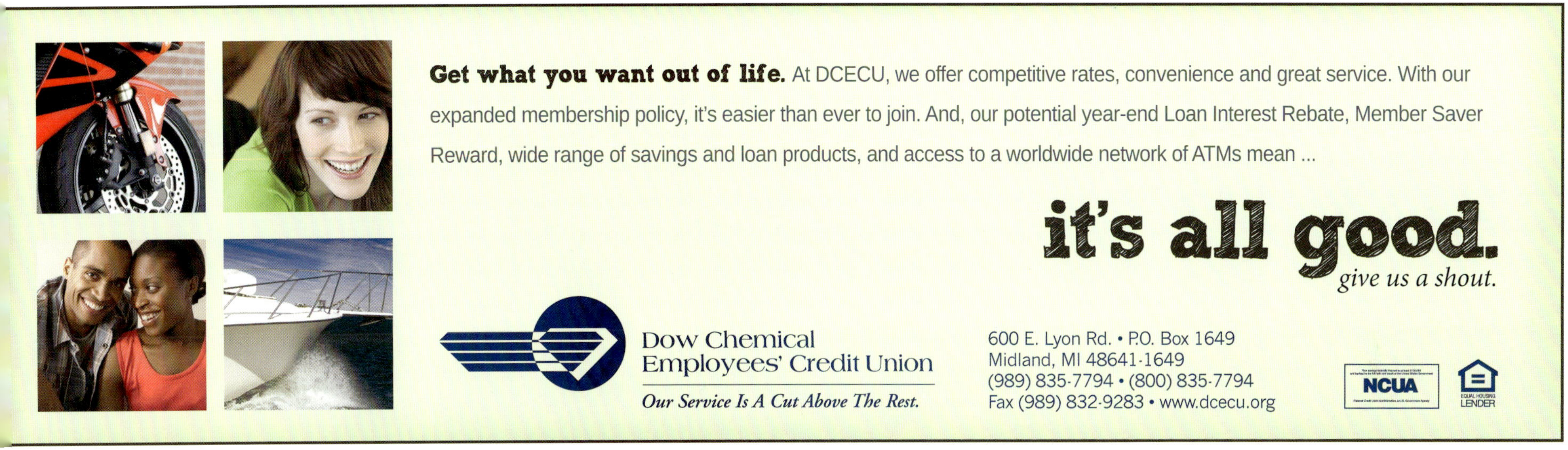
Get what you want out of life. At DCECU, we offer competitive rates, convenience and great service. With our expanded membership policy, it's easier than ever to join. And, our potential year-end Loan Interest Rebate, Member Saver Reward, wide range of savings and loan products, and access to a worldwide network of ATMs mean ...
it's all good.
give us a shout.
Dow Chemical Employees' Credit Union
Our Service Is A Cut Above The Rest.
600 E. Lyon Rd. • P.O. Box 1649
Midland, MI 48641-1649
(989) 835-7794 • (800) 835-7794
Fax (989) 832-9283 • www.dcecu.org
NCUA
EQUAL HOUSING LENDER

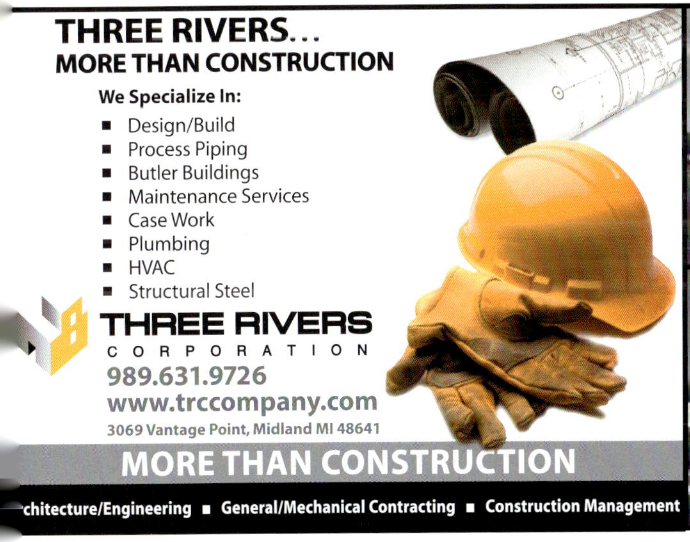
THREE RIVERS...
MORE THAN CONSTRUCTION
We Specialize In:
Design/Build
Process Piping
Butler Buildings
Maintenance Services
Case Work
Plumbing
HVAC
Structural Steel
THREE RIVERS
CORPORATION
989.631.9726
www.trccompany.com
3069 Vantage Point, Midland MI 48641
MORE THAN CONSTRUCTION
chitecture/Engineering ■ General/Mechanical Contracting ■ Construction Management

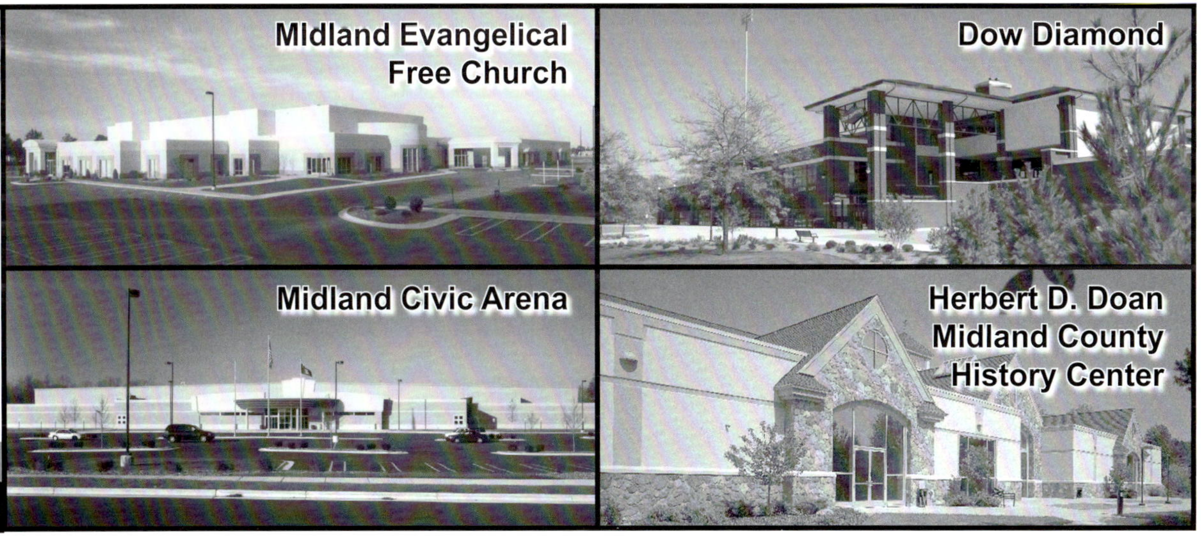
Midland Evangelical Free Church
Dow Diamond
Midland Civic Arena
Herbert D. Doan Midland County History Center

150 Years Ago, Today's Medical Miracles Were Beyond Imagination

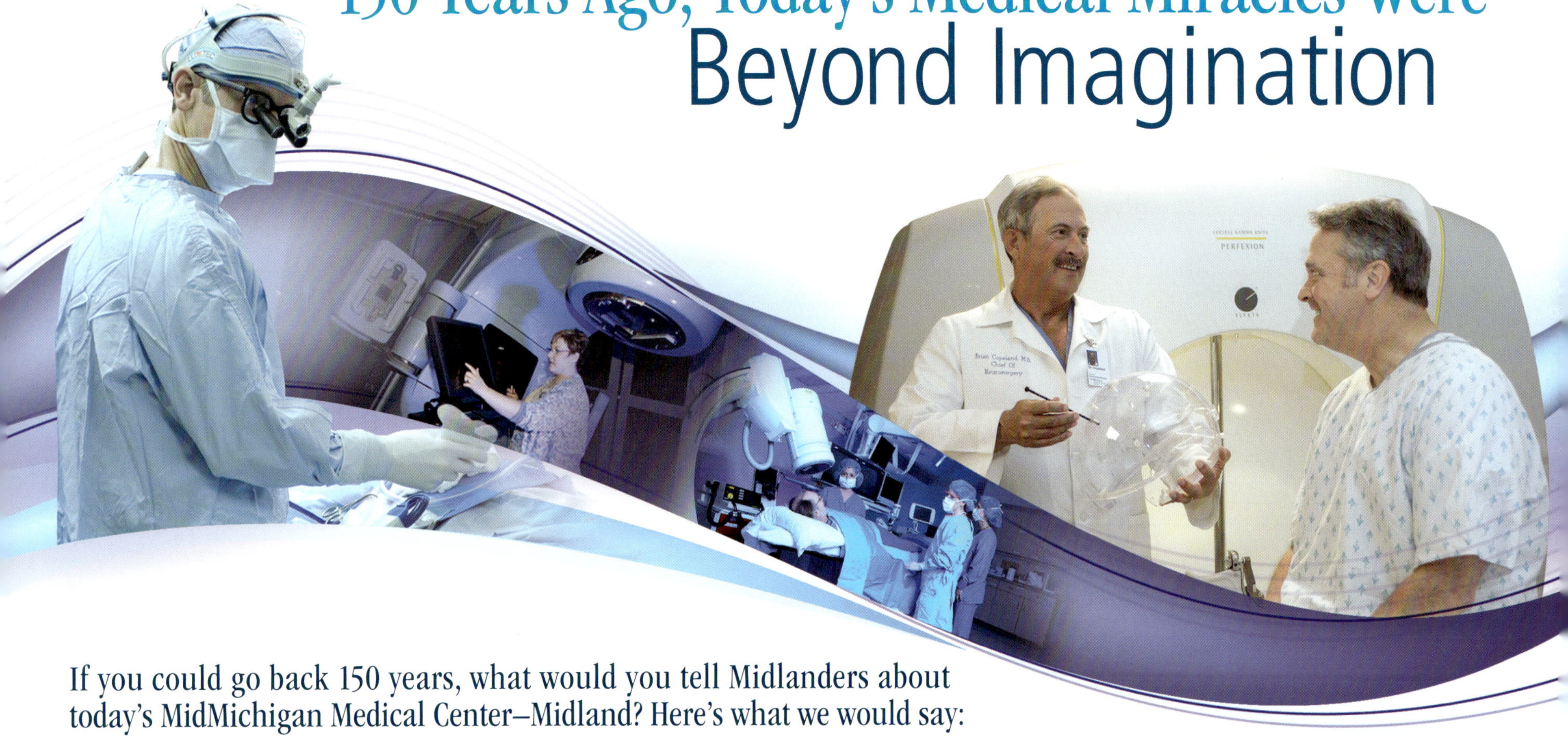

If you could go back 150 years, what would you tell Midlanders about today's MidMichigan Medical Center–Midland? Here's what we would say:

We Treat Cancer in a Radiation Oncology Center on par with the Best in the Country

We deliver tiny, precisely aimed beams of radiation to cancer in the brain and the rest of the body. With submillimeter accuracy, stereotactic radiosurgery is fast, does not involve an incision and allows the patient to go home the same day.

We Save Lives and Improve Living with Surgery on the Heart and Major Blood Vessels

Our surgeons and medical teams perform open heart surgery to repair or replace heart valves and bypass blocked blood vessels. Using the most advanced technology available experienced surgeons view real time images inside the heart as they restore blood flow and establish healthy heart beats.

We Diagnose, Treat and Help People Manage Serious Neurological Conditions

People with conditions such as epilepsy, multiple sclerosis, Parkinson's disease, stroke and many other problems involving the nervous system, including the brain and spine, have better lives and more hope because of the wide range of neurological services available from MidMichigan's advanced Neuroscience Institute.

And We Do So Much More!

While Midland's early residents couldn't find out more online, you can. Visit www.midmichigan.org/technology to learn more about MidMichigan's advanced technology. For help in finding a physician, call MidMichigan Health Line at **(989) 837-9090** or toll free at **(800) 999-3199**.

MidMichigan
Medical Center
Midland

A Lifetime of Trusted Care

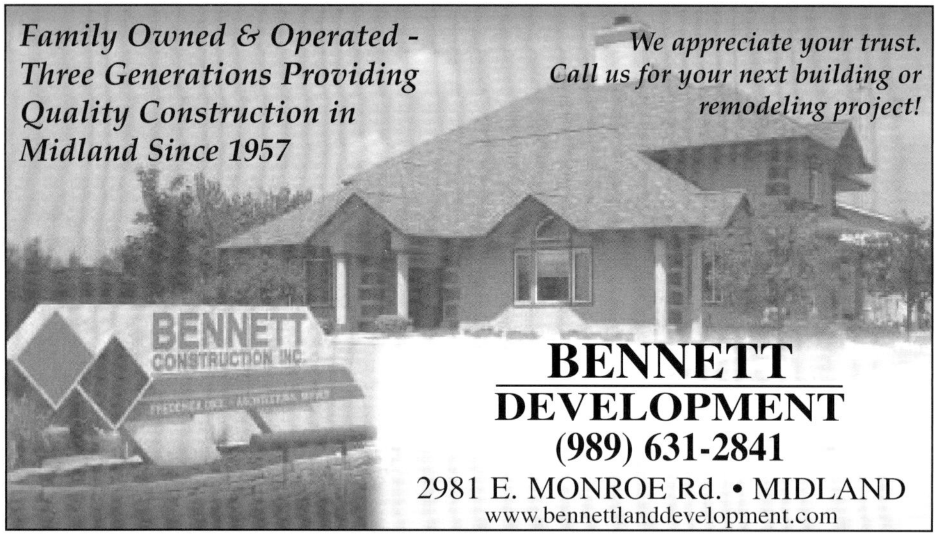
Family Owned & Operated - Three Generations Providing Quality Construction in Midland Since 1957
We appreciate your trust. Call us for your next building or remodeling project!
BENNETT CONSTRUCTION INC.
BENNETT DEVELOPMENT
(989) 631-2841
2981 E. MONROE Rd. • MIDLAND
www.bennettlanddevelopment.com

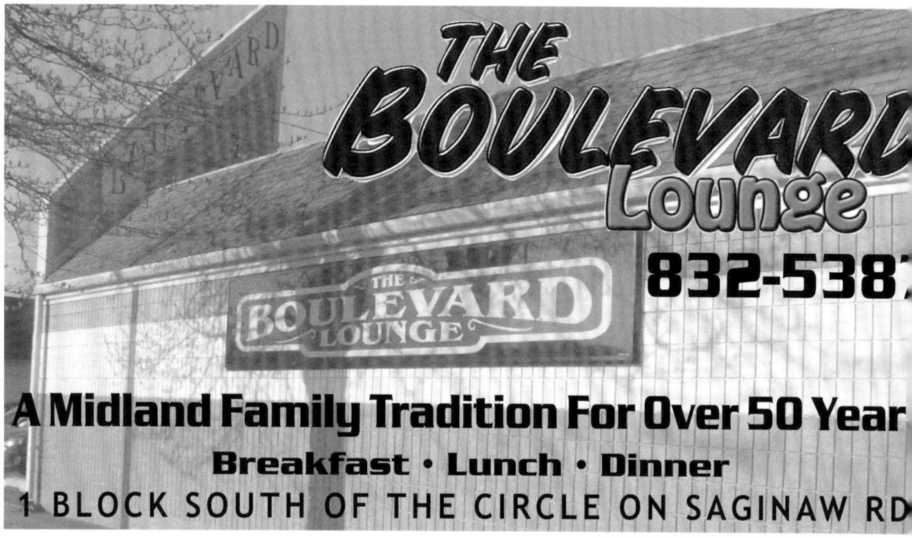
THE BOULEVAR
Lounge
832-538
THE BOULEVARD LOUNGE
A Midland Family Tradition For Over 50 Year
Breakfast • Lunch • Dinner
1 BLOCK SOUTH OF THE CIRCLE ON SAGINAW RD

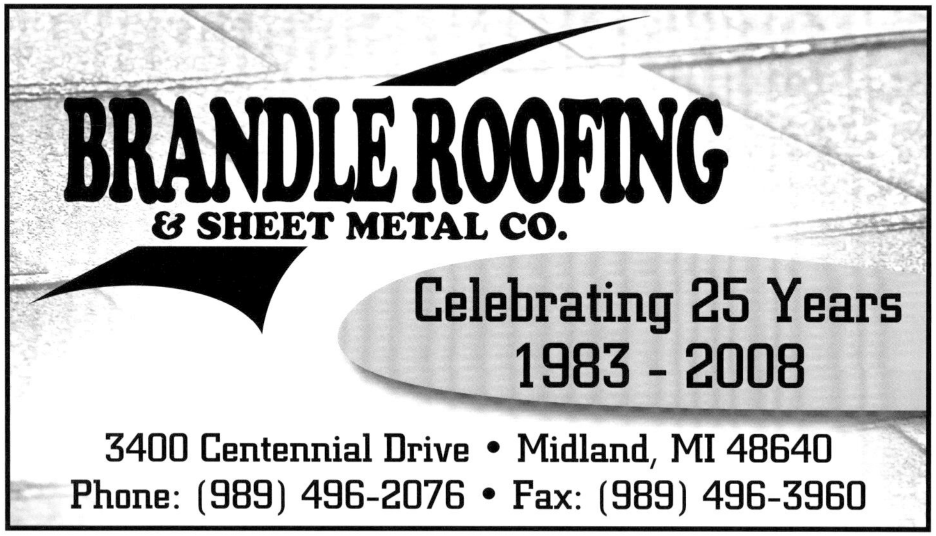
BRANDLE ROOFING
& SHEET METAL CO.
Celebrating 25 Years
1983 - 2008
3400 Centennial Drive • Midland, MI 48640
Phone: (989) 496-2076 • Fax: (989) 496-3960

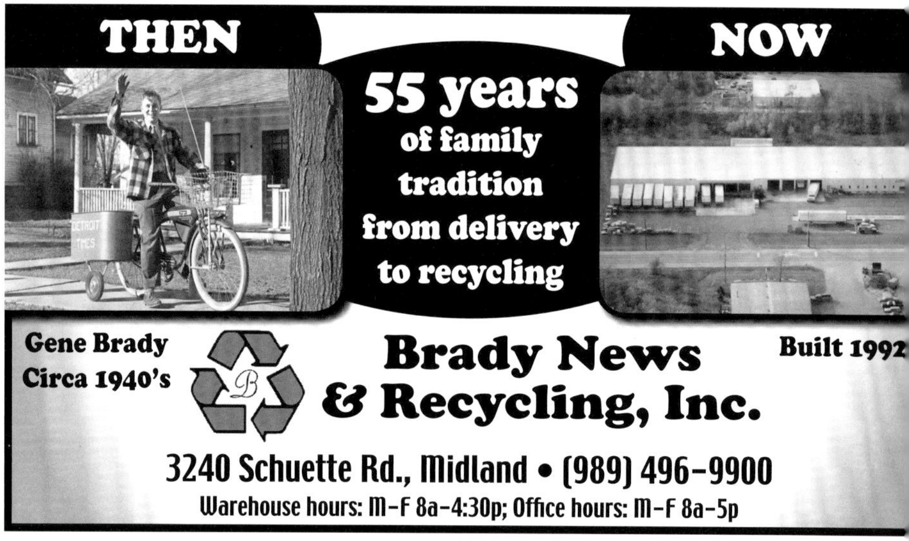
THEN
NOW
55 years of family tradition from delivery to recycling
Gene Brady Circa 1940's
Built 1992
Brady News & Recycling, Inc.
3240 Schuette Rd., Midland • (989) 496-9900
Warehouse hours: M-F 8a-4:30p; Office hours: M-F 8a-5p

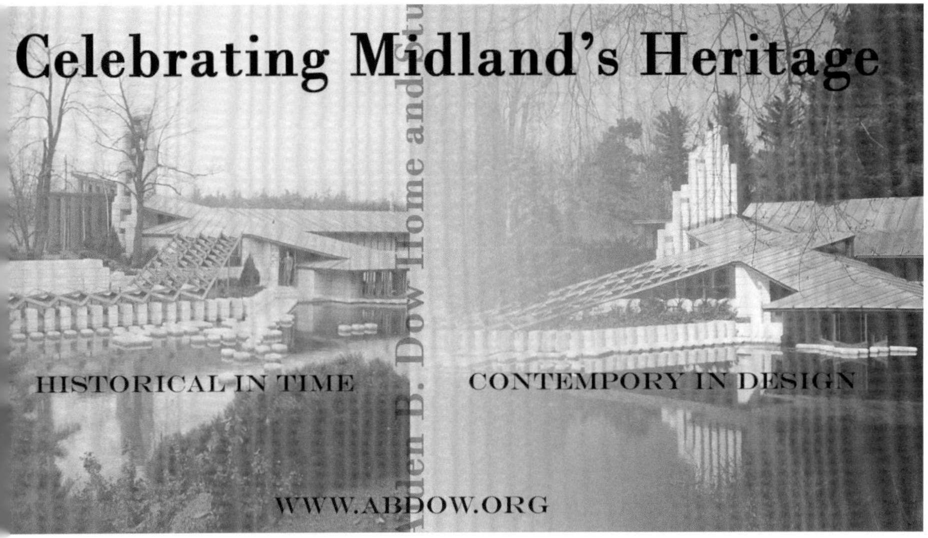
Celebrating Midland's Heritage
HISTORICAL IN TIME
CONTEMPORY IN DESIGN
WWW.ABDOW.ORG

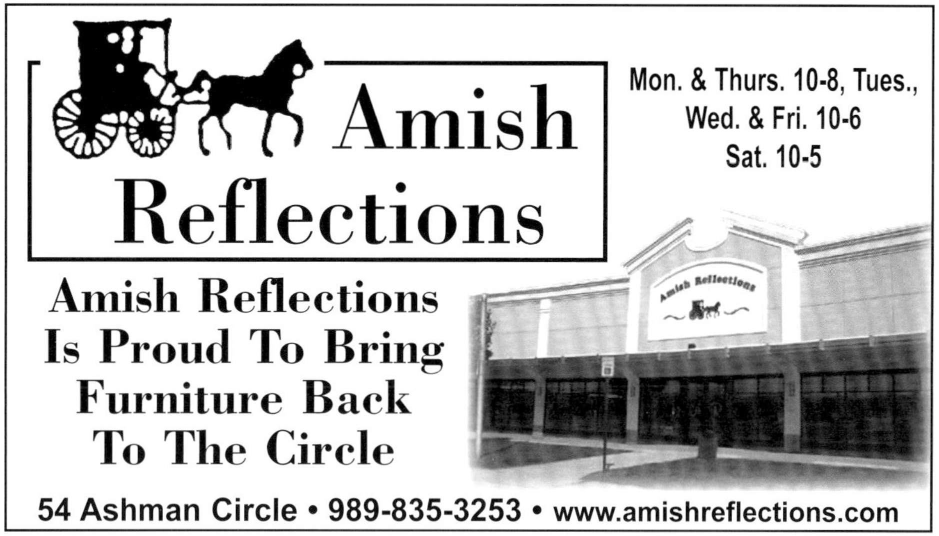
Amish Reflections
Mon. & Thurs. 10-8, Tues., Wed. & Fri. 10-6 Sat. 10-5
Amish Reflections Is Proud To Bring Furniture Back To The Circle
54 Ashman Circle • 989-835-3253 • www.amishreflections.com

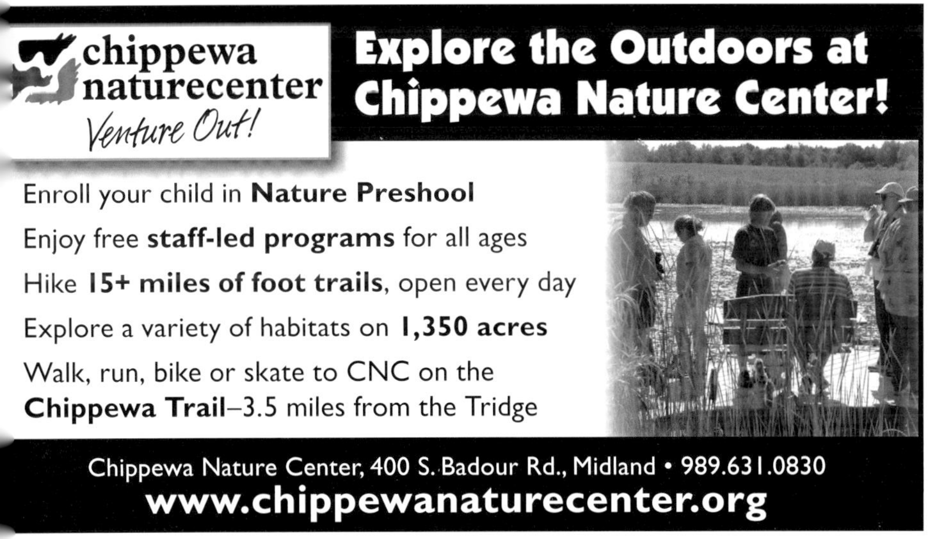
chippewa naturecenter
Venture Out!
Explore the Outdoors at Chippewa Nature Center!
Enroll your child in Nature Preshool
Enjoy free staff-led programs for all ages
Hike 15+ miles of foot trails, open every day
Explore a variety of habitats on 1,350 acres
Walk, run, bike or skate to CNC on the Chippewa Trail–3.5 miles from the Tridge
Chippewa Nature Center, 400 S. Badour Rd., Midland • 989.631.0830
www.chippewanaturecenter.org

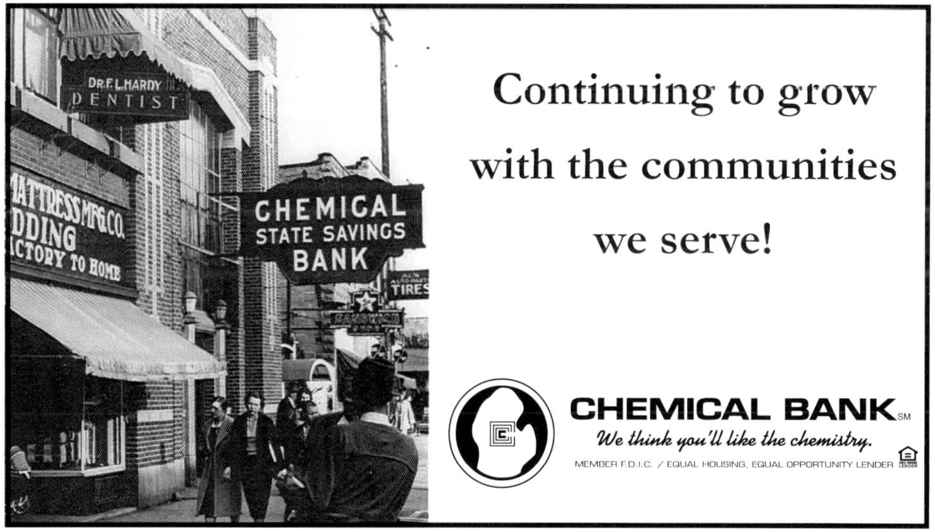
DR. F. L. HARDY DENTIST
CHEMICAL STATE SAVINGS BANK
Continuing to grow with the communities we serve!
CHEMICAL BANK SM
We think you'll like the chemistry.
MEMBER F.D.I.C. / EQUAL HOUSING, EQUAL OPPORTUNITY LENDER

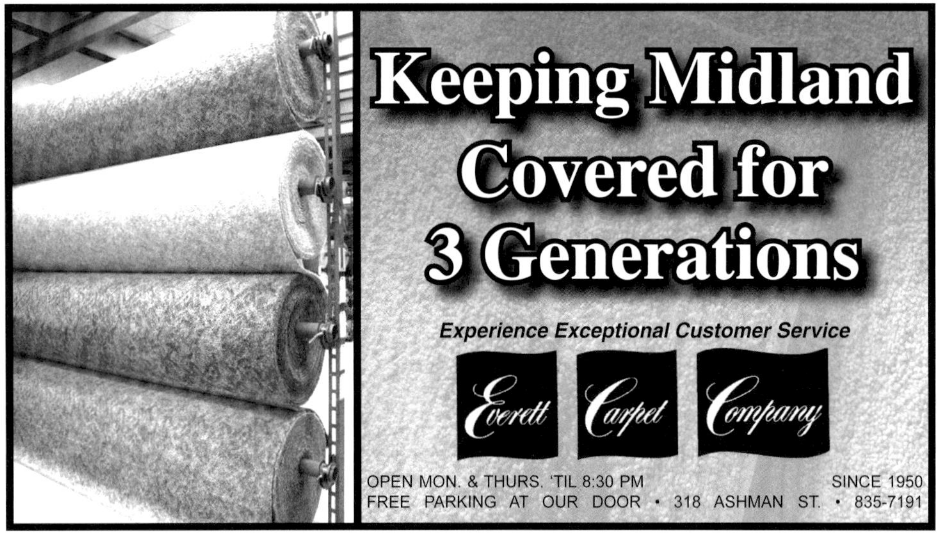
Keeping Midland Covered for 3 Generations
Experience Exceptional Customer Service
Everett Carpet Company
OPEN MON. & THURS. 'TIL 8:30 PM
SINCE 1950
FREE PARKING AT OUR DOOR • 318 ASHMAN ST. • 835-7191

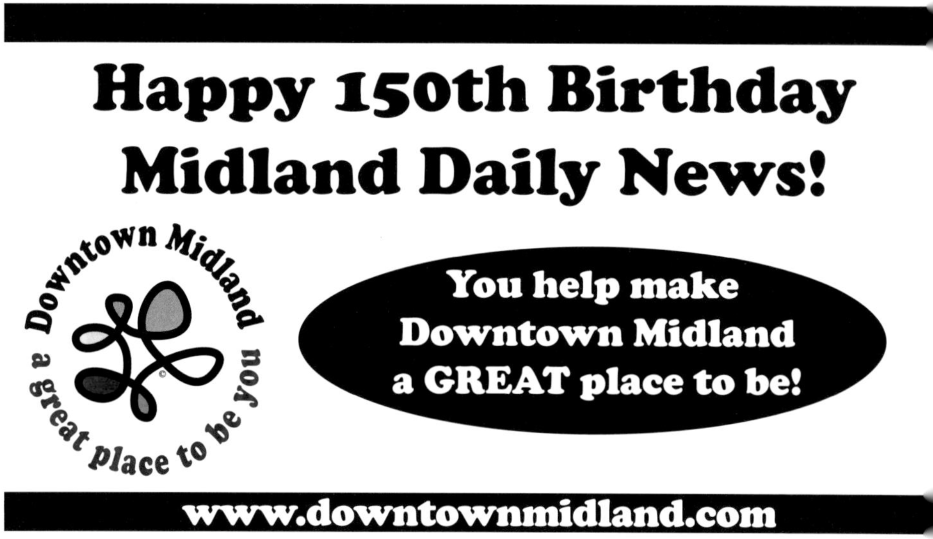
Happy 150th Birthday
Midland Daily News!
Downtown Midland
a great place to be you
You help make
Downtown Midland
a GREAT place to be!
www.downtownmidland.com

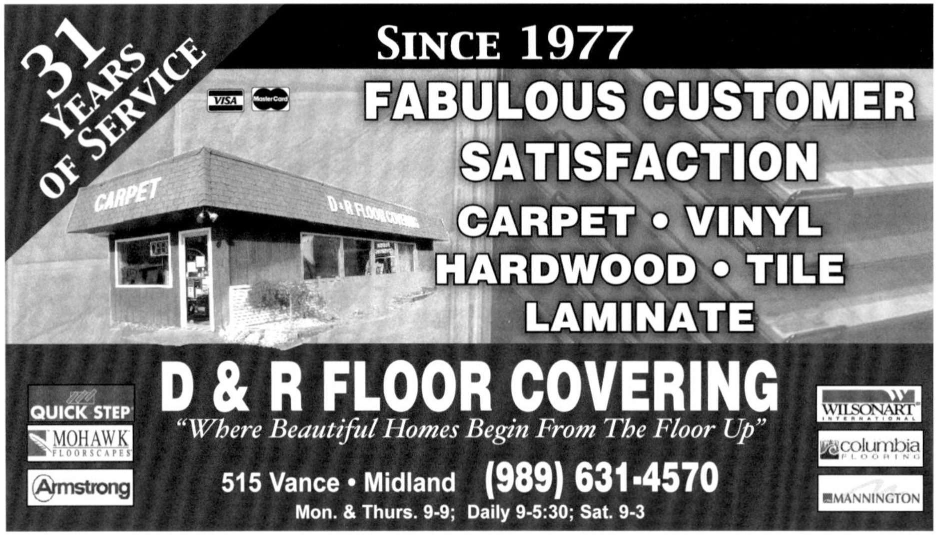
31 YEARS OF SERVICE
SINCE 1977
FABULOUS CUSTOMER
SATISFACTION
CARPET • VINYL
HARDWOOD • TILE
LAMINATE
CARPET
D & R FLOOR COVERING
"Where Beautiful Homes Begin From The Floor Up"
515 Vance • Midland (989) 631-4570
Mon. & Thurs. 9-9; Daily 9-5:30; Sat. 9-3
QUICK STEP
MOHAWK
Armstrong
WILSONART
columbia
MANNINGTON

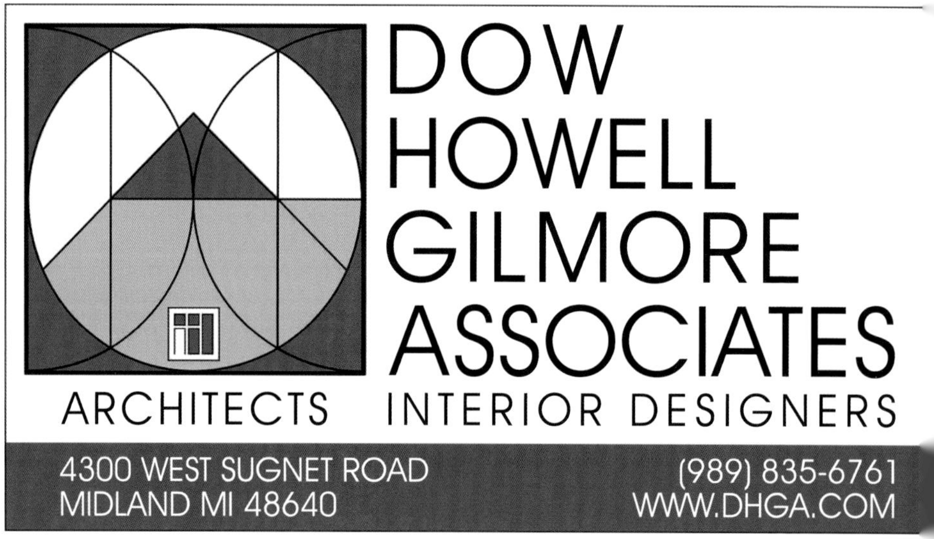
DOW
HOWELL
GILMORE
ASSOCIATES
ARCHITECTS
INTERIOR DESIGNERS
4300 WEST SUGNET ROAD
MIDLAND MI 48640
(989) 835-6761
WWW.DHGA.COM

Senior Minister
Rev. Dr. Brent McCumons

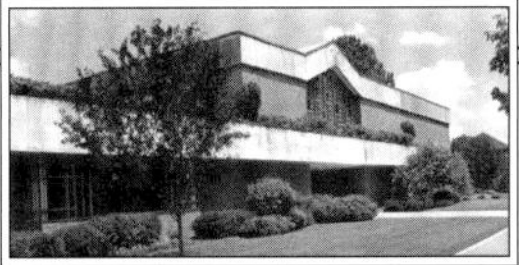

Associate Ministers
Rev. Jeremy Africa
Rev. Pam Buchholz
Rev. Dr. Charles Keyworth
Rev. Susan Kingsley

We Join You in Starting Our Second 150 Years of Service to the Midland Community!

Worship & Church School
9:15 AM & 11:00 AM and Alive@Five at 5:00 PM
Summer schedule June 15 - August 31; Sunday Worship Traditional at 9:30 AM, Contemporary 11:15 AM

Sunday Service Radio Broadcasts
Sundays on WMPX (1490 AM) at 11:00 AM

Sunday Service broadcast Tuesday at 1:00 PM & Wednesday 8 PM on Cable Channel 3 (MCTV)

Staffed Nursery, Active Programs for Children, Youth and Adults

Chapel Service at 7:00 PM on Wednesdays

LOGOS: A Midweek, Comprehensive Ministry for Youth, Children & their families on Thursdays during the school year

Alive@Five / Contemporary
A unique, celebrative, vibrant worship experience for all ages!

FIRST UNITED METHODIST CHURCH
www.fumcmidweb.org

315 W. Larkin
(Across from the courthouse)
(989) 835-6797

Celebrating 75 Years!

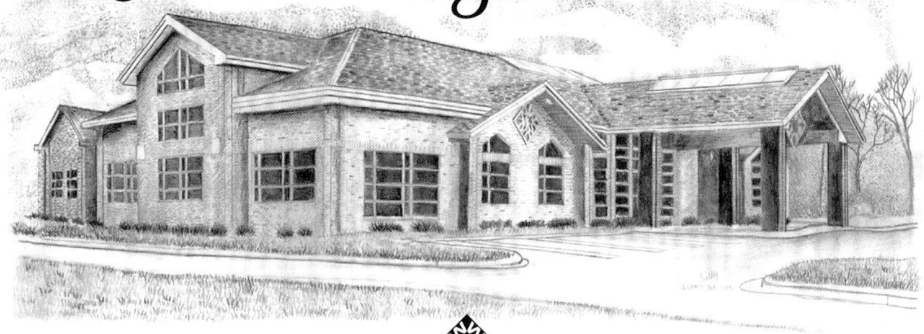

WOLVERINE BANK

Member FDIC

5710 Eastman Ave. • 118 Ashman • 1015 S. Saginaw Rd.

MICHIGAN ANTIQUE & COLLECTIBLE FESTIVALS 2008
Midland Fairgrounds US-10 @ Eastman Ave. Midland, MI

Celebrating 40 Years at the Beautiful Midland Fairgrounds!!

Visit us Online for Future Dates:
www.miantiquefestival.com

Antiques ★ Collectibles,
Classic Car Show ★ Swap Meet
4-Sale Car Lot ★ Entertainment
Specialty Coin & Sports Memorabilia Building

Over 80 Acres of Treasures, Memories & Good Times!!

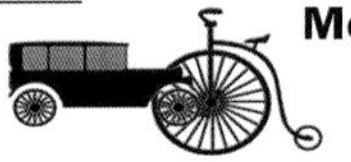

Held Rain or Shine
Free Parking
$5 Per Person
11 & Under Free

KRUSE INTERNATIONAL **Annual Classic Car Auction**

USA Demolition Derby, Inc. **FWD Figure-8 Finals**

Sat. 8am-6pm
Sun. 8am-4pm

For Info (989) 687-9001 www.miantiquefestival.com

Midland King's Daughters Home

Celebrating 50 Years in The Community

Assisted Living & Long Term Care In A Comfortable Home Like Setting.

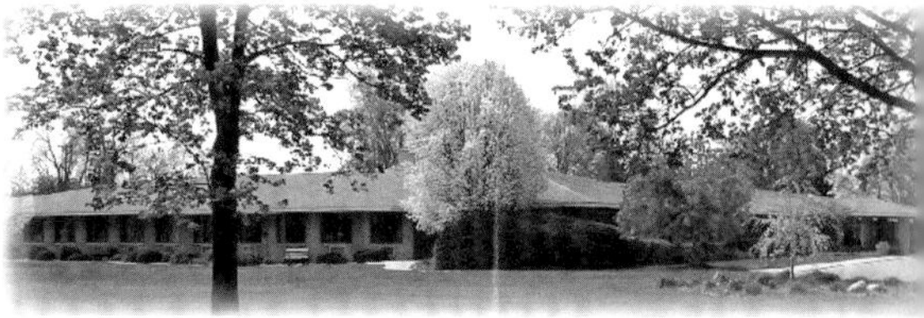

2410 Rodd Street, Midland 48640 at corner of Rodd & Nelson Streets
(989) 839-9800
Visit our website at www.midlandkdh.org

Providing Optimal Health For You, Your Family & Friends Since 1984

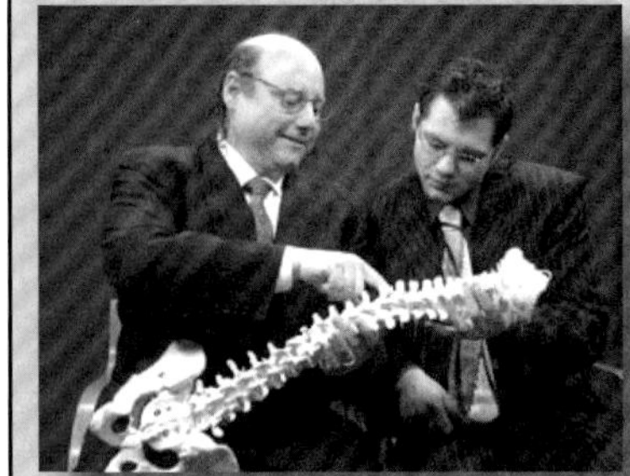

Our mission is to change the world by transforming lives: supporting as many families as possible in their quest for health, to educate everyone about their body's innate ability to heal, and how chiropractic can help achieve optimal health and to encourage them to educate others.

Chiropractic Works For all Ages and Walks Of Life

Accepting new patients. Contact us today at

832-5433

to schedule your appointment.

Rodnick Chiropractic Clinic

4604 N. Saginaw Rd. • Midland

Now 4 Locations Throughout Michigan

Congratulations On 150 Years

Pizza and Beer Go Here

Pizza Sam's

102 W. Main • Downtown Midland

631-1934

www.pizzasams.com

A Family Tradition since 1960

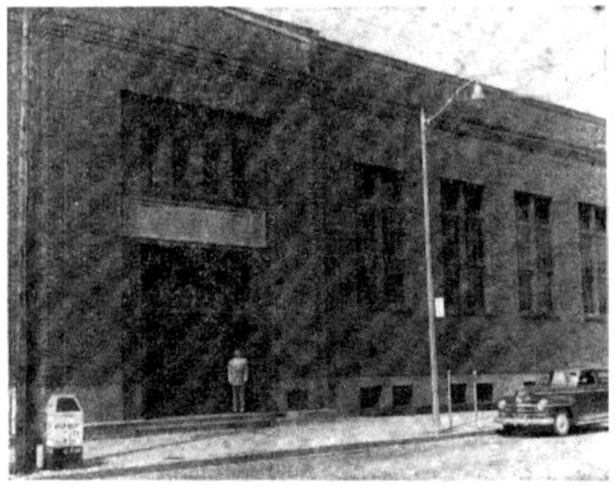

1919 - 1955

As times have changed, so has the Midland Community Center. Thanks to the generous support of many individuals, businesses, and foundations we have grown to meet the needs of the community over the years including our new campus in 2008.

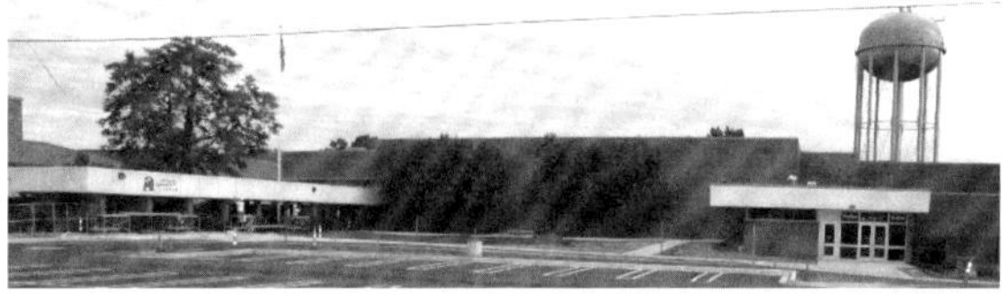

1955 - Today

Since 1919, the Midland Community Center has been the leading local non-profit organization in providing affordable and quality recreational, social, and personal development opportunities for all individuals and families.

MIDLAND COMMUNITY CENTER

2205 Jefferson Ave.
832-7937
www.MyMCC.org

Come link your lives with ours in the love of Jesus Christ.

ST. JOHN'S Episcopal Church

405 N. Saginaw Road (at St. Andrews)
Midland, MI 48640 989-631-2260

Worship on Sundays: 7:30 & 10:30 am

Christian Formation for all ages

Child care at 10:30 am service

www.sjec-midland.org

Celebrating 100 Years...*Serving Midland Since 1908*
Our Family to Your Family

Wilson MILLER
FUNERAL HOME

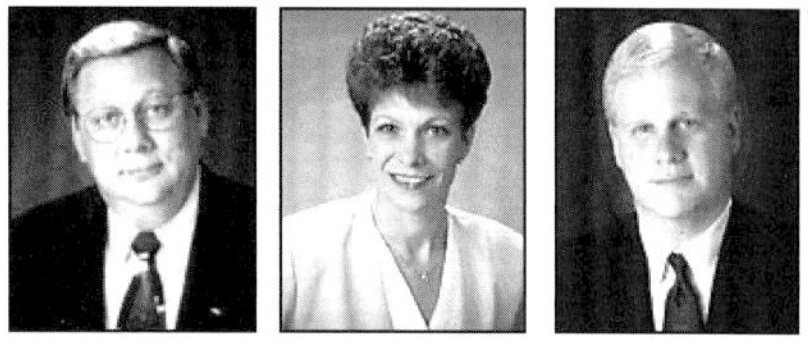

Kyran Miller Kathy Ordiway Craig Pickelman

People who know you, people you can rely on...today and tomorrow.

4210 N. Saginaw Road • Midland, MI 48640

(989) 839-9966

SELECTED *Independent* FUNERAL HOMES

On-Line Video Tributes & Obituaries
www.wilson-miller.com

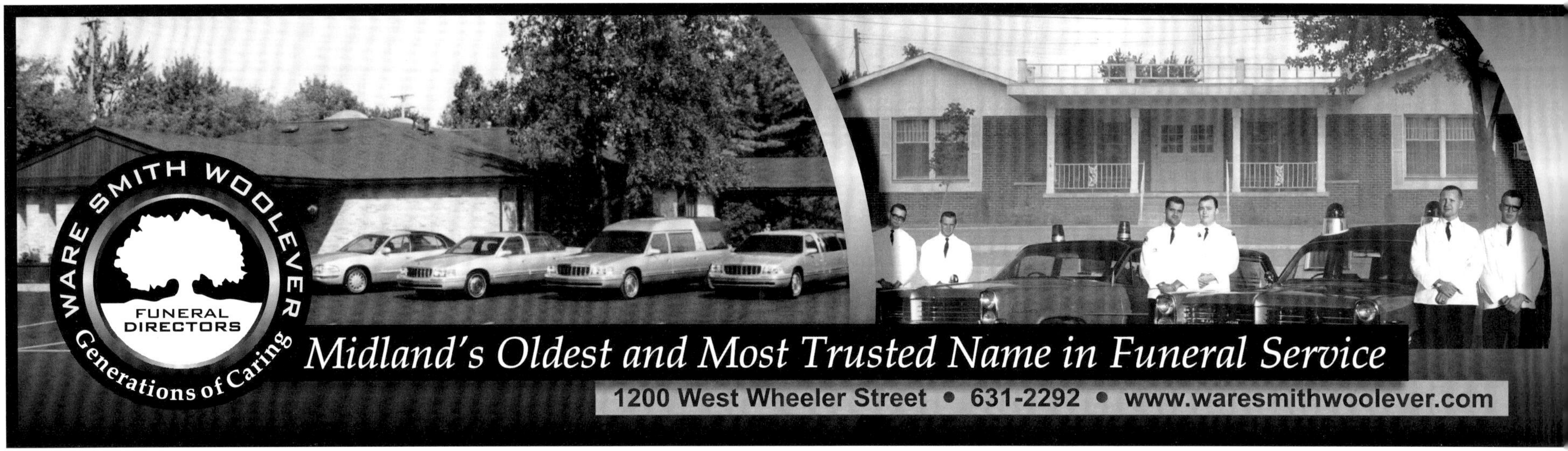